The Catonsville Nine

The Catonsville Nine

A STORY OF FAITH AND RESISTANCE
IN THE VIETNAM ERA

Shawn Francis Peters

OXFORD
UNIVERSITY PRESS

OXFORD
UNIVERSITY PRESS

Oxford University Press, Inc., publishes works that further
Oxford University's objective of excellence
in research, scholarship, and education.

Oxford   New York
Auckland   Cape Town   Dar es Salaam   Hong Kong   Karachi
Kuala Lumpur   Madrid   Melbourne   Mexico City   Nairobi
New Delhi   Shanghai   Taipei   Toronto

With offices in
Argentina   Austria   Brazil   Chile   Czech Republic   France   Greece
Guatemala   Hungary   Italy   Japan   Poland   Portugal   Singapore
South Korea   Switzerland   Thailand   Turkey   Ukraine   Vietnam

Published by Oxford University Press, Inc.
198 Madison Avenue, New York, New York 10016

www.oup.com

Oxford is a registered trademark of Oxford University Press

Library of Congress Cataloging-in-Publication Data
Peters, Shawn Francis, 1966–
The Catonsville Nine: A Story of Faith and Resistance in the Vietnam Era /Shawn Francis Peters.
p.   cm.
Includes bibliographical references (p.).
ISBN 978-0-19-982785-5 (hardcover: alk. paper)—ISBN 978-0-19-982786-2 (ebook)
1. War—Religious aspects—Catholic church. 2. Vietnam War, 1961–1975—Religious aspects. 3. Vietnam War,
1961–1975—Protest movements—Maryland—Catonsville. 4. Catholic Church—Maryland—Catonsville—History.
5. Catonsville (Md.)—Church history. I. Title.
BX1795.W37P48   2012
959.704'31—dc23 [B]   2011036895

9 8 7 6 5 4 3 2 1

Printed in the United States of America
on acid-free paper

For my father

CONTENTS

PREFACE

When people ask me how long it took to write this book, I'm never quite sure how to answer them. The truth is, I can't ever remember *not* being in the process of assembling the story of the Catonsville Nine. I guess that I've been writing this tale—in my head as well as on paper—since I was a kid.

I was born in Catonsville, Maryland—a suburb of Baltimore—late in 1966. This was about eighteen months before a group of Catholic clergy and laymen burst into the local draft board, seized hundreds of the Selective Service records housed there, and burned them in a bold protest against imperialism and injustice. The daring and provocative witness of the Catonsville Nine, as the protesters came to be known, made headlines all over the world. So too did their subsequent trial in federal court—a proceeding so singularly intense and dramatic that a play and film later were based on it.

I was too young to be fully aware of the raid when it happened, but I grew up hearing slightly garbled accounts of who the protesters were and what kind of havoc they had wrought at the local Knights of Columbus hall, where the draft board had been located. My parents, the teachers at my elementary school, the women behind the desk at the local public library, even our family's dentist—it seemed that half of the people in town had a juicy story to share with me about the Catonsville Nine (this despite the fact that none of the Nine actually were *from* Catonsville and had spent less than an hour protesting and witnessing there).

To me, these accounts always were fascinating—and slightly puzzling. I was a Catholic kid who sat through Mass every Sunday and attended a Catholic elementary school, so I knew all about priests and nuns; I interacted with them more or less every day. Likewise, we encountered Catholics of all stripes in my family's parish, including people who were passionate and outspoken about peace and social justice issues. But none of the priests and laypeople in my tranquil little Catholic world seemed capable of ransacking a federal office and then publicly burning what they had looted (in broad daylight, no less).

And, truth be told, I had a hard time believing that an event of enduring historical significance had occurred at Catonsville's Knights of Columbus hall, a building that I passed by countless times in my childhood. When I was a teenager, I went with some friends to a dingy traveling carnival that had been set up in the large parking lot behind the hall—the very spot where the Catonsville Nine had destroyed the draft records back in 1968. It seemed strange to me that we could ogle girls and eat hot dogs on what was supposed to be hallowed ground.

I became so intrigued by the stories that were floating around town that I wrote a succession of earnest reports and term papers about the Catonsville Nine as I made my way through elementary school and then Catonsville High School. In piecing together those rudimentary accounts, I discovered that much of what I heard about the Nine from people in Catonsville was not entirely accurate. Some of it, in fact, was just plain wrong.

Contrary to what people told me, the demonstrators weren't all Catholic priests or nuns. At one time or another, six of the Nine had been formally affiliated with religious orders (as priests, nuns, or brothers), but only three of them had any kind of clerical status at the time of the protest.

The Nine hadn't smeared the draft records with ducks' blood. True, two of them had used a mixture of human and animal blood to deface draft files in an earlier protest in downtown Baltimore, but the Nine had burned the Selective Service records they seized in Catonsville.

It turned out that there was more than one trial of the Catonsville Nine. Thanks to the famous play that was based on it, everyone knew about their federal trial, but there also was a separate trial in state court several months later.

And no, Father Dan Berrigan, the most prominent member of the group, hadn't masterminded the whole affair. In fact, he had been the *last* person to join the group—and only after his brother had twisted his arm.

By far the biggest single misapprehension that I encountered had to do with what, exactly, the Catonsville Nine had demonstrated against. The way I always heard it, they had attempted to cry out against the war in Vietnam and the foolhardy policies that had led to the United States becoming so hopelessly entangled in it. But this proved to be only partly true.

As a kid, I came across an immensely readable book titled *Whose Heaven, Whose Earth?* In it, two of the Catonsville Nine—Tom and Marjorie Melville—vividly described their careers as missionaries in Guatemala and the challenges they faced after being ejected from that country late in 1967 for engaging in proto-revolutionary political activities. The Melvilles explained in their book that Vietnam had been a secondary concern for them when they had protested at Catonsville. Their primary goal in burning the Selective Service files in my hometown, they wrote, had been to draw attention to the miserable plight of the Guatemalan peasantry.

Another member of the Nine, John Hogan, had been the Melvilles' colleague in Central America. It turned out that he, too, had participated in the Catonsville protest mainly because he cared so deeply about what was happening to poor people in Guatemala—and in the inner cities of the United States.

As I learned more about how Christianity evolved in the 1960s, it became clear to me that Hogan, the Melvilles, and the rest of the Nine had been swept up in the liberation theology movement, which sought to alleviate the oppression of the poor throughout the world. Somehow, though, the global dimension of their witness in Catonsville—their concern for oppressed people everywhere, from Vietnam to Guatemala to the streets of Baltimore—had been obscured in the accounts that were passed along to me.

Even if the residents of Catonsville didn't always have their facts completely straight, they tended to have strong opinions about the Nine. Growing up there in the aftermath of the draft board protest, it struck me that most people viewed them as being either modern-day saints (who had taken a heroic stand against a misguided and unwinnable war) or grandstanding vandals (who had disgraced their church and sullied the town's good name). It seemed that people either loved the Nine or detested them.

And make no mistake: many folks in Catonsville really loathed the Catonsville Nine.

My siblings and I attended a Catholic elementary school, St. Mark, that is located just a short walk from the Knights of Columbus hall, and every so often one of the nuns who taught us would allude to the draft board protest, which is probably the most noteworthy event in the town's history. Rarely were these references flattering. I can remember one nun describing for us in bleak terms what the Catonsville Nine had done and how it symbolized pretty much everything that had gone wrong in the Catholic Church since Vatican II. I don't recall her exact words as much as I remember her body language: the nun ruefully shook her head and furrowed her brow in consternation. It was as if it literally pained her to talk about the Nine.

But hearing the Catonsville Nine condemned by my teachers served only to pique my curiosity about them. My career at St. Mark was not a particularly distinguished one; the teachers at the school didn't seem to approve of *my* behavior, either. A bit of a malcontent myself, I loved hearing that a group of respectable grown-ups had flouted authority in such an outrageous way.

After all, they had stolen government property, set it on fire, and then simply waited around for the police to show up and arrest them. Later, after they had been found guilty in court, several of them had thumbed their noses at the federal government and had become fugitives. While underground, they regularly had taunted the notorious curmudgeon who led the FBI, J. Edgar Hoover. And when they were finally caught and dispatched to a federal prison, some of them had hung around with union leader Jimmy Hoffa. (Yes, *that* Jimmy Hoffa.)

Let's be honest here. What mischievous boy wouldn't find that whole saga at least a little bit intriguing?

Strangely enough, my fledgling baseball career also made me feel a bond with the Catonsville Nine. I played for many years on teams representing the town, and local sportswriters employing a traditional baseball idiom often would refer to us as the "Catonsville Nine" (because nine players comprise a team). One of my father's favorite jokes was to look up from a newspaper box score of one of my Catonsville High School games and express mock disappointment over my association with a group of wild-eyed radicals who had brought disrepute to our quiet town.

One of my longtime Catonsville teammates was able to make a handsome living out of playing baseball—Jeff Nelson, a side-arming reliever, pitched for many years with the Seattle Mariners and the New York Yankees—but I pursued a decidedly less glamorous and lucrative career in the academy. I wound up teaching and writing several books about law and religion. My interest in this area was sparked by my lifelong fascination with the Catonsville Nine, but I always felt a little too close to their story to be able to chronicle it well.

And I have to admit that I was cowed by the prospect of writing about Phil and Dan Berrigan, the two best-known members of the Catonsville Nine. For several generations of liberal Catholics, the Berrigan brothers are icons. Because of their indefatigable antiwar and social justice activism, both men have been nominated multiple times for the Nobel Peace Prize, and it is not uncommon to hear them referred to as modern-day saints. I worried that writing about these larger-than-life figures might turn into little more than an extended exercise in hagiography.

Intimidated, I was content to kick the can down the road, collecting boxes of materials about the Catonsville Nine and stowing them away for a time when I felt ready to tackle the project. I toted a small archive of books and articles with me as I bounced around the country for my academic career. The files expanded as I accessed archives and manuscript collections housed at colleges and universities, public libraries, religious centers, and historical societies. The oral histories, private letters, and unpublished accounts that I collected through these efforts both broadened and deepened my understanding of the Nine and their times.

Over time, I gathered a wealth of other materials as well—documentary films, photographs, unpublished academic papers, and recordings and transcripts of interviews. I even came into possession of a brittle reel-to-reel tape on which one of the Catonsville Nine, Brother David Darst, had recorded himself teaching a high school class. (It took me a good five minutes to explain to my children what the tape was and how one might listen to it. To kids born in the twenty-first century, it looked like a relic from an ancient civilization.)

As I compiled these materials, I also nurtured a web of contacts with the Catonsville Nine themselves and individuals who were linked to them in some fashion—their siblings and children, their friends and admirers, people who had been touched by their witness.

The surviving members of the Catonsville Nine—there are, sadly, only four as of this writing—were unfailingly generous to me. George Mische did not merely allow me to speak with him on several occasions about the case; he invited me to his home and shared a hearty breakfast of steak and eggs. He regaled me with a dizzying array of stories that deeply enriched my understanding of the Nine. Tom Melville taught me about Central American politics and intro-duced me to the wonders of Latino social networking. (I chuckled when I received an email asking, "¿Te gustaría agregarme como tu amigo?" Yes, I wanted to add him as my friend.) His wife patiently fielded questions from me that un-doubtedly struck her as being bizarre. (Had she lent Mische a safety pin after he ripped his pants during the raid on the Catonsville draft board? She had.)

Despite his failing health, Father Daniel Berrigan inspired and encouraged me as well. At one point near the end of the project, he sent me a beautiful hand-printed copy of his poem "Words, Deeds: The Penitent Speaks." In the poem, the speaker mentions his devotion to words but admits that they amount to little more than shadows of actions. After I pinned the poem to the wall above my desk, I began to reflect on its resonance—not only for Berrigan himself but also for me. Hanging near my computer monitor, it served as a useful reminder of the limitations of the historian's craft.[1]

The real turning point in writing the book came when I filed a half-dozen separate requests under the Freedom of Information Act to obtain files on the Catonsville Nine from the FBI. It is difficult for me to describe how jumbled and fragmentary these documents proved to be. The agency sent me reams of illegible and completely irrelevant material—a lot of junk, basically. But after sifting through boxes and boxes of documents for several years, I unearthed some treasures that no journalist or historian—or even the Catonsville Nine themselves—ever had reviewed.

I saw pictures of the charred remains of the files that the Nine had burned. I read the interviews that the FBI had conducted with witnesses shortly after the demonstration at Local Board 33 in Catonsville. I discovered extensive reports documenting the federal government's efforts to track the members of the Nine who became fugitives. There were other nuggets as well: a copy of Mary Moylan's application for a nursing license, an inventory of the items in Tom Lewis's pockets when he was hauled into jail after the Catonsville protest.

With stacks of such documents piling up in my cramped office at the Uni-versity of Wisconsin–Madison, I realized that I probably needed to get the book out of my system before the place was declared a safety hazard.

As I finally bore down on writing the book, my perspective on the Catons-ville Nine and their witness did not change so much as it expanded and evolved. I did not lose any respect for their creativity, their courage, or the sincerity of their ideological convictions. And I never ceased to be amazed by the array of people who have drawn inspiration from their actions. (For the first time in my career as a historian, I had to think about the common ground shared by Noam Chomsky, detective fiction authors, and the makers of pop-ular board games.)

However, as I delved deeper and deeper into the public and private lives of the Catonsville Nine, I gained a better understanding of the sharp criticisms that have been directed at them over the past four decades. By keeping an open mind, I learned why some people—including a good many Catholics—sincerely have believed that the protesters betrayed both their country and their church. While I don't necessarily agree with all of those criticisms, I have tried my best to fairly incorporate a variety of divergent viewpoints in this book.

I also have made a special effort to provide some long-overdue perspective on the lives of Mary Moylan and Brother David Darst, who probably are the two least appreciated and poorly understood members of the Nine. Both activists left the public stage—in different but equally heartrending ways—not long after they participated in the raid on Local Board 33 in Catonsville. Darst died in an automobile accident in 1969; Moylan became a fugitive in 1970 and remained underground for nearly a decade thereafter. Sadly, their respective absences from public view have been reflected in some of the previous renderings of the story of the Catonsville Nine, in which they appear as only shadowy, peripheral figures.

As the following pages show, I have found it impossible to relegate Moylan and Darst to the margins of my account of the Catonsville Nine. Their stories are too rich and tragic—too revealing about the fragility of the human condition—to be pushed to the fringes. My only regret is that the constraints of time and space have prevented me from exploring their lives more fully.

My guiding principle in assembling the story in this manner has been that I should avoid the traps of exalting the Catonsville Nine as heroes or vilifying them as charlatans. After living with this tale for most of my life, I can conclude that they were neither.

And that is precisely what makes their story so compelling.

Madison, Wisconsin, and Catonsville, Maryland
December 2011

ACKNOWLEDGMENTS

I couldn't have written this book without the support, encouragement, and forbearance of dozens of people. I'll do my best here to acknowledge their substantial contributions. (And I apologize in advance to anyone I might omit.)

My family members probably are rejoicing over the publication of this book because it means that they no longer will have to listen to me talking about researching and writing it. My wife, Susan, and my children, Fred and Maisie, have shown remarkable patience over the past several years as I have focused on far-off people and events. (To their credit, both kids ignored my suggestion that they should try to duplicate the "bathtub chemistry" feats of the Catonsville Nine and concoct a batch of napalm for their elementary school science fair.)

I am especially grateful to all of the people in Catonsville, Maryland, who helped me in ways large and small. Throughout this project, my former classmates at St. Mark School and Catonsville High School (and their spouses) were unfailingly generous and supportive. Their ranks included: Phil and Linda Bowman; Jim and Kathy Burk; Peter Keck; John and Tammy Kistler; Fred and Nancy McHugh; Scott Meacham; Maureen Murphy; Mel and Jean Sanders; Molly and Roy Santa Croce; and Eric and Rachel Wenck. Brian and Michele McFarland provided a place to stay during several of my trips back home, and Brian reminded me of the inclusion of Catonsville Nine questions in *Trivial Pursuit*. Peter Keck's parents, Mace and Maureen, got into the act as well. (Mace—a high school classmate of Tom Lewis—diligently copied for me pages from an old Mount Saint Joe yearbook.)

The Patapsco Council No. 1960 of the Knights of Columbus in Catonsville also deserves my thanks. Michael Doetzer and Nick Hasser provided me with background about the council and its history, and Wayne McCullough gave me an impromptu tour of the hall. Tim McCarthy provided some great background on the press coverage of the Baltimore Four and Catonsville Nine.

In addition to schooling me for eight years, St. Mark in Catonsville posted my call for research help in the church bulletin.

A couple of my former classmates at Rutgers University provided support. Kathleen Ogle offered feedback on the introduction, and Mark Walsh helped me think about the significance of the witness of the Catonsville Nine. (He also facilitated my contacts with Dan Berrigan.) David Willis helped me track down some material in New Jersey.

The Records Management Division of the Federal Bureau of Investigation handled innumerable inquiries from me and fulfilled my many requests for materials under the Freedom of Information Act. Staff working under David M. Hardy in the Record/Information Dissemination Section were unfailingly helpful.

Several diligent librarians and archivists made my life easier. The assistance furnished by Andrea Bainbridge (at the DePaul University Libraries Special Collections and Archives) and Amber Kohl (University of Maryland Libraries Special Collections) was priceless. The staffs at the Division of Rare and Manuscript Collections at the Cornell University Library and the Department of Special Collections and University Archives at the Marquette University Library also greatly facilitated my work.

Bryce Rumbles of the Catonsville Branch of the Baltimore County Public Library was indispensable. He did everything from facilitating my use of the library's Catonsville Room to helping me straighten out permissions with the Friends of the Catonsville Library. The Friends, too, deserve mention here, especially Cheryl Dunigan and Lisa Vicari.

Jay D. Smith, from the office of the general counsel of the Hearst Corporation, helped me gain permission to reproduce photographs from the old Baltimore *News American.*

Baltimore filmmaker Joe Tropea could not have been more good-natured and cooperative. In addition to sharing with me many of the interviews that he had conducted for his film *Hit and Stay*, Joe served as a sounding board as I muddled my way through writing this book. I am similarly grateful to filmmaker Lynne Sachs, on whose film *Investigation of a Flame* (2001) I have relied.

Whenever I asked (and that was fairly often), the Catonsville Nine and their families lent a hand. George and Helene Mische not only spoke with me—they also fed me well at their home in the Twin Cities. Tom and Margarita Melville straightened out a number of issues for me. Father Dan Berrigan was Father Dan Berrigan—gracious, profound, inspiring. I regret not having had the chance to directly interact with Phil Berrigan, Brother David Darst, John Hogan, Tom Lewis, and Mary Moylan, but members of their families capably stepped into the breach. I owe a great debt to Chuck and Guy Darst; Joan and Jen Hogan; Don Lewis; and Paula Scheye. They provided a wealth of materials that I could not have uncovered otherwise.

Several other people submitted to interviews or provided material (or both, in many cases). Debbe Orenstein Fate shared with me a treasure trove of letters she had received from Brother Darst. Joe Forgue also recounted for me some of his experiences with Darst, and he supplied a reel-to-reel tape on which Darst had recorded himself teaching. Barney Skolnik described how he (reluctantly) became involved in the prosecution of the Nine. Lane Bonner outlined how the Federal Bureau of Investigation (FBI) had searched for Moylan, and Hugh Barnhardt led me through some of the basics of the bureau's work in Baltimore in the 1960s. Joseph Sheppard schooled me on the Baltimore arts scene in the 1960s. From Grenville Whitman I learned a great deal about the activities of the Interfaith Peace Mission, the Baltimore Defense Committee, and the protest activities surrounding the trial of the Catonsville Nine. George Giese deepened my understanding of Phil Berrigan, and Sheppard informed my perspective of Tom Lewis. Joan Cavanagh provided a recording of the interview she conducted with John Hogan for the Greater New Haven Labor History Association, of which she is archivist/director. The reliable Matthew Swaye found me an important document at Columbia University. At the Brother David Darst Center in Chicago, Emily Hitchens was resourceful and patient.

I also benefited from my contacts with Willa Bickham, Michael Boover, David Eberhardt, Andrea Hellman, Ed Henson, Herman Heyn, Donna Poggi Keck, Trish Maher, Joann Malone, Mike Martin, Patrick O'Neil, Judy Porter, Mim Murphy Quaid, Jonah Raskin, Rosemary Ruether, James Smith, and Brendan Walsh.

At Oxford University Press, Cynthia Read once again proved to be both a skilled editor and a staunch advocate. Her assistant, Charlotte Steinhardt, also pitched in capably.

Joanna Griffin took on the unenviable task of shooting an acceptable author photograph. (I'm still not sure how she managed it.)

Finally, I offer my thanks to several of my academic colleagues. Arthur Eckstein (University of Maryland), J. Justin Gustainis (Plattsburgh State University of New York), and Thomas Moylan Keck (Syracuse University) furnished materials and perspective on the Nine. At the University of Wisconsin–Madison, Vice Provost Damon Williams and professors James Baughman, John Milton Cooper, Ronald Numbers, and Hemant Shah spent an inordinate amount of time bolstering my flagging confidence. (Both John and Ron are easing into retirement—partly, I think, to avoid my constant entreaties.) Mel Urofsky (formerly of Virginia Commonwealth University) and Michael Ross (University of Maryland) buoyed me as well. Mike gave me a chance to speak about the Nine in College Park, and I benefited from interacting with his students and colleagues.

ABBREVIATIONS

AITPN	James McGinnis Darst (a.k.a. Brother David Darst), *All in the Passing of Now*
BC-CU	Daniel and Philip Berrigan Collection (number 4602), Division of Rare and Manuscript Collections, Cornell University Library, Ithaca, NY
BDC-FBI	Baltimore Defense Committee FBI file
BMC	Berrigan-McAlister Collection, DePaul University Libraries Special Collections and Archives
BS	*Baltimore Sun*
CTT	Catonsville trial transcript (United States District Court for the District of Maryland, *United States v. Daniel Berrigan et al.*, October 7–10, 1968)
CU	Columbia University
DD	Francine du Plessix Gray, *Divine Disobedience*
DD-CWC	Dorothy Day–Catholic Worker Collection, Special Collections and Archives, Marquette University, Milwaukee, WI
FCLC	Friends of the Catonsville Library Collection, Baltimore County Public Library, Catonsville Branch
FTLW	Philip Berrigan, *Fighting the Lamb's War*
HAS	*Hit and Stay* film interviews (Joe Tropea)
IOAF	*Investigation of a Flame* film interviews (Lynne Sachs)
JMD-FBI	James McGinnis Darst (a.k.a. Brother David Darst) FBI file
MM-FBI	Mary Moylan FBI file
NCR	*National Catholic Reporter*
NYT	*New York Times*
PB-FBI	Philip Berrigan FBI file
PJ	Philip Berrigan, *Prison Journals of a Priest Revolutionary*
SA	Special agent
SAC	Special agent in charge
TDIP	Daniel Berrigan, *To Dwell in Peace*
TL-FBI	Tom Lewis FBI file
TOTCN	Daniel Berrigan, *The Trial of the Catonsville Nine*
WHWE?	Tom and Marjorie Melville, *Whose Heaven, Whose Earth?*

The Catonsville Nine

"Arguably the Single Most Powerful Antiwar Act in American History"

By the late 1960s the Knights of Columbus hall in Catonsville, Maryland, had come to resemble a respectable but sagging New England inn. Three stories tall and fronted by a broad porch, the white clapboard building stood just west of the center of the Baltimore suburb, on its main thoroughfare, Frederick Road. It had been built shortly after the Civil War for a wealthy Baltimore attorney; he dubbed the place "Beaumont" and used it as a country home. The local council of the Knights of Columbus had paid $13,000 for the structure in 1921. The purchase had allowed the group to move out of its temporary quarters in the hall of a nearby Roman Catholic church, St. Mark.[1]

The local branch of the Baltimore County Public Library—a building as flat and modern as the Knights' hall was tall and dignified—had been erected just across the street in 1963. For a thrill, kids walking to the library from the elementary school at St. Mark sometimes scampered along atop the low stone wall that bound the front of the Knights of Columbus property. In the summer, this same perch was well known in Catonsville as a prime spot for viewing the town's annual Fourth of July parade, for which flag-waving crowds had thronged Frederick Road since the late 1940s.[2]

Founded late in the nineteenth century in the basement of a church in New Haven, Connecticut, the Knights of Columbus is an all-male Catholic fraternal service organization. In addition to furnishing lectures on church doctrine and helping to endow scholarships at Catholic colleges, councils like the one in Catonsville—named the Patapsco Council, after the meandering river that separates the town from neighboring Ellicott City—promote Catholic education and charity.

They also give Catholic men and their families a place to socialize. The Knights in Catonsville often hosted bull roasts and crab feasts, festive occasions where local Catholics could find steady supplies of both camaraderie and cold beer. The lower levels of the Knights' rambling hall in Catonsville provided plenty of space for such activities, so they rented out several upstairs rooms. In the late 1960s their tenants included the local military draft board, which occupied two rooms on the southwest corner of the building's second floor.[3]

The main office of Local Board 33 was not much bigger than a college dorm room. There, three Selective Service System clerks warehoused and processed the draft files of young men from a wide swath of southwestern Baltimore County. With the war in Vietnam in full swing, more than thirteen thousand draft records filled rows of metal filing cabinets; hefty ledgers containing draftees' birth and registration dates sat open on tabletops.

Early in the afternoon of May 17, 1968, a group of Roman Catholics converged on the Knights of Columbus hall in Catonsville. Ironically, their destination was not the part of the building used by the Catholic fraternal organization. Instead, they were headed upstairs to Local Board 33.

They had an ambitious goal: to stage a protest so startling that it would challenge Americans of all faiths to reappraise and reinvigorate their nation's commitment to sustaining justice at home and promoting peace abroad. It wouldn't be a stretch to say that they wanted to change the world.

To avoid being spotted, eight of the protesters walked up a back staircase to the second floor of the hall. Their ranks included two priests, Dan and Phil Berrigan, brothers who were widely known for their opposition to the war in Vietnam; Tom Lewis, a Baltimore artist and social justice activist; Tom and Marjorie Melville, former missionaries in Guatemala; another former missionary named John Hogan; George Mische, at whose Washington, D.C., home much of the group had come together; and Mary Moylan, a nurse who was the sole native of the Baltimore area in the group.

The ninth member of their contingent, a member of the Christian Brothers religious order named James McGinnis Darst, stood watch on the building's front porch. It was the responsibility of Brother David, as Darst was known, to sound a warning if the police arrived before the protest had been carried out.

Once they had ascended to the second floor, the eight demonstrators barged past the trio of clerks and ransacked the cramped office of Local Board 33. They hurriedly stuffed draft files—what they lamented as "death certificates" because of the role they played in dispatching young men into combat—into large wire trash baskets. There was a minor scuffle involving Mary Murphy, the head clerk; Phil Berrigan manhandled her when she attempted to thwart the protest. Otherwise, the raid went smoothly, and the demonstrators were able to haul nearly four hundred individual draft files from the office.

But the Catonsville Nine, as they soon would be called, were not finished. They retreated to the parking lot behind the Knights of Columbus hall and doused the files they had seized with a batch of napalm. In a landmark moment of do-it-yourself arms-making, they had managed to concoct it themselves by following instructions that had been adapted from an Army Special Forces handbook.

The demonstrators had very carefully thought through this part of their protest. Napalm—a flammable liquid that was being wielded with devastating effect in Southeast Asia by the American military—was to them a symbol of the barbarity of the war in Vietnam. With their witness in Catonsville, the Nine hoped to use napalm for opposite ends—to preserve lives rather than extinguish them.

After drenching the draft files with their homemade napalm, the Catonsville Nine set the material on fire. They solemnly recited the Lord's Prayer as the records went up in flames.

Their provocative—and brazenly illegal—actions did not go unnoticed. Supporters of the Nine had tipped off reporters, and they recorded, on paper and film, the burning of the draft files outside the Knights of Columbus hall. The midday spectacle in Catonsville, suffused in religious and political symbolism, made headlines in papers throughout the country the next day.

Astonishing images accompanied these stories. Here were Catholic laymen and priests—the latter unmistakable in their dark clothes and distinctive collars—igniting a bonfire of draft records in broad daylight as a means of objecting to the shortcomings of American foreign and domestic policy. Most Americans never had seen anything like it.

The Nine, in keeping with their understanding of the norms of civil disobedience, made no effort to avoid arrest after they had torched the draft records in Catonsville. In fact, they actually *wanted* to be arrested, charged, and put on trial. That way, they would have a public forum to more fully spell out their religious and political views.

The federal government was more than happy to oblige the Catonsville Nine, charging them with a variety of crimes, the most serious being destruction of government property and interference with the administration of the Selective Service System. They stood trial together in the fall of 1968. The legal proceedings occasioned a week of demonstrations on the streets of Baltimore, the largest and most fervent antiwar protests seen in the city in the Vietnam era. Activists flocked to support the Nine from as far away as Hawaii.

Events in the courtroom were even more gripping. Prodded by their lead attorney, the iconoclastic William Kunstler, the Nine offered long and moving explanations of how their religious and political views had compelled them to besiege the draft board in Catonsville. They also provided scathing indictments of American foreign policy and the immense toll it had exacted on American society.

Their wide-ranging testimony tested the patience of the trial judge, Roszel Thomsen. Throughout the proceedings, he frequently interrupted the Catonsville Nine to remind them that *they*, and not the war in Vietnam, were on trial. Yet Thomsen wound up giving the defendants a surprising amount of latitude, and they were able to turn their trial into an extended debate about not only war but also the duty of citizens to follow their consciences—even if doing so meant violating the unambiguous letter of the law.

Their trial occurred at a time of keen social and political crisis. The ongoing carnage in Vietnam; the assassinations of Martin Luther King Jr. and Senator Robert F. Kennedy; the massive antiwar demonstrations that wracked college campuses across the country; the disruption of the Democratic convention in Chicago and the thuggish response of that city's police force—a succession of such alarming events in 1968 caused Americans from all walks of life to wonder where their country was headed, and why. Amid this tumult, the Catonsville Nine used their trial to issue a forceful call for the country to turn in a new direction, one in which justice, equality, and compassion were touchstones.

Their eloquence in making these claims showed how dramatically the Catholic Church in the United States was changing in the 1960s. One recent account of American Catholicism in this period has used terms like *revolution, maelstrom,* and *typhoon* to describe how transformations in worship and worldview swept over members of the church. The reforms of Vatican II spurred American Catholics to consider the "signs of the times," to engage in meaningful conversations with the modern world, and to embrace a spirit of open-mindedness and change. The Catonsville Nine sought to use their trial—and the protest activities that complemented it—to broadly extend these conversations to include overlapping discussions of war, imperialism, poverty, and injustice.[4]

After the jury retired, the federal trial of the Catonsville Nine climaxed in uniquely dramatic fashion. First, the defendants engaged in a lengthy colloquy with Thomsen in which they paired their critique of American foreign and domestic policy with an indictment of the legal system that had snared them. Then, in one of the most remarkable moments in the history of American law, they led everyone in the courtroom—including the judge and the federal prosecutors who hoped to convict them—in the Lord's Prayer.

If the prayer marked the high point of the trial, then the verdict marked its nadir: the jury found all of the Nine guilty on all counts. They subsequently were sentenced to terms in federal prison ranging from two to three and a half years. (Phil Berrigan and Tom Lewis received the stiffest sentences because the Catonsville demonstration was their second draft board raid in the Baltimore area in less than a year.)

But the extraordinary story of the Catonsville Nine did not end with their convictions in federal court. Several more intriguing—and unpredictable—chapters followed.

In 1970, after their legal appeals had been exhausted, four of them—the Berrigan brothers, Mische, and Moylan—refused to report for their prison sentences. Determined to continue their witness against injustice and imperialism, they went underground, relying on a loose network of like-minded activists to evade capture. Their decision to become fugitives occasioned a national manhunt that was closely monitored by J. Edgar Hoover, the director of the FBI. The length of the chase so infuriated him that he subsequently trumped up outlandish charges against the Berrigans and several other activists for their alleged roles in a wildly implausible plot to kidnap Secretary of State Henry Kissinger.

The search for Father Dan Berrigan garnered the most media coverage, in part because he often appeared in public and mocked the FBI for its inability to catch him. He remained a fugitive for several months; the FBI's prolonged embarrassment finally ended when it nabbed him in August 1970. Although Moylan's story attracted far less attention, she lasted underground even longer. After nearly a decade on the run, she finally turned herself in to federal authorities in 1979.

During Moylan's time underground, actors portraying her onstage were seen more frequently in public than she was. In 1970 Dan Berrigan published an account of the four days that the Nine spent in court explaining how the evolution of their religious and political beliefs had driven them to destroy draft files in Catonsville. *The Trial of the Catonsville Nine*, based on transcripts of the activists' celebrated trial, was turned into a play that has been produced all over the world in the last four decades. (It is a measure of the play's broad and enduring appeal that it recently enjoyed a successful run in Australia.)

The list of actors who have had parts in various productions of *The Trial of the Catonsville Nine* includes such luminaries as Sam Waterston, Tim Robbins, Peter Strauss, and Beau Bridges. Martin Sheen, who has participated in several productions of (and readings from) the play, said that he has been so drawn to the story of the Nine because they participated in "arguably the single most powerful antiwar act in American history." Such was the power of their witness that Gregory Peck, the esteemed actor, produced a film version of Berrigan's play in 1972. Although it was made on a shoestring budget, the film premiered at the Cannes Film Festival and won wide acclaim.[5]

Peck and Sheen were not alone in recognizing that the Catonsville Nine accomplished something exceptional. Scholars ranging from Noam Chomsky and Howard Zinn to Gordon Zahn and Harvey Cox have described their witness as having been a singularly daring and powerful plea for peace and social justice. (In a single essay, Cox went so far as to favorably compare them to Moses, the prophet Jeremiah, Martin Luther, and the abolitionist William Lloyd Garrison.) Journalists and social commentators like I. F. Stone, John Leonard, Francine du Plessix Gray, Amy Goodman, James Carroll, and Garry Wills have delivered similar pronouncements. "Their types are recognizable through history: the stuff of which saints are made," Stone wrote, "moved by a deeper sensitivity to human suffering." The exploits of the Nine also have been celebrated in song, poetry, literary fiction, mystery novels, children's literature, visual art, documentary film, and even board games.[6]

But the complete story of these singular activists never has been fully told. Berrigan's play, riveting though it may be, amounts to a snapshot, depicting only a few hours in a long and fascinating journey—one that involved nine distinct personalities and unfolded over several decades in such far-flung lands as Guatemala, France, and Uganda. To be sure, the lives of the two most prominent members of the group, Dan and Phil Berrigan, have been explored capably in numerous films, articles, and biographies. Yet the Catonsville Nine as a group never previously have been the subject of a book-length study. Thus, our knowledge of this seminal protest—one that gained so much international attention that officials in the Kremlin even commented on it—is woefully incomplete.

A full account of the lives of all of the Catonsville Nine represents more than simply a group biography of some quirky radical activists who briefly captured public attention and then faded back into obscurity. It demonstrates how, in perilous times, profound religious and political beliefs can coalesce and motivate sincere individuals to risk their personal freedom in order to resist state policies they deem both illegal and immoral.

The story of the Nine further reveals how broadly such selfless acts of resistance can resonate with people who question the aggressive role taken by the American government on the world stage. Today, more than forty years after they stormed into the Catonsville draft office, the example of the Nine still is often invoked by both secular and religious opponents of militarism.

In recounting this powerful story, there is a temptation to cast the Catonsville Nine as unassailably noble and pious individuals who martyred themselves for the anti–Vietnam War movement. But this characterization is misleading in two significant ways.

First, the Catonsville Nine were sinners as much as they were saints. Complex and imperfect people, they sometimes struggled to live up to the lofty ethical principles they espoused. The Nine could be self-righteous and hypocritical. They were melodramatic and drew attention to themselves. They criticized others—sometimes brutally—but often bristled when their critics returned the favor. They bickered with one another and harbored resentments that lingered for many years. They also fell into despair and questioned the paths their lives had taken. They were, in short, human beings, not one-dimensional religious icons.

Second, opposition to the American role in Vietnam was only a part—albeit a significant one—of what motivated the Catonsville Nine. Several members of the group acted primarily to express their outrage over how the United States was implicated in oppression of the poor in Central America, Africa, and other parts of the Third World. And all of them hoped that their action would draw attention to the myriad political and socioeconomic woes afflicting black Americans. For all of the Nine, Vietnam was merely one acute symptom of a pervasive illness plaguing the entire American body politic.

Within a few months of the Catonsville protest, the term *theology of libera-tion* was coined by the Catholic theologian Gustavo Gutiérrez to describe a dynamic set of beliefs and practices aimed at confronting all forms of social and economic oppression. Gutiérrez and his allies promoted an active, bot-tom-up theology that would, as he put it, "at all times protest against injustice, challenge what is inhuman, and side with the poor and the oppressed." The ideology of the American antiwar movement informed the actions of the Catonsville Nine, but so too did the emerging ethos of liberation theology, which stressed the application of the core lessons of the Gospels to the suf-fering and struggle of the poor. It provided an expansive framework that linked their concerns for the underclass in Latin America, Vietnam, and America's inner cities.[7]

The provocative manner in which the Nine brought liberation theology to suburban Baltimore was not met with universal public approval. Although some admirers likened the Catonsville Nine to the Apostles, the novelist Walker Percy wondered how much their fiery protest differed from the activ-ities of the Ku Klux Klan. Many of Percy's fellow Catholics argued that the protesters disgraced the church by engaging in a self-serving and pointless act of politically inspired vandalism. More than a few proponents of nonviolence questioned whether the Nine really had stuck to the accepted norms of civil disobedience. And some conservatives blasted them as traitors for having tan-gibly aided America's enemies in wartime.

We also should bear in mind that their protest, while it touched thousands and inspired several subsequent raids on military draft boards, did relatively little in terms of actually stopping the ongoing carnage in Vietnam or altering the central tenets of post–World War II American foreign and domestic policy. The conflict in Vietnam wore on for seven more grisly years after the Nine struck in Catonsville, and the American military became embroiled in several subse-quent misadventures (most notably in Iraq and Afghanistan) that were grounded in precisely the kind of belligerent thinking that the Nine so adamantly opposed. Yes, the Nine reached people with their witness, but they did not seem to exert widespread or lasting influence on many secular policymakers.

It is likewise crucial to note the diverging paths that the Nine followed after they came together to protest in Catonsville. The demonstration at Local Board 33 seemed to cement the reputations of Phil and Dan Berrigan as daring ecclesiastical renegades, and they remained in the public eye for the next sev-eral decades. (Dan Berrigan became such a celebrity that he once appeared in an ad for Ben & Jerry's Ice Cream.) Tom and Marjorie Melville were pursued by Hollywood heavyweights Jane Fonda and Donald Sutherland, who wanted to portray them in a film. Tom Lewis found audiences for his art and won praise for his ongoing peace and social justice activism.

But some of their compatriots—activists who were every bit as sincere in their faith and just as committed to changing American society—did not fare as well in the wake of the Catonsville protest. Brother David Darst considered leaving his religious order and struggled with thoughts of taking his own life. He died in a car wreck while the convictions of the Nine were on appeal. Mary Moylan lamented her role in the draft board protest (she felt that it had been dominated by the men involved) and suffered through a prolonged downward spiral during her time as a fugitive. For them, the Catonsville demonstration did not prove to be a launching pad into the rarified air of public celebrity. One might argue, in fact, that the protest contributed to the turmoil and uncertainty that blighted the rest of their lives.

This book explores both the triumphs and the tragedies of the Catonsville Nine. It does so by chronicling their lives both as individuals and as members of a group that engaged in a provocative and controversial iteration of social, religious, and political protest—one that still stands, for many Americans, as a signal act of civil disobedience. It also follows many of those whose paths intersected, if only briefly, with the Nine: the draft board clerk who attempted to stop their protest, the federal judge who struggled mightily to manage their trial, the firebrand attorneys who represented them in court, the supporters who aided their protest and organized the demonstrations that were staged in conjunction with their trial.

Twining together so many threads into the seamless fabric of a single narrative is an intricate task, one made all the more difficult by the fact that the Nine lived rich and varied lives that were shaped by a welter of religious, cultural, and political forces. What follows is an attempt to sort out at least some of those influences and to recount how the nine individuals who were molded by them set out to change American society.

1 }

"I Want You to Meet This Priest"

Tom Lewis had a peripatetic childhood. His family always seemed to be either getting ready to leave somewhere or just settling in.

He was born in Uniontown, Pennsylvania, on March 17, 1940—St. Patrick's Day and, in that year, a very early Palm Sunday—but his family picked up and moved before he had spent much time there. His father worked for the National Biscuit Company (now known as Nabisco), and the family relocated several times as he moved up the company ladder and helped it peddle Lorna Doones, Oreos, and Animal Crackers. The elder Lewis had started as a clerk in Akron, Ohio, but he showed so much promise that he earned a series of promotions—to auditor, branch manager, and, finally, manager. The promotions were not without a price: every four or five years, "he would pack up the family and we would move to different places," Lewis later said of his father. After Uniontown came Cambridge, Philadelphia, Louisville, and, finally, Baltimore. Tom Lewis and his family settled there in the late 1950s.[1]

The moves were hard on him, in part because of their unfortunate timing. Lewis's family relocated to Baltimore, for instance, just before his senior year in high school—a difficult juncture for a teenager to forge new friendships and become acclimated to a new school. But when he reflected on his unsettled childhood, Lewis concluded that he benefited from the disruptions and changes he so often faced. At an early age, he learned to confront new challenges and "take certain risks in order to grow and to mature artistically and also in conscience," he said. The adversity helped make him a stronger and more resilient person.[2]

Wherever the family went, faith was a constant. Lewis's mother was a staunch Roman Catholic, and she insisted that her children be raised in the church. "My mother was really, in the religious sense, kind of the father figure, in that she was responsible that we all received a Catholic education," he recalled. Because of her influence, he attended Catholic schools—Immaculate Conception in Philadelphia, St. Xavier in Louisville.[3]

Influenced by his teachers and his mother, Lewis developed an abiding—though not entirely uncritical—devotion to the church. As a boy, Lewis became fascinated with Catholic iconography and ritual, interests that bloomed during the family's time in Philadelphia, when they lived across the street from the National Shrine of the Immaculate Conception. (The Lewis kids called it "the medal factory" because miraculous medals were produced there.) On his way home from school, Lewis sometimes slipped into the back of the church while novenas were being said. He couldn't comprehend what was being uttered by the priests during these long devotions because, as he later put it, "everything was in Latin." The services touched him all the same. Transfixed, he would sit in the shrine for hours.[4]

Lewis's father, a Presbyterian, also shaped his spiritual development. At the Catholic schools he attended, Lewis often heard that non-Catholics were destined for hell, but he knew in his heart that this simply could not be true because his own father was such a sincere and caring Christian. In fact, it was Lewis's Protestant father who instilled in him a love of the Christian scriptures. The elder Lewis would read to the family from the Bible on special occasions, such as holiday meals. No one seemed to care which version of the Bible was being used; what mattered were the lessons—about love, humility, forgiveness—being invoked. These readings left Lewis spellbound, and from them he gained a lasting appreciation of the Bible. It became his touchstone.[5]

For his senior year, Lewis attended Mount Saint Joseph High School (known locally as "Mount Saint Joe") in Baltimore. Although he was far from husky—the FBI later noted that he was all of 5'6" and weighed 170 pounds—he excelled at football and became a stalwart for a team that contended for the Maryland Scholastic Association title. Wearing number 32, "Tommy" (as the *Baltimore Sun* sometimes called him) starred as both fullback and defensive back for the Gaels during the 1957 season. In one memorable November game against rival Loyola, Lewis scored two touchdowns, one coming on a spectacular 60-yard interception return. (Despite his efforts, the contest ended in a 20–20 tie.) Such were his contributions that the team named him its "unsung hero" after the season ended.[6]

One topic that never came up at Mount Saint Joe was the possibility of openly questioning the morality of war. Nor did anyone raise the idea of resisting military service on the grounds of religious conscience. In those bleak early years of the Cold War, devout Catholic kids kept their qualms about war to themselves. "We never had an anti-war discussion in any Catholic school I attended," Lewis remembered. And refusing to serve in the military on the grounds of conscience or religious faith? "I didn't even know," he recalled, "what a conscientious objector was." He never heard much about peace demonstrations either.[7]

Lewis's views about war began to evolve after he graduated from Mount Saint Joe in the spring of 1958 and gained some firsthand experience with the military. To fulfill his Selective Service obligations, he enlisted in the Army National Guard of Maryland in May 1958. He served on active duty in the Army from October 1958 to April 1959 and then in the reserves for several years thereafter.

When he entered the service, Lewis was no radical liberal. "I was not by any means what you would call left wing at that time in my life, politically," he later said. If anything, he was a conventional conservative. However, while in the military he embarked on "a slow process of waking up to the problems of war," and his political perspective changed dramatically.[8]

With the military anticipating a no-holds-barred conflict with the Soviet Union, servicemen were trained in atomic, biological, and chemical warfare. To Lewis, it seemed that the Army did not care about the welfare of the soldiers who would be imperiled when such weapons were used. Servicemen were instructed to swarm into a blast zone and search for surviving enemy soldiers immediately after a tactical nuclear weapon was deployed. The soldiers were told that they would be safe because "the radiation hadn't fallen to the ground yet," Lewis remembered. "At worst, you might lose some hair, and if it were too dangerous, the badge you were wearing would turn a particular color." This was, of course, disastrously untrue. Had they followed such harebrained instructions, Lewis and his comrades would have found themselves on suicide missions.[9]

The conduct of some of his fellow soldiers further troubled Lewis. When he was stationed at Fort Bliss, Texas, he sometimes joined groups of servicemen traveling to nearby Juarez, Mexico, to blow off steam. One night Lewis and his compatriots fell into conversation with a young woman at a bar. "She was talking about her family, that lived further down in Mexico," Lewis later said. "A large family, and she said that they had no money and that she would come up there and work, and that she had been working six months and that she was so happy that she had saved this money that she could take back to her family. And she reached down into her dress and pulled out a twenty dollar bill, and that's how much money she had, and she was so happy about that." The story appalled him. It was obvious to him that the woman was being exploited because of both her gender and her ethnicity—and that his fellow soldiers were happily complicit in this abuse during their debauches in Juarez. "[I was] beginning to realize that the military was, in fact, not what it was supposed to be," he later said.[10]

Lewis never was much of a soldier; his true love always had been art. When his family lived in Cambridge, Lewis learned that a playmate's mother was a painter, and he sometimes wandered into her studio and marveled at the shapes and colors adorning her canvases. Before long, he was rendering images of his own, often at the expense of his schoolwork. "I recall always being interested in doing little drawings, passing a lot of time in school sketching or drawing, instead of listening to certain subjects," he recalled. "Often I would be bored and do drawings." By the sixth grade, he was creating vivid watercolors.[11]

Early on, Lewis received relatively little formal art training; the parochial schools he attended offered few elective classes. It wasn't until he arrived in Baltimore for his senior year in high school that he had his first chance "to really start to study art seriously," as he later put it. At Mount Saint Joe, he befriended a talented young artist named Joe Vogelsang, who was studying under Earl Hofmann. One of a group of local artists known as the "Six Realists," Hofmann was an emerging figure in the Baltimore art scene, and Lewis quickly fell under his tutelage. For several separate periods after his high school graduation, the eager Lewis apprenticed in Hofmann's studio, observing the elder artist at work and honing his own craft. "It was similar to a kind of training that you would receive in the eighteenth or nineteenth centuries," he later said, "where you would work in a studio with the master or with the artist."[12]

After completing his active military service obligation, Lewis followed Vogelsang to Europe in order to further his training as an artist. Hoping to save money on his passage, he arranged to work as a deckhand on a freighter that was crossing the Atlantic. He ended his brief career on the high seas so that he could study at the Uffizi Gallery in Florence, widely regarded as one of the great art museums in Europe.

There Lewis had a unique chance to study the works of the Old Masters. "Through some friends who were priests in Rome, I was given total access to the collection," he later said. "I would ask one morning for, say, Tintoretto, and they would wheel in about six carts of original Tintorettos and I would just sit there and look at them. At that time you could have six original Michelangelos. . . . I was able to go in every day and ask for a particular artist. For six months I did that." For a young artist, it was a priceless opportunity.[13]

Thanks to the influence of Hofmann and another Baltimore artist under whom Lewis apprenticed, Joe Sheppard, his work was bracingly realist. Lewis's paintings, etchings, and collages starkly depicted individuals grappling with the troubles that bedeviled American society throughout the 1960s—poverty, violence, bigotry, despair. An unmistakably religious ethos informed how Lewis addressed these matters in his art. In 1966, for instance, he produced a prize-winning etching titled *Ghetto*. This disquieting image showed a Christlike figure hanging between two utility poles in a blighted Baltimore neighborhood. A work titled *Saint Martin de Porres Today* depicted the noted exponent of interracial harmony in a contemporary setting: he stood in front of a wall covered with newspaper headlines reporting incidents of war, violence, and racial injustice. If Martin de Porres were alive in the mid-1960s, Lewis explained, he surely would address such crucial issues in his ministry.[14]

As Lewis matured as an artist, Gabrielle Wise, the *Baltimore Sun*'s art critic, observed that there appeared to be few boundaries separating the major elements that defined his life. Faith, social justice, art—all were of a piece. "For Tom Lewis, there are no classifications for his varied works of art, nor are there separate compartments for religion, for art, for civil rights," she wrote. "They are fused in the whole of life."[15]

Lewis's career as a social justice and peace activist commenced in the summer of 1963. Baltimore civil rights leaders scheduled a massive demonstration to protest racial segregation on July 4 at the Gwynn Oak Amusement Park. The sprawling park long had been a target for civil rights protesters because of its refusal to admit African Americans; members of the local chapter of the Congress of Racial Equality (CORE) had been holding annual demonstrations there since the mid-1950s. Those marches had been relatively modest affairs, and they had not attracted much notice outside the local civil rights community.[16]

In size and impact, however, the 1963 demonstration organized by CORE at Gwynn Oak Park was another matter entirely. On the morning of July 4 several hundred impassioned demonstrators—some from as far away as New York and Philadelphia—gathered in downtown Baltimore at the Metropolitan Methodist Church. After the marchers made their way to the park, they organized a raucous picket line in front of its gates. As part of what the local African American newspaper later described as a "two hour assault on the racially segregated park," integrated clusters of protesters left the picket line and attempted to enter the facility. Before the day was out, hundreds were arrested for trespassing and disorderly conduct.[17]

After hearing a radio report about the protest, Lewis decided to head down to the amusement park and observe the confrontation. Initially, he wanted to watch the demonstration and sketch what he saw; he previously had sold artwork to some Catholic periodicals, and he hoped that they would be in the market for images of the protest. Lewis found himself standing among a group of white counterdemonstrators who heckled protesters as they were shoved into police vans and hauled to jail. A feeling of unease swept over him. "The people I was standing with got uglier and uglier, yelling at the demonstrators, throwing little rocks and firecrackers," he recalled. "I had this awful feeling that even though I was sketching, I wasn't really separate from them. Even though I was there as an artist, a reporter, I really wasn't separate from the crowd and what they were doing."[18]

Lewis sensed that he would be complicit in the counterdemonstrators' perverse actions if he stood aloof from the confrontation. "I went, sketchbook in hand, but while standing in the angry crowd of white bigots, sketching the demonstrators, I suddenly realized that my passivism in that particular situation actually made me part of that mob," he said. Shocked by the scene and unwilling to stand by idly as injustice surged around him, he set aside his sketchbook and resolved to join the protesters. When he approached a black marshal who was running the picket line, Lewis was asked why he wanted to join. He could say only that he felt ashamed to be white. The marshal smiled at Lewis and gave him a sign bearing the words "JIM CROW STOPS HERE."[19]

Lewis never forgot how the amusement park protest had left his heart racing. "This was quite frightening to do for the first time," he said many years later. "I think I was in a cold sweat the entire time." Part of what made the moment so unsettling was that it was transformative: he stopped observing the myriad problems plaguing American society and began taking risks aimed at solving them.[20]

Sparked by the Gwynn Oak Park demonstration, Lewis joined the Baltimore chapter of CORE. Founded in 1942 by University of Chicago students who had been active in the pacifist Fellowship of Reconciliation, CORE attacked racial segregation by following Gandhian principles of nonviolent civil disobedience. The group played a key role in several bellwether civil rights protests of the 1960s, including the March on Washington, the Freedom Rides, and the Freedom Summer. Lewis was mentored by CORE's Walter Carter, who was not known for temporizing: a militant young leader among Baltimore's civil rights activists, he often drew comparisons to H. Rap Brown, the bombastic Student Nonviolent Coordinating Committee activist who later served as a leader of the Black Panthers. But Lewis learned that Carter, for all his militancy, had the patience to move people along slowly instead of pushing them too quickly toward engaging in acts of civil disobedience.[21]

Nudged by Carter and prodded by his own conscience, Lewis began to join in antidiscrimination protests organized by CORE. (He participated in so many of these that Carter publicly recognized him for being an unsung hero in the local civil rights struggle.) Members of the organization sometimes picketed businesses that were engaging in discriminatory practices. They also attended open houses en masse to ensure that prospective black tenants and homeowners were treated equitably. Lewis participated in one such demonstration at the Colmar Apartments in Baltimore with several other CORE activists, including three African Americans. After they staged a sit-in in an apartment, the police were summoned, and Lewis and his fellow activists soon faced trespassing charges. Subsequent demonstrations at Colmar led to similar charges being filed against several other protesters.[22]

Their trial was held in Baltimore in the spring of 1966. For Lewis, the legal proceedings revealed just how many barriers still had to be surmounted before African Americans could achieve full equality in the United States. The apartment manager conceded that the complex was not integrated, but he suggested that he was mainly concerned with keeping out objectionable tenants who might be morally and financially deficient.[23]

As disturbing as these displays of thinly veiled bigotry were revelations about the city of Baltimore's efforts to rein in the activities of civil rights demonstrators. Attorney Fred Weisgal, representing the CORE defendants, elicited testimony from a state's attorney that the city selectively enforced its antitrespassing ordinance; civil rights activists like Tom Lewis apparently were the only individuals who ever faced charges under it. These disclosures—along with poignant testimony from one of the African American defendants that he "just wanted a nice apartment for my family"—seemed to turn the tide in favor of the defendants. The jury hung, and the city dropped the Colmar prosecution along with several other cases involving members of CORE.[24]

Lewis's involvement in the civil rights movement in Baltimore demonstrated for him the vast potential of nonviolent protest. His time with CORE also showed him how crucial it was for Christians to act on their most deeply held convictions and "to stand for what is correct," he explained. "To help someone who needs help. To feed the hungry. To clothe the naked." For Lewis, these weren't acts of heroism but rather simple works of mercy that were essential for all people of faith. "They're very basic acts. As I was taught. As we were all taught as Catholics [and] called to do."[25]

As the 1960s progressed, Lewis's attention increasingly turned to the war in Vietnam. The nation's foolhardy approach to foreign policy and the ongoing turmoil in its inner cities resulted, in his view, from the same maladies: unchecked greed and a mounting indifference to injustice. He argued, "Our slums, economic exploitation, world expansionism, nuclear overkill, chemical and biological warfare research, genocide in Vietnam, counterinsurgency in Latin America and street violence are the expressions of great power and isolated wealth that has no stomach for justice." These matters took on added significance for Lewis when the Air Force dispatched his younger brother to Vietnam in 1965. Until his sibling was in harm's way, he did not give serious, sustained thought to the conflict. With the reality of the war now hitting close to home, Lewis began to read critiques of the war and attend lectures given by critics of the Johnson administration. "I began to study the war, and reflect upon it," he later wrote. His opposition to the war hardened as he began to think of it as genocide. Before long, he "came to the conclusion that the war is totally outrageous, from the Christian point of view." Not only was the war politically misguided; it was immoral.[26]

This point was underscored for Lewis in 1965 when Pope Paul VI traveled to New York City. Although the sojourn was brief (it lasted scarcely more than half a day), it marked a moment of enormous significance for American Catholics: it was the first time a pope ever had visited the United States. Paul's unprecedented trip seemed emblematic of a dynamic new phase of openness and engagement for the Church.

The pontiff made the most of the occasion. Speaking at the United Nations General Assembly, he delivered perhaps the most memorable address of his tenure, referencing the memory of President John F. Kennedy and reminding the delegates that the UN had been formed in the wake of World War II to put an end to "useless slaughter and frightful ruin." The pope did not mince words.

"No more war, war never again!" he pleaded. "Peace, it is peace which must guide the destinies of people and of all mankind."[27]

Lewis was so moved by the pontiff's speech that he rendered a mixed-media painting and collage titled *October 1965*. The words "No more war, war never again" formed the background for the image, which juxtaposed scenes from the Baltimore ghetto with images of American military might and the suffering of the Vietnamese people. He meant for the piece to show that international tyranny and domestic oppression were inextricably bound together.[28]

Over time, Lewis felt his interests and priorities drifting away from the civil rights movement and toward the war. Issues of racial equality still concerned him, but he felt marginalized as advocates of Black Power came to the fore of the civil rights struggle. This was illustrated for Lewis in some stark and painful ways. At one CORE meeting in Baltimore, a militant African American speaker abruptly stopped a speech when he spotted Lewis in the crowd. He announced that, whatever the artist's sympathies, he wouldn't continue speaking in the presence of a white person.[29]

Lewis had another unsettling experience when the fiery Black Panther leader Stokely Carmichael came to Baltimore to speak. One of Lewis's paintings—a contemporary rendering of St. Peter Claver—had been put on display near the speaker's platform, and he stood nearby. Carmichael apparently didn't know what to make of the bespectacled white artist and his life-sized image of a notable Jesuit. He shot Lewis a withering look and then launched into "an incredibly violent speech against white people," as Lewis described it. The artist gradually came to the painful realization that as "black power became more powerful, the whites became—well, became the enemy. So whites who were working with blacks simply were not welcome."[30]

The antiwar and antinuclear movements were more congenial to Lewis, and he began devoting more of his energies to them. He silk-screened hundreds of signs bearing such messages as "God Is Love" and "No More War—Peace" for local picketers to carry. "This is my opposition to the war," he told a reporter who asked about the signs. "I would not go to Vietnam under any circumstances. I would go to jail rather than Vietnam." It was necessary for activists to offer such resistance because the Johnson administration was guilty of spreading "half-truths and lies," he asserted.[31]

Lewis's opposition to the war intensified after he attended an antinuclear meeting with a friend from CORE named Fred Nass. At the meeting Nass turned to him and said, "I want you to meet this priest." The suggestion surprised Lewis—he never had encountered a priest who was seriously interested in social justice issues—but he was intrigued when he was introduced to Father Philip Berrigan. After the meeting, the two men repaired to the Deutsches Haus, a German restaurant in Baltimore. Over pretzels and beer, they discussed, as Lewis later put it, "some important things." While the drinks flowed, the two men shared their views on the connections between the war in Vietnam and the ongoing turmoil in the nation's inner cities.[32]

Berrigan took a liking to Lewis and immediately sensed a kinship between them. The priest learned that the artist was at a crossroads. He and Lewis discussed the possibility of the latter studying for the priesthood, but Berrigan did not think it would be a wise choice for someone who was so devoted to confronting the great social and political problems of the day. "A seminary did not seem the place for a man already grappling with the raw stuff of human survival—poverty, race, and war," Berrigan said. "More likely, it would be a distraction and a waste."[33]

For Lewis, the chance encounter with Berrigan was a pleasant surprise. He had interacted with plenty of priests before; he was a product of the Catholic school system, and the Xavieran Brothers had put him through his paces at Mount Saint Joe. But most of these men had been formal, distant figures who seemed primarily concerned with exerting their own authority and enforcing rigid adherence to church doctrine. Phil Berrigan was different—*very* different. Lewis was drawn to how human he seemed and how deeply he cared about issues of social justice and peace.[34]

"I was just so moved by a priest that was this open, who would sit down and talk about peace issues and just relax and drink a couple of beers," Lewis later said. "So we began a kind of friendship."[35]

2 }

"You Get the Kind of Freedom You Fight For"

Phil Berrigan never was one to sugarcoat things, and in his autobiography he resisted the impulse to portray his boyhood in idyllic terms. In his telling, it was a hardscrabble life dominated by his father, Tom, a labor organizer subject to unpredictable mood swings. Though volatile, "Pop" was no bum; he worked hard, and he expected his boys—there were a half-dozen of them, no girls—to do the same. By age five, Phil Berrigan had to tackle a variety of thankless chores on the family's farm. He made sure that his father knew that he detested the work.[1]

An anti-authoritarian streak was not all that Berrigan inherited from his father. By bringing home a wide variety of books and periodicals (including the provocative *Catholic Worker*, then in its infancy), Tom and Frida Berrigan exposed their children to serious critiques of the prevailing social order, pointed challenges to both capitalist and Catholic dogma.[2]

And the elder Berrigans didn't just talk about principles of social justice; Tom and Frida acted upon them, frequently inviting hungry women and men into their home to sit at their table. "My mother didn't preach the gospels, she practiced their meaning—even if that meant her own children might have had less to eat, even if that meant we broke bread with ragged, dirty, sometimes smelly, strangers," Phil Berrigan later wrote. This, too, would be his inheritance—an urge to help the dispossessed.[3]

All of the boys attended Catholic school, but it didn't seem to have any particular impact on Berrigan's spiritual or political development. He excelled in sports and proved almost comically inept around girls. Classes were mainly exercises in learning and then "regurgitating nonsense and half-truths," as he later put it. The priests and nuns meant well, but they taught subjects like history and civics from a decidedly conventional perspective—one that stressed the valor of politicians and captains of industry and essentially ignored the fates of ordinary Americans. There was no discussion of the suppression of labor by the robber barons, no reference to the extirpation of Native Americans, no examination of the slaveholdings of the Founding

Fathers. And why had the United States entered into World War I, anyway? No one really ever said.[4]

Not that the teenaged Phil Berrigan was apt to seriously question his government's approach to foreign policy. When World War II erupted, he readily believed the prevailing rationale for American involvement. "I just accepted that the insidious Japanese and Germans had stabbed Uncle Sam in the back," he later wrote, "and needed to be defeated, even destroyed." He believed this so strongly, in fact, that the arrival of his draft notice in 1943 genuinely excited him. At that point in his life, Berrigan never gave even a passing thought to resisting the draft. At age nineteen, he was eager to serve his country and trounce infidels on the battlefield.[5]

His brother Dan was far less enthusiastic about the war and tried to dissuade him from serving. At Dan's urging, Phil attended a four-day retreat at a Jesuit novitiate before he headed to basic training. There, under the guidance of the rector, he worked through the exercises of St. Ignatius Loyola, a series of meditations, prayers, and contemplative practices. Phil asked himself some tough questions. What should he do with his life? Should he devote it to God rather than the military? Ultimately, his fervor for combat prevailed. "I wanted to join the hunt for Adolf Hitler, to hack him to pieces, and to count the demons as they flew out of his wounds," he remembered.[6]

He got his chance in Europe. Fired by his zeal to vanquish Nazis, Phil Berrigan was a model soldier. As the FBI later noted in the voluminous file it maintained on him, Berrigan's military records indicated that "his character and efficiency ratings were excellent." He earned a raft of service medals, including three Bronze Stars (awarded for bravery or meritorious service).[7]

Berrigan fought in the Battle of the Bulge and many smaller but no less brutal engagements. In the process, he mastered an array of weaponry and became, in his own estimation, "a highly skilled young killer" of German soldiers. He knew that German civilians were dying as well; his unit entered the city of Münster soon after Allied bombers essentially had razed it and killed thousands of women and children. Berrigan tried to distance himself from the immorality of those deaths by dehumanizing the enemy and minimizing his own role in the carnage. After the war, he read St. Augustine and absorbed his teachings on "just war," which are interpreted as precluding attacks on noncombatants and the indiscriminate destruction of cities. At the time, though, Berrigan wasn't thinking so deeply. "I was an ordinary soldier," he later wrote, "not a politician or philosopher." By his own admission, he was perfectly content to be "another cog in the killing machine of the United States and the Allied powers."[8]

Berrigan fell into a funk after the war, and his college experience failed to shake him out of it. He attended Holy Cross—a bastion of conformity, not a place where ideological orthodoxies were challenged. This was especially true vis-à-vis World War II. Many of Berrigan's classmates were veterans as well, and they might have welcomed a hard-nosed analysis of the origins of the war and how it had been conducted by both sides. But the college—and really the country as a whole—was unwilling to undertake that kind of inquiry. The students were fed platitudes instead.[9]

After graduating, Berrigan thought about joining the Jesuits, as his brother Dan already had done. But he instead was drawn to the Society of Saint Joseph of the Sacred Heart, whose mission centered on serving African Americans. Founded in the Reconstruction period by a group of British priests known as the Mill Hill Fathers, the Josephites evangelized recently emancipated slaves, many of whom faced insuperable social, political, and economic challenges. Nearly a century later, progress toward racial equality remained slow. Phil Berrigan had witnessed this firsthand during his time in the service. During his tour in Europe, he had been appalled at the treatment of African American servicemen, who were relegated to segregated units and routinely given such menial tasks as polishing shoes. These manifestations of inequality were not limited to the armed services, Berrigan knew; they pervaded American society. He hoped he could attack them by joining the Josephites.[10]

After his ordination, Berrigan went to New Orleans, where the Josephites had a longstanding presence. Then as now, many African Americans in the city lived in dismal conditions and attended substandard schools. In his seven years there, Berrigan did whatever he could to empower them and alleviate their despair. He became an activist, openly challenging the widespread racism he believed lay at the core of African Americans' problems.

He found inspiration in the example set by members of Catholic Worker communities and French "worker-priests," clerics who labored in ordinary jobs and participated in labor organizing (sometimes even going so far as to join striking workers in picket lines). This "commitment to ordinary men and women," as Berrigan called it, caused ripples among the Catholic hierarchy; Pope Pius XII was so disturbed by the worker-priests' spirit of innovation that he eventually threatened them with excommunication if they didn't return to more traditional parish work. Nonetheless, it appealed to Phil and to Dan Berrigan (who saw the activist priests up close during his trip to Europe in 1954). After all, hadn't Jesus himself been an activist? "Christ drove the usurers from the temple," Phil observed. "He didn't write a dissertation on the devious practices of moneychangers."[11]

Phil Berrigan adopted a similarly dynamic approach to bringing about social change. When confronted with injustice, he plunged into action.

In the early 1960s, Berrigan began to forcefully articulate his opposition to the injustices he saw being perpetrated at home and abroad. He attacked segregation in pieces written for publications like *Priest*, *Worship* (a periodical that promoted liturgical reform), and the *Catholic Worker*.[12] Convinced that the mistreatment of blacks represented a repudiation of the democratic ideals on which the nation had been founded, he argued throughout his book *No*

More Strangers that all Americans were obliged to address the country's urgent need for racial reconciliation. Berrigan pleaded for "a concerted national move to break up the racial ghetto" and an attendant effort to eliminate poverty. Passing a few laws, or desegregating a few schools, would not do the trick.[13]

It was no coincidence that *No More Strangers*, littered with calls for action, appeared in 1965, the year that the Second Vatican Council (commonly known as Vatican II) closed. Called by Pope John XXIII, the council produced no major changes in the core doctrines of the church, but its impact on Roman Catholic practices was unmistakable. The sixteen major documents generated at the conclave significantly altered how Catholics worshipped and the manner in which they related to the world outside the church. The council promoted the full participation of the laity in the church's liturgical life and encouraged Catholics join in meaningful dialogue with their non-Catholic neighbors.

In a church famous for resisting change, the developments of Vatican II seemed nothing short of revolutionary. "No other [Church] council could compare with it for direct impact on the life of every Catholic," one historian has written, "and with the sometimes considerable adjustments in religious practice and general attitude that the changes required."[14]

Journalist Garry Wills, a careful observer of postwar Catholicism, noted that Vatican II inspired a wave of social and political activism among American Catholics. "Catholics," Wills noted, "were in the very thick of things." In the vanguard of groups seeking to promote meaningful change throughout society were nuns and priests—people like Father James Groppi, a priest who brashly battled poverty and racism in Milwaukee, and Father Richard McSorley, a Georgetown University professor who told his students that Catholics were obliged to immerse themselves in the issues of the day. For Catholics, it was a time of "unparalleled American clerical radicalism," one observer wrote in 1967.[15]

Phil Berrigan personified this activist trend among Catholic clergy. He drew inspiration from Vatican II, which "was shaking the dust from scripture, challenging clergy and lay people to reexamine their commitment to social justice, and creating space for Catholics to transcend indifference and apathy," as he put it. Also important was *Pacem in Terris*, the 1963 encyclical in which Pope John XXIII argued that it made little sense to use war to ensure justice and peace.[16]

The spirit of *Pacem in Terris* and Vatican II permeated Berrigan's book *No More Strangers* and in many ways framed the witness of all the Catholic activists who became engaged in peace and social justice issues in the 1960s. Writing while the council still was in session in Rome, Berrigan noted that it addressed the obvious need for a vital process of reform in the church. Such a transformation was necessary because "impersonality, suspicion of change, reluctance to evaluate, and an aversion to the best of the democratic process" seemed to pervade all aspects of church life, from its theology and liturgy to the every-day conduct of the laity.[17]

But as the 1960s wore on, this promise of reform—both within the Church and in American society as a whole—remained unfulfilled. Berrigan's writings became correspondingly more biting as well as more overtly political. And it was not just racial injustice that he fought. With the Cold War escalating, Berrigan cast a critical eye on the many geopolitical and moral shortcomings of American foreign policy. Reading the works of authors like William Appleman Williams, the iconoclastic University of Wisconsin historian, prompted him to challenge the orthodoxies that gave rise to the Cold War.[18]

Berrigan began to trace the interconnections between America's misadventures abroad and the injustices that continued to cripple the opportunities of African Americans at home. It was obvious to him that the federal government could not provide jobs, training, and education for minorities as long as it kept devoting vast resources to the folly of the Cold War. "Blacks had to live in shacks, and their children had to die from hunger and disease," he argued, "so that the military could build bombs." The root of the problem: war, "the overarching evil in this country." If Americans repudiated militarism, they finally could address problems like poverty and racism in earnest.[19]

"All my ordained life I have fought lies, hatred and injustice," Berrigan explained in 1968. "I don't care much whether they are found in the excesses of Stalinism, Maoism in China, the Russian invasion of Czechoslovakia, the fascist murder of alleged communists in Indonesia, or our intervention in Vietnam. All are offenses against Christ, whose Body is the body of man."[20]

Berrigan's forthright activism galled his Josephite superiors. Then as later, the American Catholic hierarchy looked askance at the priest's dedication to peace and social justice issues. Matters came to a head in 1965, after he had been transferred from New Orleans to the Josephite seminary in Newburgh, New York. Berrigan raised hackles almost immediately by joining the area's fledgling antiwar community and delivering several impassioned talks about Vietnam to local civic groups. After fielding numerous complaints about his outspoken activism, his superiors ordered him to refrain from addressing controversial social and political topics. For good measure, they also transferred him to St. Peter Claver, a Baltimore parish located near the order's headquarters.[21]

Berrigan felt a moral obligation to flout the gag order. He kept speaking out, and his Josephite superiors kept trying—with little success—to shut him up. Berrigan repeatedly sparred with Father George O'Dea, who often cautioned the brash priest that the order didn't want to become embroiled in public controversies. Berrigan consistently rebuffed such efforts. "I happen to be the only man in the Society speaking and acting on the question of war and peace," he wrote in one letter. "I will neither ignore my country's mistakes, nor the failings of the Church." In another letter, Berrigan warned that he would leave the order altogether if he felt that "there is no alternative to the pursuit of what I deem to be the true voice of the Church and best interests of humanity."[22]

In 1967 Weldon Wallace, the *Baltimore Sun's* religion editor, penned a lengthy profile of Berrigan. Headlined "Father Berrigan's Two Wars," it described how the priest complemented his peace activism with a program of social betterment for the impoverished people living near St. Peter Claver. Wallace outlined how Berrigan was directing a group of seminarians in an effort to improve substandard housing and infuse the area with a sense of community spirit. Berrigan didn't necessarily get his hands dirty, but he helped motivate the young men working under him—one later called him a great "encourager of seminarians." He didn't seem to care if he had to ruffle a few feathers to get the job done. "You get the kind of freedom you fight for," Berrigan told the paper.[23]

As their friendship matured in the mid-1960s, Berrigan didn't browbeat Tom Lewis with Catholic doctrine. It was more typical of Berrigan to take Lewis to New York and introduce him to the work of Dorothy Day, who was fast becoming a kind of patron saint for liberal Catholic activists. The co-founder of the Catholic Worker movement devoted herself to aiding the poor and actively promoting pacifism. Day opposed American involvement in World War II and adamantly resisted militarism throughout the cold war. Starting in the late 1950s, she led Catholics in an annual protest of New York's civil defense drill, earning herself in the process several jail terms. Moved by the sentiments expressed in Pope John XXIII's encyclical *Pacem in Terris*, she joined a group of "Mothers for Peace" on a journey to Rome to thank the pontiff in person.[24]

Lewis was touched by the experience of visiting the Catholic Worker community in New York and observing its members' ardor for helping the poor. "I was very moved by the connection of what you believe, and what you do—the connection between the Gospel, and living the Gospel," he explained. It impressed him to see the example set by two young Catholic Workers he encountered in New York, Tom Cornell and Jim Forest. The pair had just ended a fast, and they celebrated with their visitor by ordering a repast of carryout Chinese food. (Everyone pitched in to come up with the money—a couple of dollars.) Their apartment lacked heat, but they improvised by turning on all of the stove's gas burners. Sharing such experiences with the young Catholic Workers in New York "just opened up a real other dimension to me," Lewis later said. "It showed that there was certainly a very real option, more options than I was aware of for lifestyles."[25]

Inspired by the example set by Day and her disciples, Lewis, Phil Berrigan, and other activists from a variety of religious traditions in Baltimore came together in the mid-1960s to form the Interfaith Peace Mission (IPM). The FBI called the IPM a "pacifist organization" that managed to get off the ground the "first regularly open peace office in Baltimore." Lewis himself described it as "a group of concerned people attempting to express to others what we felt about the war."[26]

In addition to offering counseling to draft resisters, the IPM took out newspaper advertisements that displayed the number of American troops who had been killed in combat in Vietnam. The group also adapted a tactic from the American Friends Service Committee, which regularly sponsored "meals of reconciliation" designed to break down denominational boundaries and bring together activists for discussions of peace and social justice issues.[27]

The IPM also went a step further and combined bread-breaking with protest. After their meals, Lewis and his fellow organizers invited people to go out on the street with signs. Some of the placards (silk-screened by Lewis himself) bore quotations from Pope Paul VI's famous UN address, including the entreaty "No More War." Lewis and his colleagues also learned how to manage media coverage by alerting reporters to their demonstrations.[28]

The press coverage intensified when the IPM—its leaders sensing the limits of simple picketing—ramped up its antiwar activities. Determined to hold public officials accountable for their roles in the expansion of the war in Vietnam, the activists decided to personally deliver letters of protest to the homes of congressmen. "It was kind of like their sacred space," Lewis said of the politicians' homes. "We were saying that with the escalation of the war, you can't really have this space." The protesters reveled in how unnerved the congressmen became by this relatively innocuous form of confrontation.[29]

Late in 1966, IPM members picketed the suburban Washington homes of two of the main architects of the Johnson administration's Vietnam policy, Secretary of Defense Robert McNamara and Secretary of State Dean Rusk. There were about two dozen clergy and laymen involved, including Lewis and Phil Berrigan; they carried placards urging a negotiated settlement to the conflict in Vietnam. At McNamara's house, the protesters knelt in the snow and prayed.[30]

The witness at Rusk's home took an unexpected turn when the secretary of state appeared and invited into his home three of the protesters, including Berrigan. The ecumenical group brought with it a proposal designed to help "cool down the runaway war in Vietnam." The plan included a call for the United States to divert one month's spending on the war (about $3 billion) to create an international police force that would occupy the demilitarized zone that supposedly separated North and South Vietnam. This wasn't a radical idea: Rusk informed the group that a nonaligned nation already had floated a similar proposal. However, the remainder of the peace group's plan seemed implausible, at least from the perspective of the Johnson administration: the trio called for the United States to end its bombing of North Vietnam and accept peace proposals outlined by United Nations Secretary General U Thant.[31]

The meeting yielded few immediate results, but Phil Berrigan was not quite ready to give up on Dean Rusk. A few weeks after their get-together, he wrote

a lengthy letter to the secretary of state. It was vintage Phil Berrigan: three relentless, uncompromising pages assailing the war. Some of his assertions dealt
with geopolitics (the United States had not given U Thant a serious chance to
broker a peace in Vietnam), while others reflected Berrigan's bedrock commitment to his faith (he could not support the large-scale use of military force
because it was inconsistent with his understanding of the Gospels). Berrigan
even went so far as to offer to the administration his services as a negotiator,
proposing that it dispatch him to North Vietnam to meet directly with Ho Chi
Minh and Prime Minister Pham Van Dong.[32]

The IPM mounted additional demonstrations at the homes of other architects of the American war effort. Among those targeted in the spring of 1967 was
Walt Whitman Rostow, President Johnson's hawkish national security adviser.
In a letter explaining its decision to picket in front of his home, the IPM said it
was censuring Rostow because of his widely known commitment to the "ruth-
less power diplomacy" that was bearing such disastrous results in Vietnam.
Indeed, thanks to Rostow and his ilk, the war had become "an enormous
moral, political and economic disaster to both Vietnamese and Americans,
and a criminal threat to world peace."[33]

It was clear from the IPM's letter to Rostow, however, that its members
already were sensing the limits of witnessing in this manner. They doubted
that the national security adviser would sit down and listen to their concerns,
as Rusk had done: "We do not even hope to meet with you as friends and
equals, since you will probably judge that your time can be better spent."
Furthermore, after seeing months of protest result in little change in the
administration's approach to the war, the members of the IPM were not sure if
there was much point in protesting any longer. "We court no special hope
about the efficacy of protest," they acknowledged, "or that foreign policy must
adjust to our opposition or that of millions like us."[34]

With their frustrations mounting, the members of the IPM became more
confrontational, more willing to risk arrest and imprisonment in their efforts
to highlight the immorality of the war. Not long after they marched in front of
Rostow's house, the IPM staged several protests at Fort Myer, an Army post
located near Arlington National Cemetery in Virginia. Members of the Joint
Chiefs of Staff lived on the base, and the activists picketed their homes. They
were ejected from the base after they attempted to have its provost deliver a
written statement of protest to the joint chiefs. When they returned to the base
three weeks later and attempted to pray around a flagpole located near the
joint chiefs' homes, they were dispatched outside the gates on a military bus.
They returned to the base in June 1967 and once more attempted to pray near
a flagpole that stood near the joint chiefs' homes.[35]

The confrontations at Fort Myer would mark a watershed in Phil Berrigan's
approach to opposing the war. "This was my first act of civil disobedience," he
later wrote, "my first step across the line separating polite discourse from

direct action." At the time, however, he hardly felt that he had accomplished very much. Berrigan was haunted by the possibility that he and his fellow activists might be devolving into little more than a bunch of well-intentioned pranksters.[36]

Their apparent lack of impact disturbed Berrigan. The Baltimore peace activists had gotten nowhere by playing by the rules. "Our efforts to communicate with the high-ranking masterminds of mass murder had been futile," he wrote many years later, still roiling with frustration. "We had attended nonviolent demonstrations, written letters to government leaders, and met with government officials, pleading with the government to end its genocidal campaign against the Vietnamese people. Nothing worked. No one listened." He reluctantly became convinced of "the uselessness of legitimate dissent." It seemed like a big dead end.[37]

Lewis shared Berrigan's sense of disillusionment. He was now convinced that "conventional politics cannot bring justice" because "even the honest politicians are too firmly wedded to the captains of finance and industry." There remained only one option for catalyzing widespread change: "creative nonviolence, directed toward the great abuses of American power—the draft, military hardware and personnel, financial centers, and the defense industry," Lewis said.[38]

Eager to hit upon new and more effective means of protesting the war, members of the IPM brainstormed. A variety of ideas were floated. The activists heard a rumor that the Army was using some ramshackle huts at Fort Howard in Baltimore County to train Green Berets for conditions they would find in South Vietnam. They wondered if they could sneak onto the base, surreptitiously demolish the huts, and thereby hinder the training. Lewis and David Eberhardt, an IPM confederate, scouted the potential target but returned with little to report; there were no huts, no Green Berets in training.

Instead of engaging in guerilla civil disobedience at Fort Howard, the IPM members resigned themselves to picketing a draft board in Baltimore's Charles Village neighborhood. Gone were the signs quoting the pope and his message of peace. The demonstrators now carried placards bearing haunting images of a skull and crossbones.

In targeting the draft, the IPM members were following a burgeoning national trend among antiwar activists, many of whom were devotees of Day and affiliated with the Catholic Worker movement. By late 1965 the public burning of draft cards was becoming a popular form of protest—and one that involved no small risk. After magazines published photographs of protesters torching their draft cards, infuriated members of Congress passed a law making such destruction a felony punishable by a $10,000 fine or five years' imprisonment, or both. The first person convicted under the new measure was David Miller, a member of the Catholic Worker community in New York who burned his card in Manhattan in 1965. Other Catholic Workers later faced prison terms for their destruction of draft cards, including Tom Cornell (who had hosted Lewis during his visit to New York).[39]

Some critics of the war went even further. In 1965 three American protesters burned themselves to death in public acts of resistance to the war. (They took their cue from Buddhist monks in South Vietnam who had self-immolated to protest the actions of their nation's government.) The first to die was Alice Herz, an elderly Quaker from Detroit. Then came another Quaker, Norman Morrison. Morrison carried out his fiery protest in front of the Pentagon; as he had hoped, Secretary of Defense McNamara witnessed his gruesome death. A week later, Roger LaPorte set himself ablaze while sitting in front of the UN building in Manhattan. On his way on the hospital (where he later died), LaPorte explained to the police, "I'm against war, all wars. I did this as a religious action."[40]

The deaths of Morrison and LaPorte shook the Baltimore activists. Morrison was a Baltimorean who had served as secretary of a local Quaker meeting; LaPorte was a Catholic Worker who had been inspired by the example of Day, just as they were. Lewis and Berrigan apparently did not know either man closely, but their deaths were significant nonetheless, demonstrating how far some individuals would go in opposing the unfolding tragedy in Vietnam.[41]

Lewis considered emulating Morrison. "Quite frankly," he later said, "I thought seriously of immolating, or burning myself in protest. And thought about it, prayed about it, thought seriously about doing it." But Lewis wondered how useful it would be to kill himself on the steps of the Pentagon. Though undoubtedly powerful, such a witness against the war would mean abandoning the world rather than attempting to reform it. After considering suicide, he settled on something that seemed more creative and effective. He would risk his freedom in another type of antiwar protest—one "that would surely put me in prison for a long time."[42]

For many young men, burning draft cards was a viable form of civil disobedience. "I myself was thinking of burning a draft card," Lewis said. "But it didn't make any sense, because I had already been in the military and I'd already been honorably discharged. The same with Phil." For them, burning draft cards "didn't make any sense because we really weren't liable," Lewis later said. "It was a gesture, with no personal risk." To engage in an authentic act of civil disobedience, they would have to find another way to place themselves in legal peril and risk going to jail.[43]

As their options narrowed, Lewis and Berrigan found themselves "searching for a really creative, positive response to what was happening," Lewis recalled, "something really strong." The protest would have to be inherently nonviolent, and it would have to result in them being arrested and imprisoned. The civil rights movement had shown the effectiveness of this tactic, and Day had argued that filling the jails with protesters would pressure the political system to address injustice. So the essential question—as Lewis later framed it—was relatively simple: "What do you do to get locked up?"[44]

It was common knowledge that files on each military draftee were held at the roughly 4,100 local Selective Service offices scattered throughout the country. In an era before widespread computerization, the creation and upkeep of these paper files—which contained a wealth of detailed data, including contact information and draft classifications—was essential to the smooth functioning of the Selective Service System, which processed an average of 300,000 draftees annually between 1966 and 1970.

At roughly the same time, Lewis and Berrigan realized that seizing and destroying these Selective Service documents might be an effective way of expressing their resistance. It was not much of a leap, in their minds, from torching draft cards. "The records, the cards, the bureaucracy—it's all pretty much the same," was how Lewis later described it. Both men felt compelled not only to join the antiwar protests engaged in by their fellow Catholics but also to extend them by further attacking the bureaucratic machinery of the draft. "We decided the way to support those young Catholic Workers who were going to prison for burning their draft cards," Lewis said, "was to destroy the draft files themselves."[45]

They were not the first antiwar activists to hit upon the idea of directly besieging draft files. In February 1966 a nineteen-year-old named Barry Bondhus expressed his resistance to the war by entering the draft office in Elk River, Minnesota, and dumping two buckets of human excrement over Selective Service files. (Bondhus and his brothers apparently had collected the feces in the preceding few weeks.[46])

Phil Berrigan was drawn to the idea of storming draft boards after he attended an antiwar conference at the University of Chicago. There was much talk at the conference about impeding the war effort by devising innovative strategies for "shutting down the Selective Service process," Berrigan recalled. One person suggested chaining the wheels of buses that transported draftees to classification centers; another said, "You know, those draft boards ought to be raided." The suggestion appealed to Berrigan. He wondered if the easiest way to protect draft-age men from the scourge of war might be to make it more difficult—through an act of vandalism—for the government to find them. He asked himself, "What if draft boards didn't exist? What if the cards all got lost, or burned, or tossed into the sea? How would the government locate military-age males?"[47]

Lewis and Berrigan were committed to nonviolent resistance. But both activists also sensed that, as Lewis put it, "doing *something* with draft records"—demolishing or defacing them in some way—would not be exactly like participating in a sit-in at a segregated lunch counter. There would be a degree of coercion and violence involved if they barged into a draft board and seized and destroyed paperwork belonging to the federal government. And there was always a chance that a bystander might inadvertently be harmed if matters got out of hand.[48]

The protesters eventually reconciled their commitment to nonviolence with their desire to destroy a cog in the war machine. They did so by focusing on the type of property they would be attacking. Indeed, they reasoned that the draft files were not even really "property" in the proper sense of the term. Lewis came to think of the draft files as macabre "death certificates"—documents that effectively sent tens of thousands of young men off to their deaths in Vietnam. "Any kind of violence against people is not nonviolent," Lewis explained. "But what about destroying a death certificate?" To him, it seemed to be an inherently nonviolent act in that it would reduce the chances of individuals—Vietnamese and Americans alike—being harmed in the war.[49]

"No, I would never do anything that would harm people physically," Phil Berrigan explained in a letter to his brother Dan, "but the property that is part of these bloody gearboxes—that's another thing."[50]

As their thinking evolved in 1967, the Baltimore activists began to consider ransacking a draft board office in the Baltimore area. The decision wouldn't be made in a vacuum; they wanted to work with the local peace community to formulate their plan. Lewis hosted a number of gatherings for a group of about ten people at the William Moore House, where he was living. "We had a number of meetings there," he later said, "talking about going to the draft board and doing something to the records, destroying the 1-A files in some way."[51]

3 }

"In Jail for the Right Reason"

As they thought about targeting a draft board, the Baltimore activists worried over the potentially broader implications of what they were planning. The men were well aware of the risks they would be taking in wrecking Selective Service files: they could be harmed in the course of the protest by security guards or police, and they were likely to be arrested and imprisoned afterward. They were willing to pay that kind of price themselves if it meant impeding the war effort and calling attention to how American foreign policy had gone haywire. But what if they inspired other protesters to take similar risks, or even greater ones? Could they shoulder moral responsibility if, even indirectly, their actions led to violence perpetrated by others? And what if Selective Service employees or bystanders were harmed during their protest?[1]

Bouncing ideas off each other in discussions that sometimes stretched late into the night, the IPM activists wrestled with all of these matters. To sharpen their thinking, they also shared their developing plans with other members of the local peace community. The concerns raised in these dialogues were both practical and philosophical. The protesters wondered where they could get their hands on a large cache of draft files and how those documents might be mutilated. They also intensely debated whether such a protest would be truly nonviolent, in the tradition of Mohandas Gandhi and Martin Luther King Jr. The men turned to their faith as well, reflecting on how their plans could be reconciled with their religious beliefs. They prayed often.[2]

Phil Berrigan kept his brother Dan (who also was immersed in antiwar activities at that time) apprised of the group's progress. He was candid about their struggles to come to grips with this new iteration of nonviolent protest. In a letter describing his collaborators in Baltimore, Phil kiddingly referenced the famously disciplined Vietcong. "The young guys," he boasted, "are coming through like old line V.C." He praised Tom Lewis and another prospective raider by noting that they "get more powerful by the day."[3]

In the end, two other men who had participated in a variety of antiwar protests at military bases—IPM secretary David Eberhardt and James Mengel, a

United Church of Christ minister—decided to join Lewis and Berrigan in targeting Baltimore's Custom House, which housed a central Selective Service office for all of the draft boards in the city. Before they struck there, the quartet of protesters traveled to Virginia to consult with Phil Hirschkopf, an attorney who was active in civil rights and civil liberties causes. They hoped that Hirschkopf would be able to outline for them some of the legal consequences they might face if they trespassed and destroyed federal property.[4]

And, at least for a time, they were considering doing far more than just demolishing draft files. According to Baltimore activist Bill O'Connor, who was present at the meeting, the group initially broached with Hirschkopf a plan for a protest that "might have gone beyond civil disobedience." In a scheme that seemed to push the outer limits of nonviolent resistance, they wouldn't merely loot the Custom House. "They were going to blow it up," O'Connor later explained. The activists told Hirschkopf that, because of their commitment to nonviolence, they wanted to make sure that the building was unoccupied and that no people would be harmed in the blast. Hirschkopf was thunderstruck; the idea of setting off an explosive device at the Custom House terrified him. His head spinning with objections, the attorney rushed to his office door, slammed it shut, and set about persuading them that they could not take such a radical step.[5]

The attorney feared that, even if they took every precaution, they might injure or even kill someone if they set off an explosive in Baltimore's main Selective Service office. He also mentioned that they could be putting themselves in harm's way—an overanxious security guard might gun them down in the middle of their foray. And what if they were put on trial and found themselves at the mercy of a judge who was convinced that they were little more than vigilantes? In a letter to his brother Dan, Phil Berrigan said of Hirschkopf, "He was horrified by our speculation and said that they'd lock us up and forget about us."[6]

Eager to minimize the activists' risks, Hirschkopf implored the men to rethink their protest. He suggested that their action at the Custom House might carry more symbolic weight—and garner less public criticism—if they despoiled the records with honey or blood. In the end, "it was the lawyer who really came up with" the idea of using blood to deface the files, according to O'Connor.[7]

At first, Phil Berrigan scoffed at Hirschkopf's idea. When the attorney nixed the bombing plan, "Phil was really pissed at him," said O'Connor. The priest grumbled that Hirschkopf was nothing more than a "goddamn liberal lawyer" who lacked the fortitude necessary to envision a truly radical assault on the draft. But after he had cooled down, Berrigan agreed that they should follow the attorney's lead and splatter blood on draft records. Shedding it, he decided, would allow the protesters to identify with the suffering of both soldiers and civilians in Southeast Asia.[8]

Tom Lewis developed a similar perspective—eventually. Initially, he wasn't entirely comfortable with the idea of defacing the draft records with blood. "It just didn't seem to sit entirely right with me," he later said. "I just didn't see it as a Christian symbol." But Lewis came to appreciate that blood would be an appropriate means of defacing the draft records because it was "a Biblical symbol and certainly a healing symbol. And also a very sobering symbol of what in fact those 1-A files were."[9]

Their chief obstacle in using blood turned out to be logistical rather than philosophical. "Our greatest mistake," Berrigan later joked, "was technical incompetence." The demonstrators had planned to rely solely on their own blood during the protest, but a sympathetic nurse was unable to draw sufficient amounts of it from them. For expediency's sake, the group obtained animal blood from a local store (the Broadway Market) and mixed it with their own. In another bow to practicality, they transported it in emptied-out bottles of Mr. Clean, the common household cleaner.[10]

On the day of their raid—October 27, 1967—Lewis's studio served as the group's staging area. The artist worked out of the William Moore House on Gay Street in Baltimore, and the Custom House was visible through his windows. As his three compatriots—along with assorted supporters and the newsmen they had alerted—stayed behind and watched, Lewis entered the building first, to see if the security guard in the Selective Service office had taken his lunch break. The plan was to have Lewis wave a white handkerchief from the draft board offices to signal that the guard had left his post. However, the view of Lewis was obscured by passing traffic and workmen. The rest of the group made one false start before finally setting off across the street.[11]

When they entered the Selective Service office, the activists had to navigate their way around several clerks. In an effort to distract them, the priest asked to review the draft file of a young man in his parish who had been classified 1-A. A clerk rebuffed him, explaining that those materials were confidential and not open to public inspection, even by a priest. Lewis and Eberhardt then joined in the charade. One asked if he could file a change of address form with his draft board; the other said he had misplaced his draft card and needed a new one. Neither was clear about which board had registered them, and this only served to make their vague inquiries even more complicated. They succeeded in sidetracking the clerk: to fulfill the protesters' bogus requests, she left her post to inspect conscription records housed on another floor of the Custom House.[12]

Once the clerks were sufficiently distracted, Phil Berrigan took the lead in looting the draft files. He opened the gate separating the office space from the reception area and approached the records of Local Board 10. But there was a glitch: the priest couldn't yank open the first filing cabinet drawer he tried. As he struggled with the drawer, one of the clerks noticed the intruder and shouted to a fellow employee that Berrigan was trying to get into the files. Not to be deterred, Berrigan searched for more forgiving filing cabinets and finally hit pay dirt with those containing the records of Local Boards 13, 14, and 24. Several clerks then saw Berrigan—now joined by Lewis—open the top drawers of Local Board 14's cabinets. "Get out of those files! You have no business in there!" a clerk yelled as she ran toward the men.[13]

Hearing the commotion, the Selective Service office's coordinator, Mabel Pearson, hurried over to the filing cabinets. There she found Berrigan and Lewis sprinkling a brownish solution—she thought it might be iodine—onto the draft files from their plastic Mr. Clean bottles. Pearson decided to focus her attention on Berrigan, grabbing the priest's right arm with her left hand in an effort to stop him from squirting any more liquid onto the draft paperwork. The supervisor used her right hand to push against the file drawers that Berrigan was still trying to pull open. Berrigan prevailed in this brief wrestling match; he was able to empty his bottle into several drawers containing the files of Local Board 13. After that, according to a FBI report on the incident, "Berrigan calmly set his bottle on the top of the cabinet."[14]

It was all over in a minute or two. Roughly six hundred draft files lay in disarray, spattered with blood. Files from seventeen of the city's twenty-six draft boards had been defaced.[15]

For Berrigan and his fellow activists, the fight put up by the clerks proved to be the biggest surprise of the protest. They had expected the women's response to be one of "screams and panic," Berrigan later wrote. "The secretaries fooled us . . . by reacting with a certain animal courage, protesting first, then trying to deter us." The priest was shocked at how quickly their reaction degenerated into violence, especially since the activists repeatedly offered assurances they did not mean to physically harm anyone.[16]

At the last minute, Mengel decided not to join the other raiders in pouring blood over the draft records. Instead, he distributed copies of *Good News for Modern Man*, a contemporary rendering of the New Testament. The draft board's besieged clerks were not in a receptive mood: a few of them flung the materials back in his face. One clerk held onto one of the books long enough to fashion it into a makeshift weapon and then rap Eberhardt on the head.[17]

The Baltimore protesters invited members of the local news media to witness their action. The reporters received a formal statement outlining the rationale behind the protest. In it, Berrigan, Eberhardt, Lewis, and Mengel made a point of explaining why they had chosen blood to deface the draft board records. "We shed our blood willingly and gratefully in what we hope is a sacrificial and constructive act," the statement read. "We pour it upon these files to illustrate that with them and with these offices begins the pitiful waste of American and Vietnamese blood, 10,000 miles away." More broadly criticizing the misplaced priorities of American policymakers, the statement further claimed that the country "would rather protect its empire of overseas profits than welcome its black people, rebuild its slums and cleanse its air and water."[18]

The protesters' statement also contained a revealing critique of the legal regime that expedited the ongoing slaughter in Vietnam. The war lacked legal legitimacy, they contended, because it was "backed up by unjust laws of conscription, tax preferences, and suppression of dissent." As these measures made a travesty of the nation's democratic ideals and purported fidelity to the basic precepts of Christianity, they had to be resisted by all Americans. The protesters called upon their fellow citizens to purge the law of such imperfections and "conform it to divine and humane law." It was this higher code that should guide the nation.[19]

The demonstrators also handed out a statement aimed at the federal employees in the building, including those working in the Selective Service office. This document contained a lengthy quotation from Henry David Thoreau's essay *Civil Disobedience*, a touchstone for many nonviolent activists of the time. Thoreau's call for resistance was applicable in a contemporary context, the protesters argued, because of the American government's reprehensible activities in Vietnam. All federal employees were complicit in such actions. "We suggest that the personnel here investigate what your government does in your name, and your own part in the brutal machinery of war," the statement urged. "Can you morally continue your work here, or must you seek other employment to be able to live with yourselves and with your families?" The document also reiterated the activists' concern for keeping their witness nonviolent. With almost childlike emphasis, the bottom line of the statement blared: "PLEASE DO NOT BE FRIGHTENED!!!!!!!! WE WILL HARM NO ONE HERE!!!!!!!!"[20]

After she subdued Phil Berrigan, supervisor Mabel Pearson summoned law enforcement. She initially told the protesters that she would call the FBI, but she figured that the Baltimore Police Department would be able to respond more quickly. "This is Selective Service, Room 131, in the Custom House on Gay Street," she said in a telephone call. "We have demonstrators here in the office who have poured [a] solution over our files. I don't know how many are involved. Send the police."[21]

Adhering to the norms of civil disobedience, the four activists made no attempt to escape after Pearson placed her call for help. "We didn't resist or try to break loose," Phil Berrigan later wrote. "We sat down and waited to be arrested."[22]

It took longer than they expected. Baltimore police officers arrived on the scene a few minutes after the raid; an FBI agent followed suit about half an hour later. He immediately noticed signs of the recent disturbance. Several file drawers remained open, and the surrounding area of the floor was "stained with a liquid resembling blood," as he put it in a report to his superiors. He approached Phil Berrigan and obtained from him a copy of the group's press statement, but the agent's efforts to question the group proved futile. The protesters were asked to sign a waiver, but Berrigan rebuffed the effort. "We aren't waiving our rights," he said, "and, therefore, there is no point in signing this." Local and federal authorities even struggled to get the protesters to divulge their birthdates and places of residence.[23]

Almost immediately after the Baltimore activists were taken into custody, the United States Attorney for the District of Maryland, Stephen Sachs, made contact with Claude DeLoach, a top aide to FBI Director J. Edgar Hoover. Sachs had no experience in handling this kind of protest, and he wanted to know if the FBI had any objection to two clergymen (Berrigan and Mengel) being arrested. DeLoach then queried Hoover, explaining that the men were being held after they "went into a draft board in Baltimore and tore it up." The FBI chief, whose loathing for radicals of all stripes was legendary, had no qualms about the two men being arrested. "I told him," Hoover recounted of his interactions with DeLoach, "to go right ahead and arrest the priest and the minister."[24]

FBI agents remained at the Custom House for several hours, collecting evidence and interviewing witnesses. Among the items taken from the scene were the Mr. Clean bottles that the four men had used. Much to Phil Berrigan's amusement, the FBI seemed deeply concerned over what kind of blood had been in the containers—so much so that the agency tested the traces of it that remained in the bottles. Lab tests later showed that the bottles "contained human blood and fowl blood," just as the protesters acknowledged.[25]

There followed a long afternoon of legal processing. Shortly after noon, the four men were taken to the Baltimore FBI office, where they were questioned once more, searched, and photographed. As the day progressed, Tom Lewis was struck by the similarities between the structures of government and those of the Catholic Church. While the four protesters awaited arrest, they sat on uncomfortable wooden benches that could have been found in any church. The FBI office reminded him of the waiting room of a rectory. ("Even the color schemes were similar—school house green," he quipped.) On the walls were framed pictures of government leaders and landmark buildings—symbols of state authority. Lewis closed his eyes for a moment and pictured religious icons—images of the Sacred Heart or crucifixes.[26]

After the FBI had finished its questioning, the men were handed over to the U.S. marshal, who in turn brought them before the federal commissioner for Baltimore. Stephen Sachs, the United States attorney, recommended that the protesters be released on personal recognizance bonds of $1,000 each. Mengel and Eberhardt posted bond, but Lewis and Berrigan refused. "Such a move was not idle heroics, as the Government believed," Berrigan explained. "It was merely an attempt to keep the initiative, to accept consequences, to shun privilege, to avoid co-optation, and above all to keep our consistency and integrity."[27]

They were dispatched to Baltimore's dank and overcrowded city jail. It was a miserable place—a rabbit hutch, Berrigan thought. Still, he felt no remorse for having taken the actions that led to his incarceration there. He was ready to accept the consequences of his witness.[28]

The presence of reporters at the Custom House assured that the raid and the protesters' arrests would receive widespread news coverage in Baltimore and beyond. The *New York Times* ran a lengthy story that was accompanied by photos showing Phil Berrigan grappling with Mabel Pearson as he tried to open the filing cabinets. A headline in the *Washington Post* proclaimed: "WAR PROTESTERS POUR OWN BLOOD ON DRAFT FILES."[29]

The Archdiocese of Baltimore not could ignore such stories, emphasizing as they did Berrigan's position as a priest. In a statement specifically decrying his conduct, it described the protest as "the kind of flamboyant gesture that is self-defeating" and contended that "its real contribution to peace is questionable." Indeed, over the long haul the raid might prove to be counterproductive. "We believe," the archdiocese's statement continued, "that such actions may be interpreted as disorderly, aggressive, and extreme and that they are likely to alienate a great number of sincere men in the cause of a just peace." Intent on distancing itself from Berrigan's increasingly radical activities, the local church hierarchy not only released its denunciation to the press but also had it read from pulpits throughout the archdiocese.[30]

Phil Berrigan tried to emphasize the positive when he explained the Custom House protest to his Josephite superiors. He pointed out to Father George O'Dea that the protesters had taken precautions to ensure that no one would be harmed during the demonstration. "We have practiced a species of nonviolence quite unknown in this country—the destruction of property necessary to continue an evil while people are fully protected from injury," the priest wrote. "Then we stand by our action, offer ourselves for arrest and take the consequences."[31]

This did not stop the Josephites from issuing a stern pronouncement of their own. The order's vicar general, Father Matthew J. O'Rourke, maintained that Berrigan had acted without the order's imprimatur and that the demonstration represented the Baltimore priest's "own thinking and his own manner of protest." O'Rourke further stated that the priest's method of opposing the war "in no way reflects the policies, the thinking or the practices of the Josephite Fathers, the religious community of which he is a member, the archdiocese of Baltimore in which he is working, the people of St. Peter Claver Church, to which he is assigned, or of the Catholic Church in general."[32]

Dan Berrigan was exultant when he learned what his brother had done. He had been involved in his own protest, participating in a massive antiwar march organized by the National Mobilization Committee to End the War in Vietnam—known as "the Mobe"—in Washington, D.C. (This demonstration had included efforts led by Abbie Hoffman and poet Allen Ginsberg to levitate the Pentagon.) Of the 100,000 protesters, nearly 700 had been arrested, including Dan, who had been held by authorities for several days before being released.

As he made his way from jail to a nearby Catholic Worker house, he heard a radio report of the Custom House witness in Baltimore. He was elated to learn that his brother had pulled off something so bold.[33]

Dan appreciated the differences between the massive Washington demonstration and the much smaller witness organized by his brother in Baltimore. These were significant, he thought. "I had taken part in a low-intensity act, together with those who, shortly thereafter, would vanish once more, into the tunnels and byways of college routine," he later wrote. "But when Philip and his friends walked through the door of the draft board, there was no exit; not for years." Carrying with it significant risks, their witness had taken exceptional physical and moral courage.[34]

When he reached the Catholic Worker house in Washington, Dan phoned his mother, Frida, and explained what had happened to his brother. She took the news calmly but struggled for a moment to understand where her activist sons were; the radio reports of Phil's arrest had confused her. "You mean that you are out of jail," she asked, "and your brother is in?" Dan confirmed their whereabouts and felt reassured that his mother would support him and Phil, wherever they were.[35]

A few years later, after his own participation in a draft board protest, Dan Berrigan reflected on the significance of the Baltimore Four (as Phil Berrigan, Eberhardt, Lewis, and Mengel would be known). He believed that the demonstrators at the Custom House inspired numerous others, including him, to take direct action to confront the immorality of the war. Phil and his accomplices "got something going," Dan concluded. "Their hands reached deeply into the springs of existence, cleared away the debris and filth, and set the pure waters running again. Some of us drank there, and took heart once more."[36]

But not all American Catholics responded so favorably to the ransacking of the Custom House. In a fairly typical reaction, the *National Catholic Reporter* voiced qualified praise for the Baltimore activists while wondering if the general public would be able to fathom the meaning of what the quartet had done. In an editorial, the liberal weekly acknowledged that in pouring blood over draft files the Baltimore Four had "devised perhaps the most vivid symbol yet found, short of self-immolation, to express what they want to say about the war in Vietnam, about the draft, [and] about war in general." Yet it was unclear to the *NCR* if their symbolic action would be understood by most Americans. Indeed, "we question whether in fact it will be discerned by any significant number of people."[37]

The reactions of individual Catholics varied widely. Catholic Worker Jim Forest admitted that the Baltimore Four's witness "really didn't turn me on, at the time." Upon hearing of the demonstration, he was left with "a feeling of profound ambiguity. It didn't speak to me." He wasn't sure how effectively it communicated the activists' message.[38]

Anthony Mullaney, a Benedictine monk, was more immediately impressed. For him, the witness was not just risky and dramatic—it even seemed to jar his consciousness. These sentiments were shared by Joseph O'Rourke, a Jesuit priest who felt that the Custom House demonstration "seemed exactly right at the time—to guys who had a history of militance and were searching for ways to protest." He was struck that the Baltimore activists had risked lengthy terms in federal prison to make a powerful statement against the war in Vietnam. "Holy shit! Five to ten years!" he thought when he learned of the possible jail sentences that the men faced. "Those guys are going to jail forever!"[39]

Secular antiwar activists took notice as well. In the late 1960s Mark Rudd was leading a series of demonstrations at Columbia University in New York. (He later became part of the Weather Underground.) "Anyone can take a building," he said after learning about the Custom House raid, "but to walk in and deface draft records, well, that takes courage."[40]

The arrest of the Baltimore Four, and the incarceration of two of them afterward, seemed to energize peace activists in the area. Berrigan and Lewis led the way by announcing that they would engage in a hunger strike in jail. Outside, their supporters showed their solidarity by picketing and telling reporters that the two men were being held as political prisoners.

The IPM also staged a succession of press conferences and released statements from several individuals connected with the witness. Tom Lewis's mother might have offered the most poignant statement of all. If she felt any ambivalence about the implications of her son's activism at the Custom House, her words did not betray it. "You are serving your country just as truly as if you were in uniform—just in a different way," she told him. "You are serving the real interest of your country, which is peace."[41]

Lewis and Berrigan fasted after they appeared at a preliminary hearing and refused to sign recognizance bonds. As the two men ratcheted up their protest, Lewis insisted that he had committed no crime in defacing the draft records and thus had no responsibility to post bond. "I am a Christian, not a criminal. I will not post bond," he told reporters. He would be happy to return to jail and continue fasting.[42]

Years later, Lewis defended his decision to escalate his witness in jail in this manner. "I think we both saw a value in being in jail for the right reason," he explained. "You might say a value in suffering for the right reason. I think that comes really from the roots of our Catholic tradition and education."[43]

When they felt they had made their point, Berrigan and Lewis ended their jailhouse fast. They were then better able to interact with their fellow inmates, the great majority of whom were black and poor. On the surface, there seemed to be little potential common ground between these streetwise men and the imprisoned protesters. But Lewis and Berrigan had long histories of civil rights activism, and they were eager to reach out to the other men in the jail. Recognizing that many of their fellow prisoners were illiterate, the activists offered their assistance in communicating with the outside world. They soon found themselves penning letters to judges, attorneys, and family members.

Writing these missives gave Lewis and Berrigan a chance to learn more about why and how so many African American men wound up in jail. It amazed the priest that these men were "treated like assassins" even though most had committed only petty crimes. They came away touched by the openness and sincerity of their fellow inmates, many of whom took the time to consider why the activists had staged their protest at the Custom House. "Only the prisoners accepted what we were and what we were attempting to do," Berrigan wrote. "Many came to thank us with embarrassing friendliness and genuine emotion."[44]

During their time in the Baltimore jail, Lewis and Berrigan often thought about the African American prisoners who filled the facility. Berrigan never believed that these men were sociopaths, nor did he think that their crimes had been committed out of sheer malevolence. He concluded, rather, that they had found themselves whipsawed between the hopeful rhetoric spouted by white officialdom and the grim reality of life in urban America. The priest thought that "they had done the only thing they could do and keep their sanity—resist." In this defiance of corrupt authority, the white activists and the African American criminals shared a great deal.[45]

But there remained an enormous gulf between them. Not long after Berrigan and Lewis arrived at the jail, a chaplain announced that the two newcomers—one of them a priest—would join in celebrating the Eucharist. "Yeah, he's one of us!" one African American prisoner said, referring to Berrigan. Although it was meant as a gesture of solidarity, the remark left the priest reeling. He was filled, he said, "with shame and something bordering on despair. Because the fact is that I had not been one of them, and was only learning gropingly that not being one of them was an inexcusable mistake." In his peace and social justice activism, Berrigan interacted primarily with elites—congressmen, Cabinet secretaries, and the like. He now realized that this strategy, premised on the assumption that those wielding power were in the best position to bring about real change, was grounded in "a fallacy offensive to both human integrity and to the democratic process."[46]

"A Great Human Act Done by Sincere Men"

In the wake of the Baltimore Four demonstration, the Interfaith Peace Mission continued to agitate. Early in 1968 it sent out a fund-raising letter proclaiming, "Now is the time for us to change our military policies as a nation whose government is by, for, and of the people." But the group faced some formidable challenges as it attempted to affect this change. One was fiscal. As the New Year dawned, its coffers contained a mere $78.[1]

Aside from its financial straits, the IPM and its members had to contend with a variety of forms of harassment. Vandals hurled rocks through the windows of both the Peace Action Center, where the IPM was housed, and the home of activist Bill O'Connor. FBI agents appeared so routinely that the IPM printed up a primer that its members could use to turn the tables on their interlocutors. Sections of the pamphlet were devoted to "General Questions" regarding the war in Vietnam and "Specific Questions" that focused on the bureau's dogged efforts to investigate peace activists in Baltimore. The latter section raised such questions as "How many agents in Baltimore are working on the Peace Issues?" and "Do you think of yourself as gathering information about us or as intimidating us?" After they became aware of the primer, FBI higher-ups realized that it would be pointless—and maybe even embarrassing—to continue overtly probing the IPM's activities. Always vigilant about protecting the bureau's image, J. Edgar Hoover instructed his subordinates, "I want no contact of any kind to be made with this outfit."[2]

While the IPM struggled to maintain its footing, Tom Lewis and Phil Berrigan decided to post bail. Lewis continued to work on his art after he was released from jail. Early in 1968 about 150 of his pieces were featured in a show at an Episcopal church in Baltimore. The opening drew a diverse crowd: according to the *Baltimore Sun*, "Anti-war sympathizers, artists and an FBI agent were among those who attended." The show demonstrated that concerns about peace and social justice issues continued to inform Lewis's work. One vivid etching showed the faces of Vietnamese children awash in a garish sea of yellow and orange hues. Lewis called the piece *Napalm*, after the weapon being used with such grotesque effectiveness by the American military in Vietnam.[3]

Meanwhile, Phil Berrigan kept up his protest activities. In November 1967, he advocated organized resistance to the draft while addressing a large gathering at Cornell University, where his brother Dan worked. Touting the disruptive impact of the Custom House raid, he urged the assembled students to take direct action to thwart the war. "You can make the draft quiver," he said. Berrigan delivered another ardent speech on the campus of Catonsville Community College in suburban Baltimore early in December 1967. "The future looks darker and darker to me," he told the crowd. "Are we going to continue this mayhem? Oh, if only everyone pursued self-determination there would be no war."[4]

As he rallied supporters to the antiwar cause, Berrigan distanced himself from a couple of peace groups that he felt had become too timid and conventional. In December 1967, in a long letter to Jim Forest, he formally broke with the Fellowship of Reconciliation (FOR), with which he had been associated for several years. "My impression has been, for well over a year, that the FOR has moved steadily to the margin of the war–peace issue," he told Forest in typically unsparing terms. "Frankly, I no longer take it seriously." Berrigan's complaints included a charge that the work of the group "seems . . . safe, unimaginative, staffish, and devoid of risk or suffering." Solemn antiwar ads in the *New York Times* were not likely to dissuade the Johnson administration from continuing the war. What the country really needed, Berrigan explained, was ongoing "social disruption, including non-violent attacks against the machinery of this war." In the same letter, Berrigan offered a similarly brutal indictment of the Catholic Peace Fellowship, lamenting that it was not "realistically facing Vietnam and/or the Cold War."[5]

As these internecine squabbles played out, the Baltimore Four formulated a defense to the raft of federal criminal charges they faced: malicious destruction of property, mutilation of records, and interference with the Selective Service process. To represent them in court, they turned to a colorful Baltimore attorney named Fred Weisgal, who had built a formidable career representing civil rights and peace activists in the area (quite often at no charge).[6]

Toward the end of his life, an admirer of Weisgal wrote that "he defended the hapless, the helpless, and the hopeless. Not a day passed that Fred, fashionably rumpled, scowling and determined, could not be seen astride his charger of the moment tilting at an assortment of windmills." Throughout the 1960s members of the local chapter of CORE repeatedly turned to Weisgal when they faced criminal charges in connection to their protest activities. The attorney's representation of Tom Lewis and his codefendants in the Colmar Apartments case typified his efforts on behalf of these activists and their social justice causes.[7]

Weisgal worked closely with the IPM activists to craft their defense. The attorney consulted so frequently with Phil Berrigan that the priest became a regular visitor in the Weisgal home. As happened so often in his life, Berrigan made an enduring impression on everyone, including Fred's eldest daughter. She thought that he "had a way of looking you directly in the eye and asking questions and you got the impression he really cared about the answers." She could understand why he had become a clergyman.[8]

The defendants also met with Weisgal in his office to plot strategy. These intense sessions continued through the Christmas holiday season—a fact that was not lost on Sidney Albert, Weisgal's law partner. At the time, it was customary for attorneys to express gratitude to their clients by offering them bottles of liquor during the holiday season. With Weisgal immersed in preparations for the Baltimore Four trial, this task fell to Albert, who soon felt harried by the procession of thirsty clients who showed up at the firm. Albert thought that Berrigan might be able to alleviate the problem. He broke into one of the conferences to jokingly ask if the priest—who presumably had the appropriate ecclesiastical connections—could make Christmas an every-other-year affair.[9]

Weisgal defended the Baltimore Four with his customary zeal. In a pretrial proceeding, he argued that his clients could not receive a fair trial because prejudice against antiwar protesters was so widespread. Weisgal, asserting that such sentiments were bound to prejudice jurors against his clients, maintained that the trial should be postponed for at least six months, or perhaps even until after the war had concluded.[10]

This was not an outrageous ploy. The Baltimore Four trial initially was slated to begin in January 1968, but federal prosecutors succeeded in moving it back for several months. As the liberal Catholic magazine *Commonweal* noted at the time, the Justice Department was wary of trying the case so soon after the succession of antidraft protests that had occurred at the end of 1967. Federal officials, according to the magazine, hoped to "put more distance between the trial and the emotions stirred up" by those demonstrations.[11]

Still, Weisgal knew he was facing an uphill battle in trying to push the trial back even further. The judge hearing the case was Edward S. Northrop, who had been appointed to the federal bench by President Kennedy in 1961. To the Baltimore activists, Northrop embodied the political establishment that had led the country so disastrously off course in recent years. Describing the vast ideological gulf separating the defendants and the judge, Phil Berrigan sniffed that Northrop was "a trust fund patriot determined to keep America safe from dissent."[12]

It thus came as no surprise to Berrigan and his codefendants when Northrop refused to further delay the start of the trial because of the war and its potential impact on jurors. Biased jurors, he ruled, could be weeded out during voir dire.[13]

That process lasted for several days early in April 1968. Northrop painstakingly questioned more than one hundred potential jurors, querying them on a variety of subjects, including their views on antiwar protests and the possible impact of those activities on the course of the war in Vietnam. He asked them,

"Have you ever been a member of a group which opposed or supported the Vietnam war?" and, "Do you believe the communists dominate the peace movement?" Unacceptable responses to these questions resulted in Northrop excusing about a fifth of the jury pool. Another group of potential jurors were released when they could not assure the judge that they would give the defendants a fair and impartial trial. Northrop's disqualifications left the attorneys in the case to squabble over the remaining forty-one potential jurors. The judge gave Weisgal fifteen challenges—five more than were required by federal law— but the defense attorney complained that he needed still more. Several of the remaining potential jurors, he claimed, were hostile to the antiwar movement, and their presence on the jury would stack the deck against his clients. Northrop wouldn't budge on the matter; he knew that the trial might never get started if he allowed Weisgal to handpick the jury. In the end, he had to live with a panel that included six former servicemen and a retiree who had worked as a civilian for the Navy.[14]

Sitting in what he later described as a "musty, paneled courtroom, impersonal as a railroad station or a mortician's parlor," Dan Berrigan looked on in dismay as Northrop impaneled the jury in his brother's trial. The Jesuit was struck by how many lives had been touched by the war in Vietnam. "It became clearer, as the jurors were questioned," he observed, "how nearly impossible it was to come upon an American who was not, in some tragic and real way, through relatives or friends or emotional bias, involved in the war game."[15]

Dan Berrigan was not the only person observing the trial. For entirely different reasons, the FBI was watching as well. The bureau's rapidly expanding file on Phil Berrigan was crammed with updates on the proceedings, from the defendants' pretrial motions through their eventual sentencing. Even something as mundane as the prolonged process of jury selection merited an "urgent" report to FBI headquarters. (The memorandum noted with annoyance Northrop's decision to award the defense so many peremptory challenges.) The government also kept tabs on the modest protests that were staged by supporters of the four men on trial.[16]

The case put on by the federal government did not include conspiracy charges; these were dropped by U.S. Attorney Stephen Sachs. Having disposed of a potentially tricky part of the case, he was able to mount a relatively straightforward prosecution. Intent on avoiding broader political and cultural issues that might cloud the trial, Sachs kept the proceedings focused as narrowly as possible on the defendants' actions in the Custom House. To that end, he put a succession of witnesses on the stand—draft board clerks, newsmen, assorted Selective Service employees—and had them describe how the four activists had plotted and executed their protest.

In making his case to the jury, Sachs also used the defendants' own words against them. With obvious relish, he introduced as evidence the public statement that the protesters had released to explain their protest. The prosecutor made much of their assertion that they would accept the legal consequences of their actions. He also attacked the quartet's claim that they should be found not legally guilty because, in taking part in the raid at the Custom House, they had been following their consciences. Pure motives, Sachs insisted, did not justify illegal actions.[17]

While Sachs sought to narrow the scope of the case, the defense attempted to broaden it as widely as Northrop would allow. Not content to limit their protest to the destruction of draft records, they hoped to use their trial as a forum to further delineate their critique of the war in Vietnam and the broader ills that were afflicting American society. In a bold gambit, Weisgal informed the court that he intended to frame the protesters' actions as a justifiable response to the illegal and immoral activities of the American government in Vietnam. The four men would claim that they had attacked the draft files in a desperate effort to prevent those criminal acts—which amounted to crimes against humanity—from continuing.

The four protesters readily admitted that the acts described in the federal criminal complaint had taken place, Weisgal said. But that would not be enough for them to be found legally guilty. Jurors also would have to assess the intent of the four men when they had entered the Custom House. "In a criminal case, it is not enough that an act takes place," the defense attorney maintained. "There must be criminal intent." And there the prosecution's case fell apart, for the government was unable to demonstrate that Berrigan, Lewis, Mengel, and Eberhardt had been "motivated by evil intent" when they defaced the conscription records. In fact, their intentions had been the noblest imaginable: they had been trying to save lives.[18]

Another pillar of the defense strategy rested on the legacy of the Nuremberg war crimes trials (officially known as the International Military Tribunal for Major War Criminals) in 1945 and 1946. There, a rogues' gallery of former Nazis had claimed that they should not be held legally accountable for their actions in World War II because they merely had been following their superiors' orders. Furthermore, everything they had done had been legal; all of it had been sanctioned under the laws of the Third Reich. These claims had been largely unsuccessful, and almost all of the defendants had been found guilty of committing crimes against peace, war crimes, and crimes against humanity.[19]

The Baltimore Four attempted to justify their actions in the Custom House by pointing to the central lesson of Nuremberg—that following orders and obeying questionable laws did not justify participation in systematic murder. Weisgal hoped to argue before the jury that the protesters had broken the law only because they hoped to stop their government's ethically and legally dubious actions. Unlike the Nuremberg defendants, they had refused to countenance illegal and immoral activity by the state.

To build this line of argument, Weisgal wanted to show that there was no legal grounding for the Johnson administration's conduct of the war in

Vietnam. He informed Northrop that he intended to call as witnesses an array of leading scholars and thinkers who would testify that the war in Vietnam was illegal because President Johnson never had received authorization from Congress. Weisgal's experts included Boston University professor Howard Zinn and Phil Berrigan's brother Dan.[20]

Like these experts, the Baltimore Four "believed their government was committing a crime," Weisgal said. "Their conscience made it a duty to try to stop their government from committing this crime. . . . Their theory was that it was not a crime to stop anyone from committing a crime." In defending the protesters' actions, Weisgal also hoped to invoke the First Amendment's protections for free speech. He wanted to claim that the actions of the four men, because of their expressive intent, amounted to a form of speech and thus merited constitutional protection. "They thought it was necessary to stop this war and they tried to adopt a more dramatic form of free speech," he explained.[21]

Northrop knocked out most of the underpinnings of Weisgal's proposed defense, including the free speech claim. Anticipating what the Supreme Court would hold a few weeks later in a different case (*United States v. O'Brien*),[22] the judge held that the First Amendment's speech provision did not protect acts of protest. The First Amendment, he found, "does not shield conduct which collides with a valid criminal statute," such as those the federal government sought to enforce against the draft protesters in Baltimore. The protesters' motives, however sincere, were irrelevant. Northrop ruled that "it makes no difference . . . that the defendants acted out of the sincerest of motives and the deepest of convictions, be that religious, moral, or political."[23]

As he reined in the defense, Northrop highlighted one of the central issues of the Custom House case: the extent to which individuals could be absolved of legal responsibility when their actions were grounded in sincere moral convictions. For the judge, this wasn't a close call. "A moral conviction is not enough to justify a violation of the law," he informed Weisgal. "This would permit the defendants to pick and choose the laws they wanted to obey. Good motives do not prevent the formation of criminal intent and indeed are no excuse for a criminal act."[24]

A writer for the *National Catholic Reporter* noted that defendants were intent "on using the federal courts as a forum for their antiwar beliefs." Northrop, though, was having none of it. In addition to blocking the First Amendment claim, the judge refused to allow antiwar scholars to testify that the war in Vietnam was illegal.[25]

He also grappled with the ghosts of Nuremberg. In a lengthy written opinion, Northrop eviscerated the defendants' claim that their actions had been a justifiable attempt to prevent the United States from committing war crimes. He determined that the defendants lacked legal standing to raise such a claim because they had not been inducted into the armed forces and thus weren't directly impacted by the government's conduct of the war.[26]

For Northrop, more serious than the matter of legal standing was the question of whether the courts should attempt to resolve such inherently political questions as the proper course of the nation's foreign policy. The Baltimore activists were not so naïve as to expect that Northrop would rule the war illegal, but they hoped that raising the question of war's legal legitimacy would at least help to justify their actions. The judge, however, closed the door on this line of argument, ruling that the war's legitimacy was a political matter that lay outside the jurisdiction of the courts. "Whether the actions by the executive and the legislative branches in utilizing our armed forces are in accord with international law," Northrop held, "is a question which necessarily must be left to the elected representatives of the people and not to the judiciary." In other words, he wouldn't allow the four Baltimore activists to put the war on trial.[27]

It was tragically appropriate that some of the momentous social issues—racism and poverty—that so disturbed the Baltimore Four wound up interrupting their trial. On April 4, 1968, civil rights leader Martin Luther King Jr. was gunned down in Memphis, Tennessee. Angered and despairing over the loss of their most eloquent advocate for equality, African Americans subsequently rioted in dozens of American cities.

In Baltimore, disturbances began in earnest two days after King's death. By the evening of April 6, Governor Spiro Agnew had declared a state of emergency, and 6,000 National Guard troops had been dispatched to the city to control widespread vandalism, looting, and arson. (On that day alone, three people died as a result of the violence, and seventy were injured.) Judge Northrop put the trial on hold for five days until order in the city could be completely restored.[28]

The unrest roiled the city's poorest and most desperate neighborhoods. Phil Berrigan's parish, St. Peter Claver, was located in one such area, Druid Heights. Berrigan returned to his church during the break in the trial and helped to man an emergency station serving the injured and those displaced by the rioting. His brother Dan had come to Baltimore from his home in New York to observe the trial, and he also tried to mitigate the suffering in the neighborhood.

Phil Berrigan's frustrations with American society bubbled over periodically during the riots. One of his superiors at St. Peter Claver extended hospitality to some of the police and National Guardsmen who were attempting to restore order in the city, feeding them sandwiches and allowing them to use the church's bathrooms. It enraged Berrigan to see his church welcoming these symbols of oppression. He felt that the church should be on the side of revolution, not repression. "Let the city burn!" he sputtered in one moment of anger.[29]

For the defendants, the rioting added another wrinkle to an already complicated case. Not only did it threaten to rip their city asunder; it also had the potential to directly affect the outcome of their prosecution. They feared that jurors would be more likely to find them guilty because members of the panel might associate their motives for engaging in protest with those of the post-assassination rioters who were running amok in the city. Northrop recognized this potential danger, and when the proceedings resumed he questioned the jurors to determine if their impartiality had been be affected by the rioting. Their answers satisfied him, and he allowed the trial to continue.[30]

Overshadowed by racial strife and the tragedy of the war in Vietnam, the trial was a serious affair, but it was brightened by a few lighter moments. A number of local activists were in attendance, including Barbara Mills (who later penned a massive biography of Weisgal). Hoping to expose her eleven-year-old son to a spirited debate over the war, one day she brought him along with her to watch the proceedings. During a break, Weisgal asked the sixth grader what he thought of the trial. He was noncommittal. "I don't know yet," the child replied. "I'll have to hear more of the evidence."[31]

Working the crowd was the least of Weisgal's worries. In essence, he needed to convince jurors to set aside their conventional understanding of how the law worked. Yes, the defendants had violated federal law; they had admitted as much. But the attorney insisted that their reasons for committing those crimes had to be taken into account in determining whether they should be punished. At one point he elicited testimony from Phil Berrigan that the defendants had acted because they were tormented by anger over the war in Vietnam.

Such claims carried little weight with Stephen Sachs. During his cross-examination of Berrigan, the no-nonsense federal prosecutor zeroed in on what the four men had attempted to accomplish when they entered the Custom House.

"You wanted to damage the Selective Service files, didn't you?" Sachs asked.

"To be perfectly honest with you, yes," Berrigan responded.

"You wanted to disrupt the clerks at the draft board, didn't you?"

"We thought that we wanted to be successful, but disrupting the work was a secondary consideration."

"You wanted to make sure you called attention to yourselves?"

"We felt we had a severe moral obligation to protest the Vietnam war."

"You used the fictitious name of a boy to gain easier access to the draft board files, didn't you?"

"I cannot excuse myself for that dissimulation," Berrigan admitted. "But the Government's conduct of the war and the reporting of it need to be taken into consideration to justify our means."

Sachs followed a similar route after Mengel stated that the four raiders had "anointed" the records at the Custom House with blood for a "cleansing effect."

"You wanted to deface the records, make them harder to read, didn't you?" Sachs asked.

Mengel replied in a philosophical vein. "In one way," he said, "we wanted to make them more clear."[32]

As the trial ended, Fred Weisgal offered a lengthy and emotional closing argument in which he confessed to feeling "really at odds with the judicial system." The defense attorney told jurors that he felt so conflicted because, while he respected the rule of law, he could not countenance its use to penalize individuals who were guilty of having followed their consciences. In doing so, the four defendants "did what's absolutely proper in the American way," the attorney said. "I honestly believe these men did something that most of us inwardly approve of." What separated Berrigan, Eberhardt, Lewis, and Mengel from most Americans was that they had been willing to risk imprisonment by acting on the basis of their beliefs. For that, Weisgal maintained, they should be celebrated, not punished. The defendants "had no evil motive, no criminal intent." They went to the Custom House to stage a "dramatic protest to an illegal war. It was a great human act done by sincere men."[33]

Sachs admired Weisgal for underscoring the loftiness of his clients' motives. But he thought that their intent, however noble, had little bearing on the narrow legal matter of their guilt or innocence. He made this plain to the jury in his closing statement. "Of course they were sincere men," Sachs explained. "But the law does not permit you to commit a crime just because you are sincere."[34]

Then came the waiting game. When he waited for a jury to return a verdict, Weisgal typically would retire to a local bar and try to relax. He often would summon his law partners for a session of drinking and piano playing. (Weisgal was an immensely talented musician and had played in jazz clubs throughout his youth.) The jury in the Baltimore Four trial gave the attorney and his colleagues relatively little time to unwind; in under two hours Weisgal was called back to the courtroom, which was packed with spectators, many of them nuns and students at nearby seminaries who had come to show their support for the defendants.

The verdict was a resounding defeat for the defendants: guilty on all counts. Northrop released the four men on their own recognizance and indicated that they later would be called back to court for sentencing.[35]

Weisgal was crestfallen. Barbara Mills saw the attorney immediately after the verdict was handed down, and she could see the anguish etched on his face. The defendants themselves were less tormented by the outcome of the trial. Phil Berrigan later wrote that Weisgal had been concerned with prevailing in a narrow, legal sense; he mainly had wanted his clients to be spared incarceration. The attorney "couldn't understand our lax view toward avoiding jail" because he hadn't prepared for, and then participated in, the protest himself. He was a lawyer, and with that role came a whole set of preconceptions that blinded him to the broader meaning of the four men's witness at the Custom House. "Fred shared the myopia of most lawyers regarding the role of the courts—to adjudicate the warmongering of the empire," Berrigan argued. "Most lawyers don't know this—their training militates against any deeper view."[36]

For Dan Berrigan, the outcome of the Baltimore Four trial never had been in doubt. He felt that a profoundly broken political system could not countenance someone like his militantly outspoken brother. Sitting in the courtroom as the verdict was handed down, "I thought how inconceivable it was that Philip should have been spared," he later wrote.[37]

Ironically, the Baltimore Four trial—even though it ended with Berrigan, Lewis, Mengel, and Eberhardt being convicted—ultimately might have done the federal government more harm than good. The proceedings fired the imaginations of activists who were sympathetic to the defendants.

George Mische and his wife, Helene, drove up to the trial from Washington, D.C, where they recently had established a communal home for Catholics interested in peace and social justice issues. The Misches listened intently in court as prosecution witnesses described how much damage the four men had done during their foray into the Custom House. In stressing the seriousness of the crime, representatives of the Selective Service System pointed out that the draft files that had been attacked were, in some sense, irreplaceable—if they were ruined, a draftee's record would be difficult for the government to piece together again because few duplicate documents were kept on file. George Mische's ears perked up when he heard this being discussed. It dawned on him that completely destroying draft records, not just defacing them, could have more than just a symbolic impact. It could slow down the draft and thereby impede the war in Vietnam.[38]

"Guatemala Smells Like South Vietnam Did a Few Years Ago"

With their convictions, the Baltimore Four faced terms in federal prison of up to fifteen years each. Given the nature of their offenses—and that two of them, Phil Berrigan and James Mengel, were clergymen—few expected the quartet to receive maximum terms from Judge Edward Northrop. Still, with the federal government increasingly eager to rein in antiwar dissent, it seemed possible that the Baltimore activists would be headed for at least short stints behind bars.

Their attorney, having spoken with Northrop and federal prosecutors, certainly thought so. "Weisgal says that we're going to get time," Phil Berrigan wrote to a family member after the trial. The priest did not fear going to jail—"Well and good!" he said of his lawyer's sentencing prediction—but first he wanted to strike another blow against the draft.[1]

The priest reasoned that if government-backed injustice at home and abroad truly stood as the central moral challenge of the time, then it mandated sustained protest. Berrigan also concluded that offering a second dramatic witness for peace—and then being put on trial for it—would give the activists another platform for speaking out against injustice and oppression. With the news media covering the protest itself and the trial that was sure to follow, their critique and call to action would be spread widely—perhaps so widely that it would begin to influence public policy and save lives. Bill O'Connor, Berrigan's IPM colleague, later summed up the priest's thinking. "Phil wasn't satisfied with the blood-pouring action," O'Connor said. "He wanted something bigger, and he wanted something that would be more difficult to discredit. And that's when they started to build for another action."[2]

Berrigan put the idea to Tom Lewis. "Let's do it again," the priest said. Lewis's heart sank. Already facing the prospect of a federal prison term, he was reluctant to break the law again and almost surely earn another sentence. Yet the artist sensed that Berrigan was right: although it had made a few headlines, their first attack on draft records had done little to stem the tide of the war, and it would be moral cowardice to give up on the idea of protesting. Staging another antidraft demonstration, Lewis realized, made sense, even if the personal cost to him would be significant. "Logically, if the war is still going on, this is the correct thing to do," Lewis decided. "Why not do it again?"[3]

Berrigan and Lewis quickly agreed that they would try to recruit others to join in a second witness against the draft that would extend and amplify what they had done at the Custom House. Lewis was concerned that Berrigan— already a lightning rod for criticism—not be further isolated by the perception that he was acting on his own. The danger of this would be mitigated by organizing a group witness that drew together an even greater number of protesters than had been involved in the looting of the Custom House.[4]

The recruitment effort began even before the Baltimore Four went on trial. In February 1968, Berrigan wrote to Catholic peace activist Karl Meyer, "We are at this time . . . planning another serious act of civil disobedience"—one that that would be "symbolic, non-violent, and highly destructive of property." He told Meyer that he hoped to involve "peace leaders from the East and Midwest (mostly Catholics, several priests)."[5]

A dynamic Catholic peace and social justice activist named George Mische played an essential role in bringing together this larger group. Mische and the confederates he helped to organize in the spring of 1968 would become the Catonsville Nine.

Mische's father had been a labor organizer with political inclinations so radical that he nearly had been deported as a communist. The family eventually settled in St. Cloud, Minnesota, where the elder Mische worked for several decades at a veterans' hospital. Being around wounded men during his boyhood brought home for George the chilling reality of World War II. In the movies, stars like John Wayne and Ronald Reagan made the conflict seem like a heroic adventure. But Mische saw something far less upbeat at the veterans' hospital in St. Cloud: men who were broken (both physically and psychologically) by the war, and families that had been shattered by it.[6]

The hospital was full of "people who have suffered the consequences of war," Mische said. "These men were there, left over from World War I and World War II; people who had really served their country, or at least thought they were serving their country, the best they could; and who for years after did not enjoy the same thing I did at home, of having an ordinary family life, but were condemned to these types of hospitals for the rest of their lives."[7]

The men relegated to the veterans' hospital received compassion and support from the Mische family. So too did the local poor. From an early age, Mische and his siblings were taught that there was "something more important in the world than just your own survival. That you had a responsibility, as a Christian and as an American, to have compassion for the poor," as he put it, "and that you just could not get hung up on pursuing your own color TV sets.

That it was very much part of the Catholic tradition in our family that, when you got out, you did not go out to seek money. You went out to find your own world, to see what you could contribute to your God, and your fellow men, and your country."[8]

These lessons took root with Mische and his siblings. One brother founded a Catholic Worker house in Chicago; another started the Association for International Development (AID), a charity that linked Catholic professionals to volunteer opportunities in the developing world. After serving a hitch in the Army and graduating from college, Mische himself worked with juvenile delinquents in the New York City area. "Since I was lucky enough to have the good family life," he said, "I felt that I should share this luck with other young people who were not so fortunate."[9]

He later went off to Central America and the Caribbean in the employ of the Alliance for Progress (AFP), the economic aid program launched by President Kennedy in 1961, and AID, the organization founded by his brother Gerald. As he promoted and implemented American-backed economic development programs, Mische sought to protect American political and economic interests and thereby prevent the contagion of communism from spreading beyond Cuba.[10]

At one point, Mische worked for the American Institute for Free Labor Development, which attempted to bolster trade unions in Latin America. "The idea was that, somehow, we had to get big government, big labor, and big business to go overseas and work hand-in-hand with the Alliance for Progress," he explained. Although Mische apparently didn't know it at the time, the group had an agenda beyond labor organizing: there were claims that it received funding from the CIA. Mische later grumbled that he unwittingly had been in the employ of a CIA front during his time in Latin America.[11]

The work proved challenging. Mische expected that he and his American colleagues, as representatives of the richest and most democratic country on the globe, would be greeted warmly when they arrived in Latin America. However, they were met with scarcely contained hostility almost everywhere they went.[12]

In time, it became clear to Mische why he and his colleagues were received so coldly in Latin America. President Kennedy's soaring rhetoric to the contrary notwithstanding, the United States was widely perceived as being a foe of genuine political democracy in the region. And from what he saw on the ground, Mische sensed that this was a valid perspective. There were, he said, "democratically elected governments . . . overthrown with Pentagon support" and replaced with brutally coercive military dictatorships. The president had promised that the United States would not deal with such regimes, but it continued backing them to the hilt—provided that they served American political and economic interests.[13]

When thinking about American policies in the region, Mische was reminded of the old notion that the cross follows the sword (meaning that armed conquest often led to the spread of Christianity). The secular, American twist on this idea was that "the sword follows the businessman," as he put it while speaking in Milwaukee in the late 1960s. "Wherever he goes in Latin America, we are there to protect him."[14]

Events in the Dominican Republic especially troubled Mische. There, strongman Rafael Trujillo exercised absolute power for more than three decades, lining his pockets and murdering his enemies at will. Mische felt that Trujillo's rule had been an unfathomable tragedy.[15]

What made the situation in the Dominican Republic doubly sad, in Mische's view, was that American politicians turned a blind eye to Trujillo's many abuses. In the name of backing a fervently anticommunist regime, the United States for decades supported a de facto kleptocracy. Trujillo's assassination in 1961 was a mixed blessing: impoverished and lacking a stable democratic tradition, the country plunged into such political and social turmoil that the United States—fearing the emergence of a second pro-Soviet government in the Caribbean—intervened directly, dispatching to the Dominican Republic several thousand Marines to restore order.

Mische thought that the United States had no business supporting dictators like Trujillo. Not only was it blatantly hypocritical; it also directly contributed to the oppression of millions of people. His conscience became so burdened by his country's meddling in the region that he left his work and returned to the United States to publicize how American foreign policy had gone horribly awry in Latin America. Colleges, churches, civic groups—his passion rarely flagging, Mische addressed them all.

Mische endeavored to tell the American people the unvarnished truth about what was happening in other parts of the world. He especially wanted to reach Roman Catholic leaders and help "them understand what was going on overseas, what the problems of white racism in this society were doing to separate people from each other." His blunt message: "Look, if you are moral leaders, speak out."[16]

As he crisscrossed the country and set out to change his own church, Mische spoke to many prominent Catholics. He urged them to address the pressing social and political issues of the day, especially racism and the ill effects of American imperialism. Like so many Catholic activists in the 1960s, he drew inspiration from Pope Paul VI. "The Holy Father, when he came to this country, said, 'War never more,'" Mische said. "The Holy Father talked about peace among men. He talked about racism. He talked about the responsibility of rich nations toward poor nations." If they had any backbone, the nation's Catholic bishops would do the same.[17]

But Mische's efforts to transform his church bore little fruit. The Catholic hierarchy's reluctance to heed his message seemed symptomatic of the church's general reluctance to address the social and political problems that threatened to tear the world apart. He had seen this same lack of engagement and compassion from church leaders during his time abroad. "Bishops throughout Latin

America are as provincial as they are here in St. Cloud," he complained while visiting his hometown in the late 1960s. "They stand by while governments are exploiting the poor, and any assistance the church gives in these countries is only to converts. . . . Throughout most of the church, the concern is not for the poor, but for building fine rectories and other buildings. The people are as exploited by the church as they are by outside business and industry which come into these poor countries."[18]

Mische cut a distinctive figure as he traversed the country. One observer described him as being "burly, quick-witted, voluble, with a blond mustache and a luminous, demonic smile." Like many of his contemporaries, he thumbed his nose at convention and wore loud clothes. (He would appear at the Catonsville Nine trial in a bright orange sweater.) And then there was Mische's frenetic manner of speaking. He had a booming voice, and the words—earnest, impassioned, forceful—poured out at a feverish clip. One listener likened his delivery to a machine gun unleashing a fusillade of bullets. Another compared his intense stare to that of a "young Lenin."[19]

Over time, Mische gravitated toward the peace movement. He shared with scores of activists the belief that the war in Vietnam was illegal because Congress had not formally declared it. He lay much of the blame for the debacle on President Johnson. "Instead of a president who would lead us through sane, Christian policies," he said, "we elected a tyrant who is leading an illegal war with total disregard for American opinion."[20]

Such were Johnson's sins that Mische believed he should be put on trial as a war criminal, as had happened to Nazi leaders at Nuremberg in the aftermath of World War II. Nuremberg had a special meaning for Mische in that it obliterated flimsy justifications for the commission of crimes against humanity while also calling for citizens to oppose governments that committed atrocities. He described the trials as "the finest precedent this country ever set" because they not only held murderers accountable for their actions but also highlighted the complicity of everyone in the slaughter of Europe's Jews. That lesson, Mische felt, should not be forgotten during the Vietnam era, when a new holocaust was under way.[21]

Mische long remembered the first large peace demonstration he attended. It was a mammoth protest that drew to Washington, D.C., hundreds of thousands of opponents of the war in Vietnam. Media reports invariably suggested that unkempt hippies thronged such demonstrations, but Mische found that many of his fellow marchers that day were professionals wearing suits and dresses, which suggested to him that opposition to the war ran deep throughout American society. Representatives of the capital's political elite were on hand as well to show their concern about the war: Mische wound up speaking with Claiborne Pell, the dovish senator from Rhode Island.[22]

The massive antiwar march inspired Mische, and he became convinced that nonviolent protest held enormous promise. "It doesn't have any bad consequences," he once explained. "To me, the most effective way to bring social change in the United States would be nonviolent forms of protest because the population here has a much higher educational means than other countries. [Americans] should be able to understand symbolism much more clearly than the person who has a difficult time even thinking because he's too busy to think, because he's so poor he constantly is caught in this struggle for survival."[23]

But Mische began to wonder if staging rallies would be enough to bring about meaningful change. It seemed that President Johnson, canny political operator that he was, was content to let demonstrators harmlessly vent their anger in the streets—provided that they did nothing to seriously impede his prosecution of the war. For Mische, it became apparent that the peace movement was being co-opted as a means of muting serious dissent. For there to be real change, he later said, something "drastic enough was needed to dramatize opposition to the war." With the war spiraling out of control and the peace movement stagnating, the time had come "to do something besides just walking up and down the streets with signs."[24]

Early in 1968 Mische moved to Washington, D.C., and established at 1620 S Street a community house that drew together a variety of Catholic activists. Bill O'Connor later described the residence as "a little collective," while Mische called it "an action-related house of Christian radicals." Like Mische, many of these individuals were motivated to resist American foreign policy because they had spent time abroad and witnessed its myriad ill effects. A nurse named Mary Moylan had lived for several years in Uganda, and former Maryknoll missionaries John Hogan and Thomas and Marjorie Melville all recently had returned from lengthy—and notoriously contentious—stints in Guatemala. Over meals and gatherings in the community house's basement, they shared their experiences and discussed how they might combat imperialism and poverty.[25]

In a newsletter, the group stated that it had come together to form "a community, not only of concern but [also] of commitment to direct action at the heart of the problems we see." These included American imperialism, the excesses of capitalism, the reluctance of religious leaders to speak out frankly on peace and social justice issues, and "the transformation of American society from a democracy to a police state."[26]

For Tom Melville—raised in what he later termed "an uncommonly religious family"—the call to the priesthood came early. By the time he had reached fifth grade, he knew that he wanted to follow in the footsteps of an uncle who served as a priest in the Boston area. But Tom hoped to venture far beyond the Hub City. Early on, he made up his mind to join the Maryknoll religious order, which focused on foreign missionary activity.[27]

Even decades later, he could pinpoint the precise moment when his desire to serve in a foreign mission first flared. It happened when he was called upon to assist at a novena being held in honor of St. Francis Xavier. The great six-teenth-century Jesuit had been an exemplary missionary, braving numerous hardships as he endeavored to spread Catholicism in India, the East Indies, China, and Japan. The priest in charge of the novena produced what Tom later described as a "first-class relic"—purportedly the saint's right arm, encased in glass—and regaled his audience with the highlights of Xavier's remarkable career, which had ended with his death on the island of Sancian, off the coast of China, in 1552. Hearing this account confirmed for Tom that missionary work, and not the life of a parish priest, was his true calling. "The life of a priest at home," he later wrote, "didn't attract me—it was too soft, I felt."[28]

After graduating from high school in 1948, Tom finally was able to join Maryknoll. But before he could emulate his heroes out in the field, he had to endure several years of training at the order's junior college and seminary. His studies were not especially difficult, and he found them dull and uninspiring. "Nothing outstanding," he observed of his lackluster performance in seminary. Always a man of action, he longed to serve on the front lines of the church's battle against the great global threat to Christianity—communism.[29]

For Maryknollers, communists were not a hypothetical menace. After taking over China in 1949, they drove the Catholic Church underground and abused missionaries there, expelling and even imprisoning several members of the order. (One of them, Bishop James Walsh, spent a dozen years in jail.) These stories, Tom said, "made our blood boil." His was still simmering when the order dispatched him to Guatemala in the early 1950s.[30]

Maryknoll had been sending missionaries to Central and South America since 1942, and by the end of the 1960s their ranks numbered approximately six hundred nonindigenous people. In addition to conducting religious services and encouraging conversions to Catholicism, the Maryknollers busied themselves with projects designed to spark economic and cultural development. They did everything from sponsoring educational radio broadcasts to conducting agricultural training programs and schooling nurses.[31]

Assigned by Maryknoll to a village in a rural area, Tom was appalled by the dismal living conditions of the native population. Every day, most Guatemalans had to grapple with malnutrition, sickness, and hunger. "I hesitate to use the word 'poverty,'" he said. "They were living in utter misery."[32]

This was not hyperbole. One observer writing in 1968 described Guatemala as a country where nearly everyone was hungry. According to some estimates, more than half the population suffered from malnutrition. With widespread hunger came poor health, particularly for children. Infant mortality rates in Guatemala were stratospheric—quadruple those in the United States. And even the Guatemalans who survived childhood could not look forward to living very long: the average life expectancy was less than fifty years.[33]

Tom Melville did not believe that Guatemalan peasants were themselves responsible for this deplorable state of affairs. Rather, he saw a more systemic cause: "a capitalist system that makes the defenseless Indian compete against the powerful and well-armed landowner." In Guatemala, this landowner typically was the United Fruit Company (or a politician in its back pocket). Protective of its vast plantation holdings, United Fruit vehemently opposed even the mildest agrarian reforms, and it convinced a succession of American presidential administrations to oppose Guatemalan politicians who threatened to implement changes. Most infamously, in 1954 it helped to persuade the Eisenhower administration to support the ouster of Jacobo Arbenz Guzmán, a democratically elected president who had promised to expropriate United Fruit lands. After quashing this threat, the corporate behemoth dealt with a series of strongmen, including, during Tom Melville's tenure in Guatemala, Miguel Ydígoras Fuentes and Julio César Méndez Montenegro.[34]

Marjorie Melville's journey to Guatemala—and, later, Catonsville—began in Mexico, where she was born in 1929. The daughter of an American electrical engineer and a Mexican woman, she spent much of her girlhood in that strife-ridden country. The 1930s were a period of intense anti-Catholicism in Mexico; dozens of priests were killed (sometimes while performing the sacraments), and soldiers desecrated altars. Mexican Catholics were forced to practice their faith in secret, and Marjorie often went to Masses performed in homes. For first grade, she attended what she later described as a "Catholic school-in-hiding," a clandestine affair housed in a succession of private residences. For fear of being discovered by authorities, the nuns who taught Marjorie did not wear their customary black garb, and they maintained hiding places for their religious texts and crucifixes.[35]

After graduating from high school and working in a succession of humdrum jobs, she joined the Maryknoll order as a nun in 1949. (The transformation necessitated a name change: she was formally known as Sister Marian Peter until she left the order two decades later.) Her father doubted that she would last six months, but she loved the order and stuck with it. She was posted to Guatemala in 1954, the year Carlos Castillo Armas overthrew Jacobo Arbenz Guzmán (with covert help from the CIA). At the time, Marjorie considered him a hero for liberating his country from the scourge of communism.[36]

During her first few years in Guatemala, Marjorie was not fully aware of the grinding poverty afflicting so many indigenous people there. Working as a teacher in a relatively prosperous section of Guatemala City, she lived a sheltered life. She had expected to experience privation; she even had wondered if she would be asked to sacrifice her life in service of Christ. It was thus something of a shock—and a disappointment—for her to discover that she and a handful of fellow sisters would have two maids to cook and clean for them.[37]

Her perspective changed as she pushed beyond the narrow limits of her role as a teacher and dug into the profound problems that bedeviled most Guatemalans. Marjorie began to wonder how, as committed Christians, she and her fellow Maryknollers could affect real change. "We were in anguish," she later said, "trying to figure out what to do with people who needed our help." There was a temptation to hang back; they had been sent to Guatemala, after all, to serve the people's spiritual needs, not to implement a radical program of wholesale political, economic, and social reform. But the impulse to "go in on the side of the people," as Marjorie later put it, proved irresistible. She began to ask herself, "What can I do to help?"[38]

Marjorie's perspective on the links between poverty and politics were influenced by her participation in a series of *cursillos* (short courses) in the early 1960s. Led by a Jesuit priest and two students who were pursuing advanced university degrees, the sessions addressed the pervasive hunger and illiteracy that wracked Latin America and created "conditions that forced human beings to live like animals," as Marjorie put it. She was appalled to learn that a full two-thirds of the people living in the region went to bed hungry every night and that millions of them lacked even the barest reading and writing skills. Such troubles were not mere abstractions, Marjorie and her fellow *cursillistas* were told; they were concrete problems that, as Christians, they had a duty to tackle.[39]

Marjorie reflected on these matters when she returned to the United States in 1964 for a kind of spiritual refresher course mandated by Maryknoll. Vatican II was in session at the time, and its reforming spirit influenced many of the gatherings that she attended over her two weeks in America. One day, she and some fellow nuns walked into a classroom and saw that their instructor, a priest, had scrawled the words "God does not exist" across the blackboard. The women were dumbfounded—until the priest walked into the room and wrote "God occurs" directly under his provocative initial notation. Marjorie thought she understood. "I was coming more and more to realize," she said, "that religion consisted, not of a collection of doctrines and church rituals, but of living with other people and sharing meaning and direction with them."[40]

Tom Melville also developed a sense of pragmatism. Upon his arrival in Guatemala in 1954, he was given a plum assignment in the parish of San Miguel Acatán. Tom ministered to two outlying towns, performing all of the typical priestly duties—celebrating Mass, hearing confessions, performing weddings, and teaching Catholic doctrine. Many in his flock clung to their indigenous religious beliefs and made but a halfhearted commitment to Catholicism, but this seemed only to stoke his enthusiasm for the work. "I was determined that these people were going to learn about Catholicism and that I was going to save their souls in spite of themselves," he later observed, "even if I had to knock people down or get killed myself in the process."[41]

He had such fervor that he literally knocked down the symbols of indigenous religion. There stood near Melville's church a cross that the local people had erected long before his arrival. Symbolizing not Christ's crucifixion but rather the directions of the wind, it held, according to community belief, the spirits of many ancestors and saints. This sacred object was an affront to

Melville; for him it was a monument to superstition and thus had no place near his church. The cross so bothered him that he toppled it over one night. (Years later, he still could remember the sound it had made as it hit the ground—"a great *whoomp*."[42])

Outrage over the priest's action earned him a new posting in Cabricán. Chastened by his recent failure, he began to reassess the way he interacted with the Guatemalan peasantry. "There I was, in Guatemala," he later wrote, "trying to impose ideas and practices, not merely of the [Catholic] Church but also of America—which I considered superior—upon a people whose basic values, lifestyle, and outlook I did not really understand in depth."[43]

He found himself opening up to the Indians and realizing that they had much to teach him about the nature of religious faith. As a Catholic, Tom always had thought that the core of religious experience involved mastering long-established principles and then preparing for the afterlife. But his time among the Guatemalan peasantry convinced him otherwise. He saw that religion could be a practical means to help people surmount real-world obstacles.[44]

Tom faced a choice: he could offer Guatemalans hope for salvation in the hereafter, or he could "do a little to ameliorate their conditions on this earth and at the same time could give a little demonstration of what Christianity is all about," as he later said. He opted for the latter. He inaugurated a pragmatic ministry aimed at giving the peasants a degree of economic—and, perhaps eventually, political—autonomy.[45]

A group of a few dozen men approached him one day and asked if he could help them purchase a truck. They wanted to further develop their own production of lime, and such a vehicle would help them immeasurably. (Without it, they were forced to carry hundreds of pounds of limestone and wood on their backs.) After Tom signed the loan, he and some local men went to fetch the truck. When they returned, three hundred jubilant villagers greeted them. For them, "it was a day of deliverance," Tom observed, "from a life of walking with back-breaking loads."[46]

Tom labored with indigenous people to set up a lime-production cooperative that drew together over a hundred members. Workers made a minimum of about a dollar per day for laboring in the limestone mines or tending to the ovens that calcinated the rock. It was a trifle by American standards, but it represented a generous wage for people who had lived in abject poverty for most of their lives. Tom's experiment in Cabricán was an undeniable success—the co-op marketed its limestone widely—and he wondered why it couldn't be duplicated throughout the country. The answer, he came to realize, was simple: in Guatemala, the indigenous people lacked land, and it was all but impossible to wrest control of it away from the United Fruit Company.[47]

The paths of Marjorie and Tom crossed in 1966, when he was working in a program to resettle landless Guatemalans in the jungles of the Petén region. On a visit to the Maryknoll Center House in Guatemala City, he encountered the nun and came away impressed with her understanding of the condition of the peasantry and her obvious desire to work for the poor. As the two became acquainted, Tom was startled to learn that Marjorie's burgeoning commitment to the dispossessed had drawn her closer to the leftist guerillas who were battling the Guatemalan government and attempting to bring about a radical change in the country's political and economic structure. (These included members of the group Fuerzas Armadas Rebeldes.) He remonstrated that the guerillas were communists and terrorists who were exploiting her and the student group she had helped form, the Crater.

"No, they are good people," she protested. "They are doing what has to be done. Nobody else is going to do it."[48]

Tom agreed to meet with some of Marjorie's radical allies, and in time he became convinced of their sincerity of purpose. What's more, the guerillas challenged his conception of Christ. Forcing the priest to go beyond mouthing Catholic doctrine, they made him think deeply about how the message of the Gospels should be lived in everyday experience. Doing so would require him to do more than just pacify people in a time of desperate need. He would have to devote himself to alleviating the obvious manifestations of human misery that were present everywhere in the Guatemalan countryside.

As Tom's respect for the guerillas grew, his esteem for American foreign policy in Latin America plummeted. The ties between the American military and the Guatemalan oligarchy—forged in the belief that antidemocratic regimes were a necessary evil in the global battle against communism—troubled him especially. By funneling money and arms to prop up a succession of repressive and exploitive regimes, Washington was pursuing "a policy that destroyed any hope of real betterment of these people's lives," he later said. "Powerful interest groups in Washington were influencing or making decisions in terms of what was good for the United States without understanding or concern for the Guatemalan people."[49]

Marjorie's militancy intensified as well. She found it unconscionable that government-backed terrorist squads were abducting, torturing, and killing reformers in Guatemala. She despaired that her efforts with the Crater, which included such valuable work as labor organizing, were being attacked as "communist inspired" by both Guatemalan authorities and wary officials in her own church.

The two Maryknollers' concern with such issues drew them into the vanguard of a broader social and intellectual movement that was bubbling up from Latin America in the 1960s. Throughout the region, theologians were making a sustained effort to interpret the teachings of the Bible through the experiences of the oppressed. Foregrounding the suffering and struggle of the poor, advocates of this emerging "theology of liberation" used the core lessons of the New Testament to offer a powerful critique of the exploitive social and political structures that denied economic opportunity to millions.

Proponents of liberation theology did more than offer ideological solidarity with the poor. They stressed liberative praxis—the active application of Christian teachings to the lives of the oppressed as a means of unshackling them. It was through action, not rhetoric, that the fundamental structures of economic, political, and social oppression would fall.[50]

Vatican II, with its spirit of reform and openness, produced a theological atmosphere in which liberation theology could flourish among Catholics in Latin America. Determined to give active meaning to their faith, Catholic theologians like Gustavo Gutiérrez and Segundo Galilea repeatedly engaged in dialogues with their Protestant colleagues in an effort to address the despair of the poor.

It was Gutiérrez who most clearly articulated the central tenets of liberation theology. In his landmark work *Teología de la Liberación* (*A Theology of Liberation*), the Peruvian priest highlighted the importance of the ongoing "struggle to construct a just and fraternal society, where persons can live with dignity and be the agents of their own destiny." Ensuring this liberation—by working to ensure economic and social equity—was no trivial matter. Indeed, for Gutiérrez it was a "question about the very meaning of Christianity and about the mission of the church."[51]

So too was it for Tom and Marjorie. Repressed by the state and increasingly marginalized by their own church, they decided that they would have to move beyond advocating for modest, incremental reforms if they wanted to fundamentally alter the structure of oppression in Guatemala. Early in November 1967, the two Maryknollers convened a meeting at an abandoned farmhouse located near the town of Escuintla. The secret gathering, which lasted over three days, drew together like-minded Christian radicals—among them Maryknollers, university students, and Indians. They hoped to determine what they "could do to bring about a meaningful revolution" in Guatemala, as Tom later put it. Their hope was to foment "a Christian revolution based on an organization of self-defense, to reoccupy the lands that had been stolen from [the peasantry] by generations of white men."[52]

They doubted that this change could be brought about by nonviolent means. The Guatemalan military—bolstered by the covert backing of the American government—would not loosen its stranglehold on the country without a fight. But the Christian plotters' immediate plans were not centered on arming the peasantry or aligning themselves with the guerilla factions that already were working to overthrow the government. Instead, they focused on forging connections with peasant leaders and readying themselves both physically and psychologically for the struggle ahead.

By Tom's own admission, the group was revolutionary, in part because it adopted a philosophy that was both militant and Christian. He wanted to bring to Guatemala "true Christianity," a faith that honored the dignity of even the lowliest peasant, but he sensed that nonviolent protest stood little chance of changing such a brutally repressive society. He counseled Guatemalans that they might have to literally battle to create a new social, political, and economic order based on the principles articulated by Jesus in the Sermon on the Mount. They were told that "no one will defend their rights if they do not defend themselves," he later said. "If the government and oligarchy were using arms to maintain the Indians in their misery, then the Indians had the obligation to take up arms and defend their God-given right to be men."[53]

As they contemplated how they might spark a revolution, Tom and Marjorie—both of whom had taken vows of celibacy—also grappled with their growing personal affection for one another. As their relationship deepened over the course of a year, both struggled to reconcile themselves with the Catholic Church's rigid strictures on sexuality for nuns and priests. If they wanted to fully commit themselves to one another and live as man and wife, they would have to leave Maryknoll, the religious order that had been their home for many years. They both knew that taking such a dramatic step was bound to give ammunition to critics who hoped to discredit their revolutionary activities. Tom's brother Art (who also was a Maryknoller in Guatemala) scolded that they were sure to be accused of joining the revolution simply because they were infatuated with one another and wanted to get married. But the prospect of such barbs was not enough to dissuade them. "After long agonizing about the effect of our marriage on our parents, Maryknoll, and our companions in the struggle for social justice," Marjorie recalled, "we decided that we had to be true to our own convictions."[54]

While Tom and Marjorie combined revolutionary and romantic activities, they drew other Maryknollers into their circle. These included a brother in their order named John Hogan. Hogan—who had taken the name "Augustine" upon joining Maryknoll and went by the nickname "Gus" in Guatemala—was a skilled mechanic and carpenter who had been dispatched by the order to help Tom with his land project in Petén. The two became fast friends. "He was a completely unaffected man who obviously enjoyed teaching the Indians," Melville said of Hogan. "The people took him to their hearts right away, and the laughter that boomed around the colony was often provoked by one of Gus's jokes."[55]

While growing up in New Haven, Connecticut, Hogan initially thought about following in the footsteps of his father and one of his elder brothers, both of whom had served in the Navy. But when he discussed the idea with one of the Dominican nuns who taught him at St. Mary's High School, he turned in a different direction. "She more or less saw that joining the Navy was kind of an 18-year-old's idea of adventure," he later explained. If Hogan really wanted to do something for people, she counseled, he should join a religious order.[56]

Hogan followed the nun's advice and signed up with Maryknoll after graduating from high school in 1953. In posts in Massachusetts, New York, and Illinois, he received training in auto mechanics, electrical repair, and plumbing. This instruction suited Hogan perfectly. "I wanted to find a community in which I would be [doing] physical work," he later said, "because I didn't care to teach."[57]

When the order decided to send him to Guatemala in 1961, his younger brother, Tom, was perplexed. Someone had told the boy that "guerillas" operated in the region—without explaining that this meant irregular soldiers, not hairy primates. Confused by the homophone, Tom worriedly asked his brother, "Why would you want to go someplace where there are gorillas? You could be eaten there!"[58]

Hogan's initial duties involved neither rebels nor animals: he worked for a time as a bookkeeper at Maryknoll's central mission. He then was dispatched to the Jacaltenango region to supervise the construction of a hospital, a nursing school, and a convent. The project presented some daunting logistical problems. Roads in the area were primitive, and the final approach to the facility required a four-hour ride on horseback. (Hogan later observed, in his typically understated way, "We were really out in the sticks.") But he loved the work because it gave him a formidable sense of accomplishment. "Probably one of the most enjoyable points of my life," he explained, "was being there at that time."[59]

After the Jacaltenango project wrapped up, Hogan was transferred to the Petén region, where he worked with Tom Melville on a variety of land distribution and economic development projects. The Maryknollers helped relocated Guatemalans work the region's rich topsoil and establish cooperatives. Conditions were brutal. "The first few months were unbearable," Melville later wrote. "The insects had everyone just bursting with boils. Food was hard to come by and expensive. . . . And of course the lands were terrible."[60]

Hogan persevered and wound up enjoying himself. "For me, it was a good opportunity, because I was working with a priest for the first time who did not have a paternalistic attitude with the people," he later said of his interactions with Melville. "It is a matter of training the people to stand on their own two feet."[61]

To clear out space in the jungle for their projects, the Maryknollers obtained a D-6 Caterpillar bulldozer. Hogan never had operated such a tractor before, so he found the manual and taught himself. After bumbling along in fits and starts for a few days, he finally got the hang of it and started knocking down trees to clear the land. He then taught the men in the cooperative how to run the machine, and they were able to do the work themselves.[62]

This was the cooperative spirit that Hogan treasured. In the Guatemalan jungle, he felt that he was able to find practical application for core Christian principles. It was "the greatest thing possible," Hogan said. "In this, through cooperatism, I was teaching the men about how they could work together in order to achieve a great project, so that they would be able to benefit themselves."[63]

Hogan was so immersed in this work—and so isolated from the outside world—that for many years he was only dimly aware of how the United States was entangling itself in Vietnam. "I didn't know anything about the Vietnam

War," he later admitted. His awareness grew, however, after a visiting Maryknoller left behind some books about the conflict. Hogan was moved by *Vietnam: A Crisis of Conscience*, which offered Protestant, Catholic, and Jewish perspectives on the morality of the war.[64]

Hogan soon began to make connections between the American military's misadventures in Vietnam and its shadowy but unmistakable presence in Guatemala. He noticed, for instance, that American transport planes sometimes landed at a nearby airfield and unloaded military equipment, including Jeeps. "What the heck is the United States Army doing here?" he asked himself. Troubled by what he saw, Hogan began to discuss with Tom Melville the behind-the-scenes role being played by the United States in propping up Guatemala's repressive oligarchy. He wondered about "the possibility of seeing another Vietnam right there in Guatemala."[65]

The two men agreed that the regime did little to help the Guatemalan people. As his worries grew, Hogan at one point told Tom that the country's indigenous people would benefit from embracing the idea of a Christian revolution, what he somewhat grandly termed "a new Crusade to recapture the Holy Land." Once Melville had determined that Hogan's commitment to reform was genuine, he suggested that Hogan attend the meeting at Escuintla, where the Christian revolutionaries would formulate their strategy for resistance. But the prospect of participating in an armed struggle gave Hogan pause. "The problem for him," Melville later said, "was the same as for the rest of us: emotional and psychological." Having lived in a religious community for his entire adult life, Hogan couldn't imagine heading into the jungle and engaging in combat. But he was sympathetic to the revolutionaries, and he told Melville that he would help them indirectly if he could.[66]

Hogan proved true to his word. Inspired by the Escuintla conclave, a group of university students resolved to explore a remote jungle area as a base of operations for the Christian guerillas. Tom was skeptical of their chances of success—the area's terrain was treacherous—but he agreed to let them take the scouting trip. Hogan offered to help: he often made resupply trips on the river that led into the region, and he thought he could ferry the young men there without arousing too much suspicion. Hogan's expertise was crucial. At one point in the trip, a craft bearing an armed man approached the students' boat. They feared the worst; in Guatemala, such confrontations frequently led to bloodshed. But Hogan's presence seemed to reassure the rifle-bearer, and he let them pass without even questioning the passengers.[67]

All of the Maryknollers' involvement in such activities came crashing to a halt late in 1967. At the time Tom and Marjorie were struggling to reconcile their burgeoning romance with their commitment to helping the Guatemalan peasantry rise up in revolution. After agonizing over their decision, they informed their respective Maryknoll superiors about their intention to marry. Both assumed that the order would ask them to leave the country, but they held out hope that they could return to Guatemala without much delay and resume their revolutionary work.

This plan went horribly awry, and the couple—along with Tom's brother Art and, eventually, John Hogan—were forced out of Guatemala under a cloud of scandal. Things began to unravel when they were summoned to a meeting before several Maryknoll officials, among them Father John Breen. Breen announced that he was aware of the details of their secret meeting at Escuintla, right down to the dates and the names of those in attendance. The infuriated Breen, the American ambassador, and the Guatemalan government all were in agreement that the would-be revolutionaries had no business interfering in political matters and should be expelled from the country immediately. Tom, Marjorie, and Art were told to report to the Maryknoll headquarters in Ossining, New York. The brothers were suspended from their priestly duties as well.[68]

Tom's ouster nearly led to a breach between him and Hogan. The Melvilles had to make a hasty exit from Guatemala, but Tom encountered Hogan before they left. Still seething from his confrontation with Breen, he demanded to know if his fellow Maryknoller had betrayed him to their superiors. "He thought that I had spilled the beans," Hogan later said. "But I didn't have any beans to spill." Hogan explained that he had known few details of their embryonic revolutionary activities, and, even if he had, he never would have violated Tom's trust and divulged any secrets. His earnestness persuaded Tom, and they parted on good terms.[69]

Tom and Marjorie never reported to Maryknoll's headquarters in New York. In fact, they only made it as far north as Miami. Determined to continue their reform work, they rerouted to Houston and from there embarked on a bus trip to Mexico City, where they met up with acquaintances in the Guatemalan exile community. And as if that wasn't a radical enough step, they also went ahead and got married.

While in Mexico, Tom penned an article for the magazine *Siempre* in which he defended his affiliation with guerillas in Guatemala, arguing that the Catholic Church "has always maintained that a human being has certain inalienable rights and that anyone can give up his own but must never permit anyone to take them from his neighbor. When Christ told me to turn the other cheek, he never meant that I remain with arms folded while my brother's face was unjustly struck." Such provocative claims—coming on the heels of the couple's well-publicized exit from Guatemala a few weeks earlier—earned the Melvilles the notice of the State Department and the FBI, which began a joint effort to determine if they could be prosecuted for having violated the Foreign Agents Registration Act.[70]

In the first months of 1968, news of the Melvilles' expulsion and their subsequent activities in Mexico made headlines in newspapers throughout Latin America and the United States. Refusing to back down, they vigorously responded to charges that they had overstepped their roles in Guatemala by engaging in political activities and committing the unthinkable sin of becoming communists themselves. While still in Mexico, Tom wrote a long and impassioned letter to the *National Catholic Reporter* in which he mocked as absurd the accusation that he and his fellow activists were in thrall to communism. "I say here that I am a communist only if Christ was a communist," he insisted. "I did what I did and what I will continue to do so because of the teachings of Christ and not because of Marx and Lenin."[71]

The Melvilles were not the only victims of the Maryknoll purge: it also claimed Blase Bonpane, who had collaborated with them in Guatemala. Because of his political activities, Bonpane was ordered out of the country in December 1967 and exiled to Hawaii. He resisted his banishment, traveling to the mainland United States in the spring of 1968 with the express purpose of speaking out on conditions in Guatemala.[72]

"Guatemala smells like South Vietnam did a few years ago," Bonpane wrote. "There are the same United States military advisers by the hundreds, the same corrupt power structure, the same fear of communism to the point of paranoia, the same group of peasants weak in themselves but firmly determined that no foreigner is going to overcome them on their land."[73]

Being connected to the Melvilles also doomed John Hogan. He was called in by his superiors in Maryknoll and asked if he had joined the notorious couple in fomenting revolution in Guatemala. Hogan—who was, by all accounts, completely incapable of dissembling—said that while he hadn't been swept up in radical activities, he could see why so many downtrodden Guatemalans appreciated the Melvilles' efforts on their behalf. His equivocal answers resulted in his being dispatched to the Maryknoll headquarters in New York. Hogan briefly worked there; he was given such dull tasks as packing and shipping supplies to foreign missions. Before long, the mundane nature of the work and his lingering qualms about the political situation in Guatemala led him to leave the order.

Like the Melvilles, Hogan found himself willing to push the boundaries of nonviolence. When he parted ways with the order, Hogan wrote to his Maryknoll superior that it was "vital that we as Christians respond to [the] invitation of the people in Guatemala and Latin America to help them in their struggle to overcome tyranny even to the point of violent revolution if necessary."[74]

"Did You Hear What We Are Planning?"

Still committed to helping the people of Guatemala, the Maryknoll exiles filtered back into the United States in the spring of 1968. Art Melville might have had the roughest trip: he was dumped over the border in Texas by Mexican authorities who were convinced that he was a dangerous radical.[1]

Tom Melville and his new wife, Marjorie, had a somewhat less harrowing journey. After four months in Mexico, they traveled to San Diego by bus. As they entered the city, they were overwhelmed by the sight of scores of warships docked in the city's harbor. "Look," Tom told her. "That's what we're fighting against. The U.S. thinks God has appointed it earth's policeman." Marjorie took the scene as a challenge: they would have to redouble their efforts to publicize the plight of the Guatemalan peasantry.[2]

They found their way to Washington, D.C., at the urging of their former Maryknoll colleague Blase Bonpane, who was hoping to persuade Congress to reassess American policies in Latin America. The Melvilles were skeptical of this approach; they believed that most policymakers were fully aware of—and indeed endorsed—American misdeeds in Latin America. Convinced that it would be a short visit, they agreed to join him in the capital.

When they arrived in Washington, D.C., from San Diego, the couple was barely scraping by; they couldn't even afford the rent for a small apartment. But they were minor celebrities among the Catholic left, and George Mische heard about their predicament. After learning from his brother (a member of the Maryknoll order) that they were "good lefties," he invited the couple to live rent-free in his house at 1620 S Street. Reflecting on the offer, Tom Melville later joked that Mische suckered the couple into participating in a draft board demonstration by providing them a free place to live.[3]

Bonpane also came to John Hogan's rescue. "If you want to come down here," he told Hogan, "there's a place for you." Bonpane needed someone in Washington to assist in his nascent lobbying efforts; he thought he could dispatch Hogan to the Library of Congress to research political, economic, and cultural conditions in Central America. At loose ends after his departure from Maryknoll, Hogan jumped at the chance to continue helping—albeit at a distance—the Guatemalan people. He, too, wound up at Mische's house at 1620 S Street.[4]

The similarities between Guatemala and Washington struck Hogan even before he touched the ground in the capital. As his plane made its final approach and circled the city, Hogan could see smoke billowing into the air. In the spring of 1968, the frustrations of African Americans in Washington finally had come to a boil: the assassination of Martin Luther King Jr. on April 4 unleashed a wave of riots that left twelve people dead, injured more than one thousand, and reduced portions of the city's black community to rubble. (Order was restored only after several thousand federal troops and National Guardsmen arrived.) "I had a bird's-eye view of Washington, and I thought they were burning down the whole city," he said of his flight. He had seen the same kind of turmoil in Guatemala, where cities went up in flames because of political unrest.[5]

Hogan noticed further parallels once he settled into the turbulent city. In addition to fires, he saw heavily armed police patrolling the streets. To quell unrest in poor neighborhoods, they fired tear gas and zealously enforced curfews. "You couldn't be on your steps," Hogan remarked. "They'd tell you to get back in your house." Such state-sponsored coercion was, he knew, commonplace in Guatemala as a means of stifling protest and reform.[6]

Determined to help the city's beleaguered African American community, Hogan complemented his research on Guatemala by becoming involved in the Poor People's Campaign, which reached its apogee in Washington in May 1968. Before his assassination, King and his colleagues in the Southern Christian Leadership Conference had called for the inauguration of a second phase of the civil rights movement, one that would cut across racial lines and attempt to address long-standing issues of economic inequality and poverty. The goal was to resolve the many problems that continued to plague America's underclass—a toxic mix of substandard housing, lackluster job opportunities, and inadequate health care—by marching on Washington and calling on Congress to implement an "economic bill of rights," the centerpiece of which was a $30 billion antipoverty package. The march went on despite King's death and drew tens of thousands to the capital. Many wound up staying for several weeks and living in an area dubbed "Resurrection City" as they unsuccessfully lobbied Congress to pass the massive antipoverty initiative.

Hogan found the march rewarding. With his commitment to social justice deepening, he pitched in by helping with planning and logistics. These contributions were small, but they made him feel connected to the cause.[7]

Poverty, race relations, and Vietnam were central topics of discussion at the living quarters that Hogan and the Melvilles found in the capital. Hogan later observed that 1620 S Street was "an interesting place," overflowing with young, idealistic people who were eager to debate—sometimes into the wee hours of the morning—issues of peace and social justice. Hogan appreciated the conviviality of his new housemates. Mische and his wife, Helene, were "very bubbly, and welcoming." So was Mary Moylan, a nurse who had connected with Mische after serving in Africa and observing the ongoing political unrest there. Many years later, Hogan fondly recalled the first time he laid eyes on Moylan's classic Irish features. Her vibrant red hair and broad face proved hard to forget.[8]

During their time in Guatemala, the Melvilles were not completely ignorant about the war in Vietnam. But their relative isolation in Central America limited their understanding of the conflict in Southeast Asia. In letters and visits home, for instance, their families discussed the war with them in positive terms, and the newsmagazines they read reported as fact many of the implausible claims made by Johnson administration officials about the American military's success. Conversely, few of their limited sources of information stressed the breadth and depth of the opposition to the war in the United States. As a result, during her time in Guatemala Marjorie was not aware of the antiwar movement. Tom was similarly oblivious: he later admitted that both he and his wife "really didn't have a feeling for the grassroots movement" against the war before they returned to the United States early in 1968.[9]

This immediately changed when they settled down in Washington in the spring of 1968. The antiwar movement suddenly was everywhere around them, including their new home on S Street. The number of people who spoke out against the war, and their intensity in doing so, proved to be a happy surprise to the couple. They were impressed by all of the grassroots activity and were eager to join in—provided that they could still maintain their commitment to publicizing and changing conditions in Guatemala. That always would be their top priority.

Alone among the group that was coalescing around Mische at 1620 S Street in Washington, Mary Moylan was a native of the area, having been born in Baltimore on August 15, 1935. That she was destined to have "a very thorough Catholic upbringing," as she described it, was perhaps evident from the moment her parents chose her name. They named her Mary Assumpta because she was born on the Feast of the Assumption, the Catholic holy day that celebrates the death of the Virgin Mary and the assumption of her body into heaven.[10]

Moylan had a conventional childhood in post–World War II Baltimore. The family's principal breadwinner was her father. Joseph Moylan worked for many years as a stenographer in the city's criminal court and was later described by the *Baltimore Sun* as "one of the most popular members of the Courthouse family." Moylan's father also was an active Catholic who belonged to the Knights of Columbus.[11]

Strong-minded and blunt, Mary could be challenging, but she proved to be a remarkable sibling. "She was different than other older sisters," her younger sister, Ella, later said. "She talked to me about things I would not have talked about. She introduced me to people I would not have known about. She was an interesting older sister to have." For all her flaws, Ella looked up to her.[12]

Moylan graduated from the Mercy Hospital School of Nursing in Baltimore and then became a registered nurse and a certified nurse-midwife. She was working at a large hospital in Maryland in the late 1950s when a colleague, Patricia O'Connor, heard a speech by Tom Dooley, the Catholic doctor who gained international fame for his humanitarian efforts in Southeast Asia. Inspired by Dooley, the two women became interested in traveling to Africa and performing missionary work. Few Catholic organizations were willing to accept lay help, but they scoured the phone book and eventually connected with the White Sisters of Africa. In 1959 it dispatched a contingent of Baltimore-area nurses, including Moylan, to Uganda. They were paid $65 a month for their services.[13]

Moylan and O'Connor wound up working with a religious mission in Nkozi. There they encountered a formidable array of hardships. Water was scarce—except in the rainy season, when the nearby river overflowed and deluged the entire settlement. Ants were so prevalent that the missionaries had to pour kerosene on their doorsteps and floors. "There were lizards everywhere, too," Moylan said, "but I didn't mind them because they ate the ants." Larger animals also proved troublesome. One day, a hippopotamus rumbled through the open-air hospital compound and sent the nurses scurrying.[14]

Working in the Nkozi clinic, Moylan quickly learned that the indigenous people were eager to embrace Western medical treatments—perhaps a little too eager, in some cases. Many of the sick Ugandans who came to the clinic were convinced that, whatever their ailment, "the needle" would cure them. Reflecting on their enthusiasm for receiving injections, Moylan mused, "They didn't seem to believe in any other form of treatment." Hypodermic needles occasionally disappeared from the clinic; Moylan and her colleagues learned that native healers were filling them with homemade concoctions (these included boiled grass water) and injecting patients. Moylan had to treat many of the resulting abscesses.[15]

Moylan saw firsthand the struggles of Uganda and the Congo, its Central African neighbor, to emerge as independent states in the early and mid-1960s. The Congo was a study in political instability. The country plunged into chaos after the assassination of Patrice Lumumba, its first prime minister, early in 1961, and a succession of coups, rebellions, and fraudulent elections marked the next several years. What one scholar described as a "corrupt, oppressive, pro-American stability" emerged by 1964 with the help of UN peacekeeping troops. Predictably, when those forces left the Congo, internecine fighting erupted again.[16]

Fearing—mistakenly, as it turned out—that the Congolese rebels were being bankrolled by the Soviet Union, the Johnson administration resolved to undermine them. This was a geopolitical calculation grounded firmly in Cold War politics, not an idealistic maneuver designed to provide the greatest good to the greatest number of Africans. Support was furnished on two levels: the United

States openly provided military aid to Prime Minister Moise Tshombe while it also covertly outfitted and managed mercenaries in the Congo. Working under the loose supervision of the CIA, this ragtag assortment of troops-for-hire waged a low-key and largely successful battle against the rebels.[17]

Living in Fort Portal, Uganda, just a few dozen miles from that country's border with the Congo, Moylan got a firsthand lesson in how American foreign policy in Africa worked. "I was there when American planes were bombing the Congo and were very close to the border," she later wrote. "The planes came over and bombed two villages in Uganda." The bombings supposedly were accidental, but they seemed completely inexplicable to her. She wondered "what the hell were American planes doing, piloted by [mercenaries], bombing the Congo when as far as I knew, the United Nations was the peacekeeping force in the Congo. Where the hell did the American planes come in?"[18]

The bombings disturbed Moylan. They made her question how the United States operated in the Third World—whose interests it served, and why. When she was underground in 1970, she reflected that the air raids by American proxies in Uganda had marked "the political turning point in my life."[19]

Soon enough, Moylan had to deal with a political clash with much more direct personal implications. Her second stint in Africa was sponsored by the Women Volunteers Association, but in time she clashed with her colleagues over the degree of control they exercised over their programs. She returned to the United States and took up residence at a home owned by the Archdiocese of Washington, D.C. It quickly drew together liberal Catholics who had been inspired by the reforms of Vatican II to more fully engage the world outside their church.[20]

The scholar and theologian Rosemary Ruether lived near Moylan in this period and was struck by her ability to bring together an emerging breed of Catholic activists, young people who were "active in the civil rights movement and the protests against the Vietnam war." As Ruether later put it, Moylan's residence "became a center for progressive Catholics in that period, people like ourselves, [who were] interested in the reforms of Vatican II, in new liturgy, and in social justice concerns. . . . Mary's living room became a gathering place for many an afternoon of talk on these subjects, sharing food and drink together while our small children scampered around in the woods that led from the house down to the creek."[21]

The Catholics brought together by Moylan tested the outer limits of the reform impulses within their church. Motivated to modernize the liturgy, they had more accessible and socially conscious Masses performed at the residence itself rather than a church.[22]

Word of Moylan's liturgical innovations eventually reached Archbishop Patrick Aloysius O'Boyle, the head of the archdiocese. Although he was a progressive on many social issues, including race and labor relations, O'Boyle was not in the vanguard of post–Vatican II liturgical experimentation. Unable to countenance the renegade services being held on archdiocese property, he came down hard on Moylan. She was ejected from the residence.[23]

Moylan was at loose ends. Appreciating her reform spirit, George and Helene Mische invited her to join the Catholic activists who were forming a new community at 1620 S Street. Moylan had some reservations: after her run-in with O'Boyle, her commitment to Catholicism was waning, and she "wasn't interested in attacking it or doing anything with it. I just wanted it to go away quietly," she later said. For the time being, though, she overcame her qualms and joined the group at 1620 S Street.[24]

The young activists who came together at the Misches' house soon learned to appreciate Moylan's liveliness, which seemed to be symbolized by the color of her hair—red. Baltimore activist Grenville Whitman used an appropriate metaphor when describing her temperament: "She was very fiery. She was very up front with her feelings and her thoughts. She was probably the most fiery of the Catonsville Nine."[25]

Moylan's spirited side was on display almost every day. Even with close friends, she could be brusque. Suzanne Ross appreciated Moylan's humility and her reluctance "to impose her ideas on anybody." But Ross, who got to know Moylan through the women's movement, knew that she could be obstinate, particularly when she discussed issues she cared deeply about. "Mary was the kind of person who stood on her own two feet and developed her own positions and stuck by them stubbornly. . . . She argued, she disagreed, she fought." It didn't matter if her opponent supposedly outranked her. "She was not awed by anybody," Ross recalled. "She laughed at people who were awed by themselves."[26]

Moylan laughed a lot, period. "She was very, very funny. She was a lot of fun to be around," Ross said. At 1620 S Street, the laughter sometimes was lubricated by alcohol. Although George Mische had a reputation as a prodigious drinker, he was not alone; Moylan joined in the drinking, enjoying beer and the occasional shot of whiskey. (Many of the activists quaffed Pikesville Rye, a single-malt whiskey that had originated in Maryland.) Moylan smoked as well—Pall Malls. Relaxing with friends, she liked to puff away at them while engaging in a lively game of cribbage.[27]

During her time in Washington, Moylan did not focus much of her attention on frivolous pursuits. She became concerned about the miserable plight of the city's African Americans. After seeing so much despair in the nation's capital, it outraged her to hear American politicians piously decry the political and economic disenfranchisement of people abroad. She came to believe, as she later said, "that we had no right to speak to foreign countries about their policies when things at home were in very sad shape."[28]

Both the scope and the intensity of the troubles afflicting Washington's African Americans distressed Moylan. Their neighborhoods were blighted and riddled with crime; their schools had fallen into disrepair. To make matters even worse, the criminal justice system treated them with contempt. When it came to African Americans, "it became obvious that 'law and order' is a farcical term," she concluded. Indeed, "justice for a black person is just about impossible." In time, she connected with black activists in Washington and contributed to their efforts on behalf of the city's beleaguered minority community.[29]

Moylan complemented her concerns with racism and imperialism with a critique of the war in Vietnam. Convinced that it was time to stand up against such an illegal and immoral conflict, she joined picket lines and "beg-ins" in which activists panhandled to raise money for the victims of the Vietnam War. (Father Richard McSorley, the antiwar Georgetown professor, took part in these efforts as well.) Moylan also participated in prayer vigils and tea and rice meals.[30]

But she was rankled by the apparent failure of such protest activities to bring about lasting change. Yes, mass marches had been essential to the success of the civil rights movement, but Moylan believed that they had lost much of their effectiveness after the epochal marches from Selma to Montgomery, Alabama, in 1965. After that, these forms of protest had become institutionalized and legalized, and by the end of the decade they were reasonably easy methods of dissent for the state to handle. New—and more provocative—methods of protest thus were needed. "You can't play your game by their rules," she insisted.[31]

The pervasiveness of violence in American life also troubled Moylan. The American military was wreaking havoc in Vietnam, and there was also bloodshed aplenty in the United States. Two leading exponents of social justice—Martin Luther King Jr. and Robert F. Kennedy—were assassinated in the spring of 1968, and ordinary people were gunned down in the nation's inner cities every single day. Americans were so constantly exposed to such carnage that they had become hardened to it. She was left to wonder, "What kind of society do we have?"[32]

For Moylan, one thing was certain: the country needed to turn in a radically new direction, and quickly. "The potential of America is fantastic," she said, "but if we continue in our madness we will destroy ourselves and the world." This could be avoided only if the country confronted the central issues of the times—poverty, violence, and injustice—and dealt honestly with them. It was up to individual Americans to take the lead in this process of healing because the country's political system was fundamentally broken. To Moylan, it just no longer seemed viable.[33]

Moylan's evolving approach to political and social justice issues was influenced by Camilo Torres Restrepo, a radical Colombian priest who is perhaps best remembered for asserting that Jesus would have been a guerrilla if he had been alive in the mid-1960s. Torres was so committed to revolutionary politics that he gave up the priesthood, left his university teaching position, and joined the guerilla fighters of the National Liberation Army (ELN). (He was killed in a firefight with government forces in 1966.) Moylan read Torres's writings and was impressed by his claim that "the people who were really going to help the poor and change things for the poor were the guerillas in the hills," as she summarized it.[34]

When discussions at 1620 S Street turned to the possibility of mounting a second draft board attack in the Baltimore area, Moylan did not require much persuading. Such an act, she knew, might be characterized as illegal because it violated the strictures of federal law. But Moylan did not believe that the rigid enforcement of such measures necessarily led to equitable results. "I think only if a law is just," she explained, "does it have the right to be enforced." And American conscription laws were anything but just.[35]

As this group of activists began to take shape in Washington in the spring of 1968, Mische indicated to Phil Berrigan—whose trial in federal court in Baltimore he had been attending—that he was beginning to assemble a group that might be willing to take part in a second demonstration at a draft board. Mische knew that the entire draft couldn't be completely crippled by such protests; there were simply too many boards to attack, too many files to destroy. But he was certain that demonstrations targeting draft boards would at least help to publicize the glaring racial and socioeconomic inequities of the military draft. Mische was eager to strike a blow against the Selective Service Act, the measure that made conscription possible. "The law itself is unjust—the very law itself," he said.[36]

At one point, the contingent from 1620 S Street traveled north to Baltimore to meet with Berrigan at St. Peter Claver and discuss what they might do to illuminate not only the horror of the war in Vietnam but also the overall folly of American foreign policy. Hogan sensed "the urgency on Phil's part. He was trying to get another action to happen before he went to jail" for his role in the Baltimore Four protest. Berrigan made clear how he wanted this second protest to proceed. "He wanted to burn files this time," Hogan recalled, "because the message of blood hadn't gotten through to people the first time." It would be "a symbol, something that would reach more people."[37]

The 1620 S Street group discussed Berrigan's proposal when they returned to Washington. Late in April 1968, they agreed to call a meeting of potential participants and obtain commitments from those who would participate in a follow-up to the Custom House demonstration. Throughout the appointed day and into the evening, activists filtered into the house's dimly lit basement; some sat on the floor, while others squeezed onto battered couches.[38]

Many of those on hand knew each other (or at least of each other) from their religious communities or their antiwar activities. There was, however, one relative stranger on hand—Brother David Darst, a member of the Christian Brothers religious order who had been teaching in inner-city high schools in Kansas City, Omaha, and St. Louis. No one at 1620 S Street ever had seen the guy before.

Darst began thinking seriously about the war in the summer of 1967, when he started poring over works like Theodore Draper's *Abuse of Power*, a book that offered a scathing indictment of the failure of American foreign policy. After reading news accounts of the Baltimore Four protest, he struck up a correspondence with Phil Berrigan. Darst was working with draft resisters in the Midwest, but eventually Berrigan asked the Christian Brother if, as Darst later put it, he "was interested in other things," such as a second draft board protest. Intrigued, Darst traveled east and presented himself at 1620 S Street.[39]

At first, the other prospective participants in the action were wary of Darst. The FBI's use of undercover agents to infiltrate the antiwar movement was common knowledge among the activists who had gathered at the house on S Street. With only a tenuous connection to the rest of the group, the clean-cut Darst aroused suspicions; some wondered if he might be an FBI plant. "People became a little worried about him," said Hogan. "People were wondering if the FBI was watching. Is he an FBI agent, or what is he?"[40]

But the disarming Darst soon laid those fears to rest. Tom Lewis and Berrigan picked him up at the airport, and they immediately realized that he was genuine. "He got off the plane and came toward us," Lewis later said, "and even before we talked to him we knew that he was correct, that he was a correct person." His obvious sincerity—and his unmistakable despair over the war—quickly convinced everyone that he had a bona fide interest in besieging a draft board. "David Darst came right out of the blue," according to Hogan. "But he had his stuff together."[41]

Darst wanted to participate in a bold antiwar protest because he was, as he described it, "terribly worried about my country and the future of mankind." American foreign policy was misguided and frightening, and the nation's priorities were completely out of order. Change was needed, but for it to occur "something completely different, something very new is going to have to happen in our country." Like Lewis and Berrigan, he had grown weary of engaging in traditional means of protest to address the many ills afflicting the country. "I for one am through *talking* about these problems; I've done enough reading, writing, discussing about how 'It's time to wake up, Americans,'" he explained. "Voluntary suffering, massive civil disobedience, the taking of many risks—these are the only hope of waking America up. . . . Something must be done to stop the storm, to shake up this system of ours so that it has the chance to radically rearrange its values."[42]

To Darst and the rest of the group that assembled at 1620 S Street, Berrigan and Mische explained there would be a second strike against a draft board in the Baltimore area. The raiding party would seize Selective Service files, take them outside the building, and burn them. Special care would be taken to ensure that none of the clerks in the office were physically harmed. And time was of the essence: Berrigan and Lewis were due to be sentenced in only a few weeks' time for their roles in the Baltimore Four action. The proposed draft board demonstration would have to take place before they were parceled off to federal prison.

It was made clear that anyone who participated in this upcoming raid could expect to be arrested, tried, and convicted, as Berrigan and Lewis had been. There would be no effort to flee the scene or evade the authorities, and the outcome of any subsequent legal proceedings seemed preordained—they were almost certain to be found guilty. Sitting in the basement of the S Street house and listening to the plan, Tom Melville got the message: "There were sure to be jail sentences after the raiders turned themselves in." Although he was enthusiastic about the proposed looting, Mische wasn't eager to twist arms to get people to participate. He saw his role as organizer as being someone who laid out possibilities and then let individuals reach their own decisions. So he simply said, "Those who will join in this action, raise your hands."[43]

Not everyone was ready to sign on. Anthony Mullaney, a Benedictine monk, confessed to having several reservations about what was being proposed. He told Mische that he wasn't sure that trying to force political changes in Washington would have much of an impact abroad. And Mullaney also had more personal fears. "I'm not sure I can handle jail yet," he said. Mische did not try to force Mullaney's hand. "Tony, everybody here tonight in this room should feel that this is their choice," he said. "Nobody should feel under pressure here that they should do that. That's gotta be a free one." Mullaney demurred but left the door open to participating in a future protest. "The next time it comes around," he said, "maybe I'll be ready."[44]

Mullaney was not the only potential recruit who blanched at the idea of spending time in prison. Interfaith Peace Mission stalwart Bill O'Connor already had been jailed for participating in antiwar and civil rights protests in Baltimore, and he wasn't eager to repeat the experience. He concluded that priests were in a better position to endure incarceration because their sexual needs presumably were less than those of laypeople. "I thought that the priests could use their celibacy for a change," he later said. "It was easier for them to get arrested." But O'Connor agreed to make other contributions to the protest: he would reprise his supporting role in the Baltimore Four action by helping to coordinate the activists' press contacts—a critical task, given their eagerness to have news of their witness widely disseminated.[45]

Many of those in attendance felt blindsided by the proposal. Some had come to the meeting believing that they were going to discuss nothing more dramatic than fairly typical antiwar or church activities—marches, prayer vigils, and the like. Suddenly they were being asked to decide, on a moment's notice, whether they were prepared to burn federal property and then spend the next several years in prison. There also was grumbling over how little input participants would have in the planning of the demonstration.

"You're trying to high-pressure us into this," one person complained, "without any discussion."

"We were invited here for a meeting on antiwar protest and church participation," another sputtered, "not to decide how many years we're willing to spend in jail!"

These objections were answered directly by those who wanted to move forward with the protest. "No one is pushing anybody," one explained. "Those who want to take part are welcome; those who don't can simply refuse."[46]

Another point of contention was the demonstrators' inclination to frame their action primarily as a protest against American misdeeds in Vietnam. "Vietnam was on the front burner," Hogan said of the discussion. "Guatemala was like a footnote." This troubled some, including Hogan and Tom and Marjorie Melville, all of whom felt a particularly strong commitment to illuminating the plight of the Guatemalan people. Did they really want to go to jail for several years—and thereby find themselves unable to speak out publicly about conditions in Guatemala—for participating in a protest that narrowly targeted Vietnam?[47]

Blase Bonpane voiced serious concerns on this score. As the group debated the plan to mount another draft board strike, Bonpane questioned if its focus would be construed too narrowly, as merely an indictment of America's wayward foreign policy in Southeast Asia. Tom Melville did his best to explain how Vietnam and Guatemala could be paired and presented to the public as symptoms of the same malady. "I tried to relate what was going on in Guatemala to Vietnam," Melville later said, "to show that Vietnam was not an isolated blunder but had resulted from a policy consistent with America's view of the world and its place in it." However, not everyone at the meeting could see the point of making such a connection at the upcoming protest. "We can't even convince people of the horror and immorality of the Vietnam War," one participant told him, "and now you want to drag in Guatemala."[48]

In the end, those with a strong commitment to Guatemala reconciled themselves to the upcoming protest in a variety ways. Although Bonpane had no real moral objection to the proposed raid, he could not shake the feeling that it was politically unwise. He would continue to focus his energies on publicizing events in Guatemala, as would Melville's brother Art. Tom and Hogan would join in the upcoming demonstration "if it were indicated that our action was related to Guatemala and Latin America," as Melville later said. According to Hogan, the Maryknollers wanted to make sure it was clear to the public that "those who worked in Guatemala were doing it not just because of Vietnam but also because of Guatemala becoming another Vietnam."[49]

Father Richard McSorley also made his way to 1620 S Street. Berrigan had contacted the Georgetown professor and, without revealing too many details, urged him to attend what promised to be an important meeting of antiwar activists. But when McSorley arrived and looked around the front room of the house, Berrigan was nowhere to be found. His annoyance growing by the minute, he eventually spied Lewis and approached him.

"I came here to see Phil," McSorley said. "He phoned and said it was important. Where is he?"

"Let's walk down to the corner and get some cigarettes," Lewis responded.

McSorley was fast losing his patience. "I don't smoke," the priest said.

"Will you walk me down? Phil will be here in a minute."

As the two men walked, Lewis apologized for his caginess. He explained to McSorley that Berrigan was in fact in the house and speaking with a group of activists about a potential antiwar protest. However, he wasn't sure everyone present could be trusted, and Lewis thought it best that they kill some time before descending into the basement and joining in the discussion. When McSorley finally entered the downstairs room, he saw Berrigan sitting around a table with a group of roughly ten people. The two priests greeted each other warmly.

"Did you hear what we are planning?" Berrigan asked.

"Not yet," McSorley said.

"All of us and a few others, we hope, are going to join in a draft file action," Berrigan told him. "At a draft board office near Baltimore we plan to get 1-A draft files and burn them. We have very good information on the place. No one will be harmed, just the draft files. We are wondering if you would like to join us?"

McSorley pressed Berrigan for details. "This means you will be arrested?" he asked.

"We are not trying to avoid arrest," Berrigan explained. "We will stay after the files are burned until the police come."

"Where will you burn the files?"

"Outside the office in the parking lot."

"Do I have to give an answer tonight?"

"No, but there isn't much time."

McSorley found himself unable to frame a quick response. Despite Berrigan's earlier hints that some kind of antiwar demonstration was in the works, the invitation took him by surprise, and he struggled to weigh all the pros and cons. The proposed raid promised to be a dramatic witness, but he had made a commitment to teach courses on war and peace at Georgetown. If he participated in the action and eventually went to prison, he would likely lose his teaching position, and he also might be marginalized by his religious order, as Berrigan had been. He also wondered if he would do more to further the cause of peace by continuing to teach. After some soul-searching, McSorley turned down Berrigan's offer. For many decades afterward, he wondered if he had made the right choice.[50]

Amid all the comings and goings at 1620 S Street that day, Tom Melville eventually realized that his wife had been quiet throughout the tumultuous proceedings. He attributed Marjorie's silence to the enormous tension of the moment, never for a moment thinking that she might harbor deep-seated reservations about joining the proposed protest. "I took it for granted," he later said, "that she agreed with the action."[51]

In fact, the discussion had set Marjorie's mind reeling. "I was angry and hurt," she later explained. "Tom had committed himself without talking it over with me at all." She had a number of serious concerns about participating in the demonstration that Berrigan and Mische were outlining. Echoing the qualms expressed by Bonpane, she wondered how such a protest could serve the cause to which they had decided to devote their lives: helping the people of Guatemala. "I couldn't see how such a raid would emphasize the immorality of the war or bring about any understanding of the situation in Guatemala." Her main concern was pragmatic: "How can the destruction of a few files end a war or get the Green Berets out of Guatemala?"[52]

And then there was the matter of the Melvilles' fledgling marriage. At that point, they had been married for only a few months. With their union still in its infancy, the idea of spending the next several years apart—and in jail, no less—held little appeal for Marjorie. She dreaded being separated from Tom.[53]

On the verge of tears, Marjorie slipped out of the meeting and went for a long, meandering walk through the streets of the nation's capital. She wound up at the Washington Mall and sat down under some trees near the Washington Monument. Marjorie had brought along a pen and paper, and with them she wrote a poem. This seemed to be only way she could adequately express her jumbled feelings.[54]

Tom noticed his wife's absence and went looking for her. After a prolonged search, he found Marjorie. Tom was surprised to discover that she was so troubled by his decision to commit to the draft board raid. It hadn't dawned on the new husband that he should have consulted his wife before deciding to plunge ahead with the protest. "It just didn't really occur to me that I should get her permission or talk to her about it," he later said.[55]

Still, Marjorie's hesitancy puzzled Tom. In the past, they had struggled with questions regarding their relationship and how it might impact their work on behalf of the people of Guatemala. In his mind, the decision to participate in the protest and risk jail time was part and parcel of the approach they had decided upon: their devotion to each other would not interfere with their commitment to confronting injustice. "Margie's reaction was inconsistent," he later explained, "and it upset me."[56]

Tom did his best to convince Marjorie that "the act of civil disobedience being proposed might shake the complacency of Americans who disliked the war but weren't willing to make personal sacrifices to end it." Still, she had difficulty coming to terms with the implications of his decision. She later explained:

> He had enthusiastically committed himself, and this had created a gap between us so big that I couldn't think about anything else. He'd agreed to something that would earn him years in jail. I couldn't begin to think what I would do meanwhile. My life had been utterly uprooted in the space of a few months, and I didn't know where and how to plant my feet firmly again. I couldn't go back to Guatemala, and publicizing the cause without Tom here in the United States would be too difficult for me alone.[57]

As the conversation continued, Marjorie began to better grasp Tom's perspective, and his rationale started to make more sense. To help clear her head, she went off by herself for another long walk. It was on this second stroll that she recognized that she "had to accept jail as testimony of my opposition to my country's intervention in Latin America and Southeast Asia," she later wrote. "I repudiated its policies, but if I remained silent I would in effect be acquiescing in them. Nuremberg came to mind." Initially, practical concerns had consumed her. "But now I saw the symbolic strength of the action—this was the best way for me to speak to people in the United States, which was precisely what I wanted to do. I couldn't understand why I hadn't thought of this before."[58]

She also knew that conventional means of protesting American imperialism had yielded few results. Marjorie had written to and met with several members of Congress, but none of these steps had done much good. "The thing continues," she explained. "We have been talking about the war in Vietnam for six years, and it is getting worse all the time."[59]

Having made up her mind to join in the upcoming protest, Marjorie went looking for her husband. "I'm going with you," she said when she found him at the S Street house. As they embraced, it occurred to Tom that they had come full circle: Marjorie had led them into radical activities in Guatemala, and now he was returning the favor in the United States.[60]

The proposed demonstration also generated some friction between George Mische and his wife, who was in the latter stages of pregnancy. When George outlined the group's plans to her, Helene was holding a long iron flyswatter that Mary Moylan had brought back as a souvenir from Africa. As it dawned on her that, if all went according to plan, her husband probably was headed to federal prison, she stood up and flailed her arms in anger. With that, the flyswatter flew from her hand and clanged off the ceiling. "You're going to *what?*" she asked him. It took some work for George to calm her fears.[61]

Lewis harbored one major reservation as the group took shape: it included only one priest. "I was afraid—and I think correctly so—that if Phil were the only Catholic priest, the government would really isolate him as somebody who was really way out," Lewis later said. "And he wasn't getting a lot of support by the Catholic Church." McSorley had been a promising candidate, but when he bowed out it looked as though Phil Berrigan might be the only priest involved. If that were the case, Lewis believed that the group shouldn't proceed. His misgivings were so strong that he was prepared to keep the raid from moving forward if a second Catholic cleric couldn't be found. He was determined to "do everything in my power to keep [it] from happening, unless there was another Catholic priest in it." Ironically, he was ready to sabotage a sabotage scheme.[62]

Phil Berrigan wanted to find another priest, too. And he had an ideal candidate in mind: his brother Dan.

"I Couldn't Not Do It"

There was nothing special about Dan Berrigan's early religious development. He and his siblings dutifully attended church and received the Catholic sacraments, but they were not transformed into especially pious lads. The Communion wafer, he recalled, "left us improved only for the hour. We remained remarkably bellicose among ourselves, prone to laziness, imaginative in avoiding duties, light-minded in reading habits." They also smoked and lied and committed acts of petty theft. Saints they were not.[1]

But unlike his brother Phil, whose circuitous journey to the priesthood included detours with the military and at Holy Cross, Dan knew from a relatively early age that he wanted to become a priest. When he was still young, he and a friend requested information from a variety of religious orders. Most of them responded with glossy brochures that showed strapping, well-scrubbed priests in a variety of idyllic landscapes. One order, however, sent only a plain brochure that appeared to be the precise opposite of a come-on. Instead of hype, the Society of Jesus—the Jesuits—offered a carefully measured sales pitch that stressed the long and rigorous training that the order required. It had all the warmth of a railroad timetable, Dan thought.[2]

But something in the materials resonated with Berrigan. The Jesuits had a rich history in upstate New York, and he had read about their exploits in a multivolume tome that had found its way onto his father's bookshelf. He was awed by the book's accounts of the exploits of Isaac Jogues, Jean de Brébeuf, and Jacques Marquette. (Awed, and perhaps slightly aghast: it was said that when Brébeuf died at the hands of the Iroquois in 1649, they mocked the baptism ritual by pouring scalding water on his head and cutting out and consuming his heart.) Berrigan was frail and undersized, and for him there was something appealing about becoming part of this hearty tradition. Both he and his friend signed up.[3]

Berrigan entered St. Andrew-on-Hudson Seminary in 1939, the year that World War II began in Europe. As the war wore on over the next six years, he and his fellow seminarians—largely cut off from the outside world—became only dimly aware of the carnage. Reflecting on his time at the New York seminary, Berrigan later said that this isolation from world events had made him and his fellow seminarians war casualties, of a sort. "How retarded our moral development was, as it touched on the first moral question of our lifetime, that of war and the war-making state!"[4]

Not even the obliteration of two Japanese cities by atomic bombs could puncture this moral bubble. By the summer of 1945 Berrigan had moved on in his training and entered the Jesuit seminary located in Woodstock, Maryland. When he learned about the bombings of Hiroshima and Nagasaki, he failed to fathom the devastation. "I read of the obscene triumph of the president, the estimated casualties," Berrigan later wrote. "And my eyes were as illiterate as the unborn." Despite the unprecedented magnitude of the blasts, he "had no sense that we had crossed a line, all of us."[5]

Berrigan's awakening was a gradual one. He read two writers who had reacted strongly to World War II, George Orwell and Ronald Knox. Just after the American military used atomic weapons to vanquish Japan, Knox published a slender and somewhat quirky volume titled *God and the Atom*, which argued that the United States, instead of dropping the first nuclear device on Hiroshima, should have first staged a demonstration of its destructive force by wiping out a deserted Pacific island in full view of a team of Japanese observers. This fantastic show of force, Knox argued, might have convinced the Japanese to surrender more quickly and thus eliminated the need to use the weapon in a manner that harmed hundreds of thousands of noncombatants.[6]

Knox's arguments impressed Berrigan—"I just ate that book up," he later said—and he tried to impart them when he began teaching at a New York–area prep school. Hoping to spark a debate over the morality of the American military's conduct of the war, he discussed Knox's ideas with his adolescent students. Much to his dismay, they were outraged that he would question the purity of American motives. It wasn't the last time Berrigan heard such vehement justifications for the use of American military force.[7]

Following his ordination as a Jesuit in 1952, Berrigan spent a transformative year in France. It was there that he began to seriously grapple with poverty, inequality, and militarism—the weighty issues that would come to define his priesthood.

A progressive Catholic theology surged from Europe after World War II. Political involvement in the resistance to Nazi occupation had led to the radicalization of the church in several countries, including France, Belgium, and Holland. French priests were especially radicalized after the war; many of them began to preach what Cardinal Emmanuel Célestin Suhard described as "a fearless involvement in the temporal and social spheres." At the vanguard of this movement were worker-priests who resisted the notion that their primary concern should be enforcing rigid theological orthodoxy. Instead, they devoted themselves to improving the material circumstances of the economically disadvantaged, working alongside laborers in factories, supporting them when they went on strike, and urging the French government to erect and subsidize affordable housing.[8]

The worker-priests astonished Berrigan. Fresh from seminary, he had a conventional sense of what a priest's role should be—and here were priests so unorthodox that they didn't even wear clerical collars. He later said that "arriving in France was like landing on a fresh-air planet after being locked up all my life in a capsule." The example set by the worker-priests was central to this awakening. "They gave me, for the first time," he later said, "a practical vision of the Church as she should be."[9]

But Berrigan's time in France also demonstrated for him how stubbornly the Catholic Church's hierarchy resisted meaningful change. The Vatican warily had given approval to the worker-priests in the mid-1940s, but it never fully embraced the movement. Its reservations mounted as they increasingly became involved in industrial unrest (and varying degrees of real and imagined entanglement with communists) in the early 1950s. Eventually, Pope Pius XII— "our icebox Pope," as Berrigan derisively called him—lost patience and cracked down on the movement, ordering all of the worker-priests to resume more traditional priestly functions.[10]

The move saddened the young American Jesuit, who was spending his year doing parish work in a small town near Lyon. It traumatized Berrigan to see such a promising movement "squashed before my very eyes." (He likened it to a Soviet-style purge.) But the suppression of the worker-priests left an indelible impression on Berrigan. "It hit me directly, it made me suffer deeply, it filled me with determination to carry on the work of the men who had been silenced," he later said.[11]

Intent on continuing this work when he returned to the United States, Berrigan forged closer ties with progressive Catholics who operated in the spirit of the worker-priests. After the Jesuits dispatched him to teach theology and French at a Brooklyn prep school, he made a point of exposing his students to Dorothy Day's Catholic Worker community on New York's Lower East Side, where they ladled out soup to the poor. On other excursions, he led his charges to the Gold Street Mission and told them to connect with children who craved interactions with older kids.

To those who knew him in the 1950s, it was clear that Dan Berrigan had little use for the barriers that traditionally separated priests and the laity. "Most priests . . . keep a guarded, closed professionalism in their rapport with laymen," one friend said. "But Dan dared to enter the relationship to a point where he was absolutely exposed. He was always ready to run behind the layman and learn from him. In the fifties, he was revolutionizing the role of the layman in the Church faster than any other priest in the country." He became active in a group called the Walter Ferrell Guild, which brought together clergy and laity in informal settings (cocktails were shared) for discussions of art and current events.

Such gatherings were not uncommon after the reforms of Vatican II, but in the mid-1950s they represented a pioneering spirit among American Catholics.[12]

Berrigan continued to challenge orthodoxy when he took up a position at LeMoyne College in Syracuse, his hometown. In an effort to focus students' energies on social justice issues, he established "something daring and new," as he later called it. International House brought together students in a community of work and worship. He enlisted his father to build the altar—and then, anticipating a Vatican II liturgical reform, he turned it toward the congregation. He also performed parts of the Mass in English. (This, too, became routine in American Catholic churches, but only later.) Such moves outraged some of Berrigan's Jesuit superiors, who "thought I was working at the family jewels with a sledge hammer," he joked.[13]

As Berrigan's iconoclasm grew, he found himself increasingly at odds with his superiors in the church, conservative men who seemed unconcerned about altering the liturgy or seriously addressing issues of poverty or peace. He grew so disaffected that, with the urging of Thomas Merton, he returned to Europe for a prolonged sabbatical in 1963. His visits to the Soviet Union and countries under its domination, including Hungary and Czechoslovakia, strengthened his commitment to serving the disenfranchised and battling for peace. The latter fight was looming larger with each passing day. "The Cold War was sinking world temperature to zero," he later wrote of that time, while "the war in Vietnam was expanding more savagely."[14]

For both Dan and Phil Berrigan, a galvanizing moment came in the spring of 1965, when they joined Merton at the Abbey of Gethsemani for retreat. One of the more unlikely literary celebrities of his time, Merton was a Trappist monk who had vaulted into prominence with the publication of his book *The Seven Storey Mountain* in 1948. Americans of all faiths revered him in the 1960s, and his standing among progressive Catholics rivaled that of Dorothy Day. For the Gethsemani retreat, Merton called together an ecumenical group to reflect on the "Spiritual Roots of Protest." People with strong religious convictions were being drawn into a broad range of protest activities, and Merton hoped to spark a meaningful conversation about the spiritual moorings of that work. "By what right do we protest?" he asked. "Against who or what? For what? Why?" This open-ended conversation helped to clarify the thinking of many of the participants. It energized them as well: several of the Catholic attendees at the retreat, including the Berrigans, came together to form the core of the Catholic Peace Fellowship.[15]

Dan Berrigan stepped up his antiwar activism in 1965 as the conflict in Vietnam worsened. He felt that with civilian and military casualties increasing with each passing day, people of faith had to start voicing their objections to the war or they might never have another chance.[16]

His opposition to the war growing, Berrigan emerged as one of the leaders of Clergy and Laymen Concerned About Vietnam (CALCAV), which one observer described as "the most powerful peace group in the United States." The group attracted an all-star roster of American religious leaders: joining Berrigan in the new group were the likes of theologian Reinhold Niebuhr, Rabbi Abraham Joshua Heschel, and Martin Luther King Jr. CALCAV made an immediate splash by calling together several hundred New York–area clergymen for a conference on the war at a Methodist church in the city.[17]

Berrigan missed the gathering. In a move that provoked a widespread outcry among liberal Catholics, his Jesuit superiors had banished him to South America for several months because of his immersion in antiwar causes. (Of particular concern was the priest's fleeting connection to Roger LaPorte, the Catholic Worker who had immolated himself in an antiwar protest.) Berrigan's banishment set off a firestorm. Lamenting his exile as "a shame and a scandal," *Commonweal* insisted in an editorial that it was "a disgustingly blind totalitarian act" that represented a clear betrayal of the spirit of Vatican II.[18]

Berrigan's tour—which lasted four months and took him to ten countries in Latin America—proved to be an ordeal. Almost everywhere he traveled he observed that the Catholic Church was serving the oligarchy but not people who were in desperate need. "The poverty I saw was overwhelming," he later explained. He wondered why the poor were condemned to live such intolerable lives. And the American government wasn't helping matters. In Rio de Janeiro, Berrigan toured a *favela*—"a city of slums burrowed into a mountain," he called it. His guide mentioned how little the United States seemed to care about the poverty and squalor. "Nine billion dollars for the war in Viet Nam," he said, "and this for us." The comment had an enormous impact on Berrigan, illuminating for him how misplaced American priorities seemed to be.[19]

Yet there were rays of hope. "Here and there, like a radioactive capsule in a diseased body," he observed, "were groups of biblically alert Christians . . . dwelling in *barrios* and *favelas*, passionately loving and beloved by the poor." He was heartened to see these practical iterations of liberation theology, and they strengthened his resolve to serve the interests of peace and social justice.[20]

The imbroglio over Berrigan's exile was a source of ongoing embarrassment for the church, and when the priest came back to the United States in March 1966 he was told that there would be no restrictions on his freedom to speak on sensitive social and political issues. Berrigan—who called this outcome "almost hilarious"—announced upon his return to the United States that he would redouble his efforts to address "the immediate and terrifying question of Vietnam." He hoped that the peace movement had gathered sufficient momentum to "get a hearing in government circles" and thereby alter the course of the war.[21]

Berrigan jumped back into the antiwar fray. Just a few weeks after his return, he helped to lead a peace march through the streets of New York. The two-hour march, which drew several dozen participants, stopped at a variety of houses of worship, including Central Synagogue and St. Patrick's Cathedral, where a ten-minute prayer service was held. (This was believed to be the first such interfaith observance in the history of the cathedral.) And in May 1966 he spoke to a crowd of approximately ten thousand opponents of the war gathered in Washington, D.C., for a demonstration organized by the Committee for a Sane Nuclear Policy (SANE).[22]

Berrigan found a secure niche at Cornell, accepting in 1967 the university's invitation to become the associate director of United Religious Work, its interfaith department. From that post he continued to oppose the war. In a whirlwind of antiwar activity, Berrigan counseled draft resisters, spoke out against the escalating violence in Vietnam, and participated in myriad protests.[23]

Berrigan emerged as something of a celebrity among progressive Catholics. He was a singular figure in the American priesthood—"a hippie cleric" (as he jokingly described himself when he took up his position at Cornell) who not only spearheaded liturgical innovations and spoke out forcefully against the war but also published award-winning poetry. (His first volume, *Time Without Number*, won the Lamont Prize in 1957.) Berrigan's physical appearance only added to his luster. Clad in a black beret and a turtleneck, his hair cropped in a bowl cut, he looked more like a beatnik poet than a priest.[24]

But Berrigan feared that he was becoming less of a true radical and more of a dilettante. As the war in Vietnam intensified, some antiwar activists began to criticize the protests organized by groups like CALCAV as being too timid to have much of a practical effect on the Johnson administration. Among those pushing for more direct and dramatic action against the war was Dan's brother Phil. The two had participated together in several protests, but Phil had grown frustrated with how little peace activists had managed to change the course of the war. He took matters into his own hands in October 1967 by defacing draft files with blood at the Custom House in Baltimore.

Although he attended the massive demonstration held that same month at the Pentagon (and wound up in jail because of it), Dan did not participate in the Baltimore Four action. He knew that a draft board protest was imminent but fell victim to "moral inertness" and failed to take aggressive steps to join his brother at the Custom House. "I was not ready," he confessed, "and Philip was."[25]

The time he spent in jail after the Pentagon demonstration—along with the guilt he felt for failing to join his brother's far bolder witness in Baltimore— helped to ready Dan Berrigan to take the next step in his opposition to the war. Being imprisoned for acting on his moral beliefs had such a deep impact on him that he wondered, "Why was I so long retarded from so crucially formative a happening?" He fasted and reflected on the duty of all people of faith to commit themselves to social and political justice. Writing from prison, Berrigan noted that his conversations with other prisoners—most of them poor and utterly powerless—reminded him that "the Church is invited to be where the action is."[26]

A few months later, Berrigan found himself in the center of the action, as least as far as American foreign policy was concerned. He went to Vietnam.

Late in January 1968 a student interrupted Howard Zinn's Boston University political theory seminar to report that someone was trying desperately to reach him via the telephone. It was no ordinary inquiry. Zinn's caller was the antiwar leader David Dellinger, who told him that he had just received a telegram from the North Vietnamese government announcing that it was prepared to release, as a sign of goodwill, three American pilots who had been captured. The captors wanted to know if the American peace movement would dispatch "a responsible representative" to travel to Hanoi and pick up the flyers. Dellinger and his colleagues thought it might be wiser to send two men on the journey. Over the phone, he said he wanted Zinn to accompany Dan Berrigan. There was no time to waste; they would leave the next day.[27]

Zinn quickly accepted the task. He met Berrigan the following day at a Manhattan apartment, where they were briefed on conditions in North Vietnam by Dellinger and Tom Hayden, another peace activist who had traveled there during the war. Zinn had only vaguely heard of Berrigan, and he was concerned that the priest might prove to be a dreary travel companion. Berrigan quickly put him at ease: he was puckish, Zinn later wrote, and demonstrated an impish wit. The priest's outfit—he wore a turtleneck and sneakers, and a silver medallion hung from a chain around his neck—also signaled to Zinn that his partner for the next sixteen days would be anything but a stuffed shirt. By force of habit, Zinn initially addressed the priest as "Father," but Berrigan insisted on being called "Dan."[28]

Like Zinn, Berrigan had to scramble to prepare for the trip. He later wrote in a poem that he left Cornell for Manhattan "with half a wit," a pile of mismatched socks, some ski underwear, and his passport. Only later did he realize that he had somehow forgotten to bring a copy of the New Testament.[29]

It took them more than a day to reach Laos. After a brief stay there, they boarded a rickety plane for Hanoi. They found a city that had been ravaged by war. "How is one to convey the atmosphere of a city rendered alien as another star by the mythology of our words, by distance, by bombs?" Berrigan later wrote. "It was like stepping out upon the threshold of another planet." The reality of the war hit close to home—literally—on their first night in the city, when an American bombing raid awakened the two men and forced them to scramble to safety in a bomb shelter. Berrigan's loathing of war was long-standing, but interacting with ordinary Vietnamese in such dire circumstances underscored for him in a new and powerful way the horrors of armed conflict.[30]

He was moved by the plight of children and the massive burden the war had created for them. There were relatively few children in Hanoi; most had been evacuated to the countryside to escape the almost constant bombings by American aircraft. But in one of their many trips to a bomb shelter, the two men encountered three youngsters who had remained in the city. Berrigan picked up the smallest of the group, a boy, and cradled him in his arms. Such gut-wrenching experiences made Berrigan even more strident in his opposition to the war.[31]

When he returned from Hanoi (having successfully shepherded home the captured airmen), Dan Berrigan might have seemed primed to engage in a more dramatic form of antiwar activism—the kind that his brother Phil had pulled off at the Custom House and planned to repeat in the spring of 1968. But Dan was still hesitant, and he resisted entreaties to join in such raids after he returned from Vietnam. Determined to persuade him, Phil visited Cornell shortly after the core of the new antidraft protest group had come together at George Mische's house in Washington, D.C.

In Ithaca, Phil did not beat around the bush: he directly asked Dan to join him in besieging another draft board in the Baltimore area. Phil and his fellow activists, including Tom Lewis, were not content to have their witness at the Custom House be "a flash in the pan, a gesture," Dan later wrote. Even as they faced serious criminal penalties for their participation in that earlier protest, they felt that it must be duplicated—and perhaps even surpassed in intensity. And they wanted Dan to help them pull it off.[32]

At first, Dan still was reluctant to take the leap and join Phil in a second antidraft plot. He felt that, in counseling and encouraging activists at Cornell, he already was doing enough to thwart the war. "I was still caught in the idea that in standing with the resisting students I was doing all that was possible, or indeed helpful," he later explained. So the brothers talked through the night, sharing a bottle of whiskey and debating the practical and philosophical implications of such a protest. They also discussed how their participation would be viewed by other Catholics and their colleagues in the peace movement. "Would the action we proposed offend the Church? Of course it would," Phil wrote in a recollection of their conversation that night. "Might it alienate us from some of our fellow peace activists? Most definitely. Would it end the war? Certainly not. Was it consistent with the spirit of Christ, Martin Luther King, and Mohandas Gandhi? We, the people who were planning this action, believed it was."[33]

The offer grew on Dan. He found himself drawn to one of the core ideas undergirding the entire plan: the notion that "the initiative of action and passion in human history belonged to the peaceable and resisting." But he still wondered if he had the moral and physical mettle to sign on. Phil had been through such a travail once already, but Dan was an admitted "coddled egg" who had only recently begun to take greater risks in his activism. Dan also struggled to clarify the ultimate goal of such an action. "Would I survive?" he asked himself. "Was my purpose sound?"[34]

As daybreak neared, Dan finally relented; he would join in the upcoming draft board action. "I couldn't not do it," he later explained. Whatever the potential risks—and for Dan these included losing his position at Cornell and being drummed out of his religious order—he needed to intensify his commitment to ending the war by taking part in a protest that would have a real impact. He said to himself, "I can't just be counseling other people to be heroic; I better do something myself."[35]

There was one caveat, though: Dan wanted a day to mull over his decision. Still hesitant, he told his brother that he needed a short time to reflect on his choice and fully come to peace with it. If Phil didn't hear from him in that period, he could assume that Dan was still committed.[36]

The next morning, Tom Lewis got the news when he met Dan for breakfast in Ithaca. The Jesuit came to the table with two cups of coffee and said simply, "Well, I'm in."[37]

At that moment, Lewis knew that the second draft board demonstration would be staged. The realization filled him with a mixture of joy and fear. Lewis was elated at the prospect of striking another blow against the draft, but he knew that in doing so he would be all but guaranteeing himself a federal prison sentence.[38]

Dan Berrigan felt that his brother and Lewis, in convincing him to join in the next draft board demonstration, had rescued him. "Like a shipwreck or a man sucked into quicksand, or a drowning man, where almost every resource of friendship and ingenuity is lacking, and yet where one emerges alive," he wrote, "I say simply that I was saved at the last moment."[39]

With this late but crucial addition, the roster of participants was set. Baltimore Four veterans Phil Berrigan and Tom Lewis would be joined by the former's brother, Dan. Accompanying them would be a trio of former Maryknollers who had served in Guatemala (John Hogan and Tom and Marjorie Melville) and George Mische, their host at 1620 S Street. Rounding out the contingent would be another member of the S Street group, Mary Moylan, and Brother David Darst, the earnest outsider who had persuaded everyone that he wasn't a FBI plant. Although dozens of people had been contacted about participating in the demonstration, only these nine would directly take part in destroying draft files in Catonsville. (A few others, like Bill O'Connor, would play important but indirect supporting roles.)

It turned out that all nine of the raiding party were Catholics, and they framed their protest as a call to rouse their church from its slumber regarding peace and social justice issues. But while their faith had drawn then into overlapping circles of activism, there did not appear to have been any kind of strict religious litmus test for joining the group. Years later, Tom Melville downplayed the role played by Catholicism in the witness. He reflected that religion might have been "almost a justification for what we were doing rather than an inspiration." For him, it was in part a political act meant to protect human rights throughout the world. As such, it transcended the confines of a particular religious tradition. Mische felt much the same way, explaining that religion was but one of several factors that motivated the protesters.[40]

As the group came together, they focused on how and where they might attack another draft board in the Baltimore area. Both were matters of serious concern, particularly for Phil Berrigan. He felt that the impact of the Baltimore Four protest had been obscured by the public's misunderstanding of why they had destroyed the draft records with blood. He wrote that some people "had trouble with blood as a symbol" and had criticized it as "uncivilized, messy, bizarre." For a second draft board raid to be effective, the records would have to be ruined in some other manner.[41]

Lewis hit upon the idea of defacing the records with napalm, the flammable liquid that was being used with devastating effect by the American military in Vietnam. In his mind, it was a symbol of the war that could be used by the activists to help preserve American and Vietnamese lives. And it was perhaps clearer as a symbol than blood had been. In using it, they would be turning an emblem of the war's savagery upon the war itself.[42]

It was not a new weapon. A sort of jellied gasoline, napalm had been employed by the American military at least as far back as World War II. (American bombers—including one piloted by Howard Zinn—used it in the firebombing of Tokyo.) A new variant, called "Napalm B," had been developed for use in Vietnam. Simple to make and cheap to produce, it had become an integral part of the American military arsenal in Southeast Asia.

A provocative article in the January 1967 issue of *Ramparts*, the liberal political and literary magazine, helped to make napalm an emblem of the war's brutality. Written by a human rights activist named William Pepper, the article chronicled the enormous toll such weapons had taken on the people of Vietnam, particularly its children. As if Pepper's narrative wasn't chilling enough, the piece featured grisly color photographs of Vietnamese children who had been horribly disfigured by napalm.[43]

After much discussion, Lewis's fellow demonstrators came to agree with him that napalm would be an ideal means of destroying draft records. According to Marjorie Melville, the activists "wished to demonstrate a better use for napalm than burning human beings to death." It struck her as strange that the Nine might be censured for using the weapon to save lives rather than take them. "It is noble, patriotic, and worthy to use napalm to burn people, 'enemy people.' It is ignoble, unpatriotic, and unworthy to use napalm to burn 'our paper,' our property," she later wrote in an exasperated summary of this critique. "Property is important; life is expendable."[44]

From a military standpoint, part of Napalm B's appeal was that it could be made so simply. Dow Chemical mass-produced it for the Army, but smaller batches could be made through what was known as "bathtub chemistry." Rudimentary instructions appeared in an Army Special Forces manual and were subsequently reproduced in antiwar publications. Lewis did the legwork, researching the recipe at a military law library at Georgetown University. There he "learned that there actually existed a way of making a kind of homemade napalm," he explained. "That was also an indictment of the sickness of the military—that they would figure out how to make their own napalm in case they ran out of the professional stuff."[45]

On the night of May 16, 1968, the entire ransacking party met at Bill O'Connor's row house in Baltimore's Charles Village neighborhood. (This was the first time that Dan Berrigan, the last addition to their ranks, met with the entire group.) O'Connor and Dean Pappas—a local physics teacher who also had agreed to play a behind-the-scenes role in the upcoming protest—descended into the basement to work on the napalm and make a reasonable approximation of what was being used abroad by the American military. O'Connor felt that the moment was "exciting, scary, important. We didn't know what was going to happen." O'Connor's wife, Marilyn, feared for the worst: she worried that the mixing might go horribly wrong and that her house would be burned to the ground.[46]

O'Connor and Pappas loosely followed the recipe that Lewis had unearthed, mixing two parts gasoline and one part Ivory Soap flakes. The instructions called for the concoction to be cooked (so that it would congeal), but O'Connor and Pappas decided to skip that step; they wanted the demonstrators to be able to easily pour it out of some gasoline cans.[47]

When they had finished mixing the napalm, O'Connor summoned the Nine downstairs. "Alright, come down," he called. "You want to see what this stuff looks like?"[48]

Choosing to use a napalm-fueled fire to burn the draft records influenced the activists' selection of a target. Some later reports suggested that the Nine targeted Catonsville—a leafy suburb located several miles west of downtown in Baltimore County—for demographic or political reasons. The writer Francine du Plessix Gray, in her account of the demonstration, suggested that the group had zeroed in on Catonsville because it was "a lily-white, middle-class suburban town of smug brick houses and pleasant oak-lined streets"—precisely the kind of placid community that needed to be shaken out of its torpor by a dramatic protest.[49]

According to a later FBI report, there also was some speculation that Catonsville "was 'symbolic' since one of the four persons who had jumped ship (from a United States aircraft carrier) in Japan was from Catonsville." This was a reference to the defection of four Navy enlisted men from the aircraft carrier *Intrepid* late in 1967. They deserted—and subsequently sought political asylum in Sweden—as an antiwar protest. One of the seamen was a Catonsville native named John Barilla.[50]

In fact, Catonsville was targeted for more prosaic reasons. All of the activists were committed to nonviolence, and they felt that they should do everything possible to minimize the risk of harming anyone during their foray; the last thing they wanted was for someone to get injured. In an effort to find the most accessible draft board, Lewis scouted several potential locations in the Baltimore area. ("We could have been called the Towson Nine, or we could have been called the Pikesville Nine," he later joked, referring to two other Baltimore suburbs that he visited during his search for a target.) Local Board 33 in Catonsville was located on the second floor of the town's Knights of Columbus hall, and Lewis investigated it by pretending to be a prospective groom interested in renting the building's downstairs hall for a wedding reception. "I looked over the whole place—looked all through the building and cased it out, so to say," he explained.

Lewis could see that the draft board in Catonsville presented, from a logistical standpoint, a perfect target. Access to the Selective Service office was relatively straightforward—a back staircase led up to the second floor of the Knights of Columbus hall—and, once they were seized, the draft records could be burned in an open area behind the building. "We picked Catonsville partly because we were able to take the records outside," according to Lewis, "and have a very open and a very safe place to burn them." It also appealed to the Nine that there would be plenty of room for members of the news media to assemble and record their witness.[51]

And then there was the fact the building in Catonsville was owned by a Catholic fraternal organization. The Nine had a special appetite for targeting a draft board in a building owned by the Knights of Columbus—"a very high-minded Catholic group," as Dan Berrigan put it. In their minds, it was important to highlight the complicity of the church's hierarchy in the war in Vietnam. The Nine realized that in targeting the draft board in Catonsville, they could speak out against the injustices perpetrated not only by their government but also by their own church. It could be a double blow.[52]

To make sure that these messages were clear, the Nine ironed out a public statement that would be distributed to the media. "When we realized that all who had finally agreed to act were Catholics, we decided to aim our statement primarily at the Catholic Church," Tom Melville later explained, "as we believed it was the most culpable of all the Christian churches in providing a moral rationale for war and exploitation." Bearing Phil Berrigan's unmistakably strident stamp, the document also offered a far-ranging indictment of how policymakers had jumbled the nation's priorities.[53]

Dan Berrigan apparently did not play a central role in crafting the statement that the Nine planned to distribute in Catonsville. His brother thought it would be unfair for him to influence the document, given that he had joined the protest at the eleventh hour. Largely shut out of this group effort, Berrigan later penned a separate meditation that, ironically, wound up gaining a far wider circulation. "Our apologies, good friends, for the fracture of good order, the burning of paper instead of children, the angering of the orderlies in the front parlor of the charnel house," he wrote. "We could not, so help us God, do otherwise. . . . We say: killing is disorder, life and gentleness and community and unselfishness is the only order we recognize. For the sake of that order, we risk our liberty, our good name."[54]

As they prepared themselves on the night before the protest, the Nine took care of other last-minute details. Marjorie Melville, figuring that she wouldn't be able to change out of her clothes for awhile after she was arrested, made sure that she had a dress that wouldn't wrinkle. She and her accomplices also reviewed the schematic diagrams of the Knights of Columbus hall that Lewis had prepared. Dan Berrigan found the plans incomprehensible. "I didn't understand anything, Philly, . . . never could read a map," he said to his brother. "I'll follow you, Philly, okay? I'll just follow you."[55]

When the meeting at O'Connor's broke up at about 1 A.M., they dispersed to the homes of various confederates in the Baltimore area. As they thought about the momentous step they would be taking later that day, rest proved elusive. "We didn't get much sleep that night," Brother David Darst admitted.[56]

On the morning of May 17, the Nine and members of their support team met at the home of Lewis's family. Lewis's mother wasn't sure what was brewing, but she did her best to be an accommodating host, setting out a meal for her son and his fellow activists. Lewis politely waved her off; he wanted everyone to focus on the task at hand. After laying out his diagrams of the Knights of Columbus hall, he reviewed how the group would enter and exit the building and where they would burn the draft files after seizing them.

For Lewis, the plan for their witness in Catonsville was like a work of art. "And what I mean by that is that my art was outside the studio," he later explained. "My creation was outside the studio. The work and the love and the articulation and the involvement that goes into one of my paintings, all of that went into Catonsville. All of the details that go into my artwork went into the whole details of Catonsville. How would we go, where we would meet. The symbols. The press."[57]

Lewis appreciated the importance of having members of the news media present when the Nine struck. He and O'Connor had arranged for selected members of the press to rendezvous with supporters of the Nine at the Hilltop Motel, located just off the Baltimore Beltway, and to proceed from there to Catonsville. Such was Lewis's attention to detail that he had driven the routes to Catonsville from both his family's home and the motel and determined that the press contingent would need to leave about ten minutes earlier if they wanted to arrive at roughly the same time as the activists. But when Lewis phoned the motel to check in with the assembling press group, he learned of a potential snag: one reporter was running late. Everyone would have to wait.

The delay drove Phil Berrigan to distraction. Impatient to leave, he pressed Lewis.

"Hurry, hurry, let's go!" he said. "Stop all this. Stop all this."

Lewis urged him to remain calm. "Phil," he told the priest, "we have to be clear what we're doing."[58]

When things settled down, the group piled into three cars for the drive to Catonsville. Brendan Walsh, a local activist who was serving the Nine in a support role, had planned to drive Phil and Dan Berrigan. But Phil was unable to take a backseat—literally or figuratively—at such an important moment. When it came time to go, the priest grabbed the keys and took the wheel. He left the house so quickly that he nearly drove off by himself.[59]

As he made the journey to Catonsville in another car, Tom Melville worried that word of the protest had leaked out and that the police would be waiting for the Nine at the Knights of Columbus hall. If that happened, they still would face punishment—but without having made their witness against war and imperialism. "They're going to pick us up for conspiracy," he thought. "There's not going to be any action, and we're going to do the time anyway, and it won't have any effect at all." His wife shared his fears. For her, too, the drive to Catonsville was absolutely nerve-racking.[60]

"My God, They're Burning Our Records!"

Mary Murphy took a job with the military draft system in the spring of 1944. With Allied and Axis forces engaging in desperate combat in both the European and Pacific theaters, it was "a very bad time for the country," she later said. Although she supported her country wholeheartedly in World War II, Murphy was reluctant to join the war effort; she had small children at home, and she was hesitant to leave them in someone else's care. But a neighbor chaired the draft board located in Irvington, an area adjacent to Catonsville, and he all but begged her to chip in at his short-staffed office. She agreed and embarked on a fulfilling career that lasted for the next several decades.[1]

Her schedule was erratic, and there were no limits on the number of hours she might work. (The clerks could count on having one day off per year—Christmas.) Sometimes she would be called into the draft board office at daybreak to guide draftees to Baltimore's Fifth Regiment Armory, where they would be subjected to physical exams and then formally inducted into the armed services. There were no special transports for the bleary-eyed recruits. Murphy shepherded them over to the car barn in Irvington, and from there they rode city streetcars to the armory.[2]

Not that Murphy or her fellow clerks felt that they were in any position to complain about their jobs. They realized that the young men they were helping to dispatch to combat were making far greater sacrifices, sometimes even with their lives. In time, Murphy came to believe that working in the draft office was part of her responsibility as a citizen to support her country in a time of crisis. "While we were tired and many times discouraged, we felt that we were doing our duty to our country," she later said. "Our country needed us in the worst kind of way and we were supporting the men that were fighting in Europe at that time." She was just doing her fair share.[3]

Murphy's resolve to help her country did not waver after World War II ended. She worked for the Selective Service System during subsequent armed conflicts, including the wars in Korea and Vietnam. Her son, John, always felt that she was simply a patriotic woman who was determined to help her country. Clerking wasn't flashy or lucrative work, but it allowed her to contribute.[4]

Although Murphy was far from the front lines, she had a few harrowing experiences. In what she later described as being "kind of a terrifying incident," a disgruntled draftee vowed to shoot her. Police took the threat so seriously that they positioned an armed officer near her desk for an entire week. (Luckily, nothing came of the threat.[5])

Starting in 1960, she worked at Local Board 33 in Catonsville. The board served an area in southwestern Baltimore County that was bound by the county's borders with Baltimore City (to the east), Howard County (west), and Anne Arundel County (south). To the north, the board's territory stretched to Dogwood Road in adjoining Woodlawn. In that area, there were about 13,750 registrants for the draft.[6]

Murphy understood that the war in Vietnam was not widely viewed as a "good war," as World War II had been. It seemed that every day the television news would feature some antiwar protest or, increasingly, some demonstration against the part of the war effort to which she contributed: the draft. But for Murphy, this was only one side of the story. "I felt that we were doing the right thing by being there [in Vietnam]," she later said, "because I was sold on the idea that we were trying to fight communism in that part of the world."

And in Murphy's work at Local Board 33 in Catonsville—which earned her a salary of $6,300 per year—she encountered many young men who were willing, if not eager, to serve. Sometimes these individuals returned to Catonsville after finishing their tours of duty and reported that they had benefited from being in the military. "We had many boys who came back and told us that [serving in the military] was the best experience they ever had in their life," she later said. "That, while they would not want to make a career of it, they wouldn't have changed their experiences in the service for any amount of money that anyone could have given them. Many of them say it made them grow up, made them more mature, made them feel more like a man."[7]

Murphy's superiors in the Selective Service System realized that not everyone shared her favorable view of the war in Vietnam and its benefits. Even before the Baltimore Four raid in October 1967, draft boards were viewed as inviting potential targets for antiwar demonstrators, and Selective Service officials attempted to prepare draft personnel on how to handle protests at their offices. In July of that year, draft boards throughout Maryland received from state field director Katherine Kindervatter a memorandum on the appropriate procedures to follow if a "local board [is] picketed or [a] sit-down strike occurs on local board premises." They were told to immediately alert the office of the state's Selective Service director, local law enforcement, and the FBI. To be fully prepared, local draft boards also were to have the telephone numbers of these agencies typed onto a single four-by-six-inch note card that could be affixed to a readily accessible desk.[8]

When it became clear that antiwar activists would target them, Maryland's draft boards received similar instructions throughout the following year. A few months after the Baltimore Four protest, for instance, Kindervatter set forth explicit instructions for securing sensitive Selective Service materials at the close of business each day. Items such as cover sheets, registration certificates, and local board stamps—all of which could be used to forge documents, if they fell into the wrong hands—were to be stored in metal file cabinets and secured with a lock. Such precautions were necessary, Kindervatter wrote, to ensure that the materials were "properly safeguarded from fire, theft, mutilation, etc."[9]

Kindervatter's worst fears about the security of Maryland's draft records were realized at Local Board 33 in Catonsville shortly before 1 o'clock on Friday, May 17, 1968.

Not everything went according to the activists' carefully laid plans. Bill O'Connor's job was to stand outside the Knights of Columbus hall as the raid proceeded and distribute copies of the demonstrators' statement to the assembled news media. But O'Connor and one local television crew ran into trouble. A driver was supposed to pick them up at the Hilltop Hotel, but he became skittish and abandoned them at the rendezvous. In the end, three carloads of reporters and supporters left the hotel after receiving a coded telephone message: "The plane has flown."[10]

The nine demonstrators, some members of their support team, and a contingent of newspaper and television reporters converged on the Knights of Columbus hall in Catonsville more or less as planned. The raiders decided that Tom Lewis would enter the draft board first; Mary Moylan and Marjorie Melville were to accompany him. Lewis was to "announce that he represented a group of clergy and laymen concerned over the Vietnam War and the United States' militaristic and imperialistic policies," Tom Melville later said. "He was to tell them that we were going to stage a demonstration and that they needn't be alarmed." Five of the other activists—Phil and Dan Berrigan, John Hogan, Tom Melville, and George Mische—would follow them a few minutes later in a second wave.[11]

Brother David Darst did not enter the hall. Assigned to be the group's lookout man, he stationed himself on the building's front porch, which provided a broad and elevated view of Frederick Road. The Nine fully expected to be apprehended, but they did not want authorities to intervene before they had seized and destroyed a sizable number of draft records. There was some fear among the group that word of their action would spread before they had finished it and that the draft board clerks might receive assistance in the middle of the demonstration. (A particular point of concern was Catonsville's U.S. Post Office, which was located just a short walk east on Frederick Road. Its personnel could quickly reach the draft board.) Darst's job was to warn the group inside the building if authorities appeared to be on their way to break up the raid. If that happened, the demonstrators would have to change their plans on the fly.

To the amusement of his fellow activists, the mild-mannered Lewis failed to raise his voice enough to attract much notice when he entered the draft board. None of the clerks lifted their heads when he walked in and started to announce that a demonstration was about to take place. Moylan was not surprised that the clerks initially paid so little attention to the protesters. She noted, "Bureaucracy is fantastic: we walked in and nobody would look at us. . . . Nobody would look up, they were so busy writing."[12]

When the second line of demonstrators came up the steps to the draft board, they found the solicitous Lewis still in the doorway; he was saying, "Excuse me, I represent some people. . . . Pardon me, can I have your attention?" Eager to engage in their witness, the Berrigans, Hogan, Tom Melville, and Mische pushed past him and confronted the clerks. They carried with them large wire wastebaskets—trash burners, they were called. Their plan was to dump the draft files into these receptacles and then carry them outside, where they could be doused with the homemade napalm and then set aflame.[13]

Three Selective Service clerks were at work in the two small adjoining rooms used by Local Board 33: Mary Murphy, Phyllis Morsberger, and Alice Phipps. (Phipps was officially retired, but she periodically came back to work at the board when things got busy.) Murphy, whose desk was nearest the door, noticed the protesters first. Hearing footsteps, she looked up from her work and saw a man—Phil Berrigan—in the doorway.

"Can I help you, sir?' she asked.

As soon as she spoke, she realized that something was wrong; she recognized Berrigan from the widely published photographs that had been taken during the Baltimore Four protest the previous fall.

"Oh, my Lord," she thought as the priest entered the room, "something is going to happen."[14]

Murphy, still unsure of the group's purpose, pleaded with them to not press into the main Selective Service office.

"Please don't all come in here," she said. "Go in the other room."

Phil Berrigan and his fellow activists ignored her and surged into the main office, leaving it crowded with people. Increasingly alarmed, Murphy asked what they were doing.

"We're clergymen [attempting] to prevent war," Berrigan told her.

Dan Berrigan and Mische took the lead in seizing draft files from Local Board 33's filing cabinets and then placing them in the wire baskets. As they rifled through the files, the men attempted to encourage and calm each other. At one point, Berrigan told Mische, "You're doing great, kid." Already thinking ahead to the planned climax of their witness—the burning of the files—they also cautioned each other against packing the material too tightly into the wire baskets. The files would burn more quickly, the two men decided, if they were left loose in the receptacles.[15]

Mische's partner was a dynamo. "I'll give Dan Berrigan credit," he later said. "That little guy, he sure knows how to pull draft files out fast out of a drawer."[16]

Most of the draft files were classified according to the registrants' status in six separate four-drawer cabinets. Dan Berrigan and Mische—who read the filing cabinet labels aloud—zeroed in on the 1-A files; these were for the most vulnerable men, those classified as "available immediately for military service." The men also seized a large number of files of men who had been classified 1-Y, meaning that they were eligible for military service only in time of national emergency. (They took three-quarters of the files in a drawer devoted exclusively to men in that classification.) They also included in their haul a number of files of men who had been classified 2-A, meaning that they were eligible for an occupational deferment from military service.

Years later, Murphy chuckled over the fact that the Catonsville Nine had targeted the draft files of some men who were not in immediate danger of being sent into combat. "At that time," she observed, "they didn't know enough not to bother with people in 1-Y and 2-A." But Murphy understood why the men had been slipshod in grabbing the draft files. "I think they were just as terrified as we were, in a way," she said.[17]

Indeed, Hogan was so nervous that he struggled to remember how to open a filing cabinet. Paired with Lewis, he yanked on the drawer's handle without first sliding the small button on the drawer's face to unlatch it. In a panic, he turned to Lewis.

"Tom, how do you open the drawer?" Hogan asked. "The drawer is locked."

Lewis, having participated in the Baltimore Four demonstration the previous fall, had some experience in rifling through file drawers, and he reminded Hogan to move the button. He did so, and the drawer popped open.[18]

Hogan and Lewis started at the top of one of the filing cabinets and worked their way down, yanking out files and cramming them into one of the wire baskets. They moved quickly, and it wasn't a neat process; some of the documents fell to the floor. "We were just pulling as much as we could," Hogan later said. Although they focused on seizing as many 1-A files as possible, they also made a point of grabbing records from other classifications.[19]

Though startled, Murphy was not paralyzed by fright, and she did what she could to stop the demonstrators. She yelled at them to get away from the draft records, and at one point she tried to fling her body across one of the open file drawers. She also endeavored to wrestle one of the file-packed wire baskets away from the men as they exited the office.

The clerks heard Phil Berrigan insist that the activists did not wish to physically harm any of the women in the room. All of the demonstrators were dedicated to nonviolence, and they intended to abuse only property, not the individuals who created and safeguarded it. "I don't want to hurt you," he told Murphy.[20]

But this proved difficult in the tumult of the raid. In attempting to keep Mary Murphy from disrupting the seizure of the draft records, Phil Berrigan manhandled her. Almost every firsthand account of the raid—offered by the activists themselves or the draft board clerks who tried to stop them—includes some mention of there being a physical altercation between the Baltimore priest and Murphy. FBI summaries of her account of the protest reported that Berrigan "shoved her out of the way when she tried to stop them" from seizing the draft files. There was also a "scuffle," as the FBI put it, when Murphy tried to grab one of the wire baskets.[21]

"I took hold of the wire basket and I pulled and tugged and tried to get it away from [Phil Berrigan and Mische]," Murphy explained. "They were two very large men, and naturally I could not do anything about it." In the fracas, she suffered a cut on one leg and a scratched finger—injuries that required minor bandaging afterward.[22]

It fell to some of Berrigan's collaborators to control the other two Selective Service clerks in the office, Morsberger and Phipps. When the protesters entered the room, Morsberger was inspecting a draft registration ledger that rested on a table opposite the door; her back was turned to the activists when they walked in. They took her by surprise. Typically, the clerks could hear the front door of the Knights of Columbus building slam shut after someone entered, and visitors to the draft board usually made some noise as they clambered up the front steps to the second floor. But, because the eight demonstrators had ascended the back staircase, Morsberger heard nothing until they were entering the room. Immediately realizing that something was wrong, she reached for the nearby telephone. She knew she immediately had to contact the police.[23]

Moylan had the task of restraining Morsberger. The two "had a little scuffle" over the telephone, as Morsberger later put it, with Moylan trying to yank the receiver out of the clerk's hands and thereby prevent her from summoning the police. Moylan later said that the two women "went through a wrestling match" over the phone. Morsberger understood that Moylan did not mean to harm her. As they grappled for the phone, Moylan repeatedly told her, "I don't want to hurt you," and begged her time and again to "please be nice." Whenever it appeared that the clerk might be gaining an advantage in the struggle, Tom Melville came over and took the phone from Morsberger's grasp. "Don't do that," he said of her efforts to call the police. "We won't hurt you."[24]

Years later, Morsberger said that the Nine had berated the clerks for their participation in the war effort. "They came in screaming, 'You're murderers. You're murderers,'" she recalled. Morsberger also remembered Tom Melville castigating her for "doing harm to these boys"—the registrants whose files she helped to collect and process. ("I'm doing a job," she told him, "and if I don't do this, someone else will.") In a 1972 interview, Murphy also claimed that she had been a target of verbal abuse during the raid. While they pilfered the draft files, the activists were "trying to convince us that we should not be working there [and] calling us murderers," she asserted. They asked "why did we work here, and did we know we were sending boys away to be killed, and all that sort of thing."[25]

Murphy couldn't remember the details of her response as much as she recalled its volume. "Both Phyllis and I," Murphy said, "screamed at the top of our lungs."[26]

The activists also prevented the third clerk in the draft board, Phipps, from attempting to stop the raid. Phipps was not exactly an imposing figure—she was in her mid-seventies, weighed all of a hundred pounds, and suffered from a heart condition—but Marjorie Melville took no chances. She blocked Phipps's movements by placing one hand on the clerk's desk and another on a nearby wall. Phipps recognized only one of the activists who burst into the room—Phil Berrigan. She had seen his picture in the newspaper after the Baltimore Four protest.

The raid was over in about five minutes. Lugging two wire baskets filled with draft files, the activists exited the crowded room and made their way down the steps. Moylan stopped tussling with Morsberger and relinquished the phone.

"It's all yours," she said as she left the room.

Morsberger went to a nearby window. She could see two workmen outside; they apparently were fixing a sign on the building. The clerk tried to open the window and alert the pair, but it had been nailed shut some time earlier. Not to be thwarted, she picked up the telephone and hurled it through the window.

"Get help!" Morsberger cried as she leaned outside through the jagged hole in the glass.[27]

The Nine knew that they would have to move quickly before that help—in the form of police officers and, inevitably, FBI agents—arrived on the scene. They had seized more than 370 draft files. They wanted to douse these documents with their homemade napalm and set them aflame before the authorities intervened.

A few days earlier, WBAL-TV reporter Patrick McGrath had heard from a contact in the local peace movement—Grenville Whitman, who worked with Phil Berrigan and Lewis at the Interfaith Peace Mission in Baltimore—that a spectacular protest was planned for May 17. Whitman wouldn't divulge much else; initially, McGrath learned nothing about the precise location of the protest or the identities of those who would participate in it. Whitman did reveal that the demonstration would involve a sizable group of Catholic clergy and laymen. He also informed McGrath that the protest would highlight the Catholic Church's silence about, and complicity in, the war in Vietnam.[28]

The tip intrigued McGrath, and he agreed to rendezvous with Whitman at Beaumont Avenue in suburban Catonsville. Accompanying him were photographer Bob Boyer and soundman Ed Smith, who would record whatever transpired. They pulled up behind two cars: one was filled with local peace activists, including Whitman; the second vehicle contained men whom McGrath quickly recognized as other reporters and photographers.

As they waited in their own car, McGrath and his colleagues speculated about what they were about to witness. McGrath thought that the protest would occur at a church and that it might be more of a religious vigil than an antiwar demonstration. The WBAL crew waited for the participants to drive by, and then the small caravan followed them down Beaumont Avenue after a few minutes. McGrath caught a glimpse of Phil Berrigan in the car and recognized him as having been one of the Baltimore Four, but he could not identify the priest's accomplices.[29]

The reporters drove for about three blocks and then stopped at the northeast corner of Beaumont Avenue and Frederick Road. There stood, as McGrath later put it, "a staid-looking, white building"—the Knights of Columbus hall. One of the activists in the lead car informed the reporters that the protest would take place there, so the newsmen dashed out of their cars. Boyer turned on his camera and began recording "a man setting fire to a pile of paper and cardboard," as McGrath later put it. "A closer view, seconds later, revealed that the fire was consuming what appeared to be draft records. Seven men and two women, all breathing hard, stood watching the fire."[30]

With several hundred draft files stuffed into their wire trash baskets, eight of the Nine—all but Brother David Darst, who had been serving as a lookout on the front porch—had descended the stairs from the second floor of the Knights of Columbus hall. Darst had joined them as they exited and walked around the building to its back parking lot. There they had placed the file-filled baskets and doused them with their homemade napalm. The man whom McGrath saw starting the conflagration was Hogan. He apparently was using a lit cigarette to ignite the fire.

"It went *whoop*," recalled Whitman. "It really exploded. Everyone jumped back."[31]

Dan Berrigan spoke first, suggesting that the activists say a prayer. "We make our prayer," he began, "in the name of God—the God of decency . . . and love." Following a brief moment of silence, all of the protesters approached the pyre with lit matches and tossed them in. They all wanted to be equally culpable for setting the materials on fire. For the activists, the fire was more than a mechanism for destroying the draft records. It was an enduring Christian symbol that evoked the Pentecost, the moment when (as recorded in the Book of Acts) the Holy Spirit took the form of fire and descended upon the apostles. Dan Berrigan later explained that the Nine hoped to spark a similar renewal that would "light up the dark places of the heart, where courage and risk and hope were awaiting a signal, a dawn."[32]

Dan Berrigan had not played a central role in the planning of the Catonsville protest, but now he came to the fore. As the draft records went up in flames, he told the assembled reporters that he wished the peace negotiators in Paris would make a serious effort to end the ongoing debacle in Vietnam. He further hoped that the example set by the Nine would demonstrate to the world that "Americans are willing to take some risks for justice. We do this in the name of the dead and the name of the unborn."

The fullest articulation of the activists' rationale came not in their off-the-cuff comments but rather in the joint statement that was distributed to the reporters on the scene. The document was not a paean to civil disobedience, nor was it a narrowly religious manifesto. However, by linking the excesses of imperialism with the worldwide subordination of the underclass, it reflected the core values of liberation theology, the social and intellectual movement that had been surging through Latin America throughout the preceding decade. The common thread connecting all of the issues raised in the statement was a concern for the poor. Reflecting Phil Berrigan's unmistakable influence, the document offered a relentless indictment of American imperialism. It explained why the activists had chosen to target the draft and the records that kept it functioning. Military conscription was contemptible, they asserted, because it "reduces young men to cost efficiency items. The rulers of America want their global wars fought as cheaply as possible." Draft files were an important cog in the war machine, and they held symbolic power as well. "We destroy these draft records not only because they exploit our young men, but [also] because those records represent misplaced power, concentrated in the ruling class of America," the statement said. "Their power threatens the peace of the world and is aloof of public dissent and parliamentary process."[33]

The activists knew that they would be condemned for defacing government property. Anticipating this line of criticism, they used their statement to advance the argument that "some property has no right to exist." The documents they were torching were akin to "Hitler's gas ovens, Stalin's concentration camps, [and] atomic-bacteriological-chemical weaponry"—tools of mass murder that merited speedy and complete destruction.[34]

The Catonsville Nine's press statement reflected the activists' sweeping concerns with injustice. The disaster of the war in Vietnam was, they argued, but one of many examples of how American foreign policy had failed to uphold the nation's core ideals. Noting how the United States had been involved in suppressing democratic reform and economic development in other countries, the manifesto argued that "Thailand, Laos and the Dominican Republic have already been Vietnams." And there were other countries where American imperialism threatened to do similar damage. Not surprisingly, the activists highlighted their concern with the ongoing troubles in Guatemala, a country where three of them (the Melvilles and Hogan) had been living until only a few months earlier. America's meddling there contributed to its entirely justified reputation as "the world's number one counterrevolutionary force."[35]

Misadventures abroad exacerbated inequality at home. Although press reports of the Catonsville demonstration stressed the participants' distress over American foreign policy, the Nine also used their statement to express their outrage over the marginalization of the poor in the United States. While the nation contributed to the oppression of the Vietnamese and Guatemalans, "colonies at home rise in rage and destructiveness," in part because the country diverted resources from its troubled inner cities and poured them into the Pentagon. It was little wonder that African Americans were taking to the streets in many urban areas and angrily demanding full political, social, and economic equality. "The black people of America have concluded that after 360 years," the statement read, "their acceptance as human beings is long overdue."[36]

The press statement also explained how the religious beliefs of the Nine had drawn them to Catonsville that afternoon. "We are Catholic Christians who take our faith seriously," it explained. The activists mentioned that they had been inspired by Pope Paul VI's recent encyclical *Populorum Progressio* ("On the Development of Peoples"). Extending the reforming spirit of Vatican II, this document had offered, for many liberal Catholics, a clear mandate for social and political activism. In a passage that the Nine quoted in their press statement, the pope had noted: "The hour for action has now sounded." Following this charge had led all of the Nine to the draft board on Frederick Road.[37]

The Nine had no intention of trying to evade capture. Confronting legal authority and taking full legal responsibility for their action was—at least at that point—a central element of their witness. While they waited for the police and FBI to arrive, they began to spontaneously interact with reporters, explaining some details of the raid.[38]

It was a tense and somewhat emotional moment for all of the Nine. They were making a meaningful statement grounded in their core political and religious beliefs, and all of them understood that they would be arrested, tried, and probably jailed for it. As McGrath observed them, he noticed that "when anyone spoke, it was in quiet tones; all seemed to be under strain as they waited to be arrested."[39]

Hogan felt anxious as the Nine burned the draft files and spoke with the media. "It was very tense," he later said. "You could almost feel your heart pounding at this point. It *was* pounding." Hogan's mind raced; he wondered what would happen when the police arrived and took the activists into custody. These thoughts so preoccupied him that he found himself speechless. "I didn't say anything. My heart was going too fast to try to say anything."[40]

But there were a few lighter moments that momentarily broke the somber mood of the afternoon. Mische later joked that there were elements of comic opera in the raid—the chief one involving his pants. At one point during the scrum in the draft board office, the activist's chino trousers were torn. "My pants ripped all the way down," he later said. "I'm standing in the room there with my pants on the floor and I can't believe this is happening." His fellow demonstrators, caught up in the moment, scarcely noticed Mische's distress. Oblivious to what had happened, Dan Berrigan kept on shoveling files into a trash container.[41]

Mische's sartorial troubles continued as the Nine made their way into the Knights of Columbus parking lot. Clutching his pants, he asked his friends if any of them had a pin. Marjorie Melville came to his rescue: while the cameras rolled, she produced a safety pin, knelt down next to Mische, and fastened his pants.[42]

After the demonstrators hauled the files from Local Board 33, draft board clerk Mary Murphy initially was too stunned to react. "Well, I was beside myself," she later said. "I didn't know what to do." She recovered quickly, though, and made her way out of the building to the parking lot, where the fire already was burning. Although they were now engulfed in flames, Murphy still felt that the files were her responsibility. After determining that the raiders were destroying the files they had seized, she went back up to the disarrayed draft board and phoned the state Selective Service headquarters.

She also told Phyllis Morsberger and Alice Phipps what was happening outside.

"My God," Murphy sputtered, "they're burning our records!"[43]

"You Hide Behind Words"

It took several agonizing minutes for the police to arrive at the scene. While everyone waited, the Catonsville Nine offered a running commentary on their witness to the reporters who had assembled outside the Knights of Columbus hall.

Tom Melville stressed the activists' displeasure with the Catholic Church. The former priest, like all of his fellow protesters, was angry that the church had done so little to resist American imperialism or serve the needs of the nation's poor. "Our church has failed to act officially, and we feel that as individuals we're going to have to speak out in the name of Catholicism and Christianity," he insisted. "And we hope our action will inspire other people who have Christian principles to act accordingly to stop the terrible destruction that America is wreaking on the whole world." As they spoke, the Nine did not lose sight of their primary practical objective—burning the conscription records. John Hogan darted into the fire and grabbed the wire baskets, shaking loose some files so that they could burn more easily. Tom Melville also braved the small conflagration and kicked the baskets.[1]

While the fire crackled, the demonstrators kept up their commentary. "May this symbolic message bring home to the American people that while people throughout the world, and especially Vietnam now, are suffering from napalm, that these files are also napalmed, to show that these lives can fall on the same fate as the Vietnamese," George Mische offered.[2]

"Not only are we killing people through violent physical war, but we are also killing them through the extension of our economic-political empire," Tom Melville said. "Let us also pray for all those people that are dying from hunger and starvation throughout the world so that Americans can have a higher standard of living." After Melville spoke, the Nine underscored the sacred dimension of their protest by joining hands and saying the Lord's Prayer.

The protesters then returned to making comments to the assembled reporters. Brother David Darst told them that the creation of the napalm had been a group effort. "We all had a hand in making the napalm that was used here today," he said. As the draft files burned, Phil and Dan Berrigan expressed their concerns over how the protesters had scuffled with the draft board clerks. Dan was troubled by the struggle put up by the three women; it saddened him that they had so zealously defended documents that facilitated the deaths of soldiers and civilians. "We regret very much the inconvenience and even the suffering that we brought to these clerks here," he said. "We had hoped that they wouldn't be so excitable over a few files. It's very hard to bring home to people exactly what they're doing by being custodians of such files. But I want publicly to say our apologies for hurting them, if we did. I don't think we did, did we?" His brother Phil explained: "We tried to interpose ourselves between them and those who were gaining the draft files from the cabinets themselves. We did have to struggle a bit with them. And I'd just like to repeat what Dan has said: We sincerely hope we didn't injure anyone." "We don't believe that nonviolence is dead," Dan Berrigan continued. "We don't believe in interposing one form of violence for another. We believe that an action like this will still speak to our fellow Americans and bring home to them that a decent society is still possible, but it's totally impossible if these files and what they represent are preserved, and even defended, as these poor women tried to."[3]

While the Nine set the draft files aflame and then explained their witness to the assembled media, members of the activists' support network took in the scene. Grenville Whitman noticed how quiet it was outside the Knights of Columbus hall. He spotted some passersby—a mother and daughter who happened to be out for a midday walk—but they watched without comment. The only sounds were the crackling of the fire and the subdued voices of the Nine. After it was all over and the supporters left the parking lot, "we realized that there had not been one shout, not one scream, not one yell" outside the hall, Whitman observed. "Revolution, sometimes, is very quiet."[4]

As the draft files burned, Whitman and the others who had volunteered to help the Nine completed several important tasks. Whitman walked east on Frederick Road and mailed a batch of press statements from the nearby post office. Phil Berrigan would not be getting behind the wheel again anytime soon, so Brendan Walsh took his keys and drove St. Peter Claver's car back to the parish.[5]

The Baltimore County police were the first law enforcement authorities to arrive at the scene of the protest. After the nearby Wilkens station received calls reporting the disturbance at the Knights of Columbus, its dispatchers contacted two patrol cars in the area—numbers 483 and 484—and directed them to the hall. The first officer showed up at about 1:05 P.M. He exited his patrol car and warily circled the group. ("Covering this kind of crime," reporter McGrath later observed, "clearly was not his specialty.") Two other patrolmen arrived soon after. One was a trainee on a scooter who, as Whitman later put it, "tried to look fierce." Working together, the officers questioned the activists. "Who is responsible for this?" one asked, pointing at the charred files. Nine hands went up. They all took responsibility.

News of the fiery protest spread quickly after police were dispatched to the scene. A number of people made their way to the Knights of Columbus hall after hearing a radio bulletin about the raid. Among them was Anthony Orban, who served on Local Board 33. Orban lived only a couple of blocks from the hall, and he rushed over to assess the damage. Orban, a retiree, had been gardening at his home, and he had been in such hurry to reach the draft board that he hadn't bothered to change out of his plaid shirt and work pants.[6]

The editor of the local weekly newspaper, the *Catonsville Times*, had not been given any advance word about the demonstration. That afternoon, Jean Walsh had gone home for lunch. An employee in the newspaper's advertising department telephoned Walsh there and reported that she had heard a report on the radio about a disturbance at the Knights of Columbus. Sensing that she had a major story on her hands, the editor bolted from her home. She found a chaotic scene at the hall. The fire already had been extinguished, but police were interviewing participants and witnesses, and other members of the news media were clamoring on the building's front porch, trying to gain entrance to the draft board upstairs.[7]

"You can't go up there," a local broadcaster told her as they milled around on the porch. "They won't let any of us up."

"Who's up there?" Walsh asked.

"Well, the police are up there and the F.B.I. and the Army, and they won't let anyone in."[8]

Walsh somehow managed to squeeze through the throng of reporters and make her way up the stairs to the entrance of the draft board. There she encountered a police lieutenant named James Scannell, who worked out of the nearby Wilkens station. Here, being the editor of the local paper worked to Walsh's advantage. Unlike the other reporters on the scene, the *Times* editor was a familiar face to Scannell. "Come on in," he said.[9]

Walsh stepped into a scene of disarray. Draft files and other materials lay strewn across the floor of Local Board 33, and the drawers of several filing cabinets remained open. Mary Murphy's arm—scratched when she had tried to wrest one of the wire baskets away from the looters—was being bandaged. Orban, the draft board member, surveyed the damage; several uniformed military officers joined him in trying to determine which materials had been seized from the office during the demonstration. Walsh had brought with her a Polaroid camera belonging to the *Times*, and with it she captured several stark images of the disorder that the Nine had left in their wake.[10]

Murphy—her voiced tinged with the distinctive twang of a Baltimore accent—recounted the incident for reporters. "The one man with a trash-burner, he went around and starting dumping my files into this trash-burner," she explained. "I tried to prevent it. . . . I tried again to stop them. . . . They indicated we were doing them harm. Of course, I was very much upset." Murphy explained that the raid would seriously disrupt the operations of the Catonsville Selective Service office. "It's going to take hours and hours and hours of intense, hard labor to reconstruct and bring back all of these [files]. And it's doing a great injustice to the boys themselves because in many instances these boys have gone through a lot of trouble to get doctor's statements—these things are all inside these files."[11]

Outside, meanwhile, the Nine waited to be arrested. They had planned on going to jail—several had brought toothbrushes with them—but at first the police seemed hesitant to take them into custody. "We stood there and we waited and we waited and we waited," Mary Moylan recalled, "and the people were watching us—the clerks from the second floor—and nobody knew what we were doing." The first police officer on the scene looked on cautiously, without moving to arrest the group. To Moylan, he seemed flabbergasted by the protest; she guessed that he was accustomed to investigating bicycle thefts. "We thought, 'My god, they're not going to arrest us; what are we going to do?'"[12]

Like all of the Nine, John Hogan had "expected cops to be coming in from all different directions" as their witness unfolded behind the Knights of Columbus hall. So he also was befuddled when the group "reached a point where nothing happened. . . . Nobody came to arrest us." And when the police finally did arrive, they seemed unsure of themselves. "They really didn't know what to do," Hogan recalled. "I don't think they knew what was going on there and what was the nature of the whole thing."[13]

The Baltimore County Fire Department responded to the protest at 1:14 P.M. Engine 4 from the Catonsville fire station sped west on Frederick Road and arrived at the Knights of Columbus within a few minutes. In a subsequent report, the firemen on the scene said that they had extinguished "draft cards burning in containers in parking lot." The blaze, they noted, had been set by "vandals."[14]

As more police officers and FBI agents converged on the scene, it became clear that the Nine would not escape arrest. For Tom Melville, the arrival of the police created a sense of relief. Before the protest, he had worried that authorities would catch the Nine before they could seize and destroy the files housed in Local Board 33. Now, with the files damaged and the police poised to take them into custody, he experienced a feeling of liberation. "I felt relieved," he later said, "that it had come off the way we had planned it."[15]

FBI agents combed through the scene and carefully gathered evidence. They marked as specimens Q1 through Q3 three boxes containing ashes removed from the parking lot of the Knights of Columbus hall. The materials were described as being

> primarily Selective Service files consisting of individual folders (SSS Form 101) each containing various Selective Service forms and other correspondence for the individual registrant whose name appears on the outside of

each folder. The folders or portions of folders were found for 323 registrants. . . . All folders and enclosed documents were burned to some
degree, from edge burning on some to almost total destruction on others.
Some burned fragments could not be associated with any specific files.[16]

Specimens Q4 and Q5 were "two cans with flammable liquid." According to
the internal FBI documents, the cans were found to have contained "a mixture
of gasoline and soap flakes." Specimen was Q6 was "one 8 x 11 piece of paper
imprinted with anti-war slogans." All of these materials subsequently were
checked for fingerprints.[17]

As the FBI collected evidence, the activists were questioned individually.
Police officers asked them whether they had participated in the destruction of
the draft records and then asked their identities. All of the Nine volunteered
this information, sometimes adding an unsolicited explanation.

"Did you burn these draft records?" an officer asked Darst.

"Yes, I wanted to make it more difficult for men to kill each other," Darst
replied.

"Your name, please?"

"David Darst, Christian Brother."

The officer then moved on to question Dan Berrigan.

"Did you burn these draft records?" he asked.

"Yes, I wanted to say 'yes' to the possibility of a human future," Berrigan
replied.

"Your name, please?"

"Father Daniel Berrigan, S. J."

"Thank you, father."[18]

After all of the Nine had been questioned and identified, a police officer told
them, "Okay, we're going to take you to the station now; please get into the
paddy wagon." The Nine did not resist; as ordered, they clambered into the
vehicle. To make sure that no one had slipped away, officers counted them off,
one through nine, as they climbed in. It was about 1:15 P.M.—about ten minutes
after the arrival of the first officers on the scene.[19]

Jean Walsh was busy snapping pictures, and she didn't notice that the Nine
had been taken into custody. When she inquired into their whereabouts, Scannell, the police lieutenant, informed her that they had been moved to the
Wilkens station for processing. Scannell seemed eager to help the local editor
follow the story. "Come on and get into my patrol car," he said, "and we'll drive
down there immediately."[20]

When Scannell and Walsh arrived at the Wilkens station, the editor found
the Nine assembled in a large room that the police department ordinarily used
for holding meetings and conducting morning roll call. Walsh noticed how
differently the protesters were dressed. Several of the men were wearing dark
suits or, in the case of the Berrigans, clerical garb. But the two women wore

more casual clothing. "They were in sleeveless dresses," Walsh said, "because it was a very warm, bright, sunny day."[21]

Polaroid still in hand, Walsh asked if she could take a group portrait. Despite the circumstances, the protesters seemed ebullient and agreed to sit for the picture. Walsh was struck by the Nine's apparent eagerness to be photographed. "This seemed all very strange for people who had just been arrested by the police, because most times those who are arrested by the police prefer to hide their heads," she recalled. "But these people were adamant and eager to be in the limelight. That was the purpose of what they had done—to bring attention to their act." There was a moment of levity as Walsh arranged the group for the picture. Sometime during the hectic day, Phil Berrigan had loosened his clerical collar, and it remained somewhat crooked. Dan Berrigan gently chided his brother for looking so sloppy. "Come on, Phil, put that collar on properly," he joked. "You don't want to look unkempt for the picture in the paper. Fix it." Although he rarely was one to care about formality, Phil complied.[22]

Milling around with their fellow activists in the Wilkens station, Tom and Marjorie Melville reflected on what had brought them to this crossroads in their lives. Tom gazed out the window and thought about the many twists and turns his life had taken over the previous few years. His experiences in Guatemala, his decision to leave the priesthood and marry Marjorie, and now his dramatic witness in Catonsville—all had changed him. He wondered, though, if everyone would accept the new direction his life had taken. "I realized that many of my friends who had supported me in my missionary work would feel threatened by all this," he later wrote, "that the transformation in my standing would be incomprehensible to most of them; yet my path was utterly logical and clear to me."[23]

Marjorie could see that Tom was thinking, and she didn't want to interrupt him by trying to engage him in conversation. Instead, she put her arm around him—a simple gesture of comfort and compassion.

Marjorie was ruminating, too. Standing in the Wilkens station, she wondered if she "could ever realize my dream of being a bridge for people," she later wrote. There were, she knew, many chasms that threatened to divide the modern world, including the immense gap in understanding "between Americans who believe themselves highly moral and Guatemalans and Vietnamese who suffer the consequences of American policy." Perhaps their action in Catonsville would bring those groups closer to understanding each other and finding some common ground.[24]

The time for such introspection was cut short by the FBI, whose agents had little interest in the Catonsville Nine's philosophizing or Walsh's portraiture. After she photographed them, Walsh scrambled to identify all of the protesters for the accompanying caption. She was still trying to sort out the names when an FBI agent entered and broke up the impromptu photo session. "All right, we don't want anyone else in here," he told the editor as he directed her toward the door. "Everybody else out, out!" (Years later, Walsh still was miffed that she had been forced to fudge the caption for the *Times*.) On her way out, Phil Berrigan handed her a copy of the Nine's press statement.[25]

For a time, the Nine were loose and relaxed. There was a piano in the squad room, and Darst managed to climb atop it and stretch out. The mood darkened when the FBI agents began interacting with the activists more closely. Phil Berrigan remembered that the FBI agents he encountered in the aftermath of the raid seemed "irritated by our insouciance and anxious to make us pay for breaking the law." Already a notorious figure because of his role in the Baltimore Four protest, Berrigan was a special target for the federal agents. One, a Catholic, became outraged when he recognized the priest. The agent brandished a fist and shouted, "Him again! Good God, I'm changing my religion."[26]

Dan Berrigan rejoiced at the prospect of the agent leaving the church. He turned to his brother and exclaimed, "That's the best thing you did all day—get him out!"[27]

After that, the Nine were processed relatively quickly. The FBI asked draft board clerk Phyllis Morsberger to come to the Wilkens station and identify the culprits. (It was decided that Mary Murphy had been so involved in grappling with Phil Berrigan that she might not have gotten a good look at everyone.) Federal agents lined up all of the activists and had them file past the clerk, and Morsberger scrutinized them, albeit somewhat tentatively. "I would not go up to them to their very faces," she recounted. "I was cowardly there." Once she had composed herself, she indicated that all nine had been present and had participated in ransacking the draft board.[28]

At about 3:30 P.M., about two and a half hours after they had burst into Local Board 33, the activists were informed that they would face federal criminal charges for their participation in the raid. United States Attorney Stephen Sachs—who had just successfully prosecuted the Baltimore Four—authorized their prosecutions under provisions of the federal criminal code dealing with property destruction and the operation of the draft. After agents informed them of these federal charges (they later would have to deal with a separate set of state charges), all nine were asked if they understood their legal rights. They indicated that they did, but, as had happened in the aftermath of the Baltimore Four demonstration, they refused to sign a form indicating that they had waived their rights. Shortly thereafter, they were given the chance to place a telephone call to an attorney, if they wanted to consult with one. All nine passed.

At about 5 P.M., the Catonsville Nine were on the move again. Federal agents loaded them into a patrol wagon and drove them from the Wilkens station in Catonsville to the FBI's offices in downtown Baltimore. They were handcuffed for the trip, but this precaution did not prove to be especially effective. Moylan, blessed with slender wrists and small hands, was able to slip off the handcuffs at will. Her trick amused everyone; it seemed to underscore the absurdity of their situation.[29]

First, the Nine were photographed. Two hours later, they were handed over to the federal marshal, who brought them before U.S. Commissioner H. Allen Metzger, who earlier had issued their arrest warrants. There was no drama in this largely perfunctory legal proceeding. The Nine discussed with Metzger the charges, their legal representation, and their bail. Sachs recommended that Phil Berrigan and Lewis—who were facing sentencing in just a few days for their roles in the Baltimore Four protest—post bonds of $7,500 each. His bail recommendation for the remaining seven defendants was somewhat less onerous: he suggested $2,500 each. Not that it mattered—none of the Nine could post bail. They would be incarcerated in the Baltimore County Jail, located north of the city in Towson, at least until their preliminary hearing, which was scheduled four days later, on May 21.

As the Nine were being transferred to the county lockup, they were reminded why they had been motivated to speak out for justice and racial equality. Several black prisoners were crammed with them into the paddy wagon for the trip. As they rumbled toward Towson, one man expressed his gratitude to the group of white, middle-class activists, telling them that their presence probably had prevented the police from beating him.[30]

When they arrived in the county jail, the men surrendered their personal property. The contents of the wallet that Phil Berrigan handed over to police spoke volumes about the priorities in his life. The items inside included membership cards for a raft of peace and social justice organizations, including the NAACP, the American Civil Liberties Union, and CORE. The wallet also contained pictures of his brother Dan and his mother.[31]

After handing over their wallets, the men were undressed and frisked for contraband. As he removed the safety pin lent to him by Marjorie Melville, George Mische had to explain to a guard why he was wearing jerry-rigged pants.[32]

Mische and the other men decided to engage in a jailhouse fast. All but Darst subsisted on liquids such as tea and fruit juice. (Darst followed the stricter Gandhian practice of fasting solely on water.) The fast was intended to draw additional attention to the Nine's witness and thereby further embarrass the establishment, much as Phil Berrigan and Lewis had done by fasting after the Baltimore Four protest. The men asked jail officials to send the money that was saved by not feeding them to a worthy charitable cause, such as the Poor People's March.[33]

The Nine found an unexpected ally in their jailer, Stanley Foster, who refused to play the part of the overbearing, authoritarian warden. From the outset, he respected the activists and their motives. It was a testament to Foster's openness and compassion that he even managed to win over the sometimes cantankerous Phil Berrigan; the priest said he was "a very, very good warden, a Catholic, and . . . this man was so human, he was so deeply understanding and sympathetic toward what we had done." As he interacted with his new prisoners, Foster made no secret of his mounting disapproval of American foreign policy. Berrigan and his fellow activists were happily surprised to learn that they were being incarcerated by a "good, caring person who was deeply concerned about the war in Vietnam."[34]

When reporters asked the warden what he thought about their fast, Foster shocked the newsmen by comparing the protesters' action to the fast undertaken by Jesus after his baptism. "It's a religious thing," he told *Newsweek*. "Like Christ in the wilderness." Foster visited his prisoners frequently during their fast. The warden didn't seem too worried that their action might reflect poorly on him. This "remarkable man," as Phil Berrigan later called him, seemed more concerned with learning what had motivated them to take such a dramatic action. "He was fascinated by the fact that Catholic priests had broken the law, and he had an open mind," Berrigan recalled. "He wanted to understand us and our actions at Catonsville."[35]

So strong was Foster's affinity for the Nine that he worshipped with them in the jail on the Sunday after the Catonsville protest. And not only did the warden provide bread and wine for the event; he also brought along his wife and five children, all of whom joined in the Mass.

Mary Moylan and Marjorie Melville were housed along with other female inmates on the second floor of the jail. When Moylan reached the facility, she desperately wanted to rest; the raid on the draft board and the activists' arrests and processing had left her physically and emotionally spent. "[When] finally we went to jail—thank God—I was so pooped," she later wrote. "I was just exhausted." She was ravenously hungry as well. "We hadn't had anything to eat—those people don't feed you—that was a big shock. I thought I'd always heard about cops giving you mugs of coffee, and I was just dying for a coffee or a Coke or something. We never got anything until 10 o'clock that night."[36]

Having anticipated spending time in jail, she had brought along some clothes and a toothbrush, and she placed them under her cot before climbing in. But her fellow prisoners—nearly all of them African American—would not let her sleep. They were baffled that a middle-class white woman had not become unglued over finding herself in jail.

"Aren't you going to cry?" one incredulous woman asked, shaking Moylan awake.

"What about?" Moylan responded

"You're in jail."

"Yeah, I knew I'd be here."

Moylan once again tried to sleep, but her fellow inmates kept waking her up and asking her why she wasn't weeping.

"I left this morning knowing I was going to be here—what's there to cry about?" she said. "I should have cried last night."

She slept between two women who were going through withdrawal from drugs and thus having difficulty resting. Moylan, at peace with herself, had no such troubles. Every morning when she woke up, the women would be watching her intently and marveling at how soundly she had slept.

"You slept all night," one woman told her.

"Yeah, and I plan to do that every night," Moylan responded.[37]

Marjorie Melville had a rougher time in jail. She struggled with a sense of being trapped. "There were bars all around, and it's a very confining, frightening kind of thing," she later said of her stay in the Towson jail. "It's like being in an elevator all day. Even though you could see outside the windows, you know you couldn't get out.[38]

Melville was further disturbed when she began to learn about the backgrounds of her fellow inmates. She quickly discerned that few of the women in the county jail had committed serious crimes. Most had been arrested for drug possession or for offenses related to their drug addictions, such as petty robberies and forgeries. What these women desperately needed, Melville saw, was not confinement in jail but rather drug treatment and counseling—"something to cure them of this terrible thing that they were in the grips of," she later said. Tragically, though, the state showed no interest in addressing these root causes of crime.[39]

According to Phil Berrigan, the Nine endeavored to create a Christian community in jail, one that was "diverse, rich, intelligent, loving. And tough." Foster had placed the men together in a roomy cell block. The space included four cubicles and a table as well as an open area where they could sit around and converse. The new inmates attempted to make the most of the time they spent there. In a project that bore Lewis's unmistakable imprint, the prisoners clipped images from magazines and assembled a ten-foot-long collage focused on peace. They also held informal seminars almost every evening, delving into such weighty topics as "Catholic Conscience and the Vietnam War," "American Imperialism in Guatemala," and "How to Move the Catholic Bishops on the War Issue." And there was physical training as well: they performed calisthenics and engaged in deep breathing exercises.[40]

Through it all, their emotions were high. "They are in better spirits," attorney Fred Weisgal reported, "than anybody on the outside."[41] Darst seemed especially buoyant. He could be heard whistling and singing while he read in the cell block's common area. Dan Berrigan noted that the Christian Brother was "as cheerful in there as he would be out on the street."[42]

A few bleak episodes punctured the generally happy mood. One day, the defendants were handcuffed and led outside so that they could appear in court. A sympathetic nun reached out and gently touched Dan Berrigan's arm in a gesture of solidarity. The contact was harmless, but the marshals were having none of it: one angrily knocked her hand away and warned, "Don't touch!" ("It was the epitome of the system; he had said it all," Berrigan observed.[43])

All of the Nine tried to devote some time every morning to writing. They shared these works with one another, and they managed to get quite a few letters smuggled out. Darst wrote to a friend, "Well, the Catonsville thing went according to plan, and here we are, right smack in the Baltimore Jail, having a wonderful time. . . . We are in the best of spirits, singing songs, carrying on, putting up a big long collage on the wall around our cells. I'm not sure the authorities know what to make of our joyousness." He related that he was passing the time by reading "great jail stuff"—Che Guevara and Albert Camus—and playing bridge.[44]

While in the county jail, Darst also penned a more somber letter for broader public consumption. In it he explained that while the Catonsville protest had been "primarily and essentially symbolic, it also had its literal side; the symbolic monkey wrench thrown into the symbolic works was also, secondarily, an honest-to-goodness iron wrench." The Nine had taken this extraordinary step because "drastic needs call for drastic actions; the man who suffers terribly cries out very loudly. This notion of a cry is very important in understanding an action like that of burning draft files. And it seems that today sensitive men are becoming desperate in their attempts to do something about the problems they see around them; many feel the urge to risk all in the hope of getting their message through."[45]

Phil Berrigan's "Letter from a Baltimore Jail" found its way into the journal *Christianity and Crisis* in the summer of 1968. "You had trouble with destruction of property, with civil disobedience, with priests getting involved this much," he wrote, directly addressing the critics of the Nine. "Let's face it, perhaps half of you had trouble with us acting at all." Berrigan refuted these claims with his customary vigor. He insisted that the activists had been driven to stage such a provocative protest in Catonsville because they had "experienced intimately the uselessness of legitimate dissent."[46]

The spirits of all the Nine rose when they learned that their supporters were taking to the streets. One day, several dozen demonstrators (including some students from St. Mary's Seminary in Baltimore) picketed at the Cathedral of Mary of Our Queen in Baltimore. They distributed fliers stating that "nine peacemakers, all Catholics, are in the Towson jail because they destroyed draft files with napalm last Friday to demonstrate that men, women and children are being killed, tortured and disfigured by Americans using napalm in Vietnam." Monsignor Thomas Whelan made plain his irritation when picketers tried to distribute literature on the steps of the cathedral, telling reporters, "I desperately disapprove of this." Many churchgoers were similarly displeased. One bluntly asked Whelan, "Why don't you put them off this property?"[47]

While their supporters rallied to their cause, the federal and state prosecutions of the Catonsville Nine began to take shape. On May 22, 1968, U.S. Attorney Stephen Sachs presented four counts to the federal grand jury in Baltimore. He alleged that the Nine had engaged in a criminal conspiracy in plotting the raid;

caused damages at Local Board 33 in excess of $100; illegally seized federal property; and interfered with the administration of the Selective Service Act. The grand jury returned indictments on all four counts. At a subsequent arraignment, Judge Roszel Thomsen allowed seven of the nine (all but Lewis and Phil Berrigan, who were awaiting sentencing for their earlier crime) to post $250 bonds after he imposed restrictions on their travel.[48]

Although he not yet initiated any formal legal proceedings, Samuel Green, the state's attorney for Baltimore County, announced that he was thinking about filing state charges against the Nine as well. "Mr. Green said that he had no desire to persecute the Catholic clergymen and laymen," the *Baltimore Sun* reported, "but that he had a responsibility to present the cases to the [grand] jury for its consideration." Green considered filing four criminal charges against all of the Nine. Among these were claims that they had violated the state sabotage prevention act and had assaulted the draft board clerks. The Nine now faced the prospect of two separate trials—one in federal court and another in state court. "Apparently, a good deal was done by the Federal authorities to forestall this," Phil Berrigan wrote to his brother Dan, "but it seems the county people want a piece of the action, and especially an opportunity to show the Feds how God-fearing people tend their own bailiwick."[49]

On the day that the federal grand jury indicted the Nine, Judge Edward Northrop sentenced two of them, Lewis and Phil Berrigan, for their roles in the Baltimore Four protest. When the two men entered the courtroom, a crowd of two hundred supporters greeted them with a thunderous ovation. After the gallery quieted down, Northrop allowed Lewis and Berrigan to make statements to the court. Berrigan was unrepentant. "Mr. Lewis and myself, while under conviction and awaiting sentence, have acted once more against the apparatus of war," he acknowledged. "And for that, many people have judged us 'irresponsible' or 'untrustworthy.'" His response to such claims? "If I know what I am about, the brutalization, squalor and despair of other men demeans me and threatens me if I do not act against its source. This is perhaps why Tom Lewis and I acted again with our friends."[50]

Tom Lewis got the sense that Sachs and Northrop were willing to pin most of the blame for the Custom House protest on Phil Berrigan. Lewis had not planned to make any comments at the sentencing, but the judge repeatedly hinted to him that he might be treated more leniently if he claimed that the charismatic priest had influenced him to break the law. For a man in serious legal jeopardy, the implicit offer was tempting, but Lewis wouldn't dissemble just to shorten his prison term.

Vexed by Northrop's questioning, he finally turned to humor, making light of the judge's hints by quoting a line from comedian Stan Laurel: "You can lead a horse to water, but a pencil must be lead."[51]

Northrop wasn't amused by Lewis's wordplay. It upset him that Lewis and Phil Berrigan had flouted the law in Catonsville just weeks after they had been convicted in his courtroom. Sternly addressing them from the bench, he said that they were guilty of "using violent means to create dissent that would destroy our society." He added that in their comments at the hearing, the two men "showed no remorse but rather a determination to bend society to their viewpoint. . . . You will not tolerate the view of others; you hide behind words." He then backed up his tough talk by sentencing both men to six years in federal prison.[52]

The severity of the sentences was roundly criticized. "Convicted thugs and murderers," the *Boston Globe* observed, "have been treated more gently." The paper asserted that Lewis and Phil Berrigan hardly presented a "mortal threat to society. The threat to society comes from the opposite direction. . . . Courts are supposed to be more equanimous than are street mobs." Another newspaper wondered if the court was "using its own means to take out of circulation those whom it judges to be a kind of public nuisance."[53]

Dorothy Day was stunned "by these harsh sentences that are being passed out," as she told Dan Berrigan in a letter. "I am convinced that sooner or later we are all going to end up in a concentration camp."[54]

Despite the criticism, Northrop stuck to his guns. Shortly after the judge sentenced Lewis and Phil Berrigan, attorney Fred Weisgal appeared in court and asked that they be released on bail while their convictions were being appealed. He managed to keep a straight face while promising that the two men would remain on their best behavior if they were granted bail. Sachs pointed out the obvious, noting that Lewis and Berrigan might "dramatically foreswear" their promise and engage in further illegal acts. Northrop needed little persuading: in denying Weisgal's motion, he said he couldn't ignore the fact that they had gone to Catonsville while awaiting sentencing for their roles in the Custom House protest. "You apparently have a tendency to escalate time after time," he told them.[55]

The two men were dispatched to Lewisburg Federal Penitentiary in eastern Pennsylvania. It reminded Lewis of the Bargello, a medieval prison and police barracks in Florence that had been turned into an art museum. "Barred gothic style windows, huge cold stone walls and floors," he said of his new home. "The lighting had a dim cast of yellow, and there was a dampness and awesome hostility in the air."

Upon arriving, the new inmates were stripped and searched. Prison officials forced them to hand over almost all of their remaining possessions. Lewis managed to keep a treasured gift from Dan Berrigan: a small fish medal that hung from a chain around the artist's neck. The priest had worn the medal (a symbol of Christ) for years before giving it to Lewis; it had gone with him to Latin America, to Hanoi, and even to Catonsville. "Now," Lewis observed, "the fish had just swum upstream to Lewisburg Penitentiary."[56]

"Crazy Like Jesus"

While the Catonsville Nine began to grapple with the next phase of their witness—the legal proceedings that would provide them with a public platform to further voice their opposition to war, imperialism, and injustice—their contemporaries tried to come to terms with what had happened at Local Board 33 on the afternoon of May 17.

For some, the Catonsville protest merited high praise. Dan Finnerty, a dedicated student activist at the University of Pennsylvania, characterized the Nine as fanatical—but, in his book, that wasn't necessarily an epithet, given the times. "These people are crazy," he wrote. "Crazy like Jesus. Crazy like Che Guevara. Crazy like all of us said we would be had we lived in Germany under Hitler."[1]

Echoing Finnerty, the chair of the Johns Hopkins chapter of Students for a Democratic Society, Stephen Shriver, said that he was astounded by the laudatory act performed by the Catonsville Nine. Shriver told a reporter, "The people who did it have a lot of courage and will succeed in making a point to the community [by] exposing the draft." It was important to have priests involved "because clergymen are highly respectable persons [and] will lend an air of respectability to it."[2]

Not everyone, though, was quite as enthusiastic about what the Catonsville Nine had done. Shortly after the protest, a longtime Baltimore disc jockey named Lee Case denounced the activists on his radio show. The city's "Morning Mayor" reflected the sentiments of many Baltimoreans when he opined, "I think they ought to lock 'em in the can and throw away the key." Although Case understood that individuals had a right to protest the war in Vietnam, he felt that the Nine had gone too far by seizing and destroying draft files. "I don't mind dissent," he said, "but this is stretching the point."[3]

In Catonsville itself, there was a mixed reaction to the protest at the draft office on Frederick Road. JoAnne Stough, a senior at Catonsville High School, was one of many young people in town who viewed the raid as a "positive example of civil resistance." The protest sparked Stough and her friends to voice their own displeasure with the war. "What changed after the Catonsville Nine, it seemed like in only a few months, was that people around me were now willing to engage in quiet acts of civil disobedience," she later said. "My friends and I began to hold sit-ins and protest marches and to engage in guerilla theater—spontaneously disrupting public events with antiwar skits and plays."[4]

But some Catonsville residents were incensed to see their town linked with a politically inspired act of vandalism. To make matters even worse for many locals, none of the perpetrators ever had resided in Catonsville. Jean Walsh, the editor of the *Catonsville Times*, summed up these sentiments in a vitriolic opinion piece in the paper. "Since none of the seven men and two women were Catonsville residents or were associated with Catonsville prior to their illegal act," she fumed, "the label suggesting that they are from Catonsville is misleading." The editor went on to denounce the substance of the protest, insisting that "if everyone felt free to interpret their consciences in violent opposition to others and to the law, this land would be an abyss without orderly civilization." Her diatribe drew an approving letter from a reader who complained that the draft board protesters were "a group of criminals [who] flouted the law and brought dishonor to our town."[5]

Political leaders in the town were no more conciliatory. Samuel Dantoni, a Catholic who represented Catonsville on the Baltimore County Council, angrily called on church authorities to "discharge from religious orders anyone involved in such activities" as the draft board protest.[6]

J. Edgar Hoover fielded numerous inquiries from people who believed that the Catonsville demonstrators should be prosecuted as common criminals—or worse. "I cannot help but feel that I, as a citizen who believes in law and order, would be tried and convicted of burglary or worse if I were to participate in such a crime," a self-described "disgusted citizen" wrote to the FBI director from Long Beach, California. "In some circles their crime would be considered treason in that it could be argued that their action aided and gave comfort to the enemy." Hoover replied that the writer's concern was perfectly understandable and assured him that the Nine would be held legally accountable for their actions.[7]

Even some allies of the Nine found their witness perplexing. Tom Lewis and Phil Berrigan had not consulted with attorney Fred Weisgal before they had gone to Catonsville, and he was apoplectic when he learned that his clients—whose sentencing for the Baltimore Four protest was scheduled for just a week later—had participated in an even more massive and destructive draft board raid. According to his wife, Jeanne, Weisgal turned to a baseball comparison when he heard that the Nine had seized and then burned the draft records at Local Board 33. "They'll never win the pennant with this one," the attorney told her.[8]

Nowhere were opinions about the Catonsville Nine more sharply divided than within the Catholic Church. Traditionalists felt that the draft board protest was emblematic of the excesses sparked by Vatican II. For them, "it was a huge kind of a cultural betrayal," according to Dan Berrigan. But many liberal Catholics viewed the Catonsville Nine as heroes for having taken such a risky public stand for peace and justice—one that was, in their minds, long overdue.[9]

According to a 1971 Gallup poll, most American Catholics disapproved of the kinds of radical and provocative actions taken by the Nine. The poll asked, "Do you think Catholics who raid draft boards to protest the war in Vietnam are acting as responsible Christians?" More than two-thirds of the poll's respondents (67 percent) said "no," and 15 percent were undecided. Only 18 percent said "yes."[10]

These numbers were reflected in the response from Catholics in the Baltimore area to the Catonsville protest. After the raid, a priest who had worked with Phil Berrigan at St. Peter Claver called him to express his dismay. "What the hell are you doing?" he demanded. Berrigan, taken aback, drew a parallel with Nazi Germany. If the priest had been given a chance to burn a list of Jewish names and thereby spare those innocents from the Holocaust, wouldn't he have done so? The destruction of draft records, Berrigan argued, had been a similarly desperate act.[11]

Trying to get a better feel for how the Nine were perceived among the members of their church, the FBI interviewed several Baltimore-area priests. One Jesuit told the bureau that he while he was in "sympathy with the current peace movement, definitely [he is] not in sympathy with any violence in furtherance of this movement." Furthermore, according to an FBI report, the priest "would certainly have notified the proper authorities if he had known such an incident would take place which could involve bodily harm and destruction to personal property." A priest at St. Mary's Seminary also was dubious about the raid, telling a newspaper reporter, "When you get into the area of destroying property which belongs to someone else, you get into a very shady area. I have misgivings about the long range good effects. I wonder about the triggering effect of large numbers of people who are not responsible for their actions and their emotions."[12]

As had happened after the Baltimore Four protest, the church hierarchy in Baltimore quickly dissociated itself from the looting of Local Board 33. Lawrence Cardinal Shehan stated, "I cannot condone and do not condone the damaging of property or the intimidation of government employees." Shehan also expressed his discomfort with the Nine's "broad and false indictment of the churches and synagogues" because of their apparent inaction regarding the war. Such was the archdiocese's displeasure that it stripped the imprisoned Phil Berrigan of his priestly faculties—"meaning in effect, that even were I free, I could not operate as a priest," he explained to a family member.[13]

The archdiocesan newspaper, the *Catholic Review*, weighed in as well. Its assessment of the Catonsville Nine was no more positive than Shehan's. "Employing technological advantages and publicity techniques not available to old-fashioned burners of effigies and witches," the paper argued, ". . . they have obscured the vital issues of peace and poverty in a great cloud of smoke." The editorial concluded, "We don't think it is necessary to burn the house down in order to dispose of the rubbish."[14]

Nationally, the activists' motives and tactics were the subject of scathing critiques from the likes of such well-known Catholics as novelist Walker Percy. In a letter published in Commonweal, Percy, a Southerner, observed that "in these parts, the Ku Klux Klan burns churches and tries to scare people in various ways. Their reasons are, to them, the best: they do it for God and country and to save us from the Communists. I would be hard-pressed to explain to a Klansman why he should be put in jail and the Berrigans [and the other members of the Nine] set free."[15]

One common complaint voiced by Catholics was that Phil and Dan Berrigan appeared to be so focused on criticizing their country—and thrusting themselves into the limelight—that they had neglected their primary duties as priests. Stella Landefeld's criticisms on this score were typical of those voiced by more tradition-minded members of the church. A Baltimore Catholic, Landefeld said that she was "tired of people, clerical and lay, breaking laws, saying 'Peace' and 'stop the bombing,' and calling my country names." Phil Berrigan's behavior was bothersome because all of his grandstanding against the war meant he was shirking his responsibilities as a priest. "Let [Father Berrigan] be a priest," Landefeld asserted. Instead of ransacking draft offices, he should "say Mass, hear Confessions, baptize babies, be there when the people need him, write, work and strive to save souls."[16]

The Catholic draft board protesters had drawn inspiration from Vatican II and the various calls to social action issued by the church throughout the 1960s. For critics of the Nine, their unruly protest showed that those reform impulses, however well-intentioned, were being carried too far. In the wake of the Catonsville raid, Catholic periodicals brimmed with angry letters from church members complaining that their faith was in danger of losing its bearings because Vatican II apparently had given priests like the Berrigans the green light to neglect their religious duties. One Catholic from Baltimore complained that Vatican II was referenced so often in church circles that it was "as if some new God brought some new religion to the world in 1962" (the year that the council convened in Rome). Weary of this discourse, she bemoaned the brothers' political activism as yet another symptom of the "creeping tendency to shift the Church's main role from the spiritual to the secular."[17]

Psychiatrist Robert Coles was involved in a research project with working-class Catholics in Boston, and they provided him with a telling glimpse of what the laity thought of church members who immersed themselves in radical political activism. One man, a gas station attendant, expressed grudging admiration for Phil Berrigan's honesty. "He's probably a damn fool, but I'll bet he's more honest than some of our big-time leaders—I'll bet he's not out to line his own pockets and become a bigger and bigger fish in the ocean," the man said. "He's probably an idealist, that's what. And let me tell you: the world doesn't like idealists."[18]

In his conversation with Coles, the gas station attendant touched on many of the themes heard throughout the psychiatrist's interviews about the Berrigans and their activist colleagues. Many of the families in Boston, for instance, expressed concern that the priests were neglecting their essential duties as priests by becoming so enmeshed in causes that were more political than spiritual. The attendant urged Coles to tell Phil Berrigan that "he should go back to being a *priest*, and stop this political agitation business." As priests, the Berrigans should have been working diligently in Catholic parishes, not organizing political demonstrations and then serving time in prison. "Tell him politics and religion don't mix. . . . Tell the poor father to mind his own business and get out of prison and speak honestly to his flock, but stay away from politics and things like that," the man told Coles.[19]

Although they were dismayed by the Berrigans' political activities, few of the Boston-area Catholics interviewed by Coles seemed willing to place much blame directly on the two wayward priests. Many suggested that the brothers were well-meaning men who had been led astray by unscrupulous (and perhaps even covertly communist) agitators on the political left. One man said that they had been "keeping the wrong company" and were "egged on by people who aren't footing the bill, people who are free while the two of them, priests mind you, are in prison." Another said, "I ask you: how could a priest ever get caught up with such people? I really wonder if he hasn't been brainwashed, this Father Berrigan. How else can you explain it, when two brothers start getting involved with people like that, the whole 'peace crowd,' and all their noise and troublemaking?" There seemed to be a sense among Coles's informants that the Berrigans needed to be rescued from these pernicious influences. One man urged Coles to "go help them—*save* them." And once they were saved, Coles could "straighten them out."[20]

Throughout the second half of 1968, the pages of Catholic periodicals were filled with editorials, columns, and letters to the editor that reflected a wide range of opinion about the Catonsville raid. Although they seemed to go out of their way to praise the sincerity of the Nine, few of these publications expressed clear support for their demonstration. Indeed, many of them published editorials sharply criticizing it.[21]

Ave Maria, a century-old Catholic periodical, offered a fairly typical rebuke in an editorial about the Catonsville Nine and the Baltimore Four. "We don't think that they've succeeded in getting their message across," the journal noted. Like many critics, the editors of *Ave Maria* asserted that the demonstrators' choices of symbols had been a distraction. "Blood and napalm—although they unquestionably help to dramatize certain values—tend to raise other questions that obscure the point the Berrigans et al. are trying to make: questions related to respect for the law and for other individuals, questions of public order and of propriety and of taste." Overall, both groups of protesters had failed to engage in "a very effective way of talking to the American people" about the war, poverty, and inequality.[22]

Even the left-leaning *National Catholic Reporter* took issue with the Catonsville protest. In a lengthy and acerbic editorial bearing the headline "SHRILL SYMBOL," the weekly mocked the demonstrators' tactics as overly strident. Their raid on Local Board 33, the *NCR* asserted, "comes through not as a serious manifesto but as an offensive sort of prank, the bizarre product of minds linked in their fanaticism with the antics of the gun-running, ammunition-stocking Minutemen" (zealots whose politics were to the right of the ultraconservative John Birch Society). The statement issued by the Nine had done little to help matters, for it had a "disabling quality of shrillness." The newsweekly did leave open the possibility that the verdict of history would be kind to the demonstrators and that, in subsequent accounts of this bleak period, such actions could "stand out as flames lighting a darkness."[23]

Rosemary Ruether and Michael Novak echoed these critiques. Ruether was no mossback. She was committed to the peace and civil rights movements, and she would become recognized as a pioneer Christian feminist theologian. (Ruether's politics were so liberal that she had been acquainted with Mary Moylan when they both had lived in Washington, D.C.) But Ruether struggled to make sense of the fiery Catonsville Nine demonstration. In an open letter, Ruether argued that the protest at Local Board 33 had been ill-conceived. It had not been, she claimed, a serious attempt to actually disrupt an inherently immoral war. Throwing down the rhetorical gauntlet, she recalled that the German theologian Dietrich Bonhoeffer had seen Nazism as such a threat to humanity that he had joined the Resistance and participated in a plot to assassinate Hitler—a crime for which he had been executed (in ghastly circumstances). Compared with this, the Catonsville protest did not amount to "serious sabotage." In Ruether's estimation, it had been only a symbolic action—and not a particularly useful one in terms of drawing people into the antiwar cause. "The . . . trouble is that your symbols don't seem be very effective in gaining converts," she wrote. "On the contrary, they alienate those who are already converted."[24]

Novak, a Catholic critic and social commentator, wrote in 1974 that the Berrigans and their followers had charted a course that was "politically misguided and morally romantic. . . . It lacked political penetration and point. For too many it was repellent rather than persuasive. In all these ways, it was morally and politically deficient."[25] Thirty-five years later, Novak's opinions hadn't much changed. Writing in 2009, he described Dan Berrigan as a friend but admitted that he had found it difficult to share "his growing anti-Americanism, romanticism, and semiviolent nonviolence."[26]

Not every Catholic, however, shared such concerns. Having grown impatient with gradual approaches to political and socioeconomic reform, many church members cheered more radical tactics of protest that were grounded in a fidelity to such core Christian principles as justice and compassion. Responding to Rosemary Ruether's critique, Father Richard McSorley—who almost had gone to Catonsville himself—argued in the *NCR* that the Berrigans and their accomplices had offered a dramatic and effective witness highlighting the ravages of "the disease of violence." As so often happened with prophets, their motives and tactics had been misunderstood.[27]

Many other Catholics joined McSorley in championing the Nine. Father Robert Drinan—the Boston College law professor who would be elected to Congress in 1970—wrote that "the destruction of draft files by the Catonsville Nine . . . may be a dramatic 'homily' against the evils of militarism, and the sincerity and heroism of those who participate in such activities is beyond dispute." For Drinan, the raid on the draft board was nothing less than a "prophetic witness" for peace.[28]

At one point in the Nine's stay in the county jail in Towson, a group of sympathetic Jesuits delivered to them a parcel of books on revolution. (The readings were not for the faint of heart: the authors included the celebrated Argentine Marxist revolutionary Che Guevara and the German philosopher and sociologist Herbert Marcuse.) It was an emotional visit, and the Jesuits expressed their admiration for the courage displayed by the incarcerated protesters. "We're embarrassed," one said through a flood of tears. "We feel we should be right in there with you."[29]

Another group of Jesuits—seminarians from nearby Woodstock, Maryland—offered more public support for the Nine. In a letter praising the "integrity and moral commitment of the nine men and women," the seminarians disputed the notion that the Catonsville protesters lacked fidelity to the country or their church. They asserted that it was inherently unfair for the activists to be condemned "outright for a lack of loyalty to their country and Church or for imprudence in the means they chose to express their protest." The Jesuits made the point that individuals voicing dissent did not necessarily lack fundamental loyalty to the institutions or churches whose policies they criticized. "Disagreement with policy assumptions and decisions—civil or ecclesiastical—particularly when based on moral convictions as it is in this case cannot be considered an act of disloyalty to one's country or to one's God," they wrote.[30]

Tom Cornell, a Catholic Worker with long-standing ties to Dorothy Day, offered a lengthy analysis of this "ingenious act of nonviolent revolution" and concluded that it might show the usefulness of "more vigorous forms of nonviolent intervention against the processes of murder and exploitation." With traditional forms of nonviolent protest failing to stop the war, the time might have arrived for "a shift in tactics, from nonviolent protest to resistance to revolution." For this, the Catonsville raid could serve as a profound example.

"The Catonsville Action may prove to be a powerful model for the next phase of the nonviolent revolution in America," Cornell argued. "Its power cuts through the fanciful rhetoric of the New Left to the core of frustration and longing for the Beloved Community that motivates those involved in the antiwar, student, and black movements."[31]

Day's opinions were murkier. Shortly after the Catonsville protest, she told Dan Berrigan in a letter that she "could only think it was a very strong and imaginative witness against conscription." And over the following months, Day publicly supported the demonstrators in their legal fight against the federal government; she spoke out on their behalf many times. At one gathering in 1968, Day urged those assembled to "meditate on the acts of witness given by Fathers Daniel and Philip Berrigan and the rest of the Catonsville Nine." By deliberately choosing to be jailed, they had engaged in a powerful act of witness against the war. "There is only one way to end this insane war," Day insisted. "Pack the jails with our men! Pack the jails!" At a later rally for the Nine, she stated, "The act of the Catonsville Nine is another desperate offer of life and freedom."[32]

But at that very same rally, Day made plain her discomfort with the tactics employed by the Catonsville Nine. Clearly troubled by how the demonstrators had seized and destroyed the draft records from Local Board 33, she fretted that relying on such methods might lead peace activists away from genuine pacifism. Day cautioned that opponents of the war "must restrict our violence to property" and that "we must hang on to our pacifism in the face of all violence." She urged activists to retain their bedrock commitment to pacifism by following in the noble footsteps of the likes of Martin Luther King Jr., the hero of the civil rights movement.[33]

Privately, Day expressed even less enthusiasm about the draft board raids and their participants. "These actions," she told one intimate, "are not ours"—meaning that they weren't done in the name or the spirit of the Catholic Worker movement. After the ransacking in Catonsville, she sniffed that Dan Berrigan "isn't a Catholic Worker; he came to us and stole our young men away" to help him undertake acts of antiwar resistance.[34]

By 1971 she had grown concerned with the antiwar movement's apparent drift away from nonviolent resistance. In that year she told the critic Dwight MacDonald that "the violent spirit [might] only be directed against inanimate objects now, but it could lead to the real thing. Bombings are the next step—and when it comes to bombs, you can't control it, no matter what your intentions, you can't be sure there isn't a late worker or a cleaning worker around." She also said of Catholic radicals: "Those priests and sisters! I admire their courage and dedication but not their arrogance."[35]

The other formidable Catholic casting a long shadow over the Catonsville Nine was Thomas Merton. Like Day, Merton was an unwavering apostle of nonviolence, and Phil and Dan Berrigan almost desperately sought his imprimatur.[36] Before the Baltimore Four protest, Dan Berrigan wrote the Trappist monk and asked him to comment on Phil's idea that the peace movement might have to commit violence against "idolatrous things" to effectively thwart the war effort. Merton was not reticent in expressing his qualms about the destruction of property and how it might result in harm being done to people. Cautioning that "we are getting toward the place where we have to be able to define our limits," Merton's reply highlighted several areas of practical and ideological concern. He pointed out that people could be injured or even killed if an attack ostensibly aimed at property spiraled out of control. Merton also wondered about the potentially muddled political implications of such actions, worrying if "we [are] just getting involved in a fake revolution of badly mixed-up disaster inviting people who are willing to do anything absurd and irrational simply to mess things up, and to mess them up especially for the well-meaning 'idealists' who want to run along proving that they are such real good hip people." Not surprisingly, Merton was ambivalent about groups wanting to "get violent." (He even asked Dan, "How nuts is this whole business?"[37])

When he learned the details of the Catonsville protest, Merton did not respond with much enthusiasm. He wrote blandly in his journal, "Dan and Phil Berrigan and some others took A-1 draft files from a draft center in a Baltimore suburb and burned them in a parking lot. Somewhere I heard they were arrested, but I've seen no paper and don't know anything." He later wrote privately of the brothers and their accomplices, "I don't agree with their methods of action." Merton could understand why the Nine had taken such an immoderate action and how they believed they could witness against the war from jail. Yet he resisted endorsing their tactics. "That is their business," he wrote. "It is certainly not a necessary teaching of the church."[38]

Merton's qualms about the Nine were manifest in a piece he published in *Ave Maria* late in 1968, shortly before his death. The circumstances of the Catonsville protest were worth scrutinizing, he argued, because they seemed to present "a new borderline situation: as if the peace movement . . . were standing at the very edge of violence." The protest "bordered on violence and was violent to the extent that it meant pushing some good ladies around and destroying some government property." Merton understood this to be "an attempt at prophetic nonviolent provocation" spurred by a sincere desire to protest the injustice of the war. It was, unfortunately, an action that "has . . . frightened more than it has edified." For nonviolence to be effective, Merton asserted, it "has to be extremely careful and clear"—and the Catonsville demonstration had been neither.[39]

Dan and Phil Berrigan realized that Merton, while congenial, was not enthusiastic about what they had done in Baltimore and Catonsville. "The clearest impression I have of his mood is a mix of alertness and bewilderment," Dan later wrote. "He was stirred, fearful, didn't know where such acts might lead." Phil felt that Merton simply hadn't understood that Catonsville was part of a laudable nonviolent tradition—a misapprehension that might have resulted from Merton living a life so closed off from the outside world.[40]

For many years after their protest, the Catonsville Nine received messages of thanks from individuals who had been touched by their witness. Sometimes these admirers indicated that they had been so moved by the demonstration at Local Board 33 that they had been inspired to engage in activism themselves. Occasionally, those expressing gratitude to the Nine asserted that their lives had been directly impacted by the activists' seizure and destruction of draft records. Late in his life, Tom Lewis said that men still approached him from time to time and thanked him for having demolished their files at Catonsville. His action, they said, had saved them from combat—and from perhaps dying in Vietnam.[41]

In fact, the practical impact of the Catonsville Nine protest—which probably destroyed no more than 5 percent of the draft records housed in Local Board 33—is difficult to ascertain. Immediately after the demonstration, it was apparent to federal officials that the Nine had temporarily interrupted the work of the small Selective Service office. "The removal of the files has seriously disrupted the work of the board," the FBI reported, "and it will require many hours of work to reconstruct the files." But the FBI, having consulted with state and local Selective Service officials, believed that this would be at worst a brief disruption and that, because backups of basic information existed, the Nine had not permanently destroyed any draft files. "There is no likelihood that any of the registrants will be 'lost' as a result of this action, as there are duplicate lists available at the board and/or at State Headquarters which will permit reconstruction of the files."[42]

The FBI noted that, ironically, the Nine might have harmed some young men by burning their draft files. The draft records housed in Local Board 33 contained a variety of information relating to individuals' draft statuses. The materials collected in these folders included affidavits from employers, statements provided by clergy, medical records, and personal correspondence. The draftees supplied these documents themselves—often in a desperate effort to avoid being classified 1-A. The Nine, in their haste to grab and burn as much paper as they could find inside the draft board, destroyed many of these personal draft archives. The FBI concluded that "the removal of the files did a great injustice to the registrants, many of whom had gone to a great deal of trouble and expense to obtain statements from doctors and employers and had made plans based on their classifications. The disruption of the files did the boys as much harm as it did the board."[43]

This seemed to be the case for many of the Local Board 33 registrants who had received classifications of 1-Y. These registrants had been deemed qualified for military service only in the event of war or national emergency—a status somewhat more desirable than 1-A, which indicated that a registrant was ready for immediate induction. (1-Y registrants often had medical conditions that were limiting but not completely debilitating. When the classification was eliminated in 1971, they all were classified 4-F—not acceptable for military service.) "Approximately three-quarters of the files in [a] drawer containing the 1-Y classifications had been removed" and destroyed by the Nine, according to an FBI report. "Also, files in another drawer containing 1-Y classifications were practically all removed."[44]

Draft board clerk Mary Murphy was viewed as a hero within the Selective Service System for her actions on the day of the Catonsville protest. She received a commendation noting that in a "splendid demonstration of devotion to responsibility" she had "exemplified outstanding courage" in trying to preserve draft records from the demonstrators. Murphy's esteem within the draft system was further bolstered by her dogged efforts to reconstruct the files that the Catonsville Nine had defaced. As she tackled this chore, she agreed wholeheartedly with the FBI's assessment of the impact of the protest at Local Board 33. The Nine stressed that they had targeted government property because of its role in expediting the war effort. But Murphy insisted that the activists misunderstood the matter of the files' ownership. The documents "actually belong[ed] to the registrants themselves," she said. "In these folders were many personal letters, from doctors, and all sorts of things that applied to that particular boy. Actually this was his folder—this was his property that they had destroyed."[45]

According to Murphy, military veterans often came back to the draft board to find copies of documents that, as civilians, they still needed. Ex-servicemen often appeared and asked for their record of discharge—a document called a DDT 214. "This is the most important paper a serviceman has," she explained. "Every place he goes, if he wants to borrow money from a bank, if he wants to buy a house, no matter what he wants to do, he must have this 214." Thanks to the Catonsville Nine, some of these essential documents went up in flames in the parking lot of the Knights of Columbus hall. Their destruction served only to complicate the lives of men who had served their country. (They were forced to request duplicate copies of records from an Army personnel center—a process that could take several months.)[46]

Piecing these materials back together took Murphy and her fellow clerks the better part of a year. (Just the preliminary work occupied six people for about three weeks.) Over that time, Murphy and her family had some contact with the Nine. At first, these interactions were cordial—at least in part because the activists felt remorse for having frightened and manhandled the clerks. Immediately after the protest, the demonstrators sent flowers and an apologetic telegram to the clerks. "We hope that is all well," the message stated. "Try to understand we had no intentions of injuring anyone." (The impact of this gesture was undercut by the condition of the flowers: they arrived wilted.[47])

But this convivial tone soon vanished, at least as far as Phil Berrigan was concerned. He appeared to develop a special contempt for Murphy and what she seemed to symbolize about middle America's unthinking support for the war effort. In his prison journals (which were later published as a book), he described the draft board clerk as a "narrow and doctrinaire functionary" whose cheerful participation in the war effort proved that she must have suffered from "resounding schizophrenia."[48]

Berrigan also pilloried Murphy in an article published in the journal *Liberation*. Even for him, it was an extraordinarily caustic piece. In recounting the demonstration at the draft board, he described Murphy as a "portly, middle-aged Irish matron" who had fought to protect the draft files with "furious dogged tenacity." Murphy and her fellow clerks had become unhinged—but not because of the demeanor of the Nine. "We talked to them gently indeed, but gentle talk had sparse effect," he wrote. The protesters had been left with no choice: "Mrs. Murphy had to be manhandled repeatedly."[49]

Liberation had a limited circulation, but word of Berrigan's diatribe spread after portions of it appeared in an article in a local newspaper. Murphy was livid when she saw Berrigan's comments, which she later described as "a vicious attack on me personally." She penned an angry letter to the president of the National Federation of Government Employees and urged him to speak out against the priest. Berrigan's observations were "not only insulting to me personally, but to every Local Board clerk in every Board in the United States," Murphy wrote. She recoiled at the assertion that her response to the Catonsville protest had been out of the ordinary. "No Local Board clerk would allow anyone to come into a Local Board and not attempt to stop any action to destroy government property," Murphy wrote.[50]

Murphy's distress over Berrigan's uncharitable comments was made clear in correspondence between her daughter and Phil Berrigan and Lewis. In a letter sent to Berrigan while he was in jail in the fall of 1968, the younger Murphy defended her mother's character and suggested that her family might pursue further criminal and civil charges against the Nine (including perhaps a defamation claim against Berrigan for his *Liberation* article).

Although the letter was not addressed to him, Tom Lewis felt compelled to reply. He did so in characteristically thoughtful fashion, praising the draft clerk's daughter for expressing her feelings so honestly (it was "a beautiful thing," Lewis observed) and drawing parallels between his own family and the Murphys. While expressing empathy for the elder Murphy, he pointed out that she was not the only mother to have been touched by the war. "I am honestly sorry for mental suffering that your Mother is experiencing, as I am sorry for the suffering the war has brought to the Mothers who[se] sons have and are dying in Vietnam. I am sorry also that my own Mother suffers while I am in jail," Lewis wrote. "But the war goes on and the people suffer; perhaps it is through this suffering that man will reconcile himself."[51]

Berrigan responded as well. Somewhat disingenuously, he expressed surprise at the suggestion that he had gone out of his way to publicly excoriate the draft board clerk. "I don't know where you got the idea I was conducting a personal vendetta against your mother," he wrote to Murphy's daughter. "Such is not the case." His tone somewhat less abrasive than it had been in his *Liberation* article, he described the elder Murphy as "an honorable and decent human being" and asked her daughter to "please convey warmest regards and love" to her. The Nine never had intended to harm her, and, had there been sufficient time, "we would have told her that we respected and revered her."[52]

Despite having been publicly and privately censured by Phil Berrigan, Mary Murphy did her best to fathom why the Nine had targeted the draft files housed in her office. She acknowledged that the activists had taken such an astonishing step because, like many Americans at that time, "they sincerely thought that war was bad, bad, bad." But it wasn't the motives of the Nine that nettled Murphy so much as it was their tactics. The clerk was troubled by "their use of violence," she said. "They used violence to preach their little sermon. . . . They used violence. To me, that was a very wrong thing to do." Employing physical coercion undercut the entire point of their witness, which ostensibly was meant to promote peace. Murphy was left to conclude that the Nine simply "do not represent peace."[53]

That Murphy was a Catholic made the Catonsville protest even more disturbing to her. She had grown up in the church, and throughout her life she had respected priests as figures of authority and stability. By victimizing her in a violent and criminal act, the Berrigans had shattered that image for Murphy. "It was a terrible, terrible experience for me," she said, "to feel that men I had always been taught to look up to, and respect, turned out to be anarchists."[54]

Murphy's feelings would not mellow after the Catonsville Nine were tried in the fall of 1968. Asked to encapsulate her views about the demonstrators and their impact on her, she said:

> To sum up, the actions of the Catonsville Nine really affected me and my family. They injected an element of fear and apprehension where there never had been any before. They insulted me in person and in print. The ordeal of the hearings, the trials, the fear of demonstrators, the personal shame I felt as a Catholic and as an American that these people of my religious faith would do such a terrible thing to their country has been an awful experience for me.[55]

It turned out that the Berrigans were not the only radicals with whom the personnel of Local Board 33 had to contend. The board eventually relocated to a slightly larger space in Catonsville, an office on Frederick Road that was adjacent to an armed forces recruiting station. Peace activists followed them there and harassed them, according to Murphy. "A couple of times, they tried to get in," she said. One group squeezed its way into the building's vestibule and celebrated a mock Mass, complete with bread and wine.[56]

Some of the demonstrations left the draft board clerks shaken. One sizable group—Murphy thought they were kids from Catonsville High School and some local colleges—milled around in front of the building, shouting protest slogans and pounding on its large plate-glass windows. One member of this ragtag assemblage brandished a two-by-four and threatened to shatter the glass with it. Another time, a large group of demonstrators—some of them costumed as grotesque figures—attempted to enter the board. The police had been forewarned about the protest, and they had to hold off the activists before they surged in. These later dustups did not result in the destruction of any draft files, and none of the clerks were harmed. Nonetheless, such incidents "were really terrifying," Murphy recalled.[57]

Demonstrators also targeted members of the Catonsville draft board at their homes. Nine days after the Catonsville Nine burst into Local Board 33, a group of their supporters decided to picket the homes of Edwin Steinwedel, Vivian Douglas, Anthony Orban, and Henry Helfrich. (In the case of Douglas, it turned out that their timing was poor; he wasn't home that day.) It was a Sunday, and, to drum up support for their protest, the demonstrators first distributed flyers at local Catholic churches like St. Mark, which was located near the Knights of Columbus hall. According to Jean Walsh, the editor of the local newspaper, the group then "formed sort of a parade with banners in front of the homes of several of the draft board members" and urged them to end their involvement in the war. Their signs read "DRAFT BOARDS REAR CANNON FODDER FOR VIETNAM" and "NAPALM PAPER . . . NOT PEOPLE."[58]

The draft board members were more annoyed by the picketers than persuaded by them. Helfrich was unmoved by the demonstrators' shouts of "Helfrich, resign!" Walsh interviewed him afterward, and he told her, "I have no intention of resigning. It is a thankless job, but somebody has to do it." Orban was defiant as well. He hated having to play a part in sending young men to war, he told Walsh, but the conflict in Vietnam was a noble endeavor, and he wanted to contribute to the American effort in whatever way he could.[59]

Draft board clerk Phyllis Morsberger wasn't in Catonsville that day. In the weeks after the raid, she struggled to come to grips with the disturbance in her workplace. "At the time it happened, I was fine, very cool and calm, but after it was all over I had a nervous reaction," she later admitted. "When I spoke it was like hysterical, or so everybody told me. I really didn't notice it, but I had to go to the doctor and he said it was natural because it was such a big shock, nothing other than that." Her husband had learned in advance that there might be additional protests in Catonsville that weekend, and, without sharing his concerns, he encouraged her to take a trip out of town with some friends. She learned only after returning home why he had nudged her to leave town. "My husband felt that I had been through enough harassment," she explained.[60]

11 }

"A Colossal Effrontery to Justice"

William Kunstler did some reckless things during his boyhood in New York City. He once crawled onto the roof of his family's synagogue, Temple Israel. He cavorted there for a bit—and then crashed through a skylight. (Kunstler was spared serious injury when he landed on some grillwork.) He developed a penchant for skinny-dipping as well, stripping off his clothes and plunging into the Central Park Lake and the Hudson River. "As I recall," he wrote later in life, "not a single day went by that I didn't misbehave in some way, large or small."[1]

And then there was the time that Kunstler led a group of kids, including his brother and sister, out for a walk along some railroad tracks. Kunstler, nine years old at the time, was blissfully unaware that he had led the group near the tracks' third rail, which was electrified and thus capable of killing the entire band of children. Fortunately, Kunstler's father saw that the youngsters were in peril and yelled at them to move to safer ground.[2]

Harrowing though they were, such experiences did not chasten Kunstler. He went on to become one of the best-known—and perhaps most reviled—radical lawyers of his generation. Throughout the 1960s and 1970s, he seemed to seek out and defend individuals who were the third rails of American society—"politically unacceptable outcasts," he affectionately called them. They included the Chicago Seven, Jack Ruby, Lenny Bruce, various Black Panthers and Freedom Riders, Adam Clayton Powell Jr., H. Rap Brown, and Larry Davis. Summing up his list of notorious clients, he once said, "I've taken on a lot of pariahs."[3]

An immutable set of principles guided Kunstler as he defended "people who could not stand up for themselves," as he described them. These ideals were grounded in his understanding of the nation's bedrock principles, among them the notion "that all people are equal and that government has a responsibility to protect our rights and freedoms described in the Bill of Rights." His critics—he accumulated so many of them through the years that a biography was titled *William M. Kunstler: The Most Hated Lawyer in America*—called him hopelessly quixotic, but Kunstler hardly cared. "While some people may view me as wildly and indiscriminately tilting at windmills," he boasted, "I see myself as a keeper of the faith, fighting for my own personal vision of America and my own personal goal: that someday, somehow, we will find the hidden path that leads to what we have always outwardly prized but never attained. Equal justice for all."[4]

Kunstler had no trouble pursuing that goal in the 1960s. For him, it was a time when "people asserted their rights and freedoms even if they weren't white or male or rich, even if they didn't follow the established ways." In the early part of the decade, the primary battleground in this struggle was in the South, and Kunstler immersed himself in a variety of civil rights cases there. As he fought against segregation and for the right of African Americans to live as full citizens, Kunstler felt "as if my entire life had led me to this time and place, to this work."[5]

In time Kunstler became dissatisfied with the "self-righteous role-playing," as he later called it, that characterized his work for the civil rights movement. For all of his courtroom posturing, he had failed to fully dedicate himself to the cause of justice. To make a genuine commitment, he would have to reappraise his role as a lawyer and break down the artificial barrier that separated him from his clients.[6]

The Catonsville Nine case forced him to do just that.

Ever the organizer, George Mische made the initial contact with Kunstler early in the summer of 1968. He asked the attorney to meet him and Dan Berrigan at a Mexican restaurant in Midtown Manhattan. Kunstler was wary; he doubted that the priest would live up to his advance billing. "Most of the people who had discussed him with me talked in such terms of awe, love, and respect that I was fully convinced that he was a monumental figment of some highly overstimulated imaginations," he confessed.[7]

At first, it seemed that Kunstler's fears about Berrigan would be realized. The priest walked into the restaurant wearing rumpled pants—Kunstler wondered if Berrigan had been sleeping in them—and a pair of tattered sneakers. Rounding out this offbeat costume was a large medallion that hung from a chain around Berrigan's neck. Before the meeting, Kunstler had wondered if Berrigan might resemble an Old Testament prophet—a Joshua or an Elijah. Instead, the lawyer found himself sharing a meal with a man who bore a striking resemblance to the oddballs he often encountered in Greenwich Village.[8]

But Berrigan won over Kunstler as he passionately outlined the rationale for the Catonsville protest and explained how the defendants hoped to approach their trial. He couldn't help but be captivated by this "effervescent and exceptionally intelligent man whose warmth of spirit and delight in life made even casual conversation an extraordinary event," as he recalled. After the meeting broke up and Kunstler made his way home, he was reminded of a previous encounter with a dynamic religious leader: the night six years earlier in Nashville, Tennessee, when he had first met Martin Luther King Jr. Such was the power of Berrigan's personality.[9]

Captivated by Berrigan and eager to put his skills to work in the antiwar effort, Kunstler agreed to take the case. He soon assembled a group of attorneys to mount a defense for the Catonsville defendants. Joining Kunstler—who assumed the role of lead attorney—were Harrop Freeman, a law professor at Cornell; Baltimore attorney Harold Buchman; and Father William Cunningham, a Jesuit and law professor at Loyola University in Chicago. Somewhat grandly, they dubbed themselves "the American Four."[10]

Freeman, a Quaker, had been active in peace causes for many years. Dan Berrigan was his colleague at Cornell, and the priest knew that Freeman had been voicing opposition to war since the World War II era. Unlike his clients, Freeman was a relatively subdued activist. He battled militarism by running for Congress in his upstate New York district—in 1962, he ran on a peace platform and garnered 4,200 votes—and writing scholarly articles that criticized American military conscription policies. It was this area of expertise that made Freeman an integral part of the Catonsville Nine's defense team.[11]

Long before the United States became involved in the war in Vietnam, Freeman wrote a seminal article in the *Virginia Law Review* on the constitutionality of military conscription. (Some six decades after its publication, legal scholars still cite it.) "It is clear," he contended, "that there are limits on the war power as there are on any federal power." He explored those limits by critiquing the draft on a variety of grounds, including the historical claim that the Founding Fathers had intended to limit the federal government's ability to raise and maintain standing armies. In addition to reviewing the resistance to war by Quakers and Jehovah's Witnesses, Freeman highlighted the necessity of protecting the civil liberties of individuals claiming religious objection to military service and compulsory patriotic rituals.[12]

Freeman zealously defended civil disobedience as a legitimate tactic of dissent. In 1966 he argued that it was "a recognized procedure for challenging law or policy" and that "the obligation to obey the law is not absolute but relative." He further said, "I cannot see any reason for jail sentences, or sentences more severe than for those who challenge law for other reasons as part of normal criminal intent. . . . It is usual to take motive into account in sentencing, and I believe the essentially 'democratic' or 'First Amendment' motive should incur nominal penalties at the most."[13]

Buchman was not the kind of attorney who researched and wrote erudite law review articles. Born and bred in Baltimore, he attended Baltimore City College and the University of Baltimore Law School before embarking on a long and contentious career in which he championed a variety of liberal causes, including labor. "I represent anybody except fascists, the Ku Klux Klanners, and the racists," he once boasted. "If they generally have a humanistic approach to people, I'll defend them even though they may have a distorted sense of history or are politically naïve, counterproductive, or even dangerous."[14]

Buchman was active in the Progressive Party and backed Henry Wallace's doomed bid for president in 1948. As an attorney for the party, he also represented political candidates who opposed a Maryland statute requiring them to swear loyalty oaths. Buchman's public opposition to the measure earned him a great deal of scrutiny during the McCarthy era. When Congress investigated communist activities in the Baltimore area, Buchman was grilled about his political associations. "That period destroyed some of the best talent in America," he later said. "Walking into a courtroom in those days was like walking [into] Dante's Inferno."[15]

Cunningham, the final member of the legal team, earned undergraduate and law degrees from Marquette University before serving as a lieutenant in the Army's Judge Advocate General's Corps. Following his stint in the military, Cunningham joined the Jesuits and pursued a career that paired religious service with legal advocacy for those on the margins of society. He settled in Chicago, where he took a keen interest in the plight of the poor and those who challenged the political status quo. (He defended a group of Chicago draft board raiders in 1970.) "Listen to dissent," he told one audience in the early 1970s. "Christ did."[16]

Harmonizing the efforts of four attorneys who lived and worked in four different cities (New York City, Ithaca, Chicago, and Baltimore) proved to be a tricky task. Over the summer of 1968, Buchman did his best to coordinate their preparations for the trial, but Freeman repeatedly complained that he was being left out of the loop. Three weeks before the trial was slated to begin, he pleaded to Buchman, "What are plans as to when we lawyers may get together? Are you planning to make any motions pretrial? If so, what? Do you need any help on law, brief, motion? . . . I understand the talk was of each lawyer speaking for one or two defendants, if Dan's information is correct. Is that the plan? Who for whom?"[17]

Fred Weisgal, who had defended the Baltimore Four, seemed like a natural choice to join the team representing the Nine, but he never became actively engaged in the case. This appears to have been the result of both circumstance—Weisgal went on a lengthy trip to Israel with his family in the summer of 1968—and a difference of opinion over how the defense was to be handled.

As Phil Berrigan wrote to Weisgal just before the trial, the Nine had become "convinced that the federal legal system is logically meant to protect the federal system and that we have no more chance under the law than a snow ball in hell. If that's the case, then the trial takes an entirely different complexion, becoming no more than a scene from which to communicate ideas and to illustrate the bankruptcy of justice in our fair nation." Weisgal had been infuriated by the timing of the Catonsville raid, and he apparently wanted little part of a defense that would privilege fulminating against injustice over actually fighting the criminal charges that had been filed against the defendants.[18]

And the defendants apparently wanted little to do with him. In the summer of 1968, Phil Berrigan wrote to Buchman from federal prison and informed him that he and Lewis had surveyed their codefendants about the prospect of Weisgal joining the defense team. The response had been somewhat less than enthusiastic. "The other seven wish to cut him loose," Berrigan reported. Although they were grateful for his efforts on behalf of the Baltimore Four, the priest and Lewis agreed "that our friend ought to be unloaded."[19]

With Weisgal largely out of the picture (he was devoting his energies to appealing the Baltimore Four convictions), the Catonsville defendants' strategy came into sharper focus over the summer of 1968. At Cornell, Dan Berrigan met with Freeman several times, and together they worked through some possible strategies for the trial itself and the atmosphere they hoped it would generate.

Dan Berrigan's concern for the latter was evident in a letter he wrote that July to George Mische and the defense team. He began by noting that activists in Ithaca recently had recreated portions of the trial of the famed pediatrician Benjamin Spock and four other antiwar activists. The trial of the "Boston Five"—who were charged with having engaged in a conspiracy to violate the Selective Service Act—had been the first major antiwar legal prosecution of the Vietnam era, and the Ithaca activists' attempt to highlight its central issues made Berrigan wonder if similar efforts could be mounted in conjunction with the Catonsville trial. He suggested that, after each day's courtroom proceedings, a group of law students might recreate the trial for the benefit of those activists who had converged on Baltimore. Such mock trials or forums, Berrigan offered, might energize sympathizers and garner media attention. "If we wanted to think big," he continued, "it might be possible to film these proceedings for TV use in other cities."[20]

Berrigan then addressed possible legal strategies. . He reported that Freeman had suggested stressing the religious rights of the three clergymen who had participated in the Catonsville raid (the Berrigans and Brother David Darst). "Members of religious orders have special responsibility to resist unjust laws," he noted, "giving example to the community." This was particularly true for members of his own religious order; the Jesuits had stressed the notion of public responsibility since the time of their founder, Ignatius Loyola. Berrigan relayed Freeman's emphasis on the "importance of [a] Jesuit presence" at the trial. Members of the order could testify as character witnesses, Berrigan suggested, or their writings could be referenced to help provide a theological rationale for the Nine's actions.[21]

Acknowledging that the defense could not limit itself to the doctrines and traditions of his own religious order, Berrigan also seconded Freeman's suggestion that the defense present "the Catholic position in general, from [a] contemporary point of view" and explain that "all the defendants acted out of their own conscience, informed by a sense of their own tradition." Lay theologians—Berrigan thought of Dan Callahan, who had published a book titled *The Mind of the Catholic Layman* a few years earlier—might be effective in making this point and help to "show that Catholic Christians belong where we were, doing what we did" in Catonsville.[22]

The Nine and their attorneys generally agreed on how the defense should be conducted. One point of contention, though, was whether they should agree to have a jury trial. "To my surprise and consternation," Kunstler noted, "Dan told me that he and his codefendants didn't want a jury at all." The lead attorney—who believed that having a jury hear the case was an absolute necessity if the defendants were to have any hope of carrying their message beyond the courtroom—and his client had a tense conversation over the matter.[23]

"We don't want a jury trial because we don't want to participate in the selection of a jury," Berrigan said. "That would make it look as if we think the legal system is legitimate."

"We've got to have a jury," Kunstler told him. "A jury gives us an audience and will also educate America because it represents the public."

Berrigan was adamant: "We don't want a jury."

"Maybe we can work out something, because as a lawyer I feel that it makes a better trial with a jury," Kunstler told him. "That way, you're not putting it all in the hands of a judge. You're going to lose, anyway, because you burned the draft records, and you never hid that fact."[24]

Berrigan and Kunstler reached a compromise: they would have a jury trial, but the defense would indicate its challenge to the legitimacy of the criminal justice system by refusing to participate in the selection of jurors from the pool. They would not question any prospective members of the panel, nor would they exercise any peremptory challenges. They would, as Kunstler put it, wind up "accepting all jurors who ended up in the box."[25]

Kunstler was struck by how he and Berrigan resolved the jury issue. An experienced and savvy litigator, Kunstler was famously persuasive, and he often was able to bully his clients into bending to his will on such strategic matters. But here he had been forced to work *with* someone he represented. "A decision had been reached on a partnership basis rather than by the authority of my expertise," he wrote, "a decision that took into consideration both the legal and political needs of what had suddenly and subtly become a group effort."[26]

As the Catonsville case progressed, Kunstler worked out numerous such compromises with his clients. They forced the attorney to rethink how he perceived the barriers that supposedly separated lawyers from the world around them. "I came to understand that, in order to represent those who speak for truth and love and brotherhood, a lawyer cannot maintain the traditional aloofness and reserve that have characterized the profession from its earliest days," he indicated.[27]

It appeared that most of the Nine agreed with the direction that Kunstler and Dan Berrigan were taking the defense. A notable exception—at least for a time—was the Jesuit's brother.

In public, Phil Berrigan effusively praised the defense team. Privately, though, he was not fully engaged in planning the group's defense, either practically or philosophically. In part, this was a function of logistics. Berrigan and Lewis spent much of the summer of 1968 in the federal penitentiary in Lewisburg, Pennsylvania (and the adjacent Allenwood prison farm), and it was an enormous undertaking for them to leave those facilities and meet with their fellow defendants and their lawyers. One trip to Baltimore in July took eight days—and relatively little of that time was devoted to actually plotting strategy for the trial. "Two days were spent traveling and going through the interminable red tape connected with leaving prison and returning to it," Berrigan noted in his journal. "Talking to our lawyers and friends took a few hours. The remaining time was spent waiting for return here." Many years later, when a documentary filmmaker asked him about his role in helping to map out a legal defense for the Nine, Berrigan curtly said that he "didn't help with the trial planning" and had "little access to the legal team" because he was incarcerated throughout the summer and fall of 1968.[28]

But even if he had been free, Berrigan probably would not have been eager to hash out strategy. The truth was, he had little enthusiasm for using attorneys to fully participate in the criminal justice system. According to Baltimore activist Bill O'Connor, "Phil objected strenuously to the [emerging legal] strategy because it was playing ball with the establishment."[29]

Berrigan's misgivings about the courts dated back to at least a year earlier. During the planning for the Baltimore Four protest, he informed his brother Dan that he and his fellow Baltimore activists already were thinking about what would happen after they were arrested and charged by the federal government. The group had been in touch with attorney Fred Weisgal, but his services might not be necessary, Phil had said, because "we're thinking now of taking a stand which makes clear that the court has no jurisdiction over us." As a means of defying the legal system—and the dysfunctional political order of which it was emblematic—they might limit their defense to the statement they would distribute when they seized and defaced the draft records. "It may," he claimed, "open up the rotten melon a bit more."[30]

Ultimately, the Baltimore Four had mounted a legal defense, but their trial had only further soured Phil Berrigan on the courts and the men and women who helped them function. This included lawyers—even the apparently well-meaning ones who rallied to the defense of the Catonsville Nine. As their trial drew closer, Berrigan lamented the intrusiveness of attorneys and highlighted how they often were complicit in a system that made a mockery of justice. "When it comes to defending political dissenters like ourselves, lawyers become accomplices in the game against us—if, that is, they play by the rules," he wrote in his journal. "They unite with the criminality of the bench in what is a court of justice—a monstrous euphemism indeed. Belief in the law is no adequate excuse for this." So low was his opinion of attorneys that he jokingly called their profession "nearly as dishonored as the priesthood."[31]

When lawyers represented activists like the Catonsville Nine in court, Berrigan expected them to take a page from the playbook of the nonviolent revolutionaries they were defending. Their goal should be "the embarrassment and exposure of illegitimate power." This entailed acknowledging from the outset that trials of political activists were little more than charades. "There is no good reason why lawyers defending an antiwar case can't realize that a guilty verdict has been passed before the trial begins and that they are morally obligated to dramatize such a colossal effrontery to justice," he argued. Taking such extraordinary actions was imperative, even if it meant jeopardizing their professional respectability. "There is no good reason," Berrigan insisted, "why there should not be as many lawyers in jail for contempt of court as there are young men imprisoned for draft resistance."[32]

For Phil Berrigan, Weisgal epitomized this problem. The Baltimore attorney came to Lewisburg in the summer of 1968 to discuss the progress of the appeal he was filing on behalf of the Baltimore Four. To Berrigan's astonishment, Weisgal was willing to consider the possibility of the activists ultimately prevailing in court. "What would you think," he asked the imprisoned priest, "if we won our appeal?" Without missing a beat, Berrigan replied that he would wonder what had gone wrong. Alluding to Weisgal's unwillingness to acknowledge the legal system's moral bankruptcy, he wrote that "such men and institutions, so profoundly entrapped in corporate exploitation and horror, can, at best, master duplicity."[33]

So it was scarcely surprising that their relationship frayed. Over the summer and fall of 1968, Berrigan and Weisgal communicated only sporadically. The Baltimore attorney phoned and visited the priest in Lewisburg, but Berrigan believed that he was being given the cold shoulder. "Fred seems to avoid us quite totally," he wrote to his brother from prison. Berrigan thought he knew why Weisgal had distanced himself: he was angry that the Catonsville Nine had turned to Kunstler and his team to mount a less conventional defense. "I suspect," he wrote, "that seeing the show in other hands has quite undone him."[34]

Trying to repair the damage, Berrigan wrote to Weisgal from prison. In a conciliatory tone, he lamented that he and Lewis felt that "our relationship with you had deteriorated to an astounding degree" and that they feared he might be at odds with them. Berrigan explained why the Nine had not tapped him to defend them in their upcoming trial. It had become obvious to them that the federal judicial system had become a sham designed to protect the state's power by throttling meaningful dissent. That being the case, they had little hope of scoring a legal victory at their upcoming trial. However, as

Berrigan noted, their trial might still prove useful if the nine Catonsville defendants, their attorneys, and their many supporters joined together to expose to the public the bankruptcy of the nation's judicial system. Weisgal had seemed ill-suited to this task, so the Nine had turned to Kunstler and the other members of the "American Four."[35]

Weisgal's biographer, summarizing the perspective of the attorney's wife, reports that he was perfectly happy with this outcome, insisting that the attorney eventually became so dismayed by Berrigan that he refused to have anything to do with the Catonsville case. And it's worth noting that Weisgal and Kunstler, who effectively supplanted him, maintained a cordial relationship both before and after the draft board cases. One of Weisgal's law partners characterized them as good friends who consulted with one another on tricky cases and socialized whenever Kunstler came to Baltimore.[36]

Whatever its ultimate cause, the breach between Weisgal and Berrigan— one of many that marked the latter's life—was not complete. A consummate professional, Weisgal dutifully continued to represent the Baltimore Four in the many appeals that followed their convictions.

While the team defending the Catonsville Nine coalesced in the summer of 1968, their courtroom adversaries came together and strategized as well. The prosecution team would work under the direction of Stephen Sachs, the United States attorney for Maryland. He was a familiar face to defendants, having successfully prosecuted the Baltimore Four earlier in the year.

Sachs, who was raised in Baltimore, seemed to have stepped out of central casting. His father taught political science and constitutional law at Johns Hopkins and directed the Baltimore Jewish Council for many years. He instilled in Sachs an abiding interest in the law; growing up, he lionized Louis Brandeis and Benjamin Cardozo, the great Jewish jurists. Sachs graduated from Haverford, spent a year at Oxford on a Fulbright, and then went off to Yale Law School. After New Haven came a blue-chip judicial clerkship and an apprenticeship under U.S. Attorney Joseph Tydings back in Baltimore. Determined to clean up the cesspool that was Maryland politics in the 1960s, Tydings and his charges went after several prominent politicians on corruption charges. Sachs contributed to some notable victories, including the conviction of the speaker of the state house of delegates. He made such cases a priority when he took over the duties of U.S. attorney for Maryland in 1967. "Rape and murder are the most serious crimes," he explained early in his tenure, "but there is no more venal crime than rape of the public trust."[37]

But nothing in Sachs's elite training had prepared him for the Catonsville Nine and Baltimore Four cases. "Protest-related crime is different than regular crime," he said. "It's less consequential and more transitory. These persons aren't criminals in the normal sense of the word." He was reluctant to see the sanctions of the state applied to some of them. He likened it to using cannons to shoot butterflies.[38]

Other factors further complicated the cases for him. For starters, Sachs never had been an enthusiastic supporter of the war in Vietnam. "I was a dove," he later said, "absolutely a dove." His personal feelings about the war aside, the ambitious Sachs probably also sensed that repeatedly prosecuting earnest opponents of an unpopular war was not likely to endear him to the liberal elites and voters who might determine his fate if he ever ran for public office in the future.[39]

But Sachs never seriously considered *not* prosecuting the Catonsville Nine. Whatever their motives—and whatever his own ambitions—the rule of law had to prevail. "The heart of the matter is that you can't take the law in your own hands. Lawlessness in a democracy is tyranny," he said. "They were courageous, but the other side of that is arrogance—that they and only they are Right, with a capital 'R.' That attitude is fundamentally contrary to the perception of American democracy."[40]

The legal position taken by the Nine—that their actions in Catonsville had been a justifiable response to the American government's crimes against humanity across the globe—failed to impress him. "Their legal position, in our judgment, even can be called frivolous," Sachs explained. "They really have no legal justification."[41]

The politically nimble Sachs delegated responsibility for trying the Catonsville Nine case to two of his lieutenants, Arthur Murphy and Barney Skolnik. There were sure to be legal complications resulting from the protests associated with the trial, and Sachs devoted his attention to managing them. But the trial itself was largely left in the hands of his assistants.

An African American who had graduated from Baltimore's Morgan State University and the University of Maryland College of Law, Murphy was the senior assistant U.S. attorney for Maryland . He had joined the office in Baltimore in 1961 and had been strongly considered for the top job when it came open in 1967. (The Baltimore branch of the NAACP had pushed Murphy's candidacy, but he had stepped aside when it became apparent that Sachs would be picked.) Murphy generally was regarded as a capable attorney—but not an overly strident one. "He was a nice guy," one contemporary later said. On the weekends he could be found with his regular foursome on the municipal golf course at Baltimore's Carroll Park.[42]

Sachs's reliance on Murphy raised a few eyebrows among the Nine and their supporters. Some believed that it was a cynical ploy designed to undercut the defendants' liberal bona fides. Phil Berrigan wondered if Murphy suspected "that his blackness is a public-relations weapon in the government's hands." Word filtered back to Mische from local activist circles that Sachs's friends had been critical of him for apparently persecuting religious opponents of the war. Mische believed that the canny federal prosecutor sought to deflect some of that heat from himself—and undercut the Nine in the bargain—by exploiting Murphy.[43]

Whatever his motives, Sachs put Murphy in charge of the Catonsville case and then recruited another assistant, Skolnik, to help him. Like Sachs, Skolnik had cut his prosecutorial teeth trying political corruption cases—while on loan from another office, he had helped Sachs prosecute former Maryland congressman Thomas Johnson a year earlier—and they always would be his first love. Not long after Skolnik started working full-time as federal prosecutor in Baltimore, Sachs called the younger attorney into his office for a one-on-one talk about the Catonsville prosecution. Sachs made it plain that, for personal and political reasons, he did not want to try the case himself. Murphy would lead the prosecution—with, Sachs hoped, Skolnik's help.[44]

The request flabbergasted Skolnik. The two men were close personally as well as professionally, and he knew that Sachs was aware of his distaste for the war in Vietnam. Skolnik never had been deeply involved in the antiwar movement, but during his time in Washington, D.C., he had joined in protest marches against the conflict. He sympathized with the views of the demonstrators that Sachs wanted to prosecute. "I was not predisposed to prosecute the Catonsville Nine," Skolnik later said. "I was one of the many Americans who were already convinced that the war was a mistake and doing infinitely more harm than good."[45]

Sachs listened patiently as Skolnik explained—with great fervor—why his ideological leanings would make it difficult for him to work on the Catonsville case. The U.S. attorney then said that he wanted Skolnik to work with Murphy precisely *because* of his sympathies.

Sachs recognized that Murphy was, in Skolnik's words, "a down-the-line, law-and-order kind of guy" who would not be likely to adopt a flexible, pragmatic approach to dealing with the defendants and the issues they were sure to raise at trial. (Murphy proceeded under the "rather naïve notion that the case should be tried as a violation of statute," according to Skolnik.) Furthermore, Roszel Thomsen, the federal judge who would hear the case, was unlikely to show much compassion for the Nine. Given the predilections of those two men, and given the abundant evidence that the Catonsville protesters were in fact legally guilty, Sachs feared that the prosecution would prove to be a little too effective; the Nine might get trounced in the trial and then face onerous prison sentences. Sachs thought that, because of his sympathy for the defendants, Skolnik might be able to temper the legal proceedings and ensure that the case was tried in a way that was tolerant.[46]

It took some time for Sachs to convince Skolnik to sign on. The top federal prosecutor in Baltimore was both a friend and a boss, and Skolnik had difficulty rebuffing him. He eventually came around and agreed to help Murphy, but it was an unpleasant experience to which he never completely reconciled himself. "I was always proud of my career as a prosecutor except for the Catonsville Nine case," he said many years later. "It was the only case I participated in that I have complex feelings about."[47]

Skolnik's reservations were no secret. The Nine were well aware of them, and apparently so was everyone else who followed the Catonsville case. Even Maryland governor Spiro Agnew (who would be prosecuted by Skolnik a few years later) heard about his qualms. He later observed, "Skolnik, who delighted in calling himself a radical, was publicly dismayed that he had been forced to prosecute the Catonsville Nine. . . . His heart really hadn't been in that case."[48]

"There Ain't No Justice, Man"

The shadow of war loomed over both the beginning and the end of the life of James McGinnis Darst. He was born late in the day on December 6, 1941. When his father appeared at the hospital the following day, he was wearing his Army uniform; the surprise bombing of Pearl Harbor by Japan meant that his unit had been called to active duty. In the frantic first days of full American involvement in World War II, he wouldn't return to see his newborn son for six months.[1]

During the war, the family followed the elder Darst's unit and hopscotched between military bases. There were stops in Tennessee, Alabama, and Texas. The Darsts settled for a time outside San Antonio at Fort Sam Houston, where they lived among the officers' families in a neat row house. Although the war was being fought with the latest technological advances, life at the base still sometimes had a nineteenth-century feel. The family lacked an electric refrigerator and thus needed to have ice regularly delivered. It was brought to their home by a man who clopped around the base in a horse-drawn wagon.[2]

For Jim and Guy, his brother, the war wasn't a distant affair. They saw troops readying for combat every day, and their father was dispatched to Europe in 1944. (He very nearly didn't make it. The Germans torpedoed his troopship in the English Channel, but he managed to escape unharmed.) And the enemy was nearby: the Army stockaded hundreds of Nazi prisoners of war at Fort Sam Houston. One day, some breathless military policemen appeared at the Darst home and announced that they were searching for a prisoner of war who had escaped the prison. The boys later learned that the manhunt had ended poignantly. A carnival had been operating near the POW camp, and the military police had found the German attempting to relive a bit of his childhood by riding the merry-go-round.[3]

Jim Darst's father returned home from the war in 1946 and took a position in the family business, a coal company. The growing family—Guy and Jim would be joined by three more brothers—settled down for a time in St. Charles, Virginia. The boys experienced the usual sibling rivalries, especially Guy and

Jim, who were only a year apart in age. Guy, more of a bookworm, focused primarily on studying and earning top grades in school. Although he was whip-smart, Jim had less of a scholarly bent. His mother, recalling his zeal for activity, once cracked that he was "born with a hammer in his hand." He applied his considerable energies to everything from sports to music. Jim played a graceful shortstop and took up the saxophone in the high school band. He worked, too, mowing lawns for neighbors, babysitting their kids, and delivering their newspapers.[4]

There weren't many Catholic churches in that part of Appalachia, so it often took some effort for the Darsts to attend Sunday services. Sometimes they drove through the mountains to worship at a church in Harlan, Kentucky, a trip that took over an hour each way. When such a journey wasn't practicable, informal prayer services were held at their home.

Early on, at least, this religious indoctrination did not appear to have much of an impact on Jim. He served as an altar boy, but, as far as his brothers could tell, he wasn't notably devout during his boyhood. According to Guy, Jim "didn't go around preaching," and they rarely engaged in serious discussions of matters of faith.[5]

Thanks to the efforts of his mother, Jim's religious training intensified as he grew older. She mandated Catholic schooling for her boys—no easy feat in coal country, where parochial schools were rare. For a time, Jim and Guy attended a Catholic school in Cumberland, Kentucky. Then, in 1956, Jim moved to Memphis, Tennessee, to live with his grandparents and enroll in a high school run by the Christian Brothers.[6]

Darst's time in Memphis convinced him that his future lay with the Christian Brothers, a religious order that traced its origins back to the educational innovator St. John Baptist de La Salle. Midway through 1959, he entered the order's novitiate in Glencoe, Missouri, near St. Louis, and a short time later he adopted his religious name, Brother David. His teachers there marveled at the spirit he showed both in the classroom and in extracurricular activities.[7]

After the year-long novitiate, Darst briefly attended the Christian Brothers College in Memphis. He then finished his academic training at St. Mary's College in Winona, Minnesota, where he fashioned an enduring friendship with another member of his religious order, Joe Forgue. The two young men operated on the same wavelength; before long, they were finishing each other's sentences. They studied theology and philosophy under Brother Basil O'Leary, who put them through their intellectual paces by having them read the likes of Martin Buber and Bernard Lonergan, the great Jesuit philosopher and theologian. He also introduced them to the work of Catholic novelist Walker Percy.[8]

After graduating summa cum laude from St. Mary's, Darst took a succession of teaching posts at schools operated by the Christian Brothers. In the mid-1960s, he found himself at a new high school in Omaha, Nebraska. Darst's writings from this period reveal that he was searching for a way to move beyond the narrow confines of his religious order and address the acute political, economic, and social challenges facing the world. Some believed, he wrote in 1965, that individuals in religious orders inevitably would be more sheltered Christians. Darst bristled at this conception; he felt that it straitjacketed members of religious orders and kept them from fully understanding God. He insisted that it would be far better for them—and for society as a whole—if they engaged in bold and risky behavior in their communities. He went on to suggest that "our most fundamental contact with God comes not primarily in prayer, but in choice and in *action*."[9]

Such concerns preoccupied Darst as he moved on to his next teaching post at a Christian Brothers high school in Kansas City, Missouri. In the 1966–67 school year, Darst taught three senior religion courses there. All of his students were at or near draft age, and many were poor and African American. With the war in Vietnam intensifying, these young men were preoccupied with the military draft. "Some of these black students were beginning to feel the black militants' opposition to the war, and some of the other students were very much in favor of the war," he explained. "They would get into giant arguments in religion class when I would try to bring up some of the moral values involved." The fervor of these debates startled Darst. "Being exposed to this fierce feeling about the war," he observed, "led me to see that I was kind of out of it and that I really didn't know the history of it and that I was not sure of what was involved."[10]

Darst explained, "I just didn't know anything about [Vietnam] and was kind of indifferent to the whole thing when I started teaching seniors high school religion in the fall of 1966. At this time I found a great many students knowing a great deal more about it than I did, and I felt obliged as their teacher and their moral guide to instruct them in conscientious matters in questions of morality. I felt called upon to study up about it, and as soon as I got into it I began to see and be convinced that [the war] was a terrible tragedy and a terrible wrong."[11]

To better understand what was happening in Vietnam, he read at a feverish pace. Darst devoured Theodore Draper's *Abuse of Power* and several articles by the Catholic philosopher and journalist Michael Novak. Immersing himself in such critiques convinced Darst that something was egregiously wrong with American foreign policy.[12]

Darst next took up a teaching position at Providence High School in St. Louis, which had an overwhelmingly African American student body. (There were maybe two white students in the entire place, Darst thought.) It was hard work, but he relished it. "I find working with the kids to be just amazing," he wrote a friend. "Them and me get along fabulous. I find teaching to be very difficult, but I feel I am doing a worthwhile job. I discover more each day that teaching is an exercise in helping to *show* people things, never to *tell* them, and to question with them some of the basic mysteries that surround us." Darst was inspired by a sense that he was having a real impact on the school's many disadvantaged African American students. He wrote, "I feel that these classes do make a difference in the lives and attitudes and feelings of those boys I teach. I feel that this work is helping kids grow in self-confidence and trust, in communicativeness, in love . . . I really feel that I'm doing as much good as I could in the Peace Corps, or in poverty work, or almost anywhere."[13]

Although he enjoyed teaching, the war still haunted Darst during his time in St. Louis. In the fall of 1967 he resolved to take action and "make some small effort to protest what was happening in Vietnam," as he later put it. Darst had been issued a draft card by the Selective Service System; it noted that, because of his clerical status, he had been exempted from military service. In an effort "to do something by publicly protesting and trying to cry out against the war," he sent the card back to his draft board in Kentucky on several separate occasions. According to a later FBI report, Darst informed the board that he was "protesting the war in Vietnam because of his own religious beliefs."[14]

This wasn't exactly a bold act of defiance on Darst's part; his friends assured him that the board wouldn't hassle a Roman Catholic cleric. "I didn't really expect to be arrested . . . because I thought that they would not mess with me given my clerical status," he later said. Still, it took some nerve for him to make even this tentative protest against the war. Many members of his extended family had served in the military, and his father was a World War II veteran who sat on several draft boards following his service in the Army.[15]

For a time, Darst's protest went unnoticed by federal draft officials. The local draft board wouldn't take action, presumably because it had to deal with more serious violations of the law. Frustrated by his inability to goad a reaction, he disseminated a letter to antiwar activists throughout the country, including Jim Forest of the Catholic Peace Fellowship. Distributed late in 1967, the letter detailed "why I was involving myself in this draft protest," Darst later said, "and telling why I refused to participate" in the Selective Service System (even though it had granted him a deferment).[16]

The letter changed the course of Darst's life. Forest forwarded his copy to Phil Berrigan in Baltimore, and he quickly recognized that the Christian Brother in St. Louis might be recruited for a follow-up to the Baltimore Four draft board raid. "He wrote asking me if I was interested in a little more direct type of thing," Darst later said. "I said yes, I'm very interested."[17]

He was hedging his bets. "There was a kind of qualification in my thinking when I first heard from Phil Berrigan," Darst admitted. "I sort of said to myself: If something happens in this local case, okay maybe I'll stick with this; if they bring charges against me for refusing induction I'll just fight and this publicity will be my part." However, if the draft board in Harlan continued to ignore him, he would explore the opportunity presented by Berrigan.[18]

Whether it was alone or as part of a larger group led by Berrigan, Darst wanted to make a brash public statement against the war. "I thought an outcry, a public outcry in the media might have some chance of being heard by people, especially young people," he said. And Darst was eager to involve his religious order—and his church as a whole—in the antiwar cause. If he became involved in a protest against the war, "it might have some chance of saying something to the powers that be about the churches, because I represented a kind of strain in the Roman Catholic church. I was a cleric and did have this Christian Brother membership. I wanted to involve my little part of the church in this protest; I wanted hopefully to reach people by this, to try to get them to think about this terrible immoral thing which we had going in Vietnam."[19]

Darst feared that his individual draft protest had stalled. FBI agents visited him in St. Louis, but nothing seemed to come from their questioning. Apparently unable to accomplish much on his own, he decided to join the group being assembled by Berrigan and George Mische for a second draft board demonstration in the Baltimore area.

After the Catonsville protest, Darst publicly explained why he had participated in it. "I have taken part in this action," he wrote in the radical journal *WIN*, "because I am terribly worried about my country and the future of mankind." In what fast became a familiar refrain among the Nine, Darst claimed that he had grown weary of merely discussing the many dire problems afflicting the United States. He had taken action in Catonsville, he wrote, because "something [had to] be done to stop the storm, to shake up this system of ours so that it has the chance to radically rearrange its values." He hoped that the Catonsville protest would be just one of many "searching actions designed to confront the whole machinery, all up and down the line, with all its oppression and slow violence."[20]

Darst also described the manner in which the Catonsville Nine viewed the law and its purpose. There was a distinction, he stressed, between "the spirit of the law, which seeks to protect and enhance the dignity of personal human beings, and the letter of the law, which says that property must not be abused." The Nine obviously had violated the letter of federal law in Catonsville; they never seriously argued otherwise. But Darst maintained that they had done so to uphold the spirit of the law. Offering a telling preview of the Nine's trial strategy, he wrote in a letter to the *National Catholic Reporter* that when their case was heard in federal court that fall, they would have "faith that our jury will not be just technical and literal in their understanding of law but [also] will count our having cried out against injustice to be as important as the violation of property we incurred in making the cry."[21]

Darst's participation in the Catonsville foray breathed new life into his individual protest against the draft. The widespread publicity generated by the Maryland demonstration prompted federal officials in St. Louis to secure a grand jury indictment of the Christian Brother for his repeated efforts to return his draft card to the board in Kentucky. He now would face some consequences for his individual protest against the draft.[22]

Two FBI agents appeared at Providence High School on June 6, 1968, after he had posted bail in Baltimore and returned to St. Louis. Darst asked if he could surrender to federal officials after the school day had ended; he wanted to administer three final exams before turning himself in. Worried that he might flee, the agents rejected Darst's request and immediately took him into custody. There was one bright spot, though. "I was happy to note that they didn't handcuff me, as they did so often in Baltimore and Catonsville," he noted . "I felt that handcuff business to be terribly degrading."[23]

As the agents hauled Darst off to the federal courthouse in St. Louis, his thoughts turned to four African American boys who lived near his apartment. The youngsters had fallen on hard times: both of their parents had died, and they lived in abject poverty. Desperate for attention and compassion, they spent several hours every day in the apartment shared by Darst and a few of his fellow Christian Brothers. "I know that something special has grown up between them and I; I know I represent a very important possibility of growth in the lives of these four boys," he wrote. "I feel needed by them in a way that I do not often feel needed." It made him heartsick to think that going to jail—for either his individual draft board protest or the Catonsville raid—would mean he couldn't be there for the boys. Yet he believed that they would benefit from his protests. "It is because I hope to make the future just a little bit safer for my four buddies who are always hanging around," he wrote, "that I must oppose this war in every possible way, even if it means going to jail."[24]

As he was being processed, Darst fell into a conversation with one of his FBI escorts. It turned out that the man was a Catholic—the FBI apparently teemed with them—who seemed to care about issues of social justice. The agent had spent some time in the Deep South, and he had been appalled by how routinely African Americans were mistreated there. The two men amicably shared their views on racism and discussed the tenuous plight of the Catholic school system. As the conversation progressed, the Christian Brother felt a genuine affinity for the man helping to keep him in custody. "He actually seemed sympathetic, this agent did," Darst recalled. When they parted ways, the agent offered Darst a firm handshake and wished him luck.[25]

Not all of Darst's interactions with the FBI were so pleasant. Although he had been taken into custody for having allegedly refused induction, one agent seemed eager to collect information about his actions in Catonsville. Perhaps hoping that Darst would implicate others in the case, the FBI agent doggedly quizzed him about when and how he had traveled to the Baltimore area. "Did you fly out there?" the agent asked. Darst acknowledged that he had flown but then cut off the conversation, saying that the relevant information would come out at trial. However, the discussion about travel got him daydreaming about journeying to Maryland to meet with the Berrigans and attorney William Kunstler. "I kept thinking and wondering how long it would take me to get there on Lake Central Airlines, using my clergy pass," he later wrote, "and in two offices I kept looking at maps of the United States, trying to figure out how Lake Central would go to the East Coast."[26]

There would be no trips to Baltimore in Darst's immediate future. He wound up before an unsympathetic federal magistrate who informed his attorney that what the Christian Brother had done in Catonsville was a national disgrace. It thus came as no surprise when the magistrate required him to post a sizable bail. Until it could be raised, Darst had to spend a few days in St. Louis's notorious city jail.[27]

The jail was overcrowded and unsanitary, and Darst found the conditions deplorable. The facility got so hot that the iron bars on the cells became warm to the touch. Darst often heard prisoners complain, "Man, don't no wind ever blow in this jail." He couldn't disagree: writing about it later, he observed that "sometimes it seemed nothing could stop our sweltering."[28]

Darst noted his fellow inmates' cynical attitudes toward the criminal justice system. African American prisoners in particular exhibited a "total distrust of the law and the courts," he remarked. "No matter what they had done, and some of them had done wrong and knew it, they were just convinced that the law would not deal with them in the same way it would with a middle-class white man."[29]

Darst became close with many African American inmates in the jail. "The black men in jail had a great respect for the Catholic clergy, and this kinda made me proud of the Church for a change," he later wrote. "They took pretty good care of me, and we had many great laughs at all sorts of funny, human things." Darst toyed with the idea of fasting during his stay behind bars, as he had done a month earlier after the Catonsville protest, but his new friends made it difficult: he could not resist when someone offered him a fried pie (a dessert pastry) or an orange drink. The men shared these treats with Darst because they felt that he, too, had been victimized by the American criminal justice system. They all sensed the truth of a lament that frequently echoed through the jail: "There ain't no justice, man."[30]

Darst was slated to go on trial on August 12, 1968, in federal district court in St. Louis. As that date approached, he received a show of support from some of his codefendants in the Catonsville case. A group of Catholic clergy and laypeople called the Christian Experiment—it was devoted to promoting social justice causes through the church—invited Dan Berrigan to St. Louis to celebrate a Mass for Darst.

The organization struggled, however, to find a location for the service. "The general objection," the *National Catholic Reporter* noted, "was that the Mass would be used for a partisan cause."[31] Among the institutions that rebuffed Berrigan were Webster College, St. Louis University, and St. Francis Xavier Church. The snubs from St. Louis University and St. Francis Xavier rankled Berrigan because both were operated by his own religious order, the Jesuits. They were "the latest in a long chain of incidents" that had convinced him that the order "has a preference for silence over courageous speech," he told a reporter.[32]

Berrigan wound up speaking on behalf of his fellow Catholic at, of all places, a Presbyterian house of worship—Berea Church, a predominantly African American congregation that had taken a leading role in civil rights causes in the St. Louis area. There were many of Berrigan's fellow Jesuits among the crowd of roughly four hundred, and he addressed them warmly in his remarks. The order's reluctance to embrace him on his trip to St. Louis made many Jesuits wonder whether they could remain in the order, Berrigan said. He had his own share of doubts, but they related primarily to the men at the top of the Jesuit hierarchy. "If I remain [in the order]," Berrigan said, "it is because of the Jesuits who are here tonight."[33]

Darst's legal horizons soon brightened. Four days before his trial was scheduled to begin, federal prosecutor Vern Riddle announced that he was dropping the charges against him. (These had included a claim that he had failed to report for induction.) Riddle didn't say as much, but the reason was obvious: the Christian Brother clearly was exempt from military service because of his status as a clergyman, and prosecuting him for the relatively minor offense of returning his draft card was unlikely to garner the federal government much praise.

This favorable denouement did not satisfy Darst and his supporters, who had hoped to turn his trial into a public forum on the draft and the war in Vietnam. At the time at which the trial had been scheduled, his backers packed the courtroom and sat silently through another trial. "Where's the trial?" one demanded afterward. "Why are they [the federal government] afraid to face the issue?"[34]

Throughout the summer of 1968, Darst and his advocates were asking the same kinds of questions about the Catholic Church, which seemed to be ignoring such crucial matters as poverty, racism, and war. To draw attention to this ongoing silence, Darst led a demonstration at the St. Louis Cathedral on Sunday, August 11. After several hundred protesters marched to the Cathedral, Darst and a small group of supporters—among them his Catonsville codefendants George Mische and Mary Moylan—filed inside and disrupted the 10:30 A.M. Mass. Darst interrupted the celebrant as he was about to read a letter from Archbishop John Carberry that urged Catholics to support the pope's adamant stance against contraception. The Christian Brother told the startled gathering that the war in Vietnam was a far more significant matter than the Church's position on birth control. He requested that the Mass be offered in the name of world peace and in honor of "our Vietnam brothers."[35] Darst and a small group of protesters returned to the Cathedral on August 25 and disrupted a Mass being celebrated by Archbishop Carberry.[36]

In the late 1960s Darst did not devote all of his attention to resisting the war in Vietnam or combating racism at home. He also thought about society's rapidly evolving attitudes toward sexuality. As a member of a religious order, Darst presumably was celibate himself, and his brothers chuckled over the idea that he would purport to offer any kind of informed perspective on matters of sexual intimacy. (Guy Darst laughed off Brother David's efforts in this realm, questioning the credibility of "advice from a virgin.") Nonetheless, Darst authored some provocative writings on sex that would further distance him from the social and political conservatives in his church.[37]

Darst published in the journal *Pastoral Psychology* an article about the place in society of extramarital sex—not a subject typically addressed in print by a member of a Catholic religious order. Darst's conclusions made his article all the more incendiary. He disputed the idea that sexual intercourse outside of marriage was "irresponsible, inauthentic, and self-deceiving." He resisted such ideas because he doubted that "unchanging absolutes of sexuality [are] revealed to us anywhere," including the Bible. Instead, all expressions of sexuality had to be judged in their modern social and cultural contexts.[38]

At the urging of the Catholic theologian Gregory Baum, Darst—collaborating with Joe Forgue, his longtime friend—extended these arguments on sexuality in an article originally published in the *Ecumenist*, a journal devoted to theology and culture. Readers who muddled through the airy passages of the article discovered that Darst and Forgue were making some daring suggestions about what was acceptable sexual behavior. These seemed to go beyond countenancing extramarital sexual relations between men and women. They wrote, for instance, that "there is more sameness than difference in the love between two men and the love between a man and a woman." This oblique passage was as close as Darst and Forgue came to explicitly referencing homosexuality. But anyone willing to read between the lines could reasonably conclude that the authors were open to the idea that homosexuality wasn't necessarily an unacceptable form of sexual expression for Christians.[39]

These articles attracted relatively little notice when they originally appeared in print. However, copies eventually found their way to Darst's superiors in the Christian Brothers order, and these conservative men responded with predictable consternation. The resulting tensions made Darst feel that he was being relegated to the fringes of his own religious community.

While Darst immersed himself in a variety of activities in the summer of 1968, his Catonsville codefendants kept themselves busy as well. The specter of their upcoming trial did not seem to dampen the spirits of Dan Berrigan. Before he traveled to St. Louis to show his support for Darst, Berrigan was visited at the Cornell campus in Ithaca by Jim Forest and his friend Linda Henry. When they reached the priest's apartment, they found the door open. Berrigan, however, was not home. After they had tracked him down, he explained that he never locked his door. "But won't someone steal your things?" Forest asked. "If they do that," Berrigan said with a grin, "I suppose they need them." Throughout their visit to Cornell, Forest and Henry found Berrigan in high spirits. He clearly had been invigorated by the Catonsville protest and the subsequent preparations for the activists' trial. While the priest prepared dinner and drinks for his two guests, he said that he had been suffering from an ulcer before the draft board raid. It had vanished shortly afterward—a sure sign that he had come to terms with joining his brother Phil in Catonsville. "I am going to send the doctor bills to the White House," he joked. "It was their ulcer, not mine."[40]

That summer, Berrigan and Forest helped set in motion another spectacular protest against the military draft. The two men traveled together to Milwaukee, Wisconsin, to speak to a large gathering of teaching nuns. They stayed at the Catholic Worker house in the city, Casa Maria, and spent a good deal of time talking with its founders, Mike and Nettie Cullen, and some other Catholic activists. It was clear to Forest that Berrigan hoped there would be another antiwar protest along the lines of the Baltimore Four and Catonsville Nine draft board raids. Logistically, Milwaukee seemed to provide an ideal target for such an antidraft action. Forest later said that "there were nine draft boards for the whole city on one floor of one office building downtown. It would be a chance to take out the files of all the city draft boards. It might actually stop the draft in one American city." The idea of mounting such an attack captivated Mike Cullen, who had been deeply affected by the Catonsville demonstration. Committed to taking a stand against the war, he felt that he had no choice but to participate in a similar act of protest. "The appeal, the invitation to me, personally, was compelling, demanding. I had to do something. I had to stand with these men," he later said. Berrigan, encouraging Cullen, said that he should contact James Harney, who was then curate of a church in Massachusetts.[41]

The Milwaukee scheme gelled with the help of George Mische, who roamed the country that summer in hopes of finding activists who would build on the momentum generated by the Catonsville protest. (With their trial date approaching, the Nine had been ordered not to travel without first asking permission from the federal judge presiding over their case, but Mische routinely ignored those strictures.) He made contact with Mike Cullen and provided both logistical support and motivation. "It amazed me," Cullen remarked, "how the word was getting around."[42]

Forest received a similar boost from Mische. When he journeyed to Washington to see Dorothy Day receive an award from the Catholic Liturgical Conference, he stayed with Mische at 1620 S Street. In her remarks, Day praised the Catonsville protest, asserting that it was fundamentally an act of prayer. Her words touched Forest. "Dorothy spoke very movingly of what [Catonsville] was about," he later said. "I felt very refreshed by what Dorothy had to say and challenged by it." Forest thus was primed when Mische approached him about participating in a draft board protest.

"Well, Jim," he asked, "are you going to be part of the next action?"

Surprising himself, Forest answered, "Yes."[43]

With the direct help of the Catonsville Nine, the Milwaukee plot continued to come together. Cullen, Harney, and Forest reached out to Robert Cunnane and Anthony Mullaney, and they expressed interest in participating. Cunnane was spurred by the examples set by Phil Berrigan and Tom Lewis, who twice had acted to impede the draft. "They moved us into a kind of creative activism in which people could figure new kinds of actions," he later said.[44]

To help bring the proposed draft board raid into sharper focus, several dozen activists, many of them priests and nuns, met in New Jersey to discuss its philosophical and religious underpinnings. Mische and Dan Berrigan played central roles in the retreat. Mike Cullen later said that Mische "did a lot of political analysis and no one could doubt his ability and qualifications." Berrigan invoked the prophet Jeremiah. "The whole idea of Jeremiah made it imperative to speak the truth, to confront evil," Cullen recalled. "The obligation of the Christian to say no to Caesar has not lessened. Murder and injustice are being perpetuated by Caesar, committed in Caesar's name."[45]

Fourteen people agreed to participate in a massive raid on Milwaukee's draft boards, which were centrally located downtown in the Brumder Building. Their number included Cullen, Harney, Forest, and Basil O'Leary, the Christian Brother who had mentored Darst at St. Mary's College in Minnesota. The size of their action—which they carried out on September 24, 1968—dwarfed the Catonsville protest. The group seized and then burned approximately ten thousand Selective Service records. One of the short-term goals of the Catonsville Nine—seeing their witness repeated and amplified—thus was realized just a few weeks before they went on trial in federal court.[46]

Tom Lewis was in the federal penitentiary in Lewisburg, Pennsylvania, when he learned of the handiwork of the Milwaukee Fourteen. He recognized that, reaffirming the acts of the Catonsville Nine, they had done something "really incredibly important" in terms of protesting the war. Although the Milwaukee protest didn't gain the notoriety of the Catonsville demonstration, Lewis concluded that "in a lot of ways it was much more important, in the sense of the amount of people [involved], who the people were, people really coming together and saying, 'Let's do something about the war,' and then doing it."[47]

"Come to Agnew Country"

While the Catonsville Nine readied for their trial, a group of dedicated supporters pieced together plans to make the proceedings—slated to begin early in October 1968—a galvanizing event for antiwar and social justice activists. Over the summer and early fall of that year they formulated a wide-ranging effort that would complement the courtroom activity in Baltimore with a variety of marches, rallies, and speeches. These events were designed to energize opponents of the war and draw public and media attention to their cause.[1]

The first group to tackle this task was the Catonsville Nine Defense Committee, a group headed by Paul Mayer, a Benedictine monk with myriad connections among antiwar Catholics. Mayer was among those who believed that traditional means of protest had exhausted their potential and that "something more radical and something more direct had to be done" to halt the war, as he informed an audience in Milwaukee in 1969. "Marching and protesting are not only not effective, they are a palliative to keep the people in the resistance happy and quiet." It heartened him to see a new direction being taken—one that highlighted the plight of poor and disenfranchised people across the globe. "It's much more than a protest against the war," Mayer explained of the Catonsville demonstration. "It's a protest against the whole American way of life or American way of death—seeing the connection between what we are doing in Vietnam and what we are doing to black people in our own country, what we are doing to poor people in Latin American and all over the world."[2]

Funded by erratic contributions and staffed by volunteers, the defense committee was a low-budget affair from the start. Mayer observed that it was operated primitively and "done out of a shoebox." When donations started trickling in, he scraped together enough money to hire some secretarial help to assist in fielding telephone calls and sorting through the mail. Jim Forest (of the Catholic Peace Fellowship and the Fellowship of Reconciliation) and a friend of both Dan and Phil Berrigan's named John Peter Grady also pitched in.[3]

Despite its lack of funds and limited manpower, the defense committee did a capable job of publicizing the upcoming trial in Baltimore. Perhaps its most prominent efforts were full-page ads published in liberal Catholic publications like the *National Catholic Reporter* and *Commonweal.* Bearing the headline "A Call to Men of Conscience," these ads described who the Nine were, what they had done in Catonsville, and why they had been motivated to act. The defense committee quoted the Nine's plea for contributions that would help to provide adequate legal representation and, in a broader sense, put the war itself on trial. "We wish to indict the war, not defend ourselves or renounce our action," they indicated. "We want to be able to bring world-respected experts to Baltimore to testify, and we want to be able to carry on an educational campaign in regard to the action."[4]

Several radicals took it upon themselves to complement the fundraising efforts of the defense committee. The documentary filmmaker Emile de Antonio eagerly raised money for the Nine, sending out dozens of letters to colleagues and friends in which he praised the accused activists for standing up for peace and social justice. Antonio—whose 1968 antiwar film *In the Year of the Pig* featured Dan Berrigan—solicited money from these contacts "not in the name of charity but for a revolution which will change the values that have polluted our heads and rivers." In a characteristically defiant move, the filmmaker sent a copy of his fund-raising missive to FBI Director J. Edgar Hoover.[5]

There was a good chance that Hoover would have received a copy of Antonio's letter anyway. Throughout the summer and fall of 1968, the FBI kept a close eye on the evolving efforts of the Catonsville Nine's many supporters. Internal bureau documents reveal that this was an intensive and widespread surveillance endeavor involving FBI agents throughout the country.

The FBI carefully tracked individuals who were responding to the defense committee's summons to Baltimore. A typical memo about following individuals who might be drawn to trial-related activities—it was dispatched to bureau offices in more than twenty major cities—warned that there was a "possibility [of a] large number of participants from out of state" coming to Baltimore for protests related to the trial. "All offices immediately contact all logical sources and informants and alert them to this proposed activity," it instructed. "Conduct necessary investigation to identify individuals and groups planning to participate." FBI agents were to make the surveillance of supporters of the Nine a top priority. "Afford this matter continuous investigation," the memo stated.[6]

And investigate they did. From Norfolk, Virginia, to Los Angeles, FBI agents kept track of activists who might be headed to Baltimore. Because of Dan Berrigan's ties there, the FBI paid close attention to the movements of student activists at Cornell. After interviewing a variety of unnamed sources, agents based in nearby Albany, New York, reported that several busloads of Cornell students planned to travel to Maryland for the trial. The Big Red contingent would not be making the trek alone: agents learned that other groups of activists would be coming to Baltimore from Seattle (via a chartered plane) and most of the major cities along the Eastern Seaboard.[7]

As the trial date drew closer, the FBI kept tabs on antiwar activists living as far away from Baltimore as Southern California. Agents in Los Angeles clipped stories on the Nine from local alternative newspapers and monitored the activities of the Southern California chapter of the activist organization Women Strike for Peace. The bureau learned that the local members of the group had discussed the Catonsville case in one of their regular meetings and that they were exploring the possibility of contributing financially to the defense committee through their organization's Washington, D.C., office.[8]

While the FBI kept tabs on their activities, backers of the Nine stepped up their efforts to augment the defense fund and organize protests. A few weeks before the trial was slated to begin, the Baltimore Defense Committee (BDC) was organized as a successor organization to the Interfaith Peace Mission in Baltimore, which had brought together many peace activists in the area (including Phil Berrigan and Tom Lewis). Headed by Dean Pappas and Grenville Whitman (both of whom had helped the Nine bring off the draft board raid), the BDC proved to be the fulcrum of organizational activity on the ground in Baltimore during the trial.[9]

From its offices on Maryland Avenue, the BDC issued a national call for supporters of the Catonsville Nine to converge on Baltimore. By expressing solidarity and demanding freedom for the accused while they stood trial, the BDC would catalyze what it called "the most complicated and militant act of civil disobedience in recent memory." The group promised to work with local peace activists and church groups to house and provide an evening meal for all those who were eager to participate in what promised to be an aggressive confrontation with local, state, and federal authorities. Organizers blended pragmatism with revolutionary idealism: they asked in one appeal, "If you can, we urge you to bring a sleeping bag to help us out."[10]

The BDC laid out its aims in a bold manifesto. Its main goal was highlighting the message of the Nine, who had endeavored to call attention to the great problems of the era. Although the war in Vietnam loomed largest, these matters were as diverse as they were stubborn. "War, racism, poverty—these are the issues which compelled nine Americans to 'napalm' about [400] draft files," the manifesto declared. "These are the issues which confront all of us today, while the trial of the Nine is impending and which will surely confront us after the Nine have been duly processed in the courts."[11]

The BDC believed that the outcome of that legal process was foreordained: the Catonsville Nine were going to be found legally guilty. The organization's propaganda thus never suggested that activists should converge on Baltimore in the hope of watching the Nine emerge with a clear-cut legal victory. Their trial would be significant all the same because, as one BDC press release put it, "it is a way to make public the illegality of the Vietnam war and the danger of American economic and military expansion abroad."[12]

The BDC's primary goal was to underscore the message of the Catonsville Nine and foster an activist community that would build upon the momentum generated by the trial. But its call made clear that it had broader aims as well. One of these was to embarrass the Republican presidential ticket, which featured Maryland's combative governor, Spiro Agnew, in the vice presidential slot. The 1968 election would take place shortly after the Baltimore trial, and activists hoped that they could influence its outcome by shaming Agnew on his home turf.

Ironically, Agnew, like the Catonsville protest, was a product of suburban Baltimore. His unlikely climb to national prominence began in Baltimore County, the entity that rings the city like a wrench around a nut. Democrats dominated the county, but a rift among them allowed Agnew to win election as county executive in 1962. He followed that surprise victory with an even more startling one, winning the governorship in 1966.[13]

Although he ran as a moderate, Agnew eventually tacked to the right and earned the enmity of liberals. The strident law-and-order speeches he delivered in the wake of the riots that engulfed Baltimore in the spring of 1968 helped put Agnew on the national political map. His stature among conservatives rose when he began taking swipes at antiwar activists. In one address, Agnew excoriated "the circuit-riding, Hanoi visiting type of leader" of the antiwar movement—an obvious reference to Dan Berrigan, who had just returned from his trip to North Vietnam with Howard Zinn.[14]

Agnew's star rose so quickly that Richard Nixon selected him for the second slot on the Republican ticket in 1968. For supporters of the Catonsville Nine, his ascendance—grounded in a malevolent blend of fear-mongering and opportunism—seemed to symbolize everything that was wrong with American politics, and they resolved to use the platform provided by the trial to call attention to Agnew's shortcomings.[15]

So the BDC invited backers of the Catonsville Nine to "Come to Agnew Country" for the trial. To expose the many foibles of "our own Marie Antoinette," protest organizers made targeting the Maryland governor one of their main objectives. "He is no friend of the black man. He is no friend of the poor man," one press release announced. "He speaks the language of sanctimonious suburbia, with little or no knowledge of the cities. His record as Governor speaks for itself, abysmally." His record on race relations was so dismal, the BDC asserted, that his name routinely was used as an epithet in Baltimore's black homes. As it assessed Agnew's suitability for the post of vice president, the nation needed to learn that his own state "is not as placid as [he] would like to believe."[16]

The Catonsville Nine also got into the act, issuing their own invitations to the trial. According to one account, Dan Berrigan wanted the proceedings to be "a morality play, a celebration, [and] a massive teach-in." To drum up interest, he sent out a letter inviting opponents of the war to "come to Baltimore for an event that will blow your minds and open your hearts." Berrigan being Berrigan, he couldn't resist a tongue-in-cheek prediction about how the trial would play out and how activists might feel connected to it. He promised pilgrims to Baltimore that the defense would defend them—and that the prosecution would prosecute them.[17]

Berrigan made a special effort to recruit prominent peace and social justice activists to Baltimore for the trial. In a letter that was sent to the likes of Dorothy Day and Rabbi Abraham Joshua Heschel, he wrote of the Nine's hope "that a certain number of 'visible' people would want to have some part in the ritual" of the trial. This would include evening sessions focusing on the many meaningful topics that were sure to be slighted in the courtroom. In that morally sterile space, "issues like the constitutionality or morality of the war, or the rights of conscience in times of public crisis, will be strenuously ignored," he wrote. "For this reason, we are trying to create, in the course of the trial itself, another forum in which the truth can raise its voice."[18]

To Berrigan's everlasting disappointment, Thomas Merton—whose teachings and counsel had influenced all of the Nine—demurred. "Impossible to get to trial," the Trappist explained in a letter; he would be traveling abroad. The best he could do was to wish the defendants luck.[19]

As they beckoned activists to Baltimore, the Nine and their allies in the BDC were determined to avoid a repeat of the trial of the Boston Five, which had unfolded earlier in 1968. Charged with conspiracy to encourage resistance to the draft, the defendants—led by pediatrician Benjamin Spock and Yale chaplain William Sloane Coffin—had approached their trial in a conventional manner, mounting an effective but narrow legal defense. To the chagrin of many antiwar activists, their attorneys had discouraged the peace movement from staging large-scale protests in conjunction with the trial. For many critics of the war, it seemed that an opportunity had been missed; the Boston Five had blown a chance to put the war on trial. The Catonsville Nine and their supporters resolved not to make the same mistake. They would, as the writer Francine du Plessix Gray described it, "take their case to the people with infinitely more drama and turmoil than had the Boston Five."[20]

This more confrontational approach appealed to many peace and social justice activists, and hundreds of people responded to the invitations issued by the BDC. As the trial date approached, organizers in Baltimore reported that they had received more than five hundred requests from out-of-towners for lodging. Hundreds more activists planned to make their own arrangements and converge on the city for protest activities related to the trial. As many as twenty states would be represented.

They hailed from a variety of backgrounds. Not surprisingly, hordes of students came, including a large contingent from Cornell. Many observers noted the sprinkling of priests and nuns in the crowds of protesters that materialized during the trial. (It was widely believed that some of the men in clerical garb actually were FBI agents in disguise.) And there were peace activists like Laurie Dougherty, the secretary of the Catonsville Nine Defense Committee in New York. Impressed by the eagerness of so many to study and celebrate life, she praised the thousands who participated with both "their minds and hearts" in the protest activities related to the trial.[21]

As these activists poured into Baltimore in early October, BDC organizers worked to minimize the chances that protests related to the trial would backfire on the antiwar movement. To that end, Bill O'Connor, Dean Pappas, and Grenville Whitman met with Stephen Sachs, the federal prosecutor, to iron out in advance some ground rules for where and how protests could be staged in downtown Baltimore. Publicly and privately, the BDC pledged to keep its protest activities outside the space where the Nine would be tried. ("We're not going to mess around [in] the courtroom," Whitman told the *Baltimore Sun*.) In discussions with Sachs, they tried to "work out what we could do, and could not do" in terms of staging demonstrations outside the courthouse, according to O'Connor. Sachs later said that he had not reached a formal deal with the BDC organizers about the scope of their protests. But he announced that he was pleased to learn that supporters of the Nine apparently had no inclination "to disrupt the normal functions of the courthouse."[22]

Despite these hopeful words, the city girded for the worst. The Baltimore Police Department announced that its officers would be working twelve-hour shifts during the week of the trial. (The change would allow them to deploy about 500 officers at a time, roughly doubling the strength of the force.) Some politicians in the city urged the police to use their beefed-up presence to keep the antiwar activists in line. Referring to the disorders that had disrupted the city earlier in the year, one conservative city councilman issued a statement calling on police to use the "necessary force ... to avoid the holocaust of last spring's riots."[23]

Through a series of moves before the trial, local, state, and federal authorities signaled their intention to keep the protesters—and the Catonsville Nine themselves—in check. O'Connor heard from WBAL-TV's Patrick McGrath that the FBI was looking for him. When he finally made contact with federal officials, he learned that he was being charged with misprision of a felony for having concealed and failed to report a crime—namely, the raid on the Catonsville draft board. Before being charged with having committed it, O'Connor never had heard of misprision of a felony, and he quickly determined that the obscure charge was a ruse designed to limit his activities during the trial of the Nine. "I think they charged me," he later said, "to keep me off the streets." The charges eventually were dropped, but they had the desired effect in the short term: O'Connor was unable to fully lend his organizational acumen to the BDC during the week of the trial.[24]

All of the Nine also faced a new round of criminal charges for their roles in the looting of the Catonsville draft board. On Friday, October 4, just three days before their trial was set to begin in federal court, the state's attorney for Baltimore County announced that he intended to follow through with his earlier threat and charge the Nine with having committed several state crimes, including robbery, larceny, destruction of property, and sabotage.

The state's move outraged attorney Harold Buchman, one of the members of the legal team defending the Nine. He had known all along about the possibility that the activists would face state charges, but it had been his understanding that they would be pursued only after the conclusion of the federal trial. Charging them just days before the federal proceedings were set to begin seemed calculated to disrupt their defense; seven of the nine defendants would have to be taken into custody, processed in the county jail, and then set free on bail. (Lewis and Phil Berrigan, serving their sentences for the Baltimore Four protest, already were in the county lockup, having been temporarily transferred there for the duration of the Catonsville trial from federal correctional facilities in Pennsylvania.) Buchman sputtered that putting them through such an ordeal would pose a "serious and unnecessary detriment to trial preparation and the conduct of their defense."[25]

The county police caught up with Dan Berrigan that Friday when he delivered a speech on the campus of Towson State College. Berrigan's appearance at Towson concerned federal and state law enforcement because Governor Agnew, in a rare Baltimore-area appearance during the 1968 campaign, was due to speak there a week later, and it was suspected that the Jesuit's talk might embolden activists on the campus to disrupt the governor's visit and thereby embarrass the Nixon campaign. While undercover police agents roamed the campus, Berrigan addressed a group of about 250 students and supporters, including a number of priests and nuns. He announced that he knew how the upcoming trial would turn out. "The outcome of next week is already written," he said. "A less poetic soul might say that it has already been written in the Justice Department."[26]

After his talk, Berrigan fielded questions from the audience. Some in attendance seemed more concerned with the priest's idiosyncratic wardrobe than with his radical politics. Berrigan was wearing a black turtleneck sweater that made him look like, in journalist Garry Wills's wry estimation, "an ecclesiastical U-boat commander."

"Why aren't you obliged to wear a Roman collar?" someone asked.

"By whom?" Berrigan asked. "By Jesus Christ?"[27]

The talk turned to politics, and Berrigan was asked what students could do to protest the war. He urged them to follow the example of the Nine and do something more dramatic than simply burn their draft cards. "Maybe someone who has worked himself up to burn a draft card ought to go out and burn draft files," the priest said. "If you're going to jail, you might as well do something big."[28]

After he finished speaking, three county policemen approached Berrigan and served him with a bench warrant for the state charges. He made no attempt to escape, but the crowd grew boisterous when police officers placed the Jesuit in a squad car. Several dozen students surrounded the vehicle, linked their arms to prevent it from moving, and sang protest songs. The stalemate ended quietly when police reinforcements arrived on the scene.[29]

When word of Dan Berrigan's arrest spread, small groups of protesters converged on the county jail in Towson, which now held three of the Nine. At midnight on Friday, a group of two dozen activists held a candlelight vigil outside the facility. The protesters included a contingent of priests and seminarians from the nearby Woodstock seminary. They were joined by a group of laymen and clergy from a community resource center for low-income families located in Baltimore's Reservoir Hill neighborhood. Protests at the county jail continued the following day, with a group of about forty demonstrators—including a few priests and nuns—marching to the facility and demanding a visit with Lewis and the Berrigans.[30]

The activities at the county jail served as a kind of warm-up for the main round of trial-related protests. These began in earnest on Sunday, October 6, the day before the trial started. During the day, supporters of the Nine distributed leaflets at almost two dozen churches in the city and county, including houses of worship in Towson and Catonsville. Late in the afternoon, a group of about eighty protesters marched in support of the Nine in front of the Basilica of the Assumption, Baltimore's landmark cathedral. They hoisted aloft signs reading "U.S. POLICY KILLS PEOPLE TO MAKE MONEY," "HUMAN RIGHTS OR PROPERTY RIGHTS," and "END THE WAR NOW."[31]

Support for the war ran deep in blue-collar cities like Baltimore, and not everyone was eager to march in solidarity with the Nine. Indeed, counterdemonstrators shadowed antiwar activists throughout the week. They were present that Sunday during the demonstration at the Basilica of the Assumption. Led by a member of Young Americans for Freedom, the conservative youth organization, a group of counterdemonstrators stationed themselves across Cathedral Street from the pro-Nine rally. As they marched in front of the Enoch Pratt Free Library, they angrily shredded a cardboard replica of the flag of the Viet Cong and chanted slogans aimed at expressing their displeasure with the "communist forces" working at home and abroad to subvert American interests. The young conservatives also delivered their own verdict on the upcoming trial, at one point intoning "guilty, guilty, guilty" in unison. A few went even further and urged authorities to "hang the Catonsville Nine."

Even for this relatively modest affair, local and federal law enforcement were out in force. A group of about thirty policemen—some of them clad in riot gear—stood nearby in case protesters did anything more violent than hurl insults at one another. FBI agents also observed the dueling demonstrations. Their subsequent reports focused as much on the counterdemonstrators as they did on the supporters of the Nine. Of particular concern to federal agents was the presence of a man known to have connections with the Ku Klux Klan and the ultraconservative National States Rights Party (NSRP), which had a tumultuous history in the city.[32]

As the trial of the Catonsville Nine loomed, federal and state law enforcement authorities felt that they had to keep close watch over the NSRP. On

October 7, the first day of the trial, Alabama governor George Wallace, who was making a third-party bid for the presidency, was scheduled to hold a campaign rally at the city's civic center. Baltimore thus would be teeming with peace activists and their bitterest political and social enemies: conservatives— some of them surely associated with the NSRP—who backed the segregationist Wallace and vehemently supported America's military presence in Vietnam. The FBI closely monitored this potentially explosive collision of politically minded activists. It followed the NSRP and shared its intelligence with a variety of law enforcement agencies, including the Secret Service and military intelligence units.

After the demonstration at the Basilica of the Assumption came the first in a series of evening rallies at the hall of St. Ignatius Church on Calvert Street. The BDC had prevailed upon Father J. William Michelman, the Jesuit pastor of the church, to make the spacious facility available for protest activities throughout the week. Explaining why he had extended the offer, Michelman described it as a simple act of "Christian charity and hospitality." It would be wrong, he said, "to deny the use of the hall to any group who made a reasonable request and who wish to give expression to assent or dissent to the critical debatable issue of our times," the war in Vietnam.[33]

Michelman's move was not without consequences for St. Ignatius. The pastoral council resigned in protest, and many parishioners were so offended by having their church taken over for a week by peace activists that they abandoned the parish. (The turmoil would force Michelman out of the parish in 1969.) But the priest became a hero to many of those who flocked to Baltimore for the trial. At several points throughout the week, the crowd at St. Ignatius chanted, "We love you Father Michelman!"[34]

More than three hundred Jesuits and laymen filled the church at St. Ignatius for the Mass that preceded the rally. The homily was offered by Father Daniel Kilfoyle, who said that they had come together "with an awareness of the moral blindness and political insanity" of the war in Vietnam and ongoing problems related to race and poverty. The Catonsville protest, and the circumstances that had given rise to it, "made us grow up as Christians in the Church because we had looked to our leaders in the Church for leadership . . . and we realize now that leadership and guidance can come even if they don't come from officialdom." The service closed with the singing of "America the Beautiful."[35]

After the Mass ended, about 750 people crowded into the basement of St. Ignatius. With the specter of a new round of arrests now hanging over the Nine, there was some discussion of what should be done to protect Tom Melville and George Mische, who were scheduled to address the throng. It was decided that supporters would form a "human sanctuary" around the two defendants and thereby thwart any attempt by county police to arrest them on state charges.[36]

This possibility seemed likely, given the number of law enforcement officials on hand. Several FBI agents were present for every demonstration organized in connection to the trial, including the Sunday night rally at St. Ignatius. Their efforts to infiltrate the activities of the BDC were the worst-kept secret in Baltimore, in part because the undercover agents were laughably conspicuous. One agent posed as a leader of the militant Black Panthers and boasted that he had under his control dozens of lieutenants who would be willing to support whatever radical activities might be in the offing. He attempted to curry favor with several of the activists who had gathered at St. Ignatius by inviting them to share drinks at a local strip club. But the agent's clumsy act fooled no one. "His black beret," one supporter on the Nine observed, "did not go too well with his solidly plump figure." Another poorly disguised agent attempted to gather intelligence while selling copies of an underground newspaper.[37]

At the Sunday night rally, supporters of the Nine spotted several unmarked police cars parked outside the hall, and more than a few plainclothes policemen conspicuously roamed through the crowd. Also present was General George Gelston, who had commanded the National Guard during the riots that had shaken Baltimore the previous spring.

Before any attempt was made to take Mische or Melville into custody, Whitman laid out the BDC's plan of action for the upcoming week, detailing the protest schedule and explaining how participants should behave. In the interests of delivering a clear and consistent message, they were not to interact directly with the media when they hit the streets, Whitman cautioned. Demonstrations would kick off the following morning with a march from Wyman Park, located near the campus of Johns Hopkins, to an open area near the Post Office and Courthouse Building, where the trial was to be held. (The irony of this particular destination—War Memorial Plaza—was not lost on the crowd; several audience members chuckled when it was mentioned.) Whitman told the crowd that the city had granted them most of the necessary permits for the proposed march but that it had not given authorization for a demonstration on the sidewalk in front of the federal courthouse. He drew approving cries when he proclaimed that protesters would take control of the sidewalk anyway. But Whitman's talk was as conciliatory as it was militant. He tempered his comments by calling for marchers to show some restraint as they paraded through downtown Baltimore. He emphasized that supporters of the Nine should avoid confronting the police and thereby discrediting the cause. "This is not a march against the police. Police are people," he said (to a smattering of boos from the crowd). "If you want to shout something about police, yell, 'More pay for cops.'"[38]

The BDC's emphasis on planning and discipline impressed many in the crowd, including Michael Ketchum, who had come down to Baltimore from the Catholic Worker house in Manhattan. Ketchum believed that Whitman and his colleagues in the BDC did the cause of nonviolent protest a great service by so strongly and consistently warning activists not to engage in confrontations with the police or counterdemonstrators.[39]

Not everyone, however, mustered enthusiasm for the BDC's approach. A Jesuit in the crowd at St. Ignatius took exception to the targeting of Spiro Agnew. He hardly favored the Maryland governor, but he had traveled to Baltimore from New York to show encouragement for Dan Berrigan, not to campaign against the Republican ticket. "I didn't come here to stage a riot or embarrass a candidate," the Jesuit said, "but to support my brother in his time of need."[40]

It pleased the Jesuit that the trial and its principals were prominently featured at the Sunday night rally. Attorney William Kunstler gave a spirited talk in which he previewed the defense's strategy. With a twinkle in his eye, he promised that their approach would be unusual. The Nine would stress the political context for their decision to destroy the draft files in Catonsville, and they would justify it by invoking their right to freedom of conscience. They would not, Kunstler promised, attempt to deny what they had done at Local Board 33. "No defendant here is going to take the position that he did not do what the government says he did," the lawyer explained.[41]

Braving the threat of arrest, two of those defendants, Melville and Mische, appeared at the Sunday night rally as well. Melville did not concern himself with the logistics of protest or the finer points of trial strategizing; his goal was to inspire and energize supporters of the Nine as they prepared for a week of demonstrations. He earned a chorus of cheers when he told those who had crammed into the basement of St. Ignatius that they had to resist the forces of oppression that threatened to undercut democracy throughout the globe. "You have to confront them, you have to confuse them, you have to upset them by acting on conscience," he said. For his part, Mische slammed a wide array of targets, including Lawrence Cardinal Shehan and presidential candidates Richard Nixon and Hubert Humphrey.[42]

Thanks to the crowd, Melville and Mische evaded the police, if only temporarily. When the two men moved to leave the Sunday night rally, a group of about seventy-five supporters formed a human shield and escorted them to a blue Volkswagen Beetle that was waiting outside the hall. Police converged on the vehicle, but it became apparent that it would take a violent struggle to reach the two men and extricate them. Gelston, the National Guard commander, wanted to avoid a confrontation; he signaled that the Beetle should be allowed to leave.[43]

The move enraged a plainclothes cop who felt that authorities had surrendered to a mob. As the vehicle bearing Melville and Mische sped off down St. Paul Street, he launched into a tirade against Gelston. "I never backed off in my life," he sputtered. "I've gone into buildings against armed men—fourteen years in the service, and I never backed off. Well, tomorrow I hand in my resignation."[44]

He needn't have worried about Melville and Mische evading police. Police followed the car and eventually pulled it over. The two men were arrested and held overnight at the Baltimore County Jail in Towson.

While these dramatic events were unfolding, a somewhat disoriented James Pike arrived at Baltimore's Friendship Airport. Critics dismissed the Anglican bishop as an eccentric—a year earlier he had participated in a televised séance designed to put him into contact with his dead son—but he boasted impeccable antiestablishment credentials. Pike had marched with Martin Luther King Jr., and he had been an early critic of the war in Vietnam. Although he had come to Maryland to support the Catonsville Nine, the details of the case were murky to him, and he had to be briefed on his way from the airport to his hotel.

"Aren't two of these people priests?" Pike said to his companion. "We don't put priests in jail in America."

At that point, Pike was told what the Berrigans and their accomplices had done to get jailed. He stiffened when he learned that they had seized and burned draft files.

"I don't think I approve that," he said. "It's illegal."

Pike (who was an attorney) then fired off a series of questions about the legal charges leveled by the federal government at the Nine. As he listened to his companion explain the government's case, the bishop raised several possible legal defenses. He perked up even more when he learned that Kunstler was leading the defense team. Pike admired Kunstler, but he insisted that the famed radical attorney might need some additional help. He would track down Kunstler the following day and offer his services.

"*We'll* get them off. There's no doubt of that," Pike told his companion. "*Imagine* bringing criminal charges against priests!"[45]

14 }

"Do They Believe in God?"

Roszel Cathcart Thomsen always had seemed destined to carve out a formidable career in the law. He didn't merely excel at Boys Latin, an all-boys school in Baltimore; he roared through the curriculum, skipping several grades along the way and graduating at the tender age of fourteen. Then came Johns Hopkins, where Thomsen earned a reputation as a ferocious debater. After graduating Phi Beta Kappa in 1919, he clerked for Morris Ames Soper, the chief judge of the Supreme Bench of Baltimore City, and attended the University of Maryland Law School at night.[1]

Determined to follow Soper's example, Thomsen complemented his devotion to the practice of law with a commitment to public service. He engaged in a wide array of civic and educational causes in Baltimore, serving as president of the Family Welfare Association and heading the board of Goucher College. Before he was appointed to the federal bench, Thomsen also led the city's school board during the tumultuous period in which it oversaw the integration of Baltimore Polytechnic Institute (Poly). The school board's move—which came in 1952, two years before the United States Supreme Court's landmark desegregation ruling in *Brown v. Board of Education*—was widely hailed a milestone for racial progress in the city, and it won acclaim for Thomsen and his colleagues.[2]

But Thomsen was no revolutionary—on matters of race or anything else. At no point in the controversy over the integration of Poly did he argue that the board should ignore as inherently inequitable state laws mandating segregation. Thomsen took a narrower, more legalistic approach, claiming that all-white Poly could be integrated only if it was shown that comparable course offerings at a segregated high school were inferior. (As everyone in Baltimore knew, they were in fact woeful.) Although he apparently abhorred racial discrimination, Thomsen's approach to the integration issue was not informed by moral outrage over the impact of segregation. He saw it primarily as a matter of adhering to judicial precedent.[3]

Thomsen spent some three decades in private practice before President Eisenhower named him to the federal bench in 1954. As a federal district court judge, he remained cautious on matters of social justice, invariably taking his lead from the rulings of the Supreme Court. In several notable instances, Thomsen rebuffed efforts by African American groups to end racial segregation in public facilities in Maryland. Not long after his appointment in 1954, Thomsen ruled against the NAACP when it attacked as unconstitutional the segregation of Sandy Point State Park and other municipal swimming facilities. The Supreme Court's freshly minted ruling in *Brown*, Thomsen held, was limited to education; the high court justices had yet to rule segregation unconstitutional in other contexts. When they did so (in a succession of rulings throughout the late 1950s and early 1960s), Thomsen applied those judicial precedents and struck down state measures mandating segregation. He earned plaudits for those opinions and myriad others, including rulings that curbed abuses of inmates at state prisons.[4]

Thomsen's brother, Ferris, was a strapping, athletic man (he coached lacrosse at Princeton and was enshrined in that sport's hall of fame). But size did not seem to run in the family: one courthouse observer wondered if the judge stood much more than five feet tall. He apparently was so bothered by his height that he ordered judicial robes that were several sizes too large and then had his secretary alter them to fit his diminutive frame.[5]

Whatever Thomsen might have lacked in physical stature, he made up for in ambition. One of his clerks later wrote that he seemed to seek out difficult or controversial cases "in order to demonstrate to the Baltimore community just how smart he was." For many years, the other federal judge in his district seemed content occupying himself with unspectacular cases centering on obscure points of law. Thomsen thus had his pick of the more exciting legal disputes in the federal court docket—cases like the prosecution of the Catonsville Nine.[6]

It was in Thomsen's courtroom, located on the fifth floor of Baltimore's Post Office and Courthouse Building, that the legal fate of the Catonsville Nine would be decided over the second week of October 1968. The spectators who streamed in to watch the proceedings—almost all of them supporters of the defendants—entered a space that had been designed to inspire reverence for law and the government that promulgated it. The courtroom's ceilings were high, the furniture oversized and impressive. Rich wood paneling covered the walls, save for the rear, where there hung a series of portraits of Thomsen's forebears on the federal bench.[7]

Throughout the trial, federal marshals carefully controlled the flow of spectators into the courtroom, which had a seating capacity of about 120. In the interest of fairness, many supporters of the Nine cycled through the courtroom in shifts, thereby giving more people a chance to experience the trial.[8]

Having been brought up to speed on the case the night before, Bishop James Pike would not be denied admission on the morning of the trial's first day.

When he arrived at the courthouse, he was told that the courtroom already was full. Thinking on his feet, he fibbed to a marshal, "I am of counsel in this matter. You can't deprive these people of counsel." The marshals took Pike at his word and allowed him in. Once inside, Pike headed straight for the defense table, where he introduced himself to the lawyers and discussed with them trial strategy. If Pike's sudden appearance caught William Kunstler by surprise, he didn't show it. The lead defense attorney asked Thomsen if the bishop might be able to join the proceedings and then related his legal credentials. This satisfied the judge, and he allowed Pike to sit in.[9]

The crowd broke into a sustained ovation when Dan Berrigan, Brother David Darst, John Hogan, Tom and Marjorie Melville, George Mische, and Mary Moylan entered the courtroom. Berrigan made what one observer described as "a spectacular stage entrance," playfully frolicking through the courtroom in a manner calculated to mock the solemnity of the occasion. He paused to autograph copies of his book *Night Flight to Hanoi*, which recounted his trip to North Vietnam. The Jesuit made a point of displaying to the crowd the medallion that would hang around his neck all week. He had mounted to it a color photograph of his brother Phil.[10]

Dan Berrigan's spirits were high as the trial began, but he remained a realist about his chances of prevailing. When a reporter asked him what he would do if the jury acquitted him, he paused for a moment and then admitted, "You know, I never thought of that."[11]

Federal marshals brought Phil Berrigan and Tom Lewis into the courtroom through a door located near the bench. (Already serving their sentences for their roles in the Baltimore Four raid, they remained in custody throughout the trial.) Upon seeing them, the crowd offered another burst of applause. Lewis acknowledged the greeting by making the widely known gesture for peace—a "V"—with one hand. Phil Berrigan recognized the cheers "with sweeping gestures, in the manner of a weary political candidate riding through crowds in a limousine," as writer Francine du Plessix Gray observed.[12]

The State of Maryland's newfound determination to serve warrants on the defendants—and take them into custody for processing—occasioned an angry motion by Kunstler, who insisted that, because of the constitutional issues involved, the matter of the state's charges should be deferred until after his clients were able to have their day in federal court. Kunstler's move led to a two-hour conference in Thomsen's chambers in which the federal judge heard from defense attorneys, federal prosecutor Stephen Sachs, and Francis Burch, Maryland's attorney general. After some wrangling, the court allowed the Nine to be arraigned on state charges and then fixed bail for them. This disposed of the state case, but only temporarily; the Nine still would have to confront it after their federal trial.[13]

With these preliminaries out of the way, the court turned its attention to the first major phase of the trial, the selection of the jury. The defense already had determined that it would not participate in the process of quizzing prospective jurors. Kunstler did not even look up from his paperwork when Thomsen began voir dire. "Any twelve are all right," he said, waving his hand indifferently. "Just take the first twelve."[14]

Kunstler explained that the Nine had concluded that it was pointless to try to obtain a genuinely fair hearing in Thomsen's courtroom. The courts, they felt, did not serve the broader causes of justice and morality but rather protected established political and economic interests. In such a setting, the defendants were unlikely to have the chance to address the issues that lay at the heart of their case, including the legal and moral illegitimacy of the war in Vietnam. "The defendants say that they do not have faith in the judicial process," he said. "They want nothing to do with the selection of the jury because they do not recognize this court as a forum in which the matter can be solved."[15]

The defense would sit out voir dire; it would be up to Thomsen and the federal prosecutors to pick the jury. To make sure that the prospective jurors understood the precise legal issues that would be involved in the trial, Thomsen read for them the indictment. For the defendants, the case centered on broad claims of justice and morality; for the federal judge, it boiled down to a discrete set of legal charges, and he wanted to make sure that the would-be jurors could fathom all of them. He informed them that they would be asked to determine if the nine defendants "did willfully injure and commit depredation against property of the United States; did willfully and unlawfully obliterate records of the Selective Service System, Local Board No. 33 located in Catonsville, Maryland; and did willfully and knowingly interfere with the administration of the Military Selective Service Act of 1967, by removing and burning the records of Local Board No. 33 located in Catonsville, Maryland, and by disrupting the official activities [there]." The indictment also charged, Thomsen told the prospective panelists, that "the defendants aided and abetted one another in committing these alleged offenses." (There would be no conspiracy charges; Sachs had dropped them in an effort to streamline his case.[16])

Dan Berrigan was appalled that so many of the prospective jurors had ties, both indirectly and directly, to the military. Among them were an employee of the National Security Administration; a World War I veteran; a World War II veteran; a woman who once worked at Maryland's Edgewood Arsenal; a management analyst with the Army; a Department of Defense employee at Fort Meade; a Korean War veteran who had been a military policeman; an Air Force veteran; and a Navy veteran. Most claimed that their experiences would not prejudice them against the defendants. When Thomsen asked the World War II veteran if there was any reason why he might not be able to decide the case solely on the basis of the evidence presented in court, the prospective juror told him, "No, sir. I am a very conscientious person."[17]

With the headstrong Kunstler on the sidelines, jury selection went relatively quickly. After weeding out the members of the pool who seemed to have made up their minds about the case ("I believe I have already formed an opinion, sir," one told him), Thomsen took about two hours to empanel a jury of seven women and five men. Their average age was fifty-six; two were over seventy. Their ranks included an engineer, a truck driver, an insurance agent, a merchandise clerk, and a management analyst for the Army.[18]

Dorothy Day—who, in her characteristically humble way, appeared in court wearing a blue bandana—was fascinated by the selection of the jury. She remarked in her diary that the prospective jurors "all looked alike," save for a few African Americans. One question put to the prospective jurors struck her as being particularly telling: "Is there anything in your experience that would keep you from making a just decision?" For Day, this query begged another, more profound question: "Do they believe in God?"[19]

Thomsen told the jurors that they would be sequestered starting the next day. He also ordered them to ignore news coverage about the trial. "In order that there shall not be extraneous matters brought to your attention, I must tell you what we tell juries in every case: do not read about this case in the newspapers," he said. "I certainly want you to know all about the World Series and everything else in which you may be interested. But do not read about the case in the newspapers, and do not listen on radio or television to any discussions about this case."[20]

After warning the jurors, Thomsen abbreviated the trial's first day, adjourning the proceedings early in the afternoon. It was clear that he wanted to give authorities plenty of time to prepare for the two vastly different demonstrations that were scheduled in the city that evening. While supporters of the Nine came together once more at St. Ignatius, their political opposites—backers of George Wallace, the segregationist candidate for president—would gather for a rally at the Civic Center.

While the trial got underway, supporters of the Catonsville Nine staged the largest antiwar march seen in Baltimore in the Vietnam era. At about 10:30 A.M., about 1,200 protesters assembled at Wyman Park and then headed down Howard Street toward War Memorial Plaza. The group gathered strength along the way; by the time the march reached its destination, there were about 1,500 participants, according to the FBI. (The marchers themselves put the number of participants slightly higher, at roughly two thousand.) The marchers arrayed themselves in more than two hundred rows of six; marshals stationed themselves in about every tenth row and maintained discipline.[21]

In addition to a broad banner demanding "FREE THE 9," at the head of the procession were two reproductions of Revolutionary-era flags meant to show a connection between that earlier revolt against tyranny and the demonstrators' own resistance to despotism. The more familiar of the two, known as the Gadsden flag, featured a coiled snake and the defiant motto "DON'T TREAD ON ME"; the other depicted a liberty tree.[22]

The procession featured myriad other signs and symbols. As they headed south, some demonstrators hoisted flags—black for anarchy, red for socialism. Others carried aloft signs bearing the Greek letter omega, for ohm, the symbol of electrical resistance (a favorite emblem among antiwar groups). Other standards were wordier: "WHITE MIDDLE-CLASS BOURGEOIS SUBURBIA FOR PEACE" and "WHAT IF THEY GAVE A WAR AND NO ONE CAME?" A group of priests displayed a sign that reflected their determination to oppose the war. "TO SPEAK OF GOD AND REMAIN SILENT ON VIETNAM," it read, "IS BLASPHEMY, BLASPHEMY, BLASPHEMY."[23]

For Barbara Deming, the pioneering feminist and exponent of social change, the march showed the potential for new techniques of nonviolent advocacy. As she participated in the procession down Howard Street, Deming noted that the marchers slowed down as they approached points of interest, including schools, a factory, and an armed forces induction center. Dean Pappas of the Baltimore Defense Committee (BDC) capitalized on these moments, taking up his bullhorn and ad-libbing some commentary—about the war, about the Nine, about the establishment—for curious spectators. These impromptu moments of instruction held enormous promise for catalyzing social change, Deming felt. "One could hold a walking teach-in through a city, it occurred to me," she later wrote, "pausing at appropriate buildings to instruct citizens about the real loci of power in this country."[24]

The march was a seminal antiwar event for Pappas, the local physics teacher who had played a supporting role in the Catonsville demonstration. "On the opening date of the trial, I'll never forget it," he said many years later. "We marched down Howard Street. [It was] the biggest local march we'd had on the war." It seemed to him that "the population was on edge, primed for some confrontation" with the marchers. But Pappas and his fellow activists resolved not to quarrel with bystanders and thereby discredit their witness. Instead, the antiwar demonstrators would communicate and instruct. Pappas proudly recalled that "when we actually got into the streets, our act was so clean. We were scrupulously into dialoguing with people on the side. If somebody was yelling at us, we didn't want to get back into a shouting match with them." He felt that during the march—and throughout the week as a whole—supporters of the Nine managed to connect "pretty positively with mainstream Baltimoreans."[25]

Authorities in Baltimore were not eager to interfere with these interactions. Mayor Thomas D'Alesandro III had resolved to avoid a reprise of the recent debacle in Chicago, where activists protesting at the Democratic convention had been brutally suppressed (in full view of the news media) by the city's heavy-handed police department. D'Alesandro, a Democrat, had been in Chicago for that disaster, and on the flight back to Baltimore a reporter had asked him how his city would handle the thousands of demonstrators who were expected to converge on Baltimore for the trial. "I'll have them greeted at the city line," the mayor had said, "and give them a police escort all the way."

D'Alesandro was true to his word, giving Baltimore police notice that he expected them to behave markedly better than their colleagues in Chicago.[26]

Still, the city prepared for the worst. Several hundred officers, many of them decked out in riot gear accompanied by police dogs, monitored the march and the subsequent demonstration at War Memorial Plaza. Just across the street, at the Post Office and Courthouse Building, their ranks were bolstered by a contingent of one hundred federal marshals, some brought in from as far away as Los Angeles. These local and federal forces worked in concert to thwart any effort that might be made to disrupt the trial. Authorities screened everyone entering the building, even those who were there just to buy stamps.[27]

For Baltimore writer Thelma Nason, the scene outside the courthouse was ominous. She noticed how menacing the police seemed as they guarded the building against the demonstrators. "Wearing plastic visored blue helmets and carrying nightsticks," she remarked, "they looked like policemen from outer space or perhaps an Orwellian world."[28]

Viva House cofounder Willa Bickham, like nearly everyone who commented on the police, noted that many officers were decked out in full riot gear, a rare sight in Baltimore. Careful observers also noticed what many police officers were *not* wearing—name plates. Demonstrators assumed that these badges had been removed or obscured so that they would not able to identify individual officers by name if they committed acts of misconduct. (Police in Chicago notoriously had done this during their recent pillorying of demonstrators.) After a reporter asked some police brass about the missing name plates, an order went out that all officers were to display them.[29]

The FBI kept close tabs on all of the protest activities organized by the defense committee during the week of the trial, including the march on Monday morning. Several agents monitored the procession down Howard Street and reported back to bureau headquarters about the demonstrators—"mainly young people of the 'hippie' type with about 150 persons in clerical garb," one noted. "Signs carried by the marchers were mainly in opposition to the war in Vietnam," according to one report. "Numerous signs were in support of the 'Catonsville Nine.' A large banner carried by two people bore the words 'SDS—Liberation.'"[30]

Despite the fears of law enforcement, the march and the demonstration proceeded relatively peacefully. In its subsequent account of the march, the *Baltimore Sun* highlighted—with a notable trace of surprise—the "relaxed and often joyous mood" of the march as it meandered down Howard Street. As would be the case throughout the week at events organized by the BDC, there were no serious run-ins with police, who were "conspicuously restrained during the demonstrations," according to the *National Catholic Reporter*. Local authorities seemed determined to prevent Baltimore from turning into another Chicago, and for the most part they succeeded.[31]

Few of the protesters dealt with anything worse than a smattering of incredulous stares or catcalls. "The crowds are curious, they mutter among themselves, but overt response is minimal," one marcher observed of her experience traveling down Howard Street. "We beckon and they stare or shake their heads." She recalled that black spectators, who presumably shared the marchers' distaste for the establishment, generally reacted more favorably, sometimes flashing the iconic "V" peace sign or shouting encouragement.[32]

One journalist walking along with the marchers collected snippets of comments from spectators, some of whom watched from the steps of Baltimore's fabled row houses. "It's indecent," one woman grumbled about the procession. Another expressed shock at seeing priests and nuns marching with ragged students and joining them in protest anthems. "I suppose *you'll* tell *us* how to live next Sunday, from the pulpit!" she offered.[33]

Perhaps because they were viewed as neglecting their proper religious duties, the priests in the march seemed to take a disproportionate share of abuse from spectators. At one point, a well-dressed man approached a Jesuit and brandished his fist. "Filthy communist!" he thundered. "You're a disgrace to your religion." The outburst startled the priest, but, like all of the marchers, he maintained his cool. Ignoring the man who had accosted him, he kept walking and resumed an ecumenical conversation with an Episcopal priest.[34]

Father Jack Eagan, a Catholic priest from Jersey City, New Jersey, found the march frightening. Many in the crowd, he later said, were uptight because so many priests had decided to participate. "They were calling people fairies and communists," he remembered. "They were angry as hell. I really thought we were going to be beaten up."[35]

If the demonstrations rattled Eagan, they exhilarated Neil McLaughlin, a young priest from Baltimore. For him, the protests presented a welcome opportunity to connect with like-minded reformers from a variety of backgrounds. "The community that came together around the trial was, to a sort of lonely priest, exceedingly good news," he later said. "A lot of beautiful people had come together. It was a refreshing experience." McLaughlin realized that the activists coalescing in Baltimore represented "a Catholic element that was potentially very powerful within the church."[36]

Many priests and seminarians regretted that they weren't able to make it to Baltimore for the opening day march or any of the events surrounding the Catonsville Nine trial. They tried to keep track of events by reading accounts published in newspapers and liberal religious publications like the *National Catholic Reporter*. James Carroll obsessively followed the trial from St. Paul's College, the Paulist Fathers' seminary in Washington. Carroll had been brought up to revere the law enforcement authorities who were clumsily tracking the protesters—his father had served as an FBI agent and then as director of the Defense Intelligence Agency—but he developed a tremendous admiration for the Berrigan brothers and their many collaborators. Experiencing the trial in an "intensely private way" at his seminary deepened

Carroll's nascent commitment to social justice, and he resolved to model his priesthood on the ministry of the Berrigans.[37]

Baltimore writer Thelma Nason stumbled upon the march when she ventured to a sale at a Howard Street shoe store. In the weeks leading up to the trial, she had heard that supporters of the Nine would stage a succession of protests on the streets of Baltimore, and she had wondered if the recent debacle in Chicago would be replayed. Her curiosity got the better of her, and she ventured closer to the demonstrators to determine if they were "as long-haired, disheveled, and provocative" as she had been led to believe. The activists surprised Nason. They weren't "as unkempt or hippy as I expected," she later wrote. She noticed several nuns and priests "as well as three older women—motherly types." They hardly looked like rabble.[38]

What's more, they were well-mannered and clearly committed to peacefully advocating for their cause, even in the face of taunting from counterdemonstrators. Their devotion and sincerity so impressed Nason that she ventured into the courthouse and attended the trial—that day and for the rest of the week. She never made it to the sale at the shoe store.[39]

Shortly after noon, the marchers reached War Memorial Plaza, which had opened in 1927 as a tribute to soldiers who had fallen in World War I. The rally that followed featured the reading of statements of gratitude from several of the Nine, including Phil Berrigan. The priest sounded a joking note of caution: "First of all, a warning—no insults from visitors. We Baltimoreans, native or adopted, resent outsiders calling us 'Baltomorons.' Doing that makes agitators of outsiders, and we have passed a statute against agitators. So there'll be no name-calling in Baltimore. Those of you who are guests, mind your manners."[40]

A parade of speakers voiced support for the defendants and sought to put their actions in Catonsville within a broader context of peace and social justice activism. One excoriated the establishment for its role in perpetuating inequality and called on workers to join in the activities that the BDC had planned for the remainder of the week. In one of its many reports on the rally, the FBI noted that this speaker had invoked the example set by radical protesters in other parts of the world, pointing out "that students who had recently been active in the revolutionary uprisings in Paris, France, had been backed by the French working class."[41]

Counterdemonstrators—many of them affiliated with the ultraconservative National States Rights Party (NSRP)—did their best to disrupt the march and rally. Members of the NSRP brandished placards with such provocative messages as "KILL THE VIETCONG AND STEP UP THE BOMBING," "WE WANT DEAD REDS," "DIP THE YIPS," and "WALLACE FOR PRESIDENT." Joseph Carroll, a young NSRP leader from suburban Lutherville, was the most confrontational counterdemonstrator, at one point grabbing a red flag from one of the marchers and burning it. Police did not arrest Carroll for this act of vandalism, but eventually they removed all counterdemonstrators from the area.[42]

As the rally wore on, the counterdemonstrators became increasingly belligerent. A few heckled incessantly, demeaning supporters of the Catonsville Nine as traitors and communist dupes. At one point, an assertive counterdemonstrator—news reports later identified him as a middle-aged contractor from Baltimore—demanded to use the activists' microphone and address the throng, presumably to castigate the assembled radicals for their disloyalty. When organizers brushed aside his request, a brief altercation ensued, and police had to intervene.[43]

The counterdemonstrators' disruptions were not all that irritated supporters of the Nine. Organizers of the rally had hoped to continue their protest outside the Post Office and Courthouse Building, located two blocks to the west on North Calvert Street, but they were cautioned that this might violate federal law (presumably because it could be viewed as an effort to influence the trial). Sensing that the demonstrators might have *wanted* to be arrested in an act of civil disobedience, federal officials backed off, permitting a picket line in front of the courthouse on the theory that the marchers wouldn't be trying to influence the outcome of the trial.[44]

Some enterprising demonstrators also set up shop on the small, elliptical island that lay in front of the courthouse in the middle of Calvert Street. Officially known as Monument Square, this football-shaped piece of land, framed by the street on either side, featured a 52-foot-high marble battle monument designed by Maximilian Godefroy, a noted nineteenth-century Baltimore architect, to honor soldiers who had died in Baltimore during the War of 1812. Demonstrators transformed this area into what they called the "Island of Life" and mobilized there daily throughout the week.[45]

While their compatriots occupied the Island of Life, picketers circled in front of the courthouse for several hours. As the afternoon progressed, the protest lost some of its momentum. "By the ninth time around," one sardonic reporter observed of the picketing, "the whole thing was a bore." A few counterdemonstrators dogged the picketers, but ridicule failed to deter them, and they trudged on until about 3:30 P.M. Before the protesters left the scene, BDC organizers addressed them a final time, reviewing the day's successful activities and urging them to attend that night's festivities at St. Ignatius. A few hours later, a group of about a thousand crowded into the church's hall to hear from a few of the defendants and an all-star roster of speakers, including Bishop Pike, Noam Chomsky, Dorothy Day, Harvard Divinity School's Harvey Cox, and Rennie Davis (who soon would be on trial himself for his role in the disruption of the Democratic convention).[46]

At St. Ignatius, Dan Berrigan provided some perspective on the trial. It had been a dynamic day for the supporters of the Nine; they had marched and picketed and chanted until they had grown weary. The defendants themselves, however, had suffered through a far less exhilarating experience. The proceedings in Thomsen's courtroom, Berrigan told the crowd, had been more stultifying than uplifting. He said that as the trial began, he and his fellow defendants became "like persons without movement, immobilized by that horrible courtroom."[47]

Outside the hall, a reporter from the *Catholic Review*, Baltimore's archdiocesan newspaper, approached Berrigan and asked him if he considered himself to be a man of law. "Yes, I am a man of law," Berrigan responded. "I have been a man of law for 47 years. Now in my 47th year, the law has become lawless."[48]

The FBI, in one of its many memoranda on the Monday night rally at St. Ignatius, flatly noted that Bishop Pike "stated that he was publicly counseling young men to avoid the draft and wanted it known that he was in complete agreement with any attempt made to destroy draft records." Pike's actual words—which drew repeated shouts of encouragement from the audience— were far more impassioned. He admitted to the crowd that he had been mistaken about a number of things: "I supported that damn war in the beginning because I believed the lies we were told about it . . . but *I* was wrong and *you* were right!" he said. "I came to Baltimore last night certain in my own mind that the Catonsville Nine should not have burned draft records because it was illegal . . . but *I* was wrong and *they* were right!"[49]

A brief intermission followed Pike's fusillade. The break allowed for some housekeeping: pamphlets were distributed, petitions signed, announcements made. Someone read telegrams of support for the Nine from such luminaries as Coretta Scott King, Benjamin Spock, and William Sloane Coffin. Seemingly oblivious to the carnival-like tumult around them, a few bedraggled students from California lurched into the hall, unfurled their sleeping bags on the floor, and fell asleep.

The break ended with the appearance of Day, the vaunted Catholic pacifist. "I hadn't been expected to be invited to speak," she joked. "I'm over thirty, you know." (She celebrated her seventy-first birthday a few weeks later.) Day drew applause when she voiced her support for the defendants. "I came here to express my sympathy for this act of nonviolent revolution," she said, "for this act of peaceful sabotage which is not only a revolution against the state but against the alliance of Church and state, an alliance which has gone on much too long." Such an action—she characterized it as a "desperate offer of life and freedom"— was necessary not only to impede the brutal business of war but also to provoke the Catholic Church "to speak out when the state has become a murderer."[50]

Unable to shake her worries about the potential for violence in the antiwar movement, Day then sounded a cautious note, warning that "we must restrict our violence to property." At this point she halted briefly, as if to underscore the importance of what would follow. "I've been in jail for civil disobedience more often than any of you, and I know more clearly than any of you the courage it entails . . . and I know that we must hang onto our pacifism in the face of all violence. We must retain our pacifism the way Gandhi, Martin Luther King, and Cesar Chavez retained it. It's the most difficult thing in the world and the one that requires most faith."[51]

Chomsky, the Massachusetts Institute of Technology polymath, followed Day to the podium and spoke on American imperialism. Next came Cox, who likened the Nine's immolation of draft records to several other acts of fiery— and thoroughly justified—resistance to tyranny. He reminded the audience that William Lloyd Garrison had publicly burned the Constitution because it countenanced slavery and that Martin Luther had set aflame volumes of canon law and supporting sacramental theology. Richard John Neuhaus, the Lutheran minister who was Dan Berrigan's colleague in Clergy and Laymen Concerned About Vietnam, earned a prolonged ovation when he launched into a scathing indictment of the Johnson administration.[52]

No one in the hall, save for perhaps the poorly disguised FBI agents, disagreed with Neuhaus's indictment of Johnson as a war criminal. But as the evening rally progressed, a few ideological disputes threatened to fragment the crowd. Chomsky's talk occasioned a heated discussion about the many manifestations of imperialism. Dan Berrigan—having given some thought to this very matter during the first day of the trial—weighed in, griping that some of his fellow Jesuits had said that they would pray for, but not overtly support, him. "That is a form of spiritual imperialism," he asserted.[53]

Blase Bonpane, the Melvilles' collaborator in Guatemala, directed this conversation to the issue of nonviolence. Like the Melvilles, Bonpane had concluded that nonviolent resistance would not free the Guatemalan peasantry from oppression; given the dire circumstances, they probably had no choice but to arm themselves and fight. Casting a confrontational glance at Day, the patron saint of pacifism, Bonpane thundered, "Nonviolence is an imperialist solution! Only guerilla warfare will alleviate the misery of the masses in underdeveloped countries. . . . The peasants do not start the violence—it is inflicted upon them, and they have the Christian right to retaliate!" The Maryknoller's proclamation horrified some in the crowd; a few wondered if he really was a Catholic cleric.[54]

A more direct challenge to the principle of nonviolence soon presented itself. A splinter group of demonstrators had resolved to picket that night's rally at the Civic Center for Wallace, the demagogic presidential candidate who seemed to represent an even greater threat to democracy and equality than the much-reviled Spiro Agnew. Some of the demonstrators confined themselves to marching outside the building (one of their signs read, "If you like Hitler, you'll love Wallace"), but a few daring souls ventured inside and heckled the Alabama governor.

Wallace noted the activists' presence and entertained the boisterous crowd by ridiculing them. "You young people seem to know a lot of four-letter words," he drawled. "But I have two four-letter words you don't know: S-O-A-P and W-O-R-K." He also jokingly invited them to join him onstage after the rally ended to have their sandals autographed.[55]

Things went downhill from there. Wallace supporters scuffled with the picketers, and police—their patience exhausted by a long day of peacekeeping— responded by manhandling them and attempting to cart them off to jail. Word of the debacle soon reached St. Ignatius. Two men rushed into the hall and announced that the picketers were under siege. "Our brothers are being bitten by dogs and trampled by horses!" one said. "It is our duty to go downtown and give them our support!" Spirited debates erupted over the wisdom of such a move, which was almost certain to turn the situation even more violent. "What to do?" one member of the crowd wondered. "March to the police station?"[56]

A few of the Catonsville Nine stepped forward to ensure that there would be no additional violence. Following a brief discussion, they walked through the hall and counseled their supporters to stay put. George Mische was adamant, at one point grabbing the microphone and proclaiming, "Anybody who wants to call Wallace a pig, and cops pigs, should stay here and not go down. If we get caught in this, we're playing the same game they are." He then drew a line in the sand: "Anybody who wants to get out of hand and spoil the whole thing is going to have to walk over some of the Catonsville Nine to do it."[57]

Not everyone was placated by Mische's counsel. One young protester, referring to the recent disruptions at the Democratic convention, complained, "If they had talked like this in Chicago, we would not have had Chicago." Another pleaded, "Do you *want* kids to get beat up?"

Despite this tough talk, there would be no reinforcements dispatched to the Wallace rally. Instead, a contingent of clergymen made their way over to the city jail and negotiated for the release of any demonstrators who had been picked by police. In time, the meeting quieted down, and people filtered out of the church hall.[58]

FIGURE 1. Father Philip Berrigan in Baltimore in the mid-1960s. Special Collections and Archives, DePaul University Libraries, Chicago, IL.

FIGURE 2. The Baltimore Four being questioned after their arrest in October 1967. Seated in the background, from left: Philip Berrigan, Tom Lewis, and David Eberhardt. James Mengel is seated, far right. © Hearst Corporation; Baltimore News-American Photograph Collection, Special Collections, University of Maryland Libraries.

FIGURE 3. The remains of the draft files burned by the Catonsville Nine. Courtesy of Jean Walsh; Catonsville Room, Catonsville Area Branch, Baltimore County (MD) Public Library.

FIGURE 4. Selective Service employees regroup after the raid on Local Board 33 in Catonsville. From left: head clerk Mary Murphy; draft board member Anthony Urban; and clerk Phyllis Morsberger. Courtesy of Jean Walsh; Catonsville Room, Catonsville Area Branch, Baltimore County (MD) Public Library.

FIGURE 5. The Knights of Columbus Hall in Catonsville after the raid. Clerks broke one of the windows (upper left) to call outside for help. Courtesy of Jean Walsh; Catonsville Room, Catonsville Area Branch, Baltimore County (MD) Public Library.

FIGURE 6. The Catonsville Nine after being taken into custody. Front row, from left: Brother David Darst, Mary Moylan, John Hogan, Marjorie Melville, Tom Melville. Back row, from left: George Mische, Philip Berrigan, Daniel Berrigan, Tom Lewis. Courtesy of Jean Walsh; Catonsville Room, Catonsville Area Branch, Baltimore County (MD) Public Library.

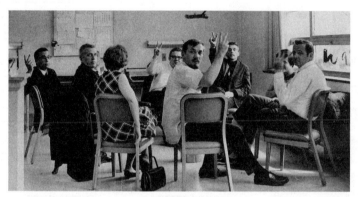

FIGURE 7. The Catonsville Nine in custody. From left: Brother David Darst, Philip Berrigan, John Hogan (partially obscured), Mary Moylan, Tom Lewis, George Mische, Daniel Berrigan, Marjorie Melville, Tom Melville. © Hearst Corporation; Baltimore News-American Photograph Collection, Special Collections, University of Maryland Libraries.

2745.9 *pag 4*
2745.9

REPORT OF FIRE

BALTIMORE COUNTY FIRE DEPARTMENT

STATION *Catonsville* Election District No. *1st* Date: *May 17, 1968*

FIRE REPORT NO. *161* Begin with No. 1 – January 1st.

Box Alarm No.: _____ Phone: *Hilgto* Radio: _____ Automatic Alarm: _____ Personal: _____

APPARATUS RESPONDING	RESPONSE NO.	RESPONDED TIME	RETURN TIME	ALARM	TRANSFER TO	MILEAGE	GAS	OIL
Engine 4	*189*	1 *pm*	2 *pm*			.09		

TYPE NO. OF FIRE: *# 8 Draft Cards*

FIRE ORIGINATED: BASEMENT: _____ FLOOR NO.: _____ OTHER: _____

DESCRIPTION OF FIRE: *Draft cards burning in containers on*
parking lot

FIRE CAUSED BY: *Vandals*

OCCUPIED BY: *Parking Lot*
ADDRESS: *1010 Frederick Rd. K of C Grounds*
OWNED BY: *Draft Board of Federal Government*
ADDRESS: *1010 Frederick Rd - Draft Board -*

Record Damage When Fire Is In Your Station Area.

ESTIMATED DAMAGE TO: Building $_____ Contents $_____ ?

INSURANCE ON: Building $_____ Contents $_____

If total loss, mark "X" in block [   ] . If damage is over $2,000, check this block
If either of the above are marked, forward to Headquarters IMMEDIATELY.

HOURS PUMPING: *Booster* HOSE LINES LAID: 2½" ____ Ft. ____ 1½" ____ Ft. ____
ASSISTED BY FOLLOWING COMPANIES: *B.C. Mosberger, F.B.I*

ACCIDENTS OR INJURIES: _____ REPORT FILED: _____

ADDITIONAL INFORMATION: *Used Booster, salvage covers.*

When fire is in your own station area, submit original (White copy).
When fire is in another station area, submite duplicate (Yellow copy).

FIGURE 8. The Baltimore County Fire Department's report on the destruction of draft files at the Knights of Columbus Hall in Catonsville.

FREE THE CATONSVILLE 9

fighters against racism & war

MARCH TO WIN JUSTICE & PEACE
MONDAY, OCTOBER 7

assemble 9 AM in WYMAN PARK
Charles & 29th

For further information, contact:
Baltimore Defense Committee
Peace Action Center
2525 Maryland Avenue
Baltimore, Md.   21218
889-0065

FIGURE 9. A flier issued by the Baltimore Defense Committee to publicize protest activities related to the trial of the Catonsville Nine. In the photo, from left to right: Daniel Berrigan, Tom Melville, John Hogan, Philip Berrigan, George Mische, and Tom Lewis. Courtesy of Catonsville Room, Catonsville Area Branch, Baltimore County (MD) Public Library.

FIGURE 10. The Post Office and Courthouse Building in Baltimore during the trial of the Catonsville Nine. © Hearst Corporation; Baltimore News-American Photograph Collection, Special Collections, University of Maryland Libraries.

FIGURE 11. Protesters marching through Baltimore in support of the Catonsville Nine. © Hearst Corporation; Baltimore News-American Photograph Collection, Special Collections, University of Maryland Libraries.

FIGURE 12. Protesters at a rally staged in conjunction with the trial of the Catonsville Nine. © Hearst Corporation; Baltimore News-American Photograph Collection, Special Collections, University of Maryland Libraries.

FIGURE 13. Marjorie Melville affixes an armband honoring the Milwaukee 14 to Mary Moylan. Brother David Darst is middle left, with head turned. © Hearst Corporation; Baltimore News-American Photograph Collection, Special Collections, University of Maryland Libraries.

FIGURE 14. From left: Mary Moylan, George Mische, and Daniel Berrigan. © Hearst Corporation; Baltimore News-American Photograph Collection, Special Collections, University of Maryland Libraries.

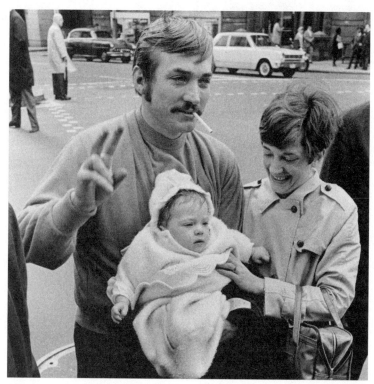

FIGURE 15. George Mische, his daughter, and his wife, Helene, at the trial of the Catonsville Nine. Special Collections and Archives, DePaul University Libraries, Chicago, IL.

FIGURE 16.   John Hogan in the late 1960s. Special Collections and Archives, DePaul University Libraries, Chicago, IL.

FIGURE 17. Mary Moylan and Brother David Darst at the state trial of the Catonsville Nine. © Hearst Corporation; Baltimore News-American Photograph Collection, Special Collections, University of Maryland Libraries.

FIGURE 18. Marjorie Melville reporting for her federal prison term in 1970. © Hearst Corporation; Baltimore News-American Photograph Collection, Special Collections, University of Maryland Libraries.

FIGURE 19. Philip (left) and Daniel Berrigan during their time as fugitives. Special Collections and Archives, DePaul University Libraries, Chicago, IL.

"They're Proud of It"

By the end of the week, long lines of spectators would be forming before dawn outside the federal courthouse in Baltimore. However, on the trial's second day—Tuesday, October 8—the queue was modest, and supporters of the Catonsville Nine were able to file into the building with relative ease; they merely had to line up in the hallway outside the courtroom. Some students had brought their breakfasts along, and they sat cross-legged and ate while waiting for the trial to start. Taking offense at this breach of decorum, a federal marshal moved toward them and muttered, "This isn't a mess hall, you know."[1]

A few opening rituals already had taken root. It became customary for the gallery to offer a prolonged and raucous ovation for the Catonsville Nine as they entered the courtroom. (Spectators couldn't help but notice that the applause lasted a bit longer each day.) This outburst usually was followed by the judge taking his seat on the bench. Flanked on both sides by large American flags, Thomsen offered a cheery "good morning" to the defendants, their supporters, and the teams of lawyers who were preparing to do battle before him.[2]

After everyone settled in, the trial began in earnest. Assistant U.S. Attorney Arthur Murphy, delivering the opening statement for the prosecution, surprised absolutely no one as he laid out the federal government's workmanlike case against the Catonsville Nine. He told jurors that he would be able to introduce irrefutable evidence showing that the nine defendants had willfully destroyed government records and had interfered with the operation of the Selective Service System. There was no getting around it: the federal government had an airtight case.

Murphy stressed that the jurors were to assess the legality of actions of the defendants in Catonsville— and not those of the American military in Vietnam. He further insisted the defendants' opinions about the war in Vietnam were, in the context of the trial, irrelevant. In Murphy's view, the defendants' critique of that conflict had no bearing on whether they should be found legally guilty of the specific charges leveled at them by the federal government.[3]

"I want to specifically say that this trial is not one involving an issue as to these defendants' [views] of this country's participation in the war in Vietnam," he said. "This trial, members of the jury, is not one involving the prosecution of these defendants for protesting the involvement of the United States in this conflict. Likewise, the issue in this trial is not one involving the prosecution of these defendants for their respective social, political, religious, or moral views."[4]

Murphy's opening exposition infuriated Phil Berrigan, who scowled at the prosecutor from the crowded defense table. Although he had expected it, he recoiled at Murphy's effort to reduce the case to a run-of-the-mill criminal prosecution. In his journal, he offered a glum summary of the prosecutor's argument: "Conscience is not an issue; neither is morality or sincerity. Law and justice are not issues; the Vietnam War is not an issue; neither is ghetto poverty."[5]

As Murphy's opening statement had promised, the federal government put on a straightforward case. Prosecutors would not ask jurors to ponder the wisdom or legality of American foreign policy, nor would they discuss the role of conscience or civil disobedience in bringing about political or social change. Instead, they would focus almost exclusively on the details of what had transpired at Local Board 33 in Catonsville on May 17, 1968, and how it had contravened federal law.

Special Agent James Anderson had been one of the first FBI agents to arrive at the Knights of Columbus hall in Catonsville. During his testimony, Murphy was able to show the jury some of the physical evidence that Anderson and his colleagues had recovered from the crime scene. These items included the wire baskets that the Nine had used in taking the draft files from the Selective Service office and then burning them in the parking lot. Jurors also saw a gas can; it had contained some of the homemade napalm that the Nine had poured over the conscription records. And Anderson identified the contents of four boxes that, for Murphy, represented the key piece of physical evidence in the case.

After looking over the boxes, Anderson told the jury, "These contain the burned records of Local Board 33 in Catonsville."[6]

On cross-examination, defense attorney William Kunstler did his best to portray Anderson as a functionary who refused to consider the morality of the government's actions. He asked at one point, "Do you know what napalm is, special agent Anderson?" The FBI man replied, "I've heard of it." The matter-of-fact nature of Anderson's response—highlighting as it did the prosecution's apparent lack of perspective on the war —drew derisive laughter from the crowd.[7]

Murphy also put WBAL-TV's Patrick McGrath on the stand and asked him to show the jury the footage he and his crew had shot at the Knights of Columbus building. As Phil Berrigan put it, the film had "an interesting history." Hinting that it might bring conspiracy charges, the federal government had prevailed upon the station not to air the footage or share it with other media outlets. With the jury out of the courtroom, Thomsen held a hearing to determine if the footage should be admitted into evidence, and under what circumstances. Prosecutors wanted the footage to be shown silently; they were reluctant to have the defendants' religious and political justifications aired in the courtroom. But defense attorneys insisted that the sound be turned on. Doing so, they argued, would provide a more complete and accurate sense of what had happened in Catonsville. Kunstler prevailed: Thomsen ruled that during the admissibility hearing, the footage would be accompanied by audio.[8]

Before the film was shown, Thomsen proposed that the defendants sit in the vacant jury box.

Dan Berrigan, speaking for the group, demurred.

"We already had part in this film," he said. "We are the actors in it, and we know what is there. We would be much happier if certain members of the audience would see it in the jury box."

The priest's comments rankled the judge.

"This is not a circus," Thomsen scolded. "This is not a propaganda matter. This is a trial of justice. . . . You do not have to sit there, if you do not want to. But, if you wish to sit there, you may." (The defendants decided to stay put.[9])

During the hearing held to determine the admissibility of the footage, about half of the audience could not view the projection screen. A bit later, when the film was shown for the jury—Thomsen ruled that it was admissible, sound and all—spectators exchanged seats so that those who had missed it the first time would have the chance to see it. As the footage showed the Nine saying the Lord's Prayer, many in the audience joined in—a spontaneous act that one spectator later said was "fitting, right, and just."[10]

The prosecution's star witnesses were two of the clerks the Nine had overpowered to seize the Selective Service files from Local Board 33. They described in detail what had transpired inside the Catonsville draft office on the day of the protest.

Supporters of the Nine found in Mary Murphy and Phyllis Morsberger irresistible targets for mockery: recounting their testimony, writer Francine du Plessix Gray sniffed that the two "matrons" were "confused and drawling . . . models of outraged respectability" who furnished nothing more useful than "comic relief." For the two women themselves, however, testifying at the trial was anything but amusing. Although they had been victimized by the Nine, they wound up having to defend themselves and were forced to justify their small roles in the war effort. They felt as though *they* had been put on trial.[11]

Because of concerns for her safety, federal marshals escorted Murphy through a back door when she arrived at the courthouse, and the clerk was kept in Thomsen's chambers until it was her turn to take the stand. Although she was anxious and frightened, Murphy did her best to explain to the jury what had happened in her office.

"They utterly terrified us. We were just terrified," she testified. "Of course, they went immediately to the files . . . I begged them not to take the files. I begged them."[12]

The activists had spoken with Murphy while they had sacked her files. "There was a lot of conversation: 'We don't want to hurt you. We have no intention of hurting you,'" Murphy told the jury. "Some of it was about the war in Vietnam; that this is not a good war, and that we shouldn't be there." They also had berated Murphy for her role in the war effort. "One of them said: 'You send boys away to be killed,'" she testified.[13]

Murphy had made one final effort to stop them, grabbing one of the baskets and trying to wrest it away. "I took hold of the trash burner and tried to pull it away, but I could not get it away from them, naturally," the clerk said from the witness stand. "And in the scuffle I cut my leg and my hand." Murphy explained that she had recovered from this skirmish quickly and had followed the activists down the stairs from the second floor of the Knights of Columbus building. She then had seen them burning the files.[14]

In recounting the details of the draft board protest, Murphy insisted that she had been mistreated during the raid at Local Board 33 in Catonsville. She noted that she had "never been treated with such bad manners in my whole life, and with such disrespect or uncharity." At one point, a defense attorney asked Murphy about the flowers and note of apology that the Nine had sent to Local Board Number 33 shortly after they had ransacked the place. He seemed to be suggesting, as Murphy later told an interviewer, that "this should have bought me over or made me feel better towards the Berrigans. All of this was very disconcerting." Thomsen didn't think much of the query, either. He disallowed the question, stating, "We are not trying the defendants for their manners, either good or bad."[15]

Phil Berrigan also found Murphy's testimony distressing, but for radically different reasons. Watching from the defense table, he felt that the draft board clerk came off as "a narrow and doctrinaire functionary" who had been brainwashed by "twenty-two years of federal propaganda" into thinking that she was providing a valuable service to her country. Murphy's obvious pride in her service to the government appalled Berrigan, as did her tendency to describe as "boys" the draftees she helped to dispatch to the killing fields of Vietnam, "ignoring the fact that they are men enough to kill and be killed," as he angrily put it in his diary.[16]

Phil Berrigan was further nettled by Murphy's distress when prosecutors showed her the small boxes—Berrigan felt as though they resembled little coffins—containing the ashes that had been recovered from the Knights of Columbus parking lot.[17] The containers of charred draft files also made a strong impression on Dan Berrigan, evoking for him memories of the devastation he had seen on his trip to North Vietnam.[18]

Dan and Phil Berrigan did not encounter Murphy after she had delivered her testimony. But when she exited the courtroom, Murphy saw several of the nuns and priests who had come to Baltimore to show their support for the Nine. Two people approached her; they turned out to be members of the Berrigan family. Their reaction comforted her. "They were very solicitous and offered their sympathy," Murphy later said. "They told me that they were very, very sorry that the whole thing had happened."[19]

Morsberger followed Murphy to the stand. She identified the nine defendants as the culprits in the draft-burning episode. "There was no problem of identifying them in a courtroom," she later said of her time on the witness stand, "because as soon as their name was mentioned they would wave or smile or something so that I would know." The clerk then recounted for jurors the havoc the demonstrators had wrought in the Selective Service office and in the parking lot of the Knights of Columbus building.[20]

In one of the few understatements uttered during the entire week of the trial, she began her account of that tumultuous afternoon by saying, "Well, we had a little visit." The clerk went on to explain how several of the Nine had entered the Selective Service office and purloined hundreds of the files housed there. Morsberger informed the jury that Mary Moylan and Tom Melville had restrained her and prevented her from intervening. The clerked further testified that she had wrestled with Moylan for the telephone.[21]

Moylan finally had relented, Morsberger testified, after her accomplices had crammed their wire baskets with draft files. Rather than use the phone to place a telephone call, Morsberger had hurled it through the window to catch the attention of some workmen standing outside. After a time, she had looked outside to see what the Nine were doing to the Selective Service files they had taken. "They were out in the parking lot," she told the jury, "burning records."[22]

Morsberger's testimony capped the prosecution's case. Jurors heard from only four witnesses—Anderson, McGrath, and the two clerks—but prosecutors believed that they conclusively had established the guilt of the Nine.

The tenor and scope of the trial of the Catonsville Nine changed completely when it came time for the defense to put on its case. In his opening statement, Kunstler offered almost a total inversion of Arthur Murphy's argument for the prosecution. Unlike the government's attorneys, he wanted jurors to take into account the full context of the defendants' actions. What they had done was indisputable; the Nine freely admitted that they had seized and burned the Selective Service files in Catonsville. "So far as the facts in this case go, we agree with the government. No defendant is going to dispute that the facts occurred as the government says they have occurred," Kunstler said. "The defendants are not going to deny doing what the evidence shows they did. They're proud of it, and they think it is one of the shining moments of their own personal lives."[23]

But why they had done it? That, the defense attorney argued, was the central issue of the case.[24] Kunstler told the jurors that they should take into account the commendable goals of the Catonsville Nine and their clear lack of criminal intent. Indeed, he suggested, the Nine had intended to prevent crimes—the further expansion of the illegal war in Vietnam—by their action in Catonsville.[25]

As he touted the Nine's noble motives, Kunstler proclaimed that he was attempting to clear the air in a manner that would allow the jurors to focus less on facts and more on principles. To that end, he proposed to read the moving poem that Dan Berrigan had written earlier that year after seeing two children in a Hanoi bomb shelter. This prompted a stern warning from the judge, who cautioned that the "propriety of the Vietnam war" would not become an issue in his courtroom. Kunstler backed off, but only momentarily; he still had every intention of making Vietnam the trial's central issue.[26]

Subtlety never was Kunstler's strong suit. He had a penchant for dramatizing his clients' claims by putting their actions on a sweeping historical scale. At several points in his opening statement, he maintained that the present criminal proceedings were akin to trials involving some earlier paragons of conscience. Comparisons could be drawn, Kunstler stated, to the trials of Socrates and Jesus—men who had been condemned to death for putting morality above the letter of the law.[27]

"We are concerned with the intent to commit a criminal act, the intent to do evil," Kunstler said in his peroration. "We submit to you that our evidence will prove that the intent was totally lacking in this case, and that, therefore, these defendants should be turned out to walk the streets again, as they have in the past."[28]

The first of the defendants to testify was the only one who had not entered the office of Local Board 33 in Catonsville, Brother David Darst. When he settled into the witness box, the clean-shaven Darst hardly looked like a radical firebrand. He had parted his hair neatly to the side and wore browline-style eyeglasses that had been popular in the 1950s. One observer asserted that he appeared "ingenuous, trim, rosy-cheeked, with the spruced handsomeness of a bridegroom on a Victorian daguerreotype." His only concession to the times seemed to be a relatively modest pair of sideburns.[29]

Prodded by Kunstler, Darst explained why he had not entered the draft board's second-floor offices to seize the draft files: "Perhaps I could be called the lookout man." He had stationed himself on the front porch of the Knights of Columbus building. If the police had arrived during the raid, he was to rush upstairs and alert his compatriots.[30]

But acting as a scout had been only one part of Darst's role in what he half-jokingly described as "a Bonnie and Clyde act on behalf of God and man." He also had helped to concoct the napalm used by the Nine. Darst told the jury that, while the Nine had generally followed the recipe that had been adapted from the Special Forces handbook, they had not cooked it into a jelly as specified. There was a good reason for deviation from the military guidelines: "We left it in liquid form," he said, "so we could pour it on the files."[31]

It wasn't by accident that the activists had chosen to use napalm in Catonsville. As Darst testified, "We felt it was fitting that this agent which had burned human flesh in the war in Vietnam and in many other places should now be poured on the records which gave war and violence their cruel legitimacy."[32]

As he would with all of the defendants, Kunstler made a point of eliciting testimony from Darst about his motives in participating in the Catonsville protest. Darst responded powerfully, explaining for jurors in vivid terms how his concerns over the war in Vietnam, and its broader impact on American society, had grown over the preceding few years. Darst said that, like many of those who joined him in Catonsville, he had been influenced by reading such indictments of American foreign policy in Southeast Asia as Theodore Draper's book *Abuse of Power*. Darst also testified that his thinking had been shaped by the criticisms articulated by congressional foes of the war, including Mike Mansfield and J. William Fulbright, the Johnson administration's chief antagonists in the Senate.[33]

Darst offered emotional testimony to explain why he had gone beyond just reading about the war. He told jurors that he had hoped to "raise a cry, an outcry at what was clearly a crime, an unnecessary suffering, a clear and wanton slaughter." That Vietnam was such an expensive exercise in brutality had heightened Darst's outrage and further motivated him to act. While the country frittered away billions of dollars hunting phantom enemies around the globe, children in the nation's inner cities—some of whom Darst regularly encountered during his time in St. Louis—were starving. It was, he testified, "an astonishing thing that our country cannot command the energy to give bread and milk to children, yet it can rain fire and death on people ten thousand miles away for reasons that are unclear to thoughtful men."[34]

Beyond crying out against the war in Vietnam, he wanted to "hinder this war in a literal way, an actual physical way." Darst likened this impulse to how some Czechs, during the recent occupation of their country by the Soviet Union, had attempted to thwart the progress of tanks by hurling bricks into their wheels. Like those determined Czechs, he had meant to take some action "to halt the machine of death" in Vietnam.[35]

Kunstler also hoped to underscore for the jury—and for the far larger audience following the trial outside the courtroom—the defendants' religious motives in destroying the draft files in Catonsville. Darst did this particularly well, referencing the New Testament's portrayal of Jesus. He also "was guilty of assault and battery when he cast the money changers from the temple and wasted their property and wealth," Darst said. "He was saying [that] it is wrong to do what you are doing." The Nine had made a similar decision in confronting the employees at the Selective Service office in Catonsville and destroying the draft files.[36]

It was during Darst's testimony that Kunstler began to spar with Thomsen over what became a central legal issue in the trial of the Catonsville Nine: the extent to which the jury should consider the activists' intent in seizing and burning the draft files.

At one point, Kunstler asked Darst "whether it was your intent to commit a criminal act of burning draft files." Prosecutor Arthur Murphy quickly objected, setting off the first of many prolonged discussions of the matter with Thomsen.

"Your honor, I think the law is quite clear that a defendant, where intent is an issue, may testify as to what his intent was," Kunstler said.

"Well, did he say he did not intend to burn the files?" Thomsen asked him.

Kunstler rephrased the question, but Arthur Murphy again objected.

"He is asking for a legal opinion, in essence, from his witness, Your Honor," the prosecutor said. "If he wants to ask whether he intended to do the act, that is one thing. But to say whether he intended to commit a criminal act is asking for a legal opinion, about which this witness cannot answer."

Kunstler withdrew the question, but the exchange continued. The defense attorney attempted to explain how his line of questioning with Darst fit in with the defense's approach to all of the counts in the indictment. He argued that

> if the defendant broke a car in order let smoke out because people were dying inside from smoke, that his intent, of course, is, on the one hand, to break the window, which is a crime and could be a crime; but, on the other hand, he has the further intent, which is to save a life. And I think he is entitled to show that. And if his position here is that he is trying to save a life, a collective life in Vietnam, then he is also entitled to show the same thing, or else we have a complete difference between the two.[37]

Thomsen backed off, but not completely. He allowed the Nine to testify broadly about their motives, but he instructed the jury that the term *intent* had a very specific legal meaning that should be applied when they considered the defendants' guilt or innocence. (There was ongoing disagreement over the extent to which this compromise allowed the defendants to make their case, and it would be central to their subsequent legal appeal.)

One tragicomic moment seemed to symbolize Darst's trial testimony. Prosecutor Arthur Murphy referenced the claim made by the Nine that draft files had no right to exist because of their role in expediting an illegal and immoral war. Did Darst hold a similar view of slum properties?

"Slum properties, I would say, have no right to exist," Darst replied.

Murphy pounced on the claim, which to him suggested that Darst might be a threat to torch any number of things he found offensive. "Would you symbolically burn down slum properties?"

The question baffled Darst. "How could I symbolically burn down slum properties?" he asked.

The quip amused many spectators, and their laughter briefly interrupted Murphy's questioning. Thomsen, however, was less than pleased to have the decorum in his courtroom breached. "If we have any more demonstrations," he warned, "we are going to clear the courtroom."[38]

Darst's parents had traveled to Baltimore for the trial. The night before it started, he and his mother shared a dinner with a Christian Brother who had come to Baltimore to show his support. The defendant was relaxed, but his mother was anxious and somewhat confused. When Darst briefly left the table to speak with some well-wishers, she turned to her dinner companion and revealed to him "how truly perplexed she was as to why David got involved in this whole enterprise," as he recalled. He did his best to reassure her, explaining Darst's motivations and putting them into the context of the times.[39]

Darst's parents hid their qualms from public view. They watched his testimony from the front row of the gallery and beamed at him. Both said they were immensely proud of the stand their son had taken in opposing the war. His father was heard commenting during one break in the trial, "I have a son at Harvard, a son at Yale, another at Notre Dame, and I'm prouder of David than all of them." Darst's mother emanated pride as well. "Our David," she boasted, "is so Christ-like."[40]

For the second day of trial-related protests, the Baltimore Defense Committee chose to focus its attention on individuals it described as "Selective Slavery personnel." At noon, a group of about 250 demonstrators assembled at St. Ignatius. From there they marched in "a muted, slow procession," as a local newspaper called it, down Calvert Street toward the Custom House, which housed the city's main Selective Service office—the target of the Baltimore Four protest a year earlier. They bore a black coffin rendered from papier-mâché. It was meant to symbolize all of those who had died in Vietnam, civilians and soldiers alike.[41]

When they reached the Custom House, police allowed six protesters to enter the building and leave the coffin in a vestibule. (Incredibly, they obtained a makeshift receipt reading, "Received at the Custom House . . . one coffin.") As the Baltimore Peace Action Center later explained, "The coffin was a symbol of all the people—American and Vietnamese—who have been killed in the war so far. We gave the coffin to the Selective Slavery people because they are directly responsible for these deaths." Two demonstrators were allowed to enter the Selective Service office itself and deliver brief speeches denouncing the war. They also engaged in a terse conversation with some draft personnel.[42]

As had been the case on the first day of protests, a few hecklers taunted the peace activists. Some of them carried signs reading "HANG THE NINE." Despite this friction, the Nine were buoyed by news of the protest. Phil Berrigan was happy to hear that a large and raucous contingent of demonstrators had delivered a coffin to the Custom House. "It is impossible to explain," he wrote from jail, "what such support means to us."[43]

Throughout the week, much of that support came from young people. College students from campuses all over the country flocked to Baltimore for the trial, and more than a few local high-schoolers played hooky in order to join in the festivities. One older observer appreciated how uninhibited and joyful these "kids" seemed to be, even when they were forced to sleep on the floor. They somehow managed to transform "the atmosphere of the trial from solemn farce into carnival celebration."[44]

A few of the younger activists exhibited remarkable zeal. The FBI noted that the demonstrators' ranks at the Custom House included a sixteen-year old boy who ardently opposed the war in Vietnam. According to the FBI's subsequent report of the incident, the boy engaged in a heated exchanged with Selective Service authorities and pledged to defy them when the time came. The youth said "that although he did not have a draft card, when he came of age he would refuse to carry one and would resist induction."[45]

After demonstrating at the Custom House, the protesters broke into groups of ten and fanned out across the Baltimore area. Each group intended to confront members of local draft boards in their places of business. The BDC explained, in one of its many fiery press releases, that "local draft board members in Baltimore, hitherto virtually anonymous, must be regarded as *public* officials, subject to exposure and censure for their collusion [in] Selective Slavery." What's more, the protesters hoped to convince the draft board members to resign from their posts by alerting them to pervasive inequities in the draft system.[46]

It was rough going. "Some of us were lucky, some were not," one demonstrator commented. "Most of the Draft Board members were conveniently out." One group attempted to track down city councilman Jerome Dashner, who served on Local Board 25. Unable to find Dashner at his city hall office, protesters walked over to his law firm, but he couldn't be found there either. They did, however, encounter another partner in the firm; he reacted angrily to their presence, threatening to call the police if they didn't leave right away.[47]

The group led by Bob Dalsemer had better luck finding Harry Schuh, chair of Local Board 9. Dalsemer asked Schuh to quit, but he refused, stating that he had a responsibility to serve his country and to ensure that the draft was administered fairly. Schuh also disputed the claim that the draft was objectionable on religious grounds. The draft board chair quoted words attributed to Jesus regarding an individual's duties to the state: "Render unto Caesar the things that are Caesar's."[48]

The protesters then drifted back to the courthouse "to picket," one of them later wrote, "to talk, to proclaim our message to the gathering crowd, and to wait for our friends to join us for supper." Throughout the week, organizing that evening meal proved to be a Herculean task for organizers, who found themselves in the position of having to feed a small army. "I think every night we planned for 2,500 or so," recalled Viva House's Brendan Walsh, one of the volunteers who endeavored to feed the protesters each night at St. Ignatius. If these meals were not elaborate, they were at least festive—and nourishing.

"Only a tired and disgruntled stomach would, I suppose, have rejected the potluck supper they created one evening out of canned baked beans, cold cuts, sliced American cheese and store-bought bread," according to writer Anthony Towne.[49]

In addition to helping prepare meals at St. Ignatius, Walsh and Willa Bickham hosted many of the Nine and droves of protesters at Viva House. Throughout the week of the trial, people seemed to be packed into every room. The hustle and bustle proved to be too much for Dorothy Day. After spending a few restless nights at Viva House, she approached Walsh and Bickham and asked if they would be bothered if she found quieter quarters somewhere else in Baltimore. With their blessing, she wound up staying at the parish of Father Neil McLaughlin. Like nearly everyone who came into contact with her, the priest was moved by Day's presence. "Just experiencing her for those days was a whole new thing for me that required rethinking and attempting to understand where I fit into all that was happening," he later said. True to form, Day did not turn her back completely on Viva House: after she left to stay at McLaughlin's parish, she returned to the Catholic Worker residence to help wash the dishes.[50]

On the second night of the trial week, the basement hall at St. Ignatius hosted what organizers described as a "resistance rap and rally." Mary Moylan was the first of the Nine to address the crowd. As she approached the microphone, "a young man suddenly stepped toward her from the audience and—as if in response to her very presence—set fire to his draft card and held it high," Barbara Deming later wrote. About two dozen men followed suit over the course of the evening, burning their draft cards as the crowd chanted, "Hell no, we won't go!" (According to one count, by the end of the week more than forty draft cards had gone up in flames.[51])

But after the daring actions of the Baltimore Four, the Catonsville Nine, and now the Milwaukee Fourteen, this particular act of defiance apparently had lost some of its luster. Francine du Plessix Gray thought that "there was something cruelly jaded, tired, blasé about the gesture" of burning a draft card, which now seemed "as old-fashioned as the Charleston." The destruction of draft cards had become so passé, Gray mused, that the FBI agents observing the meeting appeared indifferent to it (or at least tried to).[52]

Dan Berrigan energized the crowd. Responding to chants of "We want Dan! We want Dan!" he bounded to the rostrum and launched into a long complaint over the trial. "I'm caught in the bind of sitting through four days of fly shit at this trial," he said, "a process not worth its weight in that commodity." He mocked the composition of the jury, saying that it failed to represent the nation's true racial, economic, and political diversity. "None of these people are black, none of them are students, none of them are poor. They've all been through three wars and lump them into one. Sunday they go to church. Monday they go to the National Guard, Tuesday they go back to church, Wednesday they go to the Rotary Club where someone is waiting with a fly net to catch them to sit in the jury box." Nor did Berrigan think much of Thomsen, "that poor guy in the black bathrobe who needs a retirement thing." By the time the proceedings were done, the judge was "going to give us a slow death by drowning us in Karo Syrup." Such criticisms probably were unfair—the defense deliberately had refused to shape the composition of the jury during voir dire, and Thomsen had given the defense plenty of latitude in putting on its case— but people in the crowd seemed not to care. Each of Berrigan's points was greeted with boisterous cheers.[53]

It was a blessing that the trial had been energized by Darst's moving testimony earlier that day. "The judge is trying desperately to preserve the atmosphere. He's been running a mortician's chapel all his life," the priest said. "Suddenly he's confronting a scene of life and heart. Brother Darst came on and the whole thing came alive. All the clocks began to start without anyone winding them." The moment rejuvenated Berrigan, who had been feeling weighed down by the oppressive mood in the courtroom. "One began," he told the crowd, "to pick up one's own heartbeat again."[54]

Boston University's Howard Zinn, Berrigan's partner in his mission to Hanoi earlier in the year, also spoke at St. Ignatius that night. Zinn argued that the American judicial system missed the forest for the trees, doggedly prosecuting individuals like the Nine for small transgressions while ignoring the nation's broader crimes. He wondered why national leaders couldn't be charged with appropriate offenses. Referring to the vice president and Democratic nominee for president, he asked, "Why don't they put Hubert Humphrey on trial for disorderly conduct—or vagrancy?"[55]

"I Am Trying to Speak as a Human Being to the Jury"

By the trial's third day, it had become clear that it would not be a replay of the trial of the Baltimore Four. Tom Lewis's mother commented that the Catonsville Nine trial was a "love-in" compared with that earlier proceeding, which she had suffered through the previous April. "Then, everyone looked at us as though we were scum of the earth," she said one day in the courtroom. "Now, look at the crowds in here and outside." The ebullient mood in the courtroom lifted her spirits; she was untroubled by the prospect of her son being incarcerated. "Tom and Phil," she said of her son and his codefendant, "are the freest men in the world."[1]

This was true only figuratively. Federal marshals bound the two men in handcuffs as they were taken to and from the trial. But even then, they felt liberated by the shows of support they received. Lewis was especially moved one morning after he had entered the courtroom and sat down at the defendants' table. Someone tapped him on the shoulder and whispered, "Look around, look around! Dorothy is here to see you."

It was Dorothy Day, one of his heroes. Smiling and gesturing a greeting, she looked radiant to Lewis. It appeared to him that she was surrounded by sunshine.[2]

The longest day of the trial—the court would hear testimony for a full ten hours—began with the testimony of Phil Berrigan. For writer Francine du Plessix Gray, his appearance on the witness stand provided one of the more unsettling moments of the entire week. Animated by a passion to combat injustice, Berrigan had seemed to be a vibrant and indestructible force in the late 1960s. But when he testified at the Catonsville trial he appeared "exhausted, browbeaten, unsure," she wrote. Berrigan's face looked wan and haggard; his suit (issued by the Federal Bureau of Prisons) fit poorly, giving him a gaunt appearance. At least for the moment, Berrigan looked like a beaten man.[3]

Berrigan's testimony "was long and dragging, with the compulsive loquaciousness of lonely men," Gray observed. Detailing for the jury his long journey to Catonsville, he recounted his upbringing, his service in World War II, and his experiences in the priesthood. He also explained why he had felt compelled to abandon more conventional means of protest against the war in Vietnam. With more than a hint of annoyance in his voice, Berrigan described his failed attempts to engage policymakers like Secretary of State Dean Rusk in meaningful discussions about the pointlessness of the war. Throughout this narrative, "his mind seemed to wander; and the judge, afraid as ever of trespassing on an idol of the young, looked both pitying and exasperated," Gray observed.[4]

But Berrigan still made some important contributions to the defendants' overall case. He offered a stirring justification for the protest at the Catonsville draft board. He also complained that some real criminals—the architects of American foreign policy—had managed to escape punishment altogether. Taking issue with accusations that the Nine were arrogant, he asked, "But what of the fantastic arrogance of our leaders? What of their crimes against the people—the poor and the powerless? Still no court will try them, no jail will receive them." These were the people who deserved to be hauled into a courtroom.[5]

Prosecutors took a dim view of Berrigan's arguments, and they did their best to demonstrate how public order might be disrupted if individuals did not feel obliged to follow the law. Assistant United States Attorney Barney Skolnik asked, "If someone, feeling just as sincerely and just as deeply and just as conscientiously as you do . . . that the war is in the interests of this country, broke into a peace action center or some other repository of papers and documents, . . . and destroyed and stole and burned and mutilated those objects, would you feel that he had violated the law and should be prosecuted for having done so?"

"Certainly," Berrigan replied. "We violated the law, and we should have been prosecuted. . . . I think that their views ought to be exposed through testing by the community . . . just as our views are being tested by this community now and by, we hope, a larger community outside."

"Should they be convicted for the violation of the law?" Skolnik asked.

"I think that is your problem," Berrigan muttered.[6]

When it was over, Berrigan despaired over the ineffectiveness of his testimony. Describing the day in his journal, he wrote in frustration, "It is fruitless to review now what I said—it is simply not worth the effort. The government outmaneuvered me." He felt that he had been knocked off his stride by prosecutors' incessant objections and the ensuing wrangling that involved the judge and both teams of attorneys. Before long, the proceedings "speedily degenerated into a three-ring legal circus, with lawyers bouncing me about like balls among trained seals." The priest complained that both he and one of his own attorneys, Harold Buchman, had contributed to this courtroom debacle by not focusing on the larger issues at stake in the trial. Berrigan wrote in his journal, "I stepped down from the stand furious with my lawyer, the prosecutors, and myself."[7]

Listening to the trial testimony of the Nine, Richard Shaull, a professor at Princeton Theological Seminary, was struck by the fact that "for several of them, the experience of living and working in . . . Africa or Latin America had been the most important factor in shaping their decision" to participate in the raid on Local Board 33.[8]

Case in point: George Mische, who took the stand after Phil Berrigan. Mische explained why he had acted in Catonsville by relating to the jury his experiences organizing labor, land, and housing programs in Latin America and the Caribbean. He testified that he initially had been surprised that he and his fellow American aid workers were not welcomed with open arms in the region. But then Mische had come to understand why the Americans were so disliked: their government, while paying lip service to the principles of representative democracy, repeatedly backed military dictatorships. Actual American policy in Latin America and the Caribbean thus proved to be exactly the opposite of what policymakers, including President Kennedy, had pledged.[9]

This had been the case in the Dominican Republic, Mische testified. There, strongman Rafael Trujillo had relied on American backing to squelch democracy and throttle economic reform. His rule had been an unbelievable tragedy for that struggling country.

Mische offered a graphic description of repression in the Dominican Republic, and it set off a minor uproar in the courtroom. While jurors and spectators murmured in surprise, prosecutor Arthur Murphy rose and objected that Mische's testimony wasn't relevant. Judge Thomsen agreed and offered yet another admonition to the defendants, telling Mische, "We are not here to try the history of the world in the twentieth century."[10]

Mische disagreed. The motives of the Catonsville Nine, he stressed, had to be viewed within an expansive historical, political, and socioeconomic context. Furthermore, the defendants had to be afforded the opportunity to address the jury as people. "I am trying to speak as a human being to the jury," Mische said, "who I hope are human beings and can understand us." For him, the case—and, in a broader sense, the fate of American society—boiled down to whether ordinary Americans could connect on this level and address the central problems facing the world. "Will the jury dare to deal with the spirit of the law and the issues we are talking about? If not, we can expect no peace, no solutions, only disorder and riots in our country and in the world."[11]

Unwilling to countenance American foreign policy in Central America and the Caribbean, Mische had quit his post and returned to the United States. He told jurors that he had traveled the country in an effort to alert American Catholic leaders to their country's transgressions in places like the Dominican Republic. Mische had hoped that, in addition to pressuring the

Johnson administration to support democracy abroad, they might use some of the church's abundant financial resources to help the poor. But the bishops had ignored Mische's bold recommendations. "As a Catholic," he told the jury, "I apologize to you for their cowardice."[12]

"We asked them, since they have $80 billion worth of property and ten times as much in investments, that, if they were really going to live in the spirit of the stable that Christ came from, then [to] get rid of the buildings," Mische testified. "Give to the poor. No. Yet the man who wanted to build the churches in Christ's time was Judas. And Christ kept saying—"

Prosecutor Arthur Murphy, feeling that that the trial was once again veering off course, stepped in.

"Your honor, may I object again?" he said. "This defendant, your honor, is doing the exact opposite of the very thing he claims he stands for in a sense. He is talking about protecting the rights of others. Now, he is infringing of the rights of the jury and the Court, who are here to consider one thing."

Thomsen cut him off.

"It is overruled," he told the prosecutor.

Still, Murphy's comments inflamed defense attorney William Kunstler.

"That is an outrageous statement and ought to be stricken, your honor, [about] infringing on the rights of the jurors," he said. "The jurors are here to listen and to reach a determination."

Both sides of the case were now testing Thomsen's patience.

"I overrule Mr. Murphy's objection and tell the jury to disregard anything Mr. Murphy may have said in it, but I will say, again, another item that we are not here to try," the judge said. "We are not here to try the Catholic bishops of the United States."[13]

Mische's anger over the Johnson administration's mishandling of the war in Vietnam matched his animosity toward the sclerotic American Catholic hierarchy. The president lacked the constitutional authority to declare war; that power resided with Congress. "The President cannot legally take us into a war," he argued. "We should never have let him." Mische felt that since Johnson had broken the law so flagrantly, it was the president who deserved to be facing criminal charges. "He should be on trial here today," he insisted. (This assertion occasioned such a loud round of applause from the gallery that Thomsen had to pound his gavel to restore order.) After all, the magnitude of Johnson's offense dwarfed that of the Catonsville Nine. "This society is getting all uptight about [us] burning 378 pieces of paper or whatever it was," Mische said, referencing the number of draft records that had been destroyed in Catonsville. "Every day they're putting napalm on people and burning them to death."[14]

Mische testified that, in an effort to draw sufficient attention to those deaths, he had felt compelled to do "something drastic, something people could see. But the act had to be nonviolent. We were not out to destroy life." He stressed that he was not lawless. "There is a higher law we are commanded to obey,"

Mische said. "It takes precedence over human laws." A desire to adhere to that higher law, and thereby to help the victims of American militarism, had driven him to take action in Catonsville.[15]

"We get hung up on law and order," Mische said from the stand. "I think we have to understand what the law is all about. . . . The intent was to follow the higher law that all of us have, as human beings, and as Americans, and as whatever we consider ourselves: humanists, Christians, Jews, Buddhists, or whatnot. That was our responsibility; that was our intent. The double intent was to save a lot of lives, Vietnamese, North and South, American lives, everybody, to stop the madness. That was the intent."[16]

During a later break in the trial, supporters of the Nine crowded around the defendant in the hallway outside the courtroom and offered their congratulations. There was discussion of the liberties that Thomsen had given Mische and his fellow defendants in their testimony. They had been able to discuss just about anything—the lessons of the Gospels, the war in Vietnam, American involvement in Central America. Someone asked the defense attorneys what they made of it. "He can't risk the possibility of a mistrial by restrictive rulings on this one," Buchman surmised. "Also, he's painfully aware of the peace sentiment in the community, of the division in the nation." Kunstler had an additional explanation. "I also think that he's fascinated to hear what these defendants have to say," he said, grinning mischievously.[17]

As Phil Berrigan later described it, Tom Melville offered "a strong indictment of national policy and tried to explain how men of goodwill—including those enforcing the law—are being co-opted by the system." The centerpiece of this indictment was a recounting of his experiences among the peasantry in Guatemala. For Melville, this was not routine background information. "I took part in that action in Catonsville," he testified, "because of what happened to me in Guatemala."[18]

Poverty blighted the entire region, Melville told the jury, and the vast majority of Guatemalans were destitute. This was not the result of any lack of initiative or ability on the part of the indigenous people there. Rather, ordinary Guatemalans lived in squalor because they were victims of an exploitive economic system in which the United States played a key role. "They live in misery because 2 percent of the population are determined to keep them that way," he said. "These 2 percent are aligned with business interests in Guatemala, especially with the United Fruit Company. The United States government identifies its interests in Guatemala with the interests of American big business and with the Guatemalan 2 percent who control the country."[19]

The integral role of the United States in subordinating poor Guatemalans was not limited to economic exploitation, Melville explained. Reformers in Guatemala were labeled communists, and many were executed with the complicity or outright involvement of the American forces that covertly operated in the country.

Thomsen interjected.

"You mean the United States government is executing Guatemalans?" he asked.

"Yes, your honor," Melville told him.

Thomsen was taken aback by Melville's claim, and the two men sparred over its plausibility. The judge displayed remarkable patience throughout the defendants' testimony, but he felt compelled to rein in Melville.

"Well, we are not trying the series of Guatemalan revolutions," he noted.

"No," Melville said, "the court is quite busy trying us."[20]

Thomsen was not unique in his apparent ignorance of events in Guatemala. When they returned to the United States early in 1968, Melville, his wife, and John Hogan had been struck by how little the American people knew about what was happening in Central America. Legitimate concerns about the war in Vietnam seemed to overshadow analogous problems in other parts of the globe. "We discussed among ourselves what we could do to bring some of the focus to Latin America," he said. "We knew that we did not want to turn it away from Vietnam, but we did want people who were upset about the morality of our government to exercise some of their concern toward Latin America, and specifically Guatemala, where we had lived." After thinking it over, they had concluded that participating in the demonstration at the Catonsville draft board would serve this purpose.[21]

Melville had considered engaging in traditional means of protest to bring attention to the plight of the Guatemalan people. But the magnitude and urgency of their problems had driven him to take the extraordinary step of participating in the Catonsville scheme. "I think writing letters and parading are great when you want to enlarge a sewer system or put in a new highway," he said. "But when people are being murdered, you have to take dramatic action."[22]

"I wish there was a magic button that we could have pushed, instead of the action in Catonsville," Melville explained. "But there is not."[23]

One of the minor mysteries of the Catonsville Nine trial involved the sound of bells in the courtroom. The defendants periodically heard a soft tinkling noise as they exited or entered. The source turned out to be Mary Moylan: she was wearing a small golden bell on a chain around her neck. Dan Berrigan thought that she wore the bells to say, in effect, "I can rejoice in the middle of this."[24] Moylan herself explained that it was "a mere tinkle against the thudding gavel, a whispered plea amid the insane clamor of war."[25]

When it was her turn to testify, Moylan recounted for the jury her formative experiences outside the United States. She had gone to Uganda in the late 1950s as a lay worker for a religious order and had held a variety of positions there over the next several years, doing everything from working as a nurse-midwife to teaching English in a secondary school. Eventually, she clashed with her superiors over the amount of responsibility that the order was willing to give to the Africans themselves. "Much of our role," she lamented, "seemed to be to provide a white face in a black community."[26]

She had returned to the United States in the mid-1960s and settled down in Washington, D.C. Over the next several years, Moylan had worked extensively in the local African American community and became aware of its economic and political disenfranchisement. It struck her that conditions for the poor in the United States were scarcely better than they were for the underprivileged abroad. It was apparent, she told the jury, "that we had no right to speak to foreign countries about their policies when things at home were in very sad shape."[27]

Moylan testified that she had developed a particular concern for the plight of African Americans during her time in Washington. Tragically, although they lived in the nation's capital, they were denied many of the most basic rights of American citizenship. "In fact, justice for a black person is just about impossible," she said.[28]

Moylan said that the core tenets of her religious faith had influenced her decision to take action in Catonsville. After observing myriad injustices both at home and abroad, she had felt compelled to "stand up. This is what it means to be a Christian, that you act on what you say you believe." Christ had done so, providing a powerful example that still had relevance in contemporary society. "This was what Christ meant when he lived," Moylan testified. "We have not only to talk, but if we see something wrong we have to be willing to do something about it."[29]

Testifying in a trial for the second time in six months, Tom Lewis recounted his experiences as a civil rights activist in Baltimore in the mid-1960s and described the growth of his interest in the war in Vietnam. He told of the efforts he and his fellow antiwar activists had undertaken to highlight the folly of the war for lawmakers, Johnson administration officials, and assorted members of the Pentagon hierarchy. This form of protest had proven ineffective, so Lewis had turned to civil disobedience. It was a legitimate form of social protest with deep roots in the Christian tradition, he said from the witness stand. "It is well documented in Christianity," Lewis maintained. "Civil disobedience was practiced by the early Christians." He offered as examples "the Apostles walking through the grain field on the Sabbath; the Apostles taking the food that was in the temple to be offered, and giving it to the poor." And then, of course, there had been Jesus himself "disrupting the temple, chasing people out of the temple because of the way the temple was being used. It was no longer used for the good of the community."[30]

Lewis's sense of responsibility first had led him to Baltimore's Custom House, where he, Phil Berrigan, and two others had chosen a symbolic means of attacking draft records. "This protest involved the pouring of blood—a strong indictment of those records," Lewis testified. "Blood in biblical terms and in contemporary terms is a symbol of reconciliation related to the blood that is being wasted in Vietnam—not only American blood but the blood of the Vietnamese." For their protest in Catonsville, Lewis and his eight confederates had chosen another emblem: napalm. They had used it "to destroy records, which are potential death certificates. They stand for the death of men; they represent men who are put in the situation where they have to kill."[31]

Before taking part in the Baltimore Four and Catonsville Nine protests, Lewis had not been blind to the risks involved. "I was well aware that in civil disobedience," he told the jury, "you take an action, you stand, you are arrested, you attempt to express your views, you are prepared to take the consequences." The severity of the consequences of the Custom House raid—a criminal conviction and a federal prison term—had not dissuaded Lewis from participating in the Catonsville demonstration. "I was aware, too, that if I became involved in Catonsville I would be summoned once more for trial. This is the trial, and a greater sentence may follow."[32]

Lewis had not made this decision precipitously; he had agonized over the apparent choice that lay before him. "In a sense, it was a choice between life and death," he testified. "It was a choice between saving one's soul and losing it. I was saving my soul."[33]

Thomsen was less concerned about the state of Lewis's soul than he was worried about the activist's respect for the federal criminal code. As he would throughout much of the trial, Thomsen interjected with a pointed question: Had Lewis been aware that it was illegal to seize and burn Selective Service records? Lewis responded frankly, telling him, "I wasn't concerned with the law. I wasn't even thinking about the law." Instead, Lewis had been "thinking of what those records meant"—the dispatch of more young men to Vietnam.[34]

As for his objective in participating in the Catonsville protest, it had been clear from the start. "My intent in going there," Lewis said, "was to save lives." And to preserve those lives, he had been willing to break federal law for the second time within the span of a year.[35]

Thomsen struggled with Lewis's reasoning. Sure, destroying a few draft records housed in Local Board 33 might delay the induction of some young men in the Catonsville area, but wouldn't they be replaced by other draftees? Would the lives of any servicemen actually be saved? Now it was Lewis's turn to be incredulous. "Why does it have to be like this?" he asked Thomsen, attacking the entire premise of the judge's query. "You are accepting the fact that if these men are not sent, other men will be sent. You are not even asking what can be done to stop this insane killing, what can be done to stop the genocide, what can be done to stop the conditions in Latin America. You are not dealing with these things."[36]

Lewis then offered that Thomsen's complaisance about the slaughter in Vietnam—and American-sponsored discord in other parts of the globe—was similar to the German citizenry's acquiescence during the Holocaust. Germans, too, had dutifully "accepted the massacre of other people." But

Lewis refused go along; he had to voice his objections, and loudly. "This is insane," he said of the senseless killing in Vietnam and elsewhere. "I protest this."[37]

Agitated by how far Lewis had roamed in his testimony, federal prosecutor Arthur Murphy broke in with an objection.

"I don't know how long he is going to continue," he said.

"How long? I have six years, Mr. Prosecutor," Lewis said, referring to the sentence he already had received for his role in the Baltimore Four protest. "I have lots of time."[38]

Although some of the Nine seemed to radiate confidence during the trial, many of them experienced—if only briefly—moments of doubt and fear. John Hogan, for instance, was unsettled by the stares of the contingent of FBI agents who kept close watch on the defendants throughout the trial. When Hogan spoke to Mische about it, he was told to maintain his composure. "They're just trying to intimidate you," Mische said. Hogan could show his mettle by staring right back at them.[39]

The prospect of being found guilty and sent to federal prison did not faze Hogan. He already had reconciled himself to that fate. What really frightened the modest, soft-spoken man was having to get up and speak at length in public about his background and beliefs. "I was kind of tense in trying to give my story," he later said of his trial testimony. "I was more nervous about being on the stand and talking and saying what I had to say."[40]

Hogan surmounted his fears and delivered stirring testimony. While Lewis had addressed the symbolism of napalm, Hogan detailed for jurors the logistics of its manufacture. "I thought it was necessary," he later said, "that the jury understand about the making of napalm." It sickened him to know that the American military was using this devastating weapon in Vietnam. (As he later said, "It was just overwhelming to think about that."[41])

When he discussed his rationale for destroying property—and thereby breaking the law—in Catonsville, Hogan offered a memorable analogy:

> I see it like if there were a group of children walking along the street, returning home from school, and a car was coming down the street and was out of control, and even though there was a driver in that car, and if I were coming along in a car, and if I could divert that car from crashing into those children, then I feel as though I would have had an obligation to divert that car from the children. Of course, the car is property. The car would be damaged. And it is also possible that something would happen to the individual in the car. But I would be thinking ten times more of these children whom the car was going to hit than I would be thinking of the individual in that car.[42]

Hogan poignantly underscored this notion when he was asked about his intent in going to Catonsville. "I want to let people live," he said. "That is all."[43]

The stress of testifying affected Hogan so much that, during one break in the trial, he left the courtroom and asked one of the federal marshals present for an aspirin.

"You guys look so calm up there," the marshal said. "I can't believe you're asking for an aspirin."

"It'll give you a headache," Hogan joked.[44]

Hogan's spirits rose once he had gotten through his testimony. After leaving the stand, he spoke with Stanley Spector, a Washington University professor who had traveled from St. Louis to Baltimore to attend the trial. "You know, Dr. Spector, I was very frightened before the trial," Hogan told him. "I kept having butter-flies in my stomach. But once I was called up, I felt fine. I feel fine now."[45]

The demeanor and poise of Hogan and his fellow colleagues left an impression on the federal marshals who observed the trial. "Reading the papers, you'd have thought they were a bunch of kooks," one was overheard saying during a break. "But they're not, they're a bunch of regular guys."[46]

The reporters on hand were amazed, too—by the defendants themselves and by the sprawling scope of their testimony. "I've been covering the court-room for forty years," a local scribe commented, "and this one beats them all."[47]

Marjorie Melville enjoyed the trial because it drew so many like-minded people to Baltimore, and they were able to protest and air their views about poverty, war, and justice. "It was fun," she later said. "It was a continuation of the sense of community, of being together." She was comforted by the presence in the courtroom of a friend from her Maryknoll days, a sister who traveled down from the order's headquarters in New York to show her support. She benefited as well from the solicitousness of defense attorney Harold Buchman, who patiently explained to her various legal maneuverings and trial proce-dures. "He'd keep us clued in," she recalled.[48]

Thomsen's forbearance with the defendants also heartened her. Although many of them grumbled about the judge's handling of the trial, she appreciated that he gave them the chance to testify at such length about how their experi-ences had shaped their evolving social, political, and religious beliefs. "The way the judge handled the trial really gave us a tremendous opportunity to speak," she later said. "He didn't have to be as open with us as he was."[49]

Marjorie recounted for the jury her experiences in Guatemala. The whole-some former missionary—one observer thought she resembled a cheerleader you might see on the sidelines at the Rose Bowl—furnished a vivid account of her activities in Central America and her awakening to the role played by the United States in the ongoing oppression of the peasantry. These had been anx-ious times for her, but she relaxed when recalling them for the jury because she realized that in Baltimore, unlike Guatemala, she was unlikely to face a death squad for speaking out openly against the government. She could argue that "Guatemala is Vietnam beginning again," as she did from the witness stand, without fearing for her life.[50]

After her expulsion from Guatemala the previous winter, she had returned to the United States and resolved to do something that would draw attention to how the American military meddled there and in other countries. "I wanted to make as effective a protest as possible to U.S. military intervention across the world, not only in Vietnam but in Guatemala, where I had seen it," she said. She acknowledged that she didn't know if burning draft files was "an effective way of stopping this war" against the people of Guatemala and Vietnam. But she knew that endlessly discussing the war had yielded negligible results.[51]

The Nine had gone beyond talking; in Catonsville they had attacked the machinery of the war itself, and for principled reasons. Confident that she had acted ethically (if not, in a narrow sense, legally), Melville did not worry about the verdicts that would be rendered by the jury and in the broader court of public opinion. "We do not ask for mercy. We do not ask that history judge us right," she offered from the witness stand. "That is a consolation for more visionary souls than ours."[52]

The defendants' testimony culminated with Dan Berrigan—somberly outfitted in black—taking the stand. His eloquence astonished even his fellow defendants. For Marjorie Melville, his testimony "was always so perfect"; she wondered if he had practiced it beforehand. Phil Berrigan was similarly impressed, but he felt that his brother could have done even better if defense attorneys hadn't so frequently interrupted the flow of his remarks with trivial questions.[53]

As he led the jury through his autobiography, Dan Berrigan underscored the importance of his trip to Hanoi. He testified that during their mission to bring back the captured American airmen, he and his colleague Howard Zinn had suffered through several American bombardments. This had brought home for him some sobering truths. "The bombings were a massive crime against man," he said. "The meaning of the air war in the North was the deliberate systematic destruction of a poor and developing people."[54]

This claim prompted another of Thomsen's periodic reminders about the parameters of the trial. "We are not trying the air war in North Vietnam," the judge said wearily. But the Jesuit stood his ground. "I must protest the effort," he retorted, "to discredit me on the stand. I am speaking of what I saw. There is a consistent effort to say that I did not see it."[55]

Berrigan also movingly described how his brother's participation in the Baltimore Four protest had impacted him. "My brother's action helped me realize," he remarked, "[that] from the beginning of our republic good men had said no, acted outside the law when the conditions so demanded." And the conditions were dire, Berrigan reported: the nation's neighborhoods were in decay, its poor were in despair, and young people found themselves in turmoil. At the Custom House, his brother had acted to call attention to those ills and thereby offered what might be recognized as "a gift to society, a gift to history and to the community." Stirred by this example, he had joined Phil in the Catonsville protest.[56]

Tying together his influences, Berrigan told jurors that he had gone to Catonsville that afternoon in May "and burned some papers because the burning of children is inhuman and unbearable. I went to Catonsville because I had gone to Hanoi, because my brother was a man and I must be a man, and because I knew at length [that] I could not announce the gospel from a pedestal." When he was asked directly about his intent in raiding Local Board 33, he said simply, "I did not want the children or the grandchildren of the jury or of the judge to be burned with napalm."[57]

Thomsen responded skeptically to the reference to concern over his grandchildren. "You say your intention was to save these children, of the jury, of myself, when you burned the records?" he asked Berrigan. "That is what I hear you say. I ask if you meant that." Berrigan was resolute. "I meant that—of course I mean that, or I would not say it," he shot back. "The great sinfulness of modern war is that it renders concrete things abstract. I do not want to talk about Americans in general."[58]

On the trial's third day, protesters maintained their presence outside the courthouse. Their fervor and numbers had diminished. Observing a subdued knot of about seventy demonstrators picketing outside the courthouse, one spectator cracked, "Yes, it's true: there are more FBI agents there than marchers." College students had begun filtering back to their campuses; more than a few priests, seminarians, and nuns had returned to their parish obligations or studies.[59]

Conflicts between the police and demonstrators remained relatively minor. At one point, the defense committee's Grenville Whitman and a fellow organizer were taken into custody by federal marshals for allegedly distributing literature inside the federal courthouse. (Federal authorities were adamant about keeping all protest and advocacy activities outside the building.) They spent about an hour in a holding cell—where they were feted with bologna sandwiches and Kool-Aid—before federal prosecutor Stephen Sachs appeared and freed them. There would be no charges filed, he said; it all had been a misunderstanding.[60]

Local officials expressed relief—and engaged in no small amount of self-congratulation—over the fact that so many activists had come and gone over the week of the trial without setting Baltimore aflame. Boasting that there had been no serious disruptions or arrests related to the trial, Mayor D'Alesandro issued an effusive congratulatory message praising police officers' "magnificent performance of duty under some of the most difficult and trying conditions that this city has faced."[61]

D'Alesandro earned the right to pat himself on the back, according to one later assessment. *Baltimore Sun* reporter Robert Erlandson had seen police in Chicago run amok during the Democratic convention, and he was impressed that their excesses weren't repeated a few months later in Baltimore. D'Alesandro, he believed, had made the difference by stressing to police their duty to act professionally.[62]

But even midweek, police still had their hands full. On Wednesday night, for instance, events at St. Ignatius were disrupted by a bomb scare. Police cleared the hall after receiving an anonymous tip that an explosive device had been placed somewhere on church property. While a group of several dozen police officers and firefighters searched for the bomb, several hundred supporters of the Nine milled around on Monument Street. They filed back in after authorities concluded that the threat was a hoax.[63]

Back inside the hall, the crowd heard from a variety of speakers, including William Stringfellow and the journalist I. F. Stone. Stringfellow, a lay theologian, might have given the most heroic performance of the week. His health had been failing over the course of several excruciating years, and he barely could walk. But Stringfellow felt that he could not fail to show his support of the Nine. He made his way to Baltimore and spoke briefly to the crowd at St. Ignatius after being coaxed by Dan Berrigan, whom he had known for many years. "I was exhausted, but this scene was exhilarating," Stringfellow later wrote. "The pain was unspeakably severe and had not been appeased by any medicine, but, amidst this congregation, it was not debilitating."[64]

Stringfellow had told Berrigan that he would deliver a brief salutation, but he unexpectedly offered something more akin to a rousing benediction. "The state can consign you to death," he said. "The grace of Jesus Christ in this life is that death fails. There is nothing the state can do to you, or to me, which we need fear." After a moment of stunned silence, the crowd burst into applause. As the frail Stringfellow shuffled away from the microphone, the audience spontaneously joined in a hymn.[65]

Stone's efforts were not quite as valorous as Stringfellow's, but they nonetheless jolted the crowd. The radical icon respected the Catonsville Nine's act of resistance, and he fulsomely praised it on the pages of his eponymous I. F. Stone's Weekly. Speaking at St. Ignatius, Stone offered a typically blunt call to arms. "More and more people must be willing to get in trouble with their own tribe or class, in short to be more human," he said. "That is just what the Catonsville Nine have done."[66]

"You Have Just Convicted Jesus Christ"

For Tom Lewis and Phil Berrigan, the trial's final day began in the marshal's cage, a cramped space located in the bowels of the Post Office and Courthouse Building. As they waited to be handcuffed and led into the courtroom, the two men discussed what they and their codefendants might do to cap off the trial. Writing later in his journal, Berrigan summarized his thinking at that moment: "We want to leave behind one clear and final action as a kind of legacy—bearing witness that what we did was both reasonable and obligatory."[1]

Before they entered the courtroom, the defendants had a bit of extra time to consider what this coup de grâce might be, as their entry was delayed while attorneys for both sides conferred with the judge. Meeting in Thomsen's chambers, they engaged in a prolonged debate over what defense attorney William Kunstler might say in his closing argument. Although he had indulged Kunstler throughout the trial, Thomsen was wary that the firebrand attorney might go too far in encouraging jurors to disregard his instructions and engage in jury nullification. The federal judge used the conference to warn Kunstler that he would not be given free rein to pull such a stunt in his closing.[2]

When the defendants filtered into the courtroom, the customary standing ovation lasted even longer than usual—a good seven minutes. "It was more elated, more theatrical than ever," one spectator reported, "having the style of an encore, ending with the rhythmical, measured clapping that celebrates a great performance."[3]

George Mische stood with his wife and held his infant daughter. Dan Berrigan took a moment to thank the crowd for having nurtured "such an extraordinary sense of community in this courtroom." He then hinted that, however the trial turned out, they had not heard the last of the Catonsville Nine. "We shall continue, by other means of communication, to share the experience which we have shared together in the past four days. I am not allowed by natural law, or the law of the Jesuits, or the law of the court, to say what these means of communication will be, but—" Then he smiled and said, "Hang in."[4]

The trial's final day began with closing arguments. For the prosecution, Assistant U.S. Attorney Arthur Murphy delivered a "predictable but tolerably short summary of the government's case," as Phil Berrigan called it. Murphy began by asking jurors to focus exclusively on the legal issues presented by the Catonsville case. He reminded them that, even though Thomsen had allowed hours of testimony about the war in Vietnam, the legality and morality of that conflict were not at issue in the trial. Instead, the case revolved around what the defendants had done in Catonsville—by seizing and destroying federal property, they had interfered with the military draft. There was no denying it.[5]

Murphy recognized that the defendants had been motivated to act out of sincere opposition to American imperialism and the nation's apparent unconcern for the poor. But they could have remained within the law in expressing that resistance. Although all of them had testified that they had tried such methods and found them ineffective, Murphy argued that the defendants had at their disposal a variety of legal means to voice their opposition to government policy. "You are allowed to speak in public places," he said. "You can write all the letters you want to your congressmen, to your legislators. You can write letters to the editor. . . ." Murphy waved his hand in the direction of the demonstrators outside the courthouse. "You can picket. You can debate. You can write books. You can write articles."[6]

Murphy's main point was simple: there would be anarchy if having noble intentions absolved all wrongdoers of legal responsibility for their crimes. So, whatever their motives, people had to be held accountable by the state when they broke the law.[7]

"The government has no dispute in terms of their sincerity. We do not question it," Murphy said. "We believe that these defendants are sincere." But they still were legally culpable, he argued. "A man may be ever so sincere, but, once the degree of that sincerity and that motive drives him beyond the boundaries of protest recognized by law, then he has to pay the penalty."[8]

"They have no defense, because they have, purposely, violated laws of the United States," he concluded. "And, finally, members of the jury, we only ask that you decide this case solely on the evidence that you have heard in the courtroom: testimony from the witnesses, photographs, the film which you have seen, the records which have been mutilated and destroyed and which have had to be reconstructed, a job which has not yet been completed." Murphy was confident about the result: "The government knows that justice will be done."[9]

While Murphy was calm and methodical in delivering the federal government's closing statement, Kunstler was animated and impassioned, pacing and gesticulating as his final arguments for the Catonsville Nine poured forth. One spectator thought that he prowled around the courtroom like a caged tiger. It was as if he hoped to strike an emotional chord with jurors by overwhelming them with the sheer physicality of his performance.[10]

Kunstler began with the obvious, telling the jury that the Catonsville case was anything but a run-of-the-mill criminal prosecution. In fact, it was a historic moment that deserved to be put into proper historical and political perspective. As he endeavored to do this, Kunstler admitted that he had ignored his law school professors' advice that attorneys never should identify too closely with their clients. "For myself," he said, "I must confess with more heartfelt pride than I could adequately describe, that in the course of this litigation I have come to love and respect the men and women who stand before this court." Kunstler said that he long would treasure the memory of the "transcendent witnesses they have given . . . in an attempt to persuade this court to bend in their direction."[11]

The Catonsville Nine were singular defendants because they were involved in such an extraordinary case. Everyone involved, including Thomsen, agreed that "this is a unique case," Kunstler stated. "It shares the historic meaning of other great contests of law. The trial of Socrates was not merely a question of a man sowing confusion and distrust among the youth of Athens; the trial of Jesus could not be reduced to one of conspiracy against the Empire." The Catonsville trial could join this vaunted list because of the profound issues that were at its core: conscience, compassion, and courage.[12]

There was absolutely no question that the Nine had seized and burned Selective Service records in Catonsville, as the federal government alleged. "In the first place, we agree with the prosecutor as to the essential facts of the case," Kunstler said frankly. "The defendants did participate in the burning of records." But Kunstler implored the jury to look at the case a bit more broadly and assess why the defendants had in engaged in such conduct. That, for Kunstler, was the heart of the case: the intent of the Nine.[13]

"The defendants weren't burning files for the sake of burning files," Kunstler averred. Nor did they "go to Catonsville to act as criminals, to frighten Mrs. Murphy, or to annoy or hinder her." Rather, they had two primary reasons for taking such a dramatic action. First, "they wanted, in some small way, to throw a roadblock into a system which they considered murderous, which was grinding young men, many thousands of them, to death in Vietnam," Kunstler said. "Also, they wanted, as they said, to reach the American public, to reach you. They were trying to make an outcry, an anguished outcry, to reach the American community before it was too late. . . . It was a cry of despair and anguish and hope, all at the same time. And to make this outcry, they were willing to risk years of their lives."[14]

The Selective Service records housed in Local Board 33 were not just ordinary government property, Kunstler told the jury. The files targeted by the Nine helped the government determine which young men might be used "for cannon fodder, if the government so dictates," he stated. "We are not talking about driving licenses or licenses to operate a brewery. We are speaking of one kind of records. No others so directly affect life and death on a mass scale, as do these. They affect every mother's son who is registered with any board. These records stand quite literally for life and death to young men."[15]

In targeting these files, the Catonsville Nine had two goals. One was practical: they hoped to slow down, if only in a modest way, the machinery of the war. The Nine aimed "to impede and interfere with the operation of a system which they have concluded (and it is not an unreasonable belief, as the government has told you) is immoral, illegal, and is destroying innocent people around the world," Kunstler explained. Their other goal was more symbolic: they wanted to exercise their First Amendment right to free speech and express their opposition to myriad injustices at home and abroad.[16]

Of course, there were other methods of protesting war and injustice. But the defendants had tried these and found them ineffective, Kunstler reminded the jury. "All the words, writing, marching, fasting, demonstrating—all the peaceable acts of the defendants, over a period of some years—had failed to change a single American decision in Vietnam," Kunstler stated. "All their protests had failed to prevent a single innocent death, failed to end the anguish of napalm on human flesh, failed even momentarily to slow the unnatural, senseless destruction of men, women, and children, including the destruction of our own sons—a destruction wrought in the name of a policy that passes all human understanding."[17]

The most provocative portion of Kunstler's closing involved his reference to the trial of John Peter Zenger, a New York printer who famously had been charged with having printed seditious libels in the mid-eighteenth century. Most observers had considered Zenger's case hopeless, but his acquittal had been won by a Philadelphia attorney named Andrew Hamilton. In his final statement to the jury, Kunstler quoted Hamilton as having said at the Zenger trial, "Jurors are to see with their own eyes, to hear with their own ears, and to make use of their conscience and understanding in judging of the lives, liberties, and estates of their fellow subjects."[18]

"Ladies and gentlemen of the jury," Kunstler said, "that is what we are asking you to do." The Nine wanted jurors to rely on their consciences—and not a mechanical understanding of how federal law should apply to their conduct in Catonsville—in deciding the case.[19]

Roszel Thomsen, however, was having none of Kunstler's appeal "to the jury to make their decision on the basis of conscience," as the judge described it. After Kunstler alluded to jury nullification, the judge interjected that he had warned the defense attorney about taking his closing argument in that direction. "This morning, I said to you that if you attempt to argue that the jury has the power to decide this case on the basis of conscience," Thomsen said, "the court will interrupt to tell the jury their duty." He now had no choice but to follow through on that threat. "The jury may not decide this case on the basis of the conscience of the defendants," Thomsen said from the bench. "They are to decide this case only on the basis of the facts presented by both sides."[20]

After Thomsen scolded him, Kunstler wrapped up his closing argument by asking the jury to consider the possibility that "this cataclysm of our times can be understood only in the lives of a few men who, for one moment, stand naked before the horrified gaze of their fellow men." Few people had done this with more sincerity than Dan Berrigan, and Kunstler, expressing the hope that "some understanding of the truth of things can come through," quoted a mournful poem that the Jesuit had written during his trip to Hanoi.[21]

It was perhaps this ending that inspired Brother David Darst to later write a poem about Kunstler's bravura performance in court. In it, the Christian Brother remarked that "we burning types" cherished the passion and commitment of "our own electric pepper counsel, Bill Dylan, poet." Kunstler later returned the poetic favor, penning a verse praising the Nine for having "tried to illustrate . . . that, after all, morality controls."[22]

There was some fidgeting in the courtroom after Kunstler finished. At the defense table, Dan Berrigan passed his brother a stick of chewing gum. A white-haired female juror took a handkerchief and wrapped it around her index finger. A colleague of Dan Berrigan's from Cornell sat with his head in his arms, either praying or crying. Overcome with emotion, another cleric in the gallery wept quietly.[23]

The prosecution then had a final chance to make its case to the jury. Assistant U.S. Attorney Barney Skolnik hammered away at the Nine, accusing them of superciliousness. "There is, in the government's mind, a fantastic arrogance that goes along with the sincerity of these nine people," he said. "They hold their views so sincerely and so deeply that they feel they have the right to impose their views upon people who disagree. Now that, ladies and gentlemen, is not just sincerity. That is an arrogance which the people of this country simply cannot abide."[24]

Throughout the trial, the defense had compared the crisis gripping America to earlier moments that also might have called for individuals to follow their consciences rather than the law. There had been, for instance, numerous references to the resistance to tyranny in Nazi Germany. (Kunstler, in his closing, had mentioned Anne Frank.) Skolnik bristled at such analogizing. "Ladies and gentlemen of the jury," he proclaimed, "this is not Hitler's Germany!" A variety of legal protections ensured that opponents of government policy in the United States could make their voices heard without fear of oppression from the state. "It is an empirical fact, ladies and gentlemen," he observed, "that the antiwar movement in this country has grown . . . because of the legal expression of views protected by the First Amendment."[25]

The nation had its share of woes, but the best way to address and resolve those troubles did not involve lawbreaking. Skolnik told jurors that "the problems of the United States are not going to be solved by people who deliberately violate the duly enacted laws of the United States of America upon which all of the people of the United States rely. . . ."[26]

Thomsen ordered a recess before he charged the jury. As had happened throughout the trial, spectators filed into the hallway outside the courtroom and engaged one another in intense discussions about the trial and its broader meaning. Eager to share their perspectives on the significance of the trial, a pair of Jesuits huddled with a group of seminarians.

"It is a historic case because it seems to be expanding the judiciary's discussion of the executive's handling of the war," one of the Jesuits said. "The executive has been taking far too much power in this war, and, after all, if the judiciary does not check the executive we're heading . . . toward—. . ." He broke off the sentence and, unable to finish, raised a hand in the air.

His fellow Jesuit stepped in the breach. "Dictatorship and revolution?" he offered.

The first priest grimly nodded his head.[27]

During the break, the defendants held an intense discussion of their own. At issue was their wish to bear witness a final time before the trial concluded. All agreed that they should attempt to address Thomsen directly and express their frustration over his insistence on disregarding the wider moral issues at stake in the case. They had difficulty, however, in reaching a consensus about how they might proceed.

"Should we seek the judge's permission or not? Should we speak before the jury leaves to deliberate?" Phil Berrigan observed in his journal. "Someone observes that any attempt to speak without permission will have the marshals down on us like avenging angels."[28]

Kunstler suggested that they should try to receive Thomsen's approval and then address the court after the jury had left the courtroom. But others advocated a more confrontational approach: "disrupting the courtroom by speaking without permission and with the jury present," Phil Berrigan recalled. In the end, the Nine and their attorneys collectively agreed that this plan was too risky and that it "would destroy the tiny chance of acquittal, a legal victory that would have incalculable value for the peace movement. It would also destroy the opportunity for dignified communication." They would adopt Kunstler's proposal and seek the judge's permission to speak to the court after the jury had left the courtroom to begin its deliberations.[29]

This conversation was overheard by one of the federal marshals who was guarding the Nine during their breaks, and he reported it to U.S. Attorney Stephen Sachs. Before Thomsen reconvened the trial, Sachs met in the judge's chambers with Kunstler and Harold Buchman. Sachs summarized the marshal's comments, stating that Kunstler apparently had told the Catonsville Nine that they needed to engage in a provocative act to cap off the trial. According to Sachs, the defense attorney had insisted that the trial "was going to be lacking unless something were done." Some of the Nine had strongly supported the idea. "The defendant Mische is said to have been the most vocal among the defendants in feeling that some kind of courtroom drama was . . . both necessary and desirable," Sachs reported.[30]

Kunstler was livid and "shocked" (he used the word repeatedly during the session in Thomsen's chambers) that the marshal had eavesdropped on his conversation with his clients and then reported it to the prosecutors. It seemed like a clear violation of attorney-client privilege. To make matters worse, Sachs was misrepresenting the discussion that had taken place. "I cannot understand," Kunstler sputtered, "how remarks get so falsified." Although a variety of possible actions had been discussed, he never had urged the defendants to create disorder in the courtroom, as Sachs seemed to be hinting to Thomsen. And in the end they had settled on the relatively harmless idea of having one of the Nine ask to address the court a final time after the jury had retired.[31]

Buchman backed up Kunstler's version of events, and this seemed to satisfy the judge. Thomsen determined that "if there is no disorder [in the courtroom], there will be no further investigation." He then led the attorneys back into court.[32]

When Thomsen reconvened the trial at 3:45 P.M., the courtroom crackled with tension. The contingent of federal marshals on hand seemed to have doubled over the lunch break. Phil Berrigan knew why: "The story quickly gets around [that] the marshal guarding Tom and me at lunch had informed his chief that we were preparing for civil disobedience." Alert for trouble, a contingent of several dozen marshals bracketed one side of the courtroom. "They scanned the courtroom nervously," a reporter noted, "their insignias gleaming on their businessmen's suits, their pistols lurching in their side pockets."[33]

As the crowd tried to settle in, several spectators heard a faint jingling sound. This persistent noise fed a rumor about the Nine's alleged plans to engage in a final act of civil disobedience: if the jury returned a guilty verdict, they would chain themselves together and force federal marshals to carry them en masse out of the courtroom. The rumor fizzled when the source of the noise became apparent. The jingling hadn't come from chains; it was just Mary Moylan's noisy bell pendant.[34]

It was in this anxious environment that the judge delivered his charge to the jury. In it, Thomsen "knocked the props out from under the defense," as the *National Catholic Reporter*'s Thomas Blackburn noted. Although he had given all of the defendants the chance to speak extensively about how their experiences had shaped their religious and political views, he now instructed the jury to disregard almost all of that testimony. "If you find the defendants intended to injure the property of the United States," he said, "then it is no defense that he or she had other intentions such as to raise an outcry or protest against the Vietnam War or acted from high religious motives or because he or she believed his intent was justified by a higher law." In their deliberations, jurors were to disregard the notion of higher law—the lynchpin of the defense—altogether. "The law does not recognize political, religious, moral convictions, or some higher law, as justification for the commission of a crime, no matter how good the motive may be. A person may not select the laws which he is willing to obey and those which he is not willing to obey, according to those beliefs."[35]

Thomsen, echoing a claim made by prosecutors throughout the trial, told the jury that the defendants had not been compelled to break the law in order to voice their objections to the war in Vietnam or American depredations in Guatemala. There were other methods of protest at their disposal. "People who believe that the Vietnam War is illegal, or unconstitutional, or morally wrong, have the right to protest in various ways, such as by demonstrations, parades, and legal picketing," Thomsen said. He gestured toward the protesters outside the courthouse; those individuals, unlike the Nine, had chosen to protest lawfully. "But they have no right to protest by destroying government property or violating valid laws, such as those protecting the operations of the Selective Service System."[36]

Kunstler had asked jurors to take a sweeping view of the case and consider the defendants' actions through the prism of history. For Thomsen, however, only one standard of judgment was applicable: the letter of federal law. "The protester . . . may, indeed, be right in the eyes of history, or morality, or philosophy. These are not controlling in the case which is before you for decision." The central issue of the case was not the defendants' right to freedom of conscience but rather, Thomsen suggested, "the state's duty to arrest and try those who violate the laws designed to protect private safety and public order."[37]

Phil Berrigan cringed at Thomsen's instructions to the jury, which he found interminable. For Berrigan, there was something paradoxical about the judge's charge. "He offers them a contradiction for solution: judge us according to the law, he says, and judge us according to the full range of evidence," he wrote in his journal. "But do it in such a way that guilt is decided, while sincerity is merely acknowledged."[38]

The jury left the courtroom and began its deliberations at about 4:30 P.M. Thomsen—who knew from the earlier conference in his chambers that something was brewing among the defendants—then queried prosecutors about his handling of the case. He asked Arthur Murphy if he had said or done anything that might have hindered the federal government from putting on a viable case. From the prosecution's perspective, the judge probably had said and done too little, at least in terms of controlling the defendants' expansive testimony, but Murphy held his tongue. Kunstler responded differently when Thomsen posed a similar question to him. Sensing that the defendants were being given the perfect opportunity to proceed with their plan to address the court, he asked Thomsen if the Nine might be permitted to speak, and the judge seemed amenable.[39]

There followed an extraordinary colloquy between the judge and the Catonsville Nine. For more than half an hour, they sparred over how the trial had been conducted. The judge later crowed that this lofty and wide-ranging post-trial discussion was without precedent in the annals of American law, and he probably was right.

Speaking for the Nine, Tom Melville complained that the trial had more obscured than clarified the central issues of their case. But Thomsen took issue with the suggestion that the Nine had been precluded from fully making their case; the defendants had been given ample opportunity to advance their arguments in his courtroom. The problem, as the judge saw it, was that the defendants had grounded their case in a theory of law—that higher law trumped the federal statute books—that had no place in the courts. "I cannot allow somebody to argue something which is entirely contrary to the law," he said. "That would be to ask the jury to disregard their oath. I cannot allow that."[40]

Although he respected the defendants' devotion to their principles, Thomsen felt that such a commitment in no way absolved them from legal responsibility for their actions. "I am not questioning the highness of your motive. I think that one must admire a person who is willing to suffer for his beliefs," the judge said. "But people who are going to violate the law in order to make a point must expect to be convicted."[41]

Thomsen sparred with Mische over whether he had informed the jury that they could not reach a verdict based on conscience. The two men had a sharp disagreement over the implications of the judge's critical comments when Kunstler referenced the Zenger trial.[42]

Dan Berrigan then stepped in.

"Your Honor," he said, "we are having great difficulty in trying to adjust to the atmosphere of a court from which the world is excluded, and the events that brought us here are excluded deliberately, by the charge to the jury." He was disappointed that the defendants' moral passion had been discounted in the proceedings. In one of the many vivid metaphors employed by the defendants throughout the trial, Berrigan said that it was "as though we were subjects of an autopsy, were being dismembered by people who wondered whether or not we had a soul. We are sure that we have a soul. It is our soul that brought us here. It is our soul that got us in trouble. It is our conception of man. But our moral passion is banished from this court. It is as though the legal process were an autopsy."[43]

The man who wielded the scalpel in this figurative surgical procedure was not moved by Berrigan's comparison. "Well," Thomsen told Berrigan, "I cannot match your poetic language." At this, the gallery broke into applause. The outburst embarrassed Thomsen, and he warned that he would clear the courtroom if spectators engaged in any additional demonstrations.

"Father Berrigan, you made your points on the stand, very persuasively," Thomsen continued. "I admire you as a poet. But I think you simply do not understand the function of a court."

"I am sure that is true," Berrigan admitted.[44]

Thomsen then spelled out for Berrigan why the court's functions in the case were so straightforward: "You admitted that you went to Catonsville with a purpose which requires your conviction. You wrote your purpose down in advance. Your counsel stood and boasted of it." Having broken the law and then admitted it in open court, they were lucky to find their case adjudicated in a legal system that afforded them the right to due process of law. "If you had done this thing in many countries of the world, you would not be standing here," the judge admonished. "You would have been in your coffins long ago."[45]

Dan Berrigan continued to press Thomsen, suggesting that the criminal justice system should take into account significant questions of conscience when sincere individuals engaged in acts of civil disobedience. This prompted Thomsen to make an extraordinary admission about his views regarding the far-reaching impact of the war in Vietnam. "As a man, I would be a very funny sort if I were not moved by your sincerity on the stand and by your views. I agree with you completely, as a person," he said. "We can never accomplish what we would like to accomplish, or give a better life to people, if we are going to keep spending so much money for war." But Thomsen felt that he could not allow his personal sympathies for the defendants' views to influence the way he ran the trial. Even though he agreed with them that the war had exacted too great a cost on American society, he could not allow the trial's focus to shift from the defendants' legal culpability to the legal or moral legitimacy of American foreign policy. He told the defendants that "a variety of circumstances makes it most difficult to have your point of view presented. It is very unfortunate, but the issue of the war cannot be presented as sharply as you would like. The basic principle of our law is that we do things in an orderly fashion. People cannot take the law into their own hands."[46]

"You are including our president in that assertion," Dan Berrigan offered.

"Of course," Thomsen replied, "the president must obey the law."

"He hasn't, though," Tom Lewis protested.[47]

Brother David Darst weighed in as well, criticizing Thomsen's instructions to the jury. "Your Honor, the instruction you gave the jury bound them to the narrow letter of the law," he said. "And a verdict according to the spirit of the law was strictly prohibited. It is my feeling that the spirit of the law is important, particularly in American legal tradition and in American life. It is the spirit which counts."[48]

Thomsen maintained that he had acted appropriately in urging the jury to limit its interpretation of the law. "Well, many books have been written on the difference between the letter and the spirit of the law. There are certain situations in which the Constitution gives the judge a good deal of leeway," he said at one point. "There are other situations in which it does not. Unfortunately, in this case I concluded that I did not have very much leeway."[49]

Lewis, in a poignant exchange with the judge, noted that he "had been called an honest and just man in this courtroom. I appreciate that. But the reality is that I leave this room in chains. I am taken back to prison. How do you explain this?"

Thomsen confessed to being stumped: "Good character is not a defense for breaking the law. That is the only way I can explain it."[50]

Perhaps not surprisingly, some of Thomsen's sharpest exchanges came with Phil Berrigan. The priest reminded the judge that the Nine had acted in

Catonsville out of desperation. "Your Honor, I think that we would be less than honest with you if we did not state our attitude. Simply, we have lost confidence in the institutions of this country, including our own churches," he said. "I think this has been a rational process on our part. We have come to our conclusion slowly and painfully. We have lost confidence, because we do not believe any longer that these institutions are reformable."

Thomsen was taken aback: "Well, if you are saying that you are advocating revolution—"

Berrigan interrupted him.

"I am merely saying this: we see no evidence that the institutions of this country, including our own churches, are able to provide the type of change that justice calls for, not only in this country but around the world," the priest explained. "We believe that this has occurred because law is no longer serving the needs of the people, which is a pretty good definition of morality."[51]

Thomsen then cut to the core of his fundamental disagreement with the Nine. "I can understand how you feel. I think the only difference between us is that I believe the institutions can do what you believe they cannot do," he said.[52]

After this extraordinary exchange ended, Lewis felt that there should be a final, unifying moment in the trial—something that would draw everyone together and restate their shared purpose. At the defense table, he whispered to Marjorie Melville, "What do you think of saying the Our Father?" She passed the suggestion along, and it met with approval from all of the defendants. They had said the prayer together outside the Knights of Columbus hall, and now they would be coming full circle by reciting it again in court. It fell to Dan Berrigan to broach the subject with Thomsen.[53]

"Could we finish with a prayer?" he asked the judge. "Would that be against your wishes? We would like to recite the 'Our Father' with our friends."[54]

In a trial filled with surprises, this was the biggest twist of all. Thomsen seemed thoroughly baffled. Kunstler gleefully observed that the judge was startled and clearly didn't know what to do. He sat silently for a moment and mulled over Berrigan's unprecedented request. Thomsen then spotted federal prosecutor Stephen Sachs in the back of the courtroom and asked him how he felt about Berrigan's query. Sachs had been content to leave the heavy lifting in the case to his subordinates, but he now found himself very much on the spot; he had to make a quick decision. As he stepped forward, Sachs realized that virtually everyone in the gallery sympathized with the defendants' request and that he would set off an uproar if he balked at it.[55]

"The government, Your Honor, has no objection whatsoever," Sachs said, "and rather welcomes the idea."[56]

With Sachs's blessing, everyone in the courtroom—the judge, the defendants, both sets of attorneys, and the entire gallery—then rose for a singular moment in American legal history. The defendants made the sign of the cross and then linked hands, just as they had done outside the Knights of Columbus hall in Catonsville while the draft files burned. They started the prayer, and then everyone else joined in. Solemn words—"Our Father who art in heaven, hallowed be thy name . . . . . ."—filled the courtroom. Some in the gallery, overcome with the emotion of the moment, recited the prayer between sobs.[57]

For defendant John Hogan, the prayer was an exceptionally powerful and uniting moment. It underscored the religious dimension of the Catonsville Nine's ongoing witness against injustice while bringing them together with the protest community that had evolved in Baltimore over the week of the trial. "The Our Father joined us [with] that whole courtroom in [expressing] that there was something right going on here," he later said.[58]

Few attorneys ever witnessed—or perpetrated, for that matter—more courtroom theatrics than Kunstler. But even he never had seen anything like the group prayer that punctuated the end of the Catonsville Nine trial. He later wrote, "It was one of the most stirring moments of courtroom drama I have ever experienced."[59]

But not everyone was so moved by the prayer. As it was being offered, one of Sachs's assistants leaned over and informed him, "They're violating the First Amendment right here in the goddamn courtroom."[60]

The reverie ended when the jury, after deliberating an hour and twenty minutes, returned. Thomsen—undoubtedly thinking about the report that had been received from the marshal earlier in the day—issued a final warning before the verdicts were read. "Let me warn everybody in the room that there must be no demonstrations," he said. "I have not the slightest idea what the verdict is; but never mind what the verdict is, there must be no demonstrations." He would clear the courtroom if he had to, and the marshals would deal with "any recalcitrants."[61]

For a full twenty minutes, Thomsen queried the foreman about each defendant, count by count.

"Members of the jury, what say you: Is the defendant Philip Berrigan guilty of the matters whereof he stands indicted, or not guilty, as to count number 1?"

"We find the defendant guilty."

"Members of the jury, what say you: Is Daniel Berrigan guilty of the matters whereof he stands indicted, or not guilty, as to count number 1?"

"We find the defendant guilty."

And so it went: all nine of the defendants were found guilty on all three counts. The clerk then polled the jurors individually. None of them wavered.[62]

Phil Berrigan muttered some praise for the jury: "Beautiful! It couldn't do better."

Then a voice rang out in the courtroom. "Members of the jury," a man boomed, "you have just found Jesus Christ guilty!"[63]

The outburst shocked everyone. Heads immediately turned toward the speaker. A few moments of wary silence passed before a murmur began to rise in the gallery. A few people voiced their approval of the exclamation, saying, "We second that." Others openly denounced the verdicts. A few people raised their hands and gave the "V" symbol; some members of the gallery wept. The commotion outraged Thomsen. His patience finally exhausted, he banged his gavel and announced, "Let the man be escorted from the courtroom. Clear the courtroom!"[64]

It turned out that the culprit was Art Melville, defendant Tom Melville's brother. Four marshals grabbed him and hustled him out. Meanwhile, another contingent of marshals directed the rest of the gallery toward the doors. As they exited, supporters of the Nine began to sing "We Shall Overcome," the great anthem of the civil rights movement.[65]

With the spectators now gone, Thomsen and the attorneys wrapped up the trial. There was discussion of when the Nine would be sentenced (in about a month's time) and what would become of some of the items that had been entered into evidence.[66]

Dan Berrigan managed to address the court a final time before the defendants left the courtroom.

"I would like to thank the Court and the prosecution," he said. "I think we agree that this was the greatest day of our lives."[67]

After the trial had ended, Thomas Blackburn of the *National Catholic Reporter* headed over to St. Ignatius to see how supporters of the Nine were responding to the verdicts. On the way, he struck up a conversation with a black youngster who had been in court that day for the end of the trial. The boy told Blackburn he knew Phil Berrigan well from his many efforts to help Baltimore's poor.

"I suppose they'll put him away," the youngster said, his voice tinged with sadness.

Blackburn gently explained that Berrigan already was in jail and that his time behind bars surely would be extended because of the verdict that had been rendered in Thomsen's courtroom.

"That's bad," the youngster concluded, "awful bad."[68]

"Justice Is Like God: Dead"

After the trial of the Catonsville Nine, the defendants tried to sort out every-thing that had happened. In a letter to friends, Mary Moylan jokingly an-nounced that the "verdict was resoundingly GUILTY!" She did not despair over the outcome, though, because the entire week had been so memorable and invigorating. Moylan was touched by the witness of "those BEAUTIFUL REAL LIVE PEOPLE in the streets. I cannot begin to say how proud I was to be with those people!" She hoped that their efforts in Baltimore would inspire ongoing antiwar and social justice activities throughout the country.[1]

The trial also left Dan Berrigan feeling exhilarated. Like Moylan, he cared little about the legal verdict; what mattered was that so many people had come together to take a stand against injustice and imperialism. "The trial is over; by all accounts, it was an extraordinary experience for many," he wrote to a group of friends. "For the nine of us, it was an opportunity without parallel; to 'give evidence' for our lives, to unite with the hundreds in the streets and the mil-lions across the world who are also saying 'no' to death as a social method."[2]

Although they were now convicted felons, the Catonsville Nine contin-ued to witness against war, imperialism, and poverty. The seven who were able to post bail after their trial—all but Tom Lewis and Phil Berrigan—spoke out forcefully against the war in Vietnam and other manifestations of injustice. And, hoping to score another coup for the antiwar movement, they strategized.

Before the Catonsville Nine were to be sentenced, the Berrigans, Lewis, and some of their supporters secretly discussed a plan aimed at freeing Lewis and Phil Berrigan from federal prison. They weren't plotting a breakout. Instead, they wanted to "set up a program for release of American fliers, and if possible, imprisoned peace people in the United States," as the two men explained in a letter. This would "use creative nonviolence against the United States, to em-barrass it, to expose its weakness and duplicity. And finally, to force it to be honest, insofar as this can be accomplished." Under the plan (which harked back to the trip taken by Dan Berrigan and Howard Zinn earlier in the year), the federal government would free Lewis and Phil Berrigan so that they could travel to Hanoi and take custody of American servicemen who had been captured by the North Vietnamese.[3]

But the plan was too fantastic to gain much traction. Lewis and Phil Berrigan remained in the Baltimore County jail in Towson, where they would be held until their sentencing by Thomsen early in November 1968.

Lewis passed the time by focusing on his art. He hoped to letter and illustrate eleven poems that the ever-prolific Dan Berrigan had written during the Catonsville trial. It was a challenging task. His access to art supplies was limited: he could manage only to obtain a few pieces of sketch paper and a pitifully small bottle of India ink. Finishing the project thus required some improvisation. Lewis stretched out the ink by mixing ground cigarette ashes and water. "For the brown background I mixed a combination of instant coffee and cocoa," he explained. "Finally I shaped a few popsicle sticks into pens."[4]

Equipped with these makeshift supplies, Lewis went to work. "At times I would be on my hands and knees," he later explained, "swirling ink around the paper with the popsicle stick and blending the colors with my fingers, so involved that I was completely unaware of some prisoners watching me, unaware of a curious guard watching me at a distance through the bars." As he worked on the project, Lewis felt deeply connected to Berrigan's poems; he often dreamed of some of the images described in them. When he finished, he had the work smuggled out of jail. (The collaboration with Berrigan was published by Boston's Beacon Press in 1970.) Many years later, Lewis still marveled over what he had done as "an artist without materials." He later told an audience at Milwaukee's Catholic Worker house that it had been a sublime experience.[5]

A month after their trial, Lewis, Berrigan, and their accomplices in Catonsville had to face Judge Roszel Thomsen for their sentencing. When the Nine entered the federal courtroom, appreciative spectators showed their approval by clapping rhythmically for several minutes. There were several dozen federal marshals on hand—they patrolled the grounds outside the courthouse, its interior hallways, and the courtroom itself—but they made no effort to stop the impromptu demonstration.[6]

As the crowd filed in, some observers felt anxious about how the Nine were going to fare before the federal judge. Entering the courtroom, one onlooker commented to a friend, "I never realized how much courtrooms look like churches."

His companion said, "Justice is like God: dead."[7]

Federal prosecutor Stephen Sachs did little to allay such misgivings when he addressed Thomsen. The defendants were "good men, sincere men, honorable men," Sachs said (forgetting, as often happened, that two of the Nine were women). However, they had acted dishonorably when they burst into Local Board 33 in Catonsville the previous May. In a startling comparison, Sachs argued that "what they did was, in principle, exactly what a lynch mob does. They arrogantly took the law into their own hands. Their act was something more than symbolic. So should the punishment be." The analogy did not play well with the crowd: hisses erupted in the gallery. There were similarly disapproving murmurs when Sachs disparaged Dan Berrigan as "the patron saint of all those whose conscience compels them to take the law into their own hands."[8]

When it was his turn to address the court, defense attorney William Kunstler insisted on revisiting his squabble with Thomsen over jury nullification. This had been a major sticking point at the trial—the judge had barred the defense from making a thorough argument about it before the jury—and Kunstler signaled at sentencing that he was not willing to let it go. He complained that he should have been able to tell the jury that "it had the power to decide this case . . . as it saw fit, and that no one, not judge nor legislator nor executive, could question its decision, no matter how contrary to law and fact it might have been." Kunstler closed with a typically dramatic flourish—and in the process flatly contradicted his earlier claim that he would not ask Thomsen to mitigate his punishment for the Nine. Throwing back his head, he implored the judge to "suspend their sentences . . . not because they are good and noble people or because they deserve mercy or special consideration but solely because such an act on your part could affect the lives of your own grandsons as well as those of countless men, women and children."[9]

"The power is in your hands," Kunstler said, "if the glory is in your heart."[10]

All of the Catonsville Nine addressed the court as well. George Mische mourned the recent election of Richard Nixon as president—he had edged out Hubert Humphrey a few days earlier—and what it might signify for American foreign policy. Now "it looks like we're not going to have anything really different" in terms of the conduct of the war in Vietnam, Mische predicted. Brother David Darst explained once more why the Nine had targeted Selective Service records. "We have come to know draft files as death's own cry; and, somehow, we have not been able to let sacred life and total death live together quietly within us," he said. "We have cried out on behalf of life and our brothers in Vietnam and all around the world. The government seems to have chosen to see our cry as anarchy and arrogance, but the act of men and women who turn themselves in for jail terms will not inspire many others to anarchy."[11]

Like Darst, Marjorie Melville related that the Nine had taken action in Catonsville because the country had been led so wildly astray by its leaders. "Burning files is our attempt to awaken our sleeping citizenry to their obligation to be on their guard about the doings and undoings of our government," she said. "We are in danger of losing our precarious democracy; we've grown comfortable and sluggish. . . . I see around me hate and discrimination, and war, a war industry, a war culture. Our nation doesn't enslave thousands of people. It helps others to do so, and it rains death and desolation on those who would resist."[12]

Her husband struck a humble note when he spoke at sentencing. Tom Melville told the court that he had resolved to "speak in my own bumbling way to the court once more the words we tried to sear into the conscience of our society last May 17." He did so by repeating the Catonsville Nine's call for global political and economic justice. The United States continued to shirk its responsibilities in this realm, Melville argued, by ignoring the needs of its poorest citizens. Worse still, in the rankest form of hypocrisy imaginable, it denounced other countries for engaging in overt acts of imperialism. Although Americans criticized the Soviets for their recent foray into Czechoslovakia, we "feel that our own invasion [of Vietnam] and our atrocities are somehow more excusable because they are far more subtle even while being far more devastating."[13]

Phil Berrigan shot for the moon in his statement, saying that he wanted lawyers of all stripes, including federal prosecutors, to join in the antiwar cause. Sachs and his colleagues should "refuse to indict and to try opponents of the war, and prefer resignation and private practice to doing so." He urged Thomsen and his colleagues on the bench to take a similarly bold step and give antiwar activists suspended sentences so that they might be able "to work [on] justice and peace." If they failed to do so, they should resign. Echoing Martin Luther King Jr.'s famous "I Have a Dream" speech, Berrigan said that he had a dream of his own, one featuring a new coalition in which federal judges, federal prosecutors, and marshals banded together against the war in Vietnam.[14]

Thomsen knew that the sentences he imposed would not be popular with the gallery, which was packed with supporters of the Nine. To head off the possibility of any disruptions, he had conferred with federal authorities before he took the bench and arranged for a row of deputy federal marshals to stand between him and the spectators. Their ranks included a hulking man who was recognized by many in the gallery: Jim Parker, the enormous former offensive tackle for the Baltimore Colts. The future Hall of Famer now guarded Thomsen as he once had protected quarterback Johnny Unitas.[15]

Thomsen determined that there would be no suspended sentences for the Nine, as both Phil Berrigan and Kunstler had urged. "Liberty cannot exist unless it is restrained and restricted," the judge said. "None of us can have the freedom guaranteed to us by the Constitution unless people who disagree with the policy of the government express their disagreement by legal means rather than by violation of the law." Thomsen was perplexed by the defendants' lack of contrition. "None of you has shown any remorse for your illegal acts," he said. "You have repeated your previous statements." Thomsen further argued that the defendants' "attitudes as well as the nature of the offense require the imposition of a prison sentence."[16]

As repeat offenders, Lewis and Phil Berrigan received the harshest sentences: three and a half years, with no bail. There were slightly less onerous terms for Dan Berrigan, Tom Melville, and Mische : three years each. Thomsen imposed sentences of two years each on the two women involved, Marjorie Melville and Moylan, as well as John Hogan and Darst. For all but Lewis and Phil Berrigan, bail was set at $5,000 ($2,500 on the federal charges and $2,500 on the still-pending state charges).[17]

Thomsen's sentencing of the Nine, like the trial that had preceded it, gained international attention. News of the prison terms even attracted interest in the Soviet Union. In the fall of 1968, a group of representatives from American peace organizations were hosted in Moscow by the Soviet Peace Committee (SPC), which sought to burnish the Kremlin's image by sponsoring discussions of U.S.-Soviet relations. At one point in the proceedings, Yuri Zhukov (a commentator for *Pravda* and the SPC's vice chair) produced a cable describing the recent sentencing of the Catonsville Nine by Thomsen. "These nine are courageous champions of peace working in difficult conditions," Zhukov said. "Our conditions here are quite different. We are free to engage in work. . . ."[18]

Closer to home, the sentencing of the Catonsville Nine also stirred up debate. A number of newspapers editorialized about the demonstrators' crimes, their motivations, and their treatment by the criminal justice system. Reflecting the view of much of middle America, some of the editorials bluntly condemned the Nine and mocked their claim that their protest was a form of free speech that merited legal protection. "But this was not free speech," the *Albuquerque Tribune* concluded. "It was burglary, violence, destruction of official records, and self-righteous arrogance." Worse still, the Nine, like many contemporary dissenters, were "wholly intolerant of any other view."[19]

The sentencing of the Nine also gave the *National Catholic Reporter* a chance to revisit their case. Earlier that year, the liberal weekly had chided the demonstrators for providing little more than a shrill symbol for the antiwar movement. However, the Nine had impressed the *NCR* by offering such thoughtful and wide-ranging testimony at their trial and sentencing. Furthermore, their provocative witness against war and imperialism had served as a personal challenge to everyone concerned with issues of social, economic, and political justice. In raising such serious questions about America's place in the world, the Nine had succeeded where others, such as the major party candidates for president, had failed. Humphrey and Nixon had engaged in a campaign notable chiefly for its "postures and slogans, irrelevance and studied ambiguity."[20]

Despite their ambivalence about the criminal justice system, the Catonsville Nine responded to their sentencing by producing a flurry of legal appeals. Lewis and Phil Berrigan immediately challenged Thomsen's denial of bail. At first, the gambit appeared hopeless. The United States Court of Appeals for the Fourth Circuit denied their appeal, as did Chief Justice of the United States Earl Warren (who reviewed appeals from that federal circuit). But a month after he sentenced the Nine, Thomsen relented. In an unusual move, he and federal judge Edward Northrop (who had presided over the Baltimore Four case) held a special joint hearing to reconsider the two defendants' bail status.

To the consternation of federal prosecutor Arthur Murphy, who argued that the two men were poster boys for recidivism, the federal judges agreed to release both Lewis and Berrigan on bail after they promised not to publicly advocate for civil disobedience or to engage in illegal acts themselves.[21] (It wasn't until February 1969 that the matter was resolved, with a circuit court judge canceling their bail altogether.[22])

As Lewis and Phil Berrigan sorted out their idiosyncratic bail issues, the Nine and their legal team framed an appeal of their convictions. A memo drafted in the fall of 1968 (mostly likely by Dan Berrigan) neatly summarized their approach: "The question: Jury conscience!" Sketching out possible approaches to the appeal, the document summarized some of the main points emphasized by Kunstler at trial and at sentencing. The lead defense attorney had tried to stress that "juries ought to be informed that they have power to acquit when defendants are clearly guilty" and that "juries should be permitted to use their conscience" in deciding the outcomes of criminal cases. The members of a "jury many times don't realize they have absolute power to acquit," and Thomsen should have allowed Kunstler to remind them.[23]

According to the defense memo, the appeal would highlight Thomsen's error in refusing to allow Kunstler to tell the jury that they could follow the "jury nullification principle" and acquit the Nine despite the weight of the legal evidence presented against them. There were notable historical precedents for this, the memo claimed. It was "done in the slave days where [juries] wouldn't convict people in the North who helped the slaves" escape, despite the fact that these abolitionists had violated the letter of the federal Fugitive Slave Act. On appeal, the Catonsville defendants could argue that Kunstler should have been able to inform the jury that only they could give laws life. "You can put all sorts of laws on books but if [a] jury doesn't convict, [the] law dies. It is nullified."[24]

When the Catonsville Nine appealed their convictions to the Court of Appeals for the Fourth Circuit early in 1969, the jury nullification claim comprised a main pillar of their case. Their brief hammered away at the importance of "the time honored doctrine of jury nullification." As the brief described the activists' central assertion, "Their argument is, essentially, a simple one. If the jury is, ideally, a representative cross-section of the community, and the defendant is willing to admit that he is indeed guilty of the acts in question, why, then, may he not be acquitted if the community, represented by the panel, approves of their commission?" Thomsen, however, had deprived the jurors of this chance—and thereby denied the Nine a fair trial—by essentially tying their hands with his narrow instructions. "The rule of law cannot mean," the brief noted, "that there shall be an unbroken, inflexible pattern of squaring fact with law to reach, in every instance, a mechanistic, almost computer-like conclusion."[25]

As their appeal moved forward, the Catonsville Nine remained active in antiwar and social justice causes. Although none of them took a lead role in anything as dramatic as the draft board raid in Catonsville, all of them continued to participate in protest-related activities throughout late 1968 and 1969. The FBI, concerned that the Nine might again engage in civil disobedience, closely monitored the activists' comings and goings.

In March 1969, for instance, federal agents noted that Lewis and Phil Berrigan attended a program on "Peace and Freedom" at a Unitarian church in Baltimore. Berrigan addressed the gathering, and Lewis showed a film that he had made about the deployment of National Guard troops in Baltimore to quell the rioting that had erupted in the spring of 1968. The low-budget production—it cost $30 to make—left the FBI feeling underwhelmed. "This film," a report on the event sniffed, "was of poor quality."[26]

That same month, Lewis and Moylan attended a Baltimore Defense Council meeting held at First Unitarian Church. Moylan read statement from the D.C. Nine, activists who had followed in the footsteps of the Catonsville Nine and looted the offices of Dow Chemical in the nation's capital. Also on hand that evening was David Dellinger, the antiwar activist who had been indicted for his role in the disruption of the Democratic convention in Chicago. According to an FBI report on the meeting, Dellinger told the gathering that individuals who were committed to ending the war in Vietnam should imitate the Catonsville Nine, the Milwaukee Fourteen, and the D.C. Nine by participating in additional acts of civil disobedience.[27]

The Nine could not attend as many of these antiwar events as they would have liked because Thomsen had attached some strings to their bail. The defendants' movements generally were restricted to the states where they lived. The judge told Dan Berrigan that he would be able to travel only between Maryland and the Cornell campus in upstate New York. Berrigan loathed the limits and resisted them at every turn. The most peripatetic and voluble of the Nine—the Jesuit seemed to constantly hop from one speaking engagement to the next—he eventually informed Sachs of his "selective response" to the federal prosecutor's enforcement of the judge's order. He agreed to cancel his participation in events such as "poetry readings, discussions on the arts, on student movements, on peace developments—all areas which, in the sensitive eye of your office, are considered politically dangerous." But Berrigan stated he "must of course refuse compliance" with the restrictions that might interfere with his "duties as a minister of the Gospel."[28]

Berrigan seemed incapable of not speaking out against the injustices that were undermining the nation's purported commitment to justice and equality. When unrest rocked the Cornell campus early in 1969, he delivered an impassioned speech before members of the local Junior Chamber of Commerce (or Jaycees). Seeking to counteract negative depictions of student activists that had appeared in the news media, Berrigan insisted that the country was not being harmed by "those who are struggling and going to jail and going into exile in order to say no to death." The real problem? Reactionaries who feared losing their grip on power. Berrigan claimed that it was "those who are saying no to human change who are bringing down the country."[29]

Nor did Thomsen's speech and travel restrictions dissuade some of the Nine from traveling to Wisconsin in May 1969 for the trial of the bulk of the Milwaukee Fourteen defendants. Darst made light of his decision to violate the conditions of his bail by wearing a preposterous American Indian disguise as he attended the trial. "He was the most conspicuous person in the courtroom," his friend Maggie Geddes later said, "but even his friends didn't recognize him." Darst and the other spectators were treated to a gripping trial that lasted nearly three weeks (and ended, predictably, with guilty verdicts).[30]

Soon thereafter, the Catonsville Nine had another legal proceeding to worry about—their own state trial. Although they already had been found guilty in federal court, the Catonsville activists still faced a host of charges that had been filed by the State of Maryland. Phil Berrigan argued that he and his fellow defendants were victims of double jeopardy, and he derided the charges as a political ploy concocted by Samuel Green, the Baltimore County state's attorney. Green backed off a bit, dropping some of the charges, including conspiracy to commit sabotage, but he insisted on trying the Nine on the remaining counts (which included sabotage, robbery, and assault) before Judge Kenneth Proctor in Baltimore County Circuit Court. Seeing little point in rehashing the entire federal trial, both sides agreed to stipulate to the facts contained in the record of that earlier proceeding. There was little nuance in the document: it stated that "all nine defendants in these cases preconceived a plan to go on 5-17-68 to Selective Service Board 33 at 1010 Frederick Avenue, Catonsville, Baltimore County, for the express purpose of seizing a number of Selective Service Records."[31]

The state trial—held in Towson, Maryland, early in June 1969—lacked much in the way of drama. There were no extended reflections on imperialism and poverty, no group prayers offered, no rowdy public demonstrations out in the street. (Several hundred county policemen and state troopers ringed the county courthouse, but they had little to do; no protests materialized outside.)[32]

Proctor was no Thomsen, but he did permit all of the Nine to offer a few brief statements on their own behalf to supplement the federal trial record. The defendants reiterated much of what they had been claiming throughout the case. Moylan described the war in Vietnam as "indeed a war, but . . . an illegal war." Phil Berrigan said that although the defendants were "more than willing to go to jail" for their beliefs and actions, they were "not willing to be railroaded by the State of Maryland." Later in the trial, Tom Melville, hoping to signal his solidarity with the people of Guatemala, attempted to address the court in Spanish, but Proctor shut him down.[33]

The Catonsville Nine suffered a defeat in Proctor's courtroom, but only a partial one. The judge convicted them on two counts of assault and one count of robbery. "This country is exceptional," Proctor said in announcing his verdict.

"It is a country of laws, and not of men." If those laws were disregarded, he warned, "we will experience . . . chaos and revolution." However, Proctor dismissed the charge that the state considered most important, sabotage; he agreed with the defendants' argument that it was preempted by federal law in that realm. Furthermore, the Nine would not really feel the sting of the state charges. Proctor sentenced them to terms identical to those imposed by Thomsen for the federal convictions, and he ruled that they could be served concurrently—meaning that there would be no additional jail time.[34]

As they awaited the outcome of their federal appeal, the Nine continued to think about the political, economic, and social issues. Lewis spent the summer living with Brendan Walsh and Willa Bickham at Viva House in Baltimore. The ongoing carnage in Vietnam still haunted him. On trips to the beach or to Baltimore's notorious red-light district, he would pause and reflect on the conflict and its meaning. "The war is continually in my eyes and mind," Lewis wrote of that period. "At a Maryland beach this summer I saw the Vietnamese beaches around Cam Ranh Bay where my brother was stationed with the Air Force. The bars and neon lights on Baltimore Street scream and echo the corruption and prostitution, the jungle of electric technocracy this country has made of Saigon."[35]

Lewis understood that he would not be a free man for much longer. While staying at Viva House in the summer of 1969, he noticed that the surrounding downtrodden neighborhood was brightened by paradise trees, stubborn and hearty plants that grew even in the worst conditions. He knew that he soon would be seeing elms—trees that were common near the federal penitentiary in Lewisburg, Pennsylvania. "Next summer," he acknowledged, "I fully expect to be back in prison."[36]

While Lewis worked on his art, Tom and Marjorie Melville returned to school. Flouting Thomsen's travel restrictions, the couple spoke widely to antiwar groups, repeating their critique of American foreign policy before a wide range of sympathetic audiences. In their travels, they encountered Brady Tyson, an American University professor whose experiences in Latin America had mirrored their own. (A Methodist minister, Tyson had worked in Brazil for several years in the 1960s until that country's government expelled him because of his work to curb human rights abuses.) Tyson came to think of the Melvilles as cultural refugees in the United States: they were Americans by upbringing, but they had lived abroad for so long that they weren't fully attuned to all of the country's cultural currents. This wasn't necessarily a curse, in Tyson's view; he believed that the couple possessed an extraordinary perspective on events in Guatemala. He encouraged them to enroll in a graduate program in Latin American studies, and they began their studies under his tutelage.[37]

Nor did the prospect of returning to prison seem to slow down Phil Berrigan. If anything, it motivated him to redouble his efforts to combat imperialism and poverty. But as he kept charging forward, fissures developed between Berrigan and some of his allies. One involved a Catholic activist in Washington, D.C., with whom the priest had closely collaborated for several years. Bill O'Connor genuinely admired the activist for his unwavering dedication to peace and social justice causes. But he became convinced that this radical, for all of his zeal, had become more a liability than an asset to the activist community that revolved around Berrigan. O'Connor believed that their associate had become too sloppy and reckless; he was fumbling the organizational tasks that had been delegated to him. He thereby had lost the trust of others in the antiwar movement.[38]

Matters came to a head in a meeting held at O'Connor's house in Baltimore. On hand were Phil Berrigan, Moylan, Hogan, and O'Connor. He made it clear that he had reached his breaking point with the Washington radical, who had ties to the house at 1620 S Street (where several of the Catonsville Nine had lived). "I was particularly insistent that I could no longer work with [him]," O'Connor later said. He laid out for Berrigan all of the lieutenant's alleged shortcomings and explained the threat they posed—not only to those in the room but also to the broader antiwar cause that all of them held so dear. "If I'm going to jail, I want to go to jail out of my own efforts," O'Connor announced, "not because some guy fucks up."[39]

Berrigan had his own share of concerns about the Catholic activist and his colleagues in the nation's capital. Both before and after the Catonsville protest, the priest had funneled contributions to the 1620 S Street community—a few thousand dollars in the first half of 1968 alone, Berrigan reckoned. While he was happy to support the group's activities, their approach seemed lacking. "I don't think they're making mature enough provisions for themselves," he had written to his brother Dan not long after the Catonsville protest. "They ought to be getting off their asses to make that a self-sufficient community."[40]

Still, O'Connor's accusations flabbergasted Phil Berrigan. Like many in the antiwar movement, he had come to respect and trust the accused activist for his invaluable legwork in organizing several draft board demonstrations. Initially, Berrigan disputed the charges and suggested that they might have been the result of nothing more substantive than a personality conflict. But Hogan spoke up and suggested, in his typically gentle manner, that O'Connor was just articulating misgivings that were shared by many of those who had worked with the Washington radical.[41]

The heated discussion lasted until early the following morning. Berrigan grew frustrated, hurled a book against a wall, and angrily stormed out of O'Connor's house, slamming the door behind him. When Berrigan made his angry exit, Moylan was scrambling some eggs in the kitchen. The noises startled her; she poked her head into the living room and asked what had occasioned the racket. As they reflected on the confrontation, she and Hogan asked O'Connor what would happen next with Berrigan. "It's obvious," O'Connor told them. "He'll be on that phone tomorrow morning calling, saying, 'Well, come on, let's get together.'"[42]

And that is precisely what happened: a contrite Berrigan called O'Connor later that day. In a meeting at the latter's home, they discussed how they might deal with the problem. Berrigan agreed that, for the greater good, they would have to express their gratitude to their apparently wayward collaborator but then ease him out of their loosely knit activist community. The showdown with the Washington man took place in an unoccupied church in New York City. In this cold, desolate space, Berrigan, O'Connor, and a few of their close allies convened what O'Connor later described as a "kangaroo court." Berrigan apparently lost his nerve for the confrontation, and it fell to O'Connor to lower the boom. "Look, we can no longer work with you," he explained to the man. "I'm very sorry." O'Connor took no satisfaction in this unpleasant task. He later called it one of the most difficult things he had ever done.[43]

Such internecine disputes began to take their toll on Phil Berrigan. Midway through 1969, in describing the community of peace and social justice activists that he had assembled, he admitted to a friend, "Immense internal difficulties begin to plague us." He then rattled off a laundry list of problems that were limiting their effectiveness: there were "not enough of our people to sustain what they have done, they are anti-organization to a paranoiac degree, we have no provisions to maintain continuity." To make matters even worse, many activists had soured on the idea of going to jail.[44]

Despite these conflicts, throughout 1969 and 1970, activists inspired by (and connected to) the Catonsville Nine mounted a series of memorable assaults on draft boards and military-related facilities throughout the country. The filmmaker Joe Tropea, who has chronicled these demonstrations in his gripping documentary *Hit and Stay*, has argued that they were critically important in that they both legitimized and sustained the American peace movement in that period.[45]

On March 22, 1969, the D.C. Nine—aided by Bill O'Connor and Grenville Whitman, the stalwart activists from Baltimore—targeted the Washington offices of Dow Chemical, the maker of napalm. In a bold midday demonstration, the group destroyed reams of documents and vandalized the corporate giant's offices, at one point even splattering blood on the walls. Late in May, a group calling itself the Chicago Fifteen attacked several draft boards on the city's South Side over a single weekend. Like the Catonsville Nine, they burned the draft records after seizing them; the resulting conflagration was massive, with flames shooting high in the air.

These strikes against conscription were not carbon copies of the Catonsville protest. The denominational composition of the raiding parties varied; non-Catholics became involved as a way of expressing their opposition to the war. The form of the demonstrations changed as well, with the activists often leaving the scene of their protest before police could arrive and arrest them. "Both [changes] represented a decline in emphasis on Christian witness and symbolic action," according to scholar Patricia McNeal, "and a greater desire for political effectiveness."[46]

In the first eight months of 1970 alone, the Selective Service System reported 271 separate "antidraft occurrences" at draft boards across the country. Some of these incidents were relatively minor—sometimes rocks were thrown through windows—while others caused serious damage to draft offices and the files stored inside them. Repairing this damage slowed down the work in many Selective Service facilities. Late in 1969 draft offices in New York City began closing every day at 2 P.M. so that clerks could recreate and reorganize files that had been damaged in three separate raids. And in Chicago, it took forty extra employees a total of four months to recreate all of the files that had been destroyed.[47]

"People were burning and shredding files all over the place," Dan Berrigan later crowed. The priest once appeared on a television talk show with General Lewis Hershey, the head of the Selective Service System. "He was so furious he could hardly talk," according to the priest. "He said he couldn't keep the war going very well because of what we had started." At hearing this, Berrigan broke into an ear-to-ear grin.[48]

Writing to the rest of the Catonsville Nine in May 1969, Berrigan marked the first anniversary of their raid on Local Board 33 by noting that others were following in their footsteps and attacking the machinery of the draft. "Imagine! With our baby barely a year old, another fiery birth in the Los Angeles Induction Center!" the priest wrote. "The fruit is now bearing fruit."[49]

But Selective Service officials downplayed the overall significance of these post-Catonsville attacks. Federal officials insisted that the protests did not seriously hinder the functioning of the draft. Duplicate lists of the names and classifications of registrants were supplied by local boards to state headquarters, making it difficult to completely obliterate a draftee from the records. Draftees' inductions thus were slowed down but never really stopped; the system eventually caught up with them. And delays caused by attacks at one draft board simply were made up for by other draft boards that weren't hit by protests. "A man who should have been inducted in March might have been inducted in June," one field supervisor in Pennsylvania explained. "If they stop some kid from Philadelphia from being inducted, all they do is put the burden on some poor kid somewhere else. They say the draft is inequitable, but they made it more inequitable."[50]

In 1970 the Selective Service System issued a report on the attacks and concluded that they were counterproductive because they diverted time and resources from draft board employees who otherwise might have been helping draftees navigate the system quickly and fairly. "Instead of 'stopping the draft,'" the report claimed, "they merely impeded personnel who otherwise could be giving more attention to individual registrants' problems. The losers, then, are the kids."[51]

"There Are So Many Reminders of Death"

Few things were more important to Brother David Darst than staying in close contact with his friends and family members. Irrepressibly gregarious, he worked hard at nurturing relationships with a wide variety of people—his fellow Christian Brothers, his biological brothers, young people he had met during summer school sessions, like-minded social and political activists. To maintain these connections, he often embarked on long, meandering trips that included stops in multiple cities. One routine journey he took from his home in Kansas City in the late 1960s included stops in St. Louis, Nashville, and Chicago, with a second stop in St. Louis on the way back. Darst spent forty hours on the road and loved every minute of it.[1]

Darst also was a fanatical correspondent. He scrawled long and sometimes rambling letters and distributed them widely. Late in the summer of 1969, he sent a letter to a list of several dozen recipients (all of whom were described in tidy capsule biographies). On the list were family members, Christian Brothers, students, high school secretaries, and textbook writers. Darst called them "the people who love me and whom I love, those people I feel close to in that great mystery and sadness and joy that is love."[2]

When it came to corresponding with this far-flung and vast network, Darst could be inventive. At one point he and his friend Joe Forgue (with whom he had attended St. Mary's College) corresponded by recording messages on small reel-to-reel tapes. Darst, hoping to give Forgue an unfiltered glimpse into his everyday life, turned into a documentarian and recorded a math class that he was teaching. Listening to the tape, Forgue could hear Darst and his students discussing the finer points of equations.

In 1969 one of Darst's regular correspondents was a young woman named Debbe Orenstein. An undergraduate at the University of Missouri in Columbia, Orenstein met Darst when some college friends took her to St. Louis for an evening with a group of Christian Brothers who lived there. That Orenstein was Jewish hardly seemed to matter; she had a "wonderful, amazing time," as she later put it, talking with the Christian Brothers and sharing a convivial spaghetti dinner. Over the next several months, she developed a close bond with Darst, whose openness and sincerity astonished her. "He was someone who totally accepted me, totally loved me," she said many years later. "He just accepted me for whatever and whoever I was."[3]

Orenstein was struggling to establish her identity as an adult, and Darst helped her immeasurably. In 1969 the two traded letters and spent time together in Columbia and St. Louis. Sometimes they were joined by Brother Joseph Stanislaus Brostowski. "Stan," as he was known, was a Christian Brother who ranked among Darst's closest friends. The three went to see a production of Thornton Wilder's *Our Town* that left Darst emotionally drained. "The last act was especially good. I wuz crying tears big as alley biscuits," he later wrote.[4]

Throughout 1969 Darst found himself reaching out time and again to Brostowski and Orenstein. It was an emotionally turbulent period for him, and he repeatedly found himself being pulled toward the "powerful magnets in my life," as he called his two friends. As he grappled with despair, their friendship provided invaluable ballast. "Thinking about you," he wrote in one joint letter to Brostowski and Orenstein, "just knowing that I'm on the same island where you are, keeps me going when I want to end it all—if not physically, then spiritually, by refusing to get so involved, by refusing to trust life, by giving up in the face of absurdity."[5]

Some of Darst's struggles in this period resulted from his discontent with his religious order. Publicly, the Christian Brothers had closed ranks around Darst after his struggles with his draft board and his involvement in the Catonsville protest, but he began to feel a mounting sense of estrangement from the order. The tension resulted in part from the Christian Brothers' apparent reluctance to allow him to enroll in a graduate program at the Harvard Divinity School, which had offered him a fellowship. The reasons for him not going to Cambridge to study remain murky, although some Christian Brothers believed that it was in retaliation for his activism. His friend Forgue later downplayed the significance of this dispute, but Darst wrote to Orenstein that he "argued fantastically" with a superior in the Christian Brothers over "my Harvard business."[6]

In the spring of 1969 Darst expressed some of his misgivings with the Christian Brothers in a letter to Dan Berrigan. "Staying with them is terribly complicated and paradoxical—there's so much blindness, deception, exploitation through stocks, etc.," he wrote, referencing the order's financial holdings. "I often think about complicity in the bullshit which this order—as any order— represents." So strong were Darst's qualms with the Christian Brothers that he began to imagine a future outside the order. "I wonder if maybe to be honest and clean with myself," he told Berrigan, "I shouldn't sever the umbilical cord to security, gradualism, oppression, etc."[7]

Darst found himself at odds with the Christian Brothers over how they were running their schools. He had been assigned to a high school in Kansas

City, and he was appalled at how his superiors seemed to privilege maintaining discipline over genuinely opening students' minds. He repeatedly butted heads with an assistant principal over such trivial matters as the length of students' hair. Administrators told Darst that if students were allowed to sport long hair and moustaches, the school's image would suffer, and parents would be angered. "I can't imagine anyone more hung up on hair and authority (their own)," he mused in a letter to a friend, "than the administration of this school."[8]

Being so powerless to change the oppressive culture at the Christian Brothers' schools weighed on Darst. Frustrated by administrators' misplaced priorities, he seriously considered quitting his teaching post. "I keep feeling that the honest thing for me to do is make clear my reasons for leaving and then just leave," he told Brostowski and Orenstein. "I disagree *totally* with our three administrators on what a Christian school means, and right now I can see no use in going crazy trying to do something good in a high school situation that may be *impossible* to change." He daydreamed about becoming a postman and having more free time to think or connect with friends.[9]

By the fall of 1969 Darst seemed to have reached the end of his rope with his religious order. He described the order's novitiate in Glencoe, Missouri, as "the heart of absurd-land" and joked that visiting Christian Brothers College in Memphis made him feel like "Vietcong in the Embassy." (During the Tet Offensive in 1968, the Vietcong had swarmed onto the grounds of the American embassy in Saigon.) Darst's persistent struggles at his school left him wondering if he could remain a teacher there—or if he could stay in the order at all. He admitted to friends that he felt he soon would "have to let go of the Christian Brothers, or at least working in our high schools."[10]

Darst's turmoil in this period transcended his concerns with his place in his religious order. In letters to his friends, he repeatedly showed signs of profound emotional anguish. "I know I give everyone the impression of being happy-go-lucky, joyful, bouncey [sic], full of humor," he wrote. "But often times when I walk into my room and close the door a wave of despair hits me and bowls me over." He admitted that his moods often swung wildly, alternating between exhilaration and misery. "I can be utterly depressed, and a few minutes later back to my old happy-go-lucky self, laughing and joking about everything," he told Orenstein. "Is this just the way I am? Sometimes this seems so unreal." In another letter he confessed to being "up and down as a roller coaster myself, depressed half the time, so happy I'm crazy as hell the other half."[11]

Darst used ominous terms and imagery when he described his despair. At one point in mid-1969, he told Brostowski and Orenstein, "Sometimes I feel like I'm going under." He wrote to them a short time later, "I don't know how much longer I can stand it. I feel like I'm hanging on to this school, and the Christian Brothers, and so many things, life itself, by a thread."[12]

It seemed that Darst could not avoid the specter of death in 1969. Early in September, he was buffeted by news that one of his Christian Brothers superiors had been killed in a plane crash. A few weeks later, he learned that some young protesters had been killed in Chicago. "It brought up the question of death again," he wrote to his friends. "There are so many reminders of death."[13]

When his moods were particularly dark, Darst alluded to his own death, sometimes very directly. The prospect of going to jail for his part in the Catonsville protest burdened him so much that he mentioned the possibility of committing suicide. Darst wrote to his friends:

> I keep wondering how I'm going to make it through jail. I get so depressed NOW, while I'm still close to so many people who love me. What am I going to do when I don't see those people for a year? How'm I gonna live without all the hugs and closeness? People seem so far away when you can't touch them, laugh with them, hold them, laugh a little with them at all the absurdity of life. Maybe I won't make it. Maybe I will commit suicide in jail.[14]

Darst immediately backtracked from this suggestion—"Then again, maybe I won't," he wrote of the possibility of taking his own life in jail—and he further downplayed it in a subsequent letter. However, even this tentative reference to suicide underscored for Darst's friends the intensity of his gloom.[15]

Darst penned a great deal of poetry, and sometimes it reflected his darkening mood. In a grim poem titled "A Passing Thought," he wrote of his response to seeing a highway wreck:

> Slowly
> I
> wind around an
> accordian car
> suicided into
> Highway EE
> overpass abutment.
> The policeman
> motions us
> deadly.
> At [Highway] HH,
> I am seized
> by
> an
> impulse.[16]

The piece was poetic rather than expository, and Darst did not clarify the impulse that had seized him. Given the context, however, it seemed that his "passing thought" might have involved killing himself in an automobile crash.

While Darst struggled to find his emotional equilibrium, the legal case of the Catonsville Nine sputtered toward its formal conclusion. Attorneys William

Kunstler and Harold Buchman scrambled to put together a brief when they appealed the activists' convictions to the U.S. Court of Appeals for the Fourth Circuit, which sat in Richmond, Virginia. Kunstler—who was immersed in several other high-profile cases at the time—hastily assembled a draft of the document "on buses, airplanes, and trains," as he admitted. After he sent the brief to Buchman for cleaning up, he offered encouragement to the attorney's secretary, who faced the unenviable task of shaping the jumble of written notes, mimeograph sheets, and other fragments into a clean, coherent document. For inspiration, she should remember that she was serving a good cause, Kunstler noted, and that he had labored over the brief intensely. "And if nothing [else] works, drink heavily—afterward!" he joked.[17]

In June 1969, Kunstler argued the case before the federal appellate panel in Virginia. He clung to his somewhat novel claim that Thomsen wrongly had cut off his appeal to the jury regarding its time-honored right to engage in jury nullification. Kunstler asserted that in times of great social and political unrest, the law should be flexible enough to allow jurors to consider a broad range of factors when determining whether crimes had been committed. Thomsen had erred at the Catonsville trial, he insisted, because his narrow instructions had kept the jurors from considering whether the defendants "did the right thing" in torching draft records.[18]

Phil Berrigan held out little hope that the appeal of his Catonsville Nine conviction would succeed. "No question of winning," he wrote to his friends Dick and Nancy Cusack in Chicago. "Just a way of making a point, and maybe uncovering a legal technicality for others." Stephen Sachs didn't think that Kunstler's arguments would fly, either. The federal prosecutor later said of the jury nullification argument, "It's an argument from non-law. It's an argument to the viscera."[19]

The task of writing the appellate court's opinion in *United States v. Moylan et al.*, as the case was formally known, fell to Simon Sobeloff, who was nearing the end of a long and distinguished legal career that had included a stint as solicitor general under President Eisenhower. The Catonsville Nine could have done worse. Governor Theodore McKeldin of Maryland once called Sobeloff "the champion of the underdog," and over the years he had experienced few qualms about overturning rulings made by Thomsen in the lower federal court. One of Thomsen's clerks observed that Sobeloff "never hesitated to substitute his findings of fact for Thomsen's when it suited him. Sobeloff, a 'liberal' Republican, had little use for Thomsen, whom he regarded as conservative and pedantic."[20]

Unfortunately for the Catonsville Nine, Sobeloff and Thomsen were in full agreement about the legal merits of their case. Handed down on October 15, 1969, Sobeloff's opinion for the appellate panel was an unmitigated defeat for the protesters. It noted that while "their sincerity is beyond question," their legal claims were flimsy. Demolishing the heart of their defense, Sobeloff wrote that "the fact that they engaged in a protest in the sincere belief that they were breaking the law in a good cause . . . cannot be acceptable legal defense or justification." He wrote that allowing acquittals on such grounds might open the floodgates to a torrent of similar claims. "If these defendants were to be absolved from guilt because of their moral certainty that the war in Vietnam is wrong," he wrote, "would not others who might commit breaches of the law to demonstrate their sincere belief that the country is not prosecuting the war vigorously enough be entitled to acquittal?" He painted an apocalyptic picture:

> To encourage individuals to make their own determinations as to which laws they will obey and which they will permit themselves as a matter of conscience to disobey is to invite chaos. No legal system could long survive if it gave every individual the option of disregarding with impunity any law which by his personal standard was judged morally untenable. Toleration of such conduct would not be democratic, as appellants claim, but inevitably anarchic.[21]

Soloff also eviscerated Kunstler's claim that Thomsen should have more fully explained to jurors the concept of jury nullification. Soboloff did not question the right of juries to acquit defendants who appeared to be legally guilty. But trial judges like Thomsen were not required to tell jurors that they could flout the law and decide cases "according to their prejudices or consciences." If that were a standard practice, "we would indeed be negating the rule of law in favor of the rule of lawlessness," Soboloff wrote. "This should not be allowed."[22]

The ruling left the Catonsville Nine with only one faint hope: an appeal to the U.S. Supreme Court. However, given how thoroughly Soboloff had dismantled their novel legal claims, it seemed extremely unlikely that the nation's highest court would take their case.

The few newspapers that took notice of the opinion seemed to relish the idea that the Nine were now probably headed to federal prison. In an acerbic editorial, the *Pittsburgh Press* derided as ridiculous the Nine's claim that they should be able to privilege their consciences over the rule of law. Soboloff's opinion, having exposed that claim as fraudulent, "should be emblazoned in plain and unavoidable sight wherever demonstrations arise and whenever protesters indicate their inclination to create trouble," the paper observed.[23]

On the same day that the Nine learned that their legal appeal had been denied, Darst was at the University of Notre Dame in South Bend, Indiana. Darst's brother Chuck was a Notre Dame undergraduate, and he had asked the cleric to participate in a massive antiwar rally and Mass. The festivities were held on the university's mall beneath the famous Jesus mosaic—commonly known as "Touchdown Jesus" because of the figure's upraised arms—adorning the campus library. "It was fantastic," Darst later wrote. "We had a great scene for peace thru-out the day, me giving a talk at the rally, Chuck and six others coming forward at the offertory of this mass to shred their draft cards before god and assembled three thousand."[24]

While in South Bend, Darst mentioned to his brother his mounting disaffection with the Christian Brothers. Because of ongoing friction with his superiors, Darst no longer was sure that he wanted to remain in the order. He informed Chuck that he might stay in the order through his prison term but then leave once he was released. The news surprised Chuck. It shocked him to think of his brother leaving the religious community that had been his home for his entire adult life.[25]

Seeing his brother and participating in the rally at Notre Dame elated Darst, at least for the time being. Writing to his friends Orenstein and Brostowski, he reassured them that he wouldn't take his own life. "I've been thinking a lot the past four days about what I wrote about maybe committing suicide in jail. Saying that has kind of bothered me; I felt that it might be letting you two down." He now believed that, with their friendship and support, he could weather imprisonment. "I'll probably be okay in jail," he wrote.[26]

But Darst's mood seemed to darken over the last few weeks of October. He was shaken when vandals hurled a rock through the window of the residence he shared with some other Christian Brothers. "Glass all over everywhere," he wrote. "Musta been some kids or something, or maybe the Neo-Nazi's, but whatever, it's frightening as shit to pick up a rock that's come flying thru your window." The incident got Darst thinking once more about leaving behind his life and "just going somewhere to live apart." He mentioned that Holden Caulfield, the idiosyncratic hero of J. D. Salinger's *The Catcher in the Rye*, ponders escaping by pretending to be a deaf-mute and working as a gas station attendant.[27]

A few days after the rock-throwing incident, Darst experienced what he called "a depression day." Things took a downward turn when he became embroiled in a heated classroom argument with a group of students over "the super-rightness of Americans and our foreign policies." Later in the day, one of his superiors complained that he recently had fielded a half-dozen complaints about Darst's teaching methods, his protest activities, and his published writings on sex. Someone apparently had brought to the attention of the local bishop the article on "non-marital sexual expressions" that Darst had published in *Pastoral Psychology*. The dustup infuriated Darst; he wondered how bishops could be so "greatly concerned about sexual ethics while the world blows up."[28]

As he recounted these travails for his friends, Darst said that he welcomed the prospect of taking a trip with Brostowski. The two men planned to drive up to Wisconsin to see Brother Basil O'Leary, who had mentored them in college (and later had participated in the Milwaukee Fourteen protest). "I can't wait," Darst wrote. "Perhaps it'll bring some relief from this madness."[29]

Brostowski came from St. Louis to Kansas City, and the two men planned to embark from there on their trip. Before they could leave, though, Darst was once again confronted with death. He had heard that the mother of a student was ill, and he and Brostowski went to visit her in the hospital. They learned upon arriving that the woman had died a short time earlier. They did their best to comfort the grieving student, and Darst worked on sorting out his own feelings. At one point he even penned a poem that was a stark meditation on life and death—topics that had preoccupied him for the previous few months. "Dying is so simple, so quick," he wrote. Reflecting on how people's lives end in a variety of ways, he noted that one "could be struck down in a horrible wreck."[30]

Several hours after he wrote those lines, Darst, Brostowski, and another member of their religious order, George Simon, were traveling in a Ford Mustang on State Highway 73–75 near Auburn, Nebraska. Their vehicle collided head-on with a Darling Transfer Company truck and burst into flames. Within minutes, Darst and Simon had burned to death. Brostowski survived and was rescued from the wreckage, but he died five days later.[31]

Darst's official death certificate laid out in cold prose the horrific circumstances of his death. The State of Nebraska's Department of Public Health listed the immediate cause of death as "incineration," and it described the interval between the crash and his passing as "instant."[32]

Once the victims were identified, word of the accident filtered out to their family and friends. Chuck Darst received a call about the crash in the middle of the night, and he found himself not wanting to believe the news. "Brother David is going to be alright, isn't he?" he asked. When the news of his older brother's death began to sink in, Chuck realized that it was "not just like losing a brother, it was like losing a father," as he later put it, because Brother David had been such an influence on him. The following morning, it fell to Chuck to inform his parents that their son had died in the Nebraska wreck. He never faced a more heartbreaking task.[33]

The funeral Masses for Darst and Simon were held at a Catholic church in suburban St. Louis. The caskets of the two men were placed in front of the altar but remained closed because they had been so badly burned in the wreck. On hand to honor them were dozens of Christian Brothers who had come from throughout the Midwest. "A chorus of men's voices echoed in the subdued atmosphere of that cathedral-like space," according to one observer, "singing mournful Latin verses from another era." After the Mass, the two men were buried at the Christian Brothers' novitiate in Glencoe, Missouri (which Darst privately had derided just a few months earlier).[34]

The burials were followed by an impromptu religious service conducted by some younger Christian Brothers. Held in the basement of a St. Louis church, this was an informal observance that evoked the earliest days of Christianity. "The celebration featured loaves of bread torn into chunks and passed among the three dozen or so participants, along with a bottle of red wine," recalled one person who attended. "There were no utensils and no glasses; no chalice and no priestly vestments." While they broke bread, Darst's friends and colleagues periodically rose from the table and shared their memories of him.[35]

These relatively somber affairs were followed by a rowdy wake at an apartment occupied by some Christian Brothers in St. Louis. A high school student named Joe Ortbal joined in the festivities. "When we arrived, I stepped into the midst of a loud and raucous party: it came as a shock to my adolescent senses which were still steeped in the somber mood of the funeral masses," Ortbal later wrote. "Here, at a traditional Irish-American wake, whiskey substituted for wine, and nuns sat unconsciously on the laps of priests and Brothers, laughing and crying in each other's arms." The high-schooler "watched in awe, unable to assimilate all the emotions on display."[36]

There were Masses and wakes for Darst in Kansas City as well. Not everyone felt comfortable with the festive atmosphere that pervaded them. Debbe Orenstein had been devastated by the news of Darst's death; she was reeling at having lost a trusted friend and confidant. She attended a wake in Kansas City but never got caught up in the jovial spirit of it. Having chosen to mourn Darst's death in a more subdued way, she wasn't feeling celebratory.[37]

After Darst's death, Orenstein couldn't help but wonder if her friend had taken his own life. After all, he had shared suicidal thoughts with her several times over the previous few months. Could he have followed through on them on the highway in Nebraska? The circumstances of the crash eventually convinced her that it had been an accident. Darst wouldn't have jeopardized the lives of other people while attempting to kill himself. This sentiment was shared by many who knew Darst well. (It is worth noting that Darst apparently wasn't driving the car, and the official cause of the crash was listed an as accident.[38])

Darst's death hit Dan Berrigan particularly hard. In a journal entry he wrote a few years later in prison, he mentioned his friend's passing as being comparable to the death of Thomas Merton, whom he admired enormously. The process of "picking up the pieces after their deaths" involved a similarly "slow, wearisome walk into a vacuum."[39]

Berrigan memorialized Darst in a eulogy written a few months after the young cleric's death. His poetic sensibilities led him to connect the circumstances of Darst's passing with the method used by the Catonsville raiders to destroy Selective Service records. "David Darst burned draft files. David Darst died by fire. Who let the symbol loose?" Berrigan wrote. "Didn't they know that fire is a wild fire, a raving beast? Cold comfort. Burning the papers in Catonsville, burned to death on the road. . . . Someone pushed his own words in his face, a burning brand. And he died of it." Darst's flesh, he observed, had been "reduced to a burnt offering." In his eulogy, Berrigan couldn't resist taking a shot at the federal government for its zeal to imprison peace activists. He wryly observed that Darst's death presented "a problem for the FBI. How in the world will they arrange for the surrender of the person of defendant Darst to the marshals, to begin the serving of a sentence under the gentle aegis of the federal prison system? Will his ashes suffice?"[40]

The federal government didn't ask for Darst's remains. However, in a quintessentially bureaucratic move, the U.S, attorney's office in Baltimore did seek definitive evidence that he had died in the automobile accident in Nebraska. The Baltimore office of the FBI reported that federal prosecutor Barney Skolnik "would like to have [the] death of Darst verified . . . to complete his records in this matter." Early in 1970, he obtained an official copy of Darst's death certificate from Nebraska's director of vital statistics. Only then was the legal case against Darst formally closed.[41]

The FBI also continued to keep an eye on the members of the Catonsville Nine who were still alive. Tom Lewis was observed at a "radical open house" held at a home on Guilford Avenue in Baltimore. Late in 1969, agents in Baltimore noted that he was "doing art work for Christmas cards with a political message to be sent to GIs in Vietnam." The cards showed black and white hands clasped together in a gesture of interracial unity; they also bore messages promoting pacifism, such as "work for peace and freedom in the '70s." The FBI heard that Lewis planned on obtaining a mailing list of servicemen from the *Baltimore Sun*, but inquiries at the paper revealed that no such list was being published.[42]

The FBI also learned early in 1970 that Phil Berrigan was traveling to Hawaii. The trip clearly violated the travel restrictions that Thomsen had imposed on the Nine, and the bureau hoped that Sachs would prosecute Berrigan for breaching the terms of his bail. Sachs decided to let it pass; all of the Nine had violated Thomsen's travel limits, and it seemed pointless to prosecute Berrigan on such a relatively minor charge when he already was facing a sizable prison term for his convictions in the Baltimore-area draft board cases.[43]

Berrigan gave several ardent speeches in Hawaii. The My Lai massacre (in which American troops had mowed down several hundred unarmed Vietnamese civilians) was in the news, and Berrigan used the outrage it had generated to highlight the nation's hypocrisy. "How can My Lai be called a tragedy by President Nixon and a nation which countenanced slavery for so long, has psychologically destroyed its black citizenry and given Hiroshima to the world?" he asked an audience at the University of Hawaii. Berrigan also called for radicals to continue their resistance. "It is clear that there is a moral and political duty to dissent, rebel, and revolutionize, and to recapture power by taking responsibility for victims of American policy," he said.[44]

Berrigan was equally strident in his private meetings with Catholic peace activists in Hawaii. He rebuked them for not doing enough to resist the war and the social ills it had spawned. "Phil gave us the sense that whenever we're not facing courts, facing jail, that means we're not being effective," one of his hosts later said. "That's what disturbed a lot of people—the sense that we all had to do much more." One session devolved into a kind of serial confession, with local activists parading before Berrigan and apologizing for doing so little to end the war. John Witteck later said that he thought the meetings were so dispiriting for the Hawaiians that they momentarily wrecked the local peace movement. Berrigan's visit, instead of energizing opponents of the war, "made us very dissatisfied with what we were doing, with leaflets and all that," Witteck recalled. The main antiwar group, known as the Hawaii Resistance, "underwent a kind of slow death after that." But Witteck believed that Berrigan's visit had a positive long-term effect. Over time, activists on the islands took his trenchant criticisms to heart and regrouped.[45]

While the surviving members of the Nine continued to agitate against the war, the FBI monitored their legal case, which seemed to be reaching its denouement. The bureau kept close tabs on their appeal to the U.S. Supreme Court to determine when (if at all) it might be heard. In the early months of 1970 agents made "a periodic check of the records" and determined that a petition for a writ of certiorari had been distributed to the justices on January 14. The high court now had to decide if it would put the case on its docket—presumably for the subsequent term—or summarily reject it and thereby leave the lower court's ruling in place.[46]

This was a last-ditch effort, and not even Harold Buchman—who had tirelessly defended the Nine for a year and a half—thought it would succeed. He sheepishly told his colleague Harrop Freeman that the petition was "dropped into my lap and under extreme pressure I had to do a hack job." He would have felt worse about submitting such a lackluster petition if he thought it stood a genuine chance of persuading the Supreme Court to hear the appeal. It was, he acknowledged, "a rather hopeless venture."[47]

There was one new wrinkle in the appeal. The Nine learned that the federal government, in the course of conducting surveillance on another antiwar activist, had electronically monitored a telephone conversation involving Dan Berrigan in 1966. In making their appeal to the Supreme Court, the Nine argued that their case should be remanded to a lower federal court to determine if the taping had affected their trial. In a memorandum submitted to the court by Solicitor General Erwin Griswold, the federal government acknowledged that the taping had taken place. Although Berrigan had not been the subject of the surveillance, "he did participate in one conversation that was overheard during the course of a surveillance, authorized by the Attorney General," the memo stated. The government argued that the revelation was irrelevant to the case of the Nine, given that the taping had occurred two years before their crime and was not directly related to it.[48]

The taping issue failed to make much of an impression on the Supreme Court. Without comment, it denied the petition for certiorari on February 24, 1970. (That same day, the high court also declined to hear the appeal of the Baltimore Four defendants.) Their legal appeals exhausted, the surviving members of the group now faced the prospect of heading to federal prison. As an FBI memo put it, "Based on the Supreme Court denial, it appears now that all individuals involved will have to begin serving time in prison."[49]

On the day the Supreme Court rejected the appeal of the Nine, Dan Berrigan wrote to his mother from Cornell. He was not saddened by the prospect of being jailed for his opposition to the war, saying that he and his brother were now "on the edge of a great honor." He was happy that his mother would be "with us for the greatest days we have known—to be in jail and protest against the destruction of innocent life in a senseless and savage war, without issue, meaning, or outcome. I thank God with all my heart that He spared you for these days at our side."[50]

Berrigan told his mother that the surviving members of the Nine would have to begin serving their sentences within a month of the Supreme Court's denial of certiorari, but they remained free through March 1970. In the middle of that month, the FBI contacted Barney Skolnik to determine when their sentences would commence. Skolnik said that there were still a few motions relating to the sentences of Tom Lewis and Phil Berrigan that needed to be sorted out in federal court. As a result, "no mandate has yet been issued for the subjects to commence serving their sentences." Knowing J. Edgar Hoover's interest in the case, the special agent in charge in Baltimore assured him, "This matter will be followed closely, and the Bureau will be kept advised."[51]

"America Is Hard to Find"

Long before their legal case reached its conclusion, Dan Berrigan wondered what he and the other surviving members of the Catonsville Nine should do if they exhausted their appeals and were ordered to report to federal prison. The issue was very much on his mind late in the summer of 1969, when he paid an extended visit to his longtime friends William Stringfellow and Anthony Towne, who lived together on Block Island, a speck of land located off the southern coast of Rhode Island.[1]

According to Towne, Berrigan "raised with us the query whether, when all appeals had duly exhausted themselves and a date was fixed for getting to jail, he and his brother and the others of the Catonsville Nine should, in fact, render themselves to Caesar" (that is, surrender to federal authorities). The priest's primary concern was how the Nine might continue to effectively witness against the war and agitate for peace. Conventional disobedience strategy indicated that, "having made one's point, one goes meekly off to prison to take the consequences," as Towne described it. But Berrigan questioned whether capping their witness with this type of surrender would do anything to stop the war in Vietnam. Might it not in fact bolster the state's authority by demonstrating that dissenters could be locked away?[2]

At the time, Towne believed that Dan Berrigan was more speculating about his options than he was formulating firm plans for the future. "I did not have the impression," he later said, "that he really then contemplated not surrendering when the day came." Towne did not think that the priest had yet seized upon the notion of becoming a fugitive for peace.[3]

Dan Berrigan's plans came into focus early in 1970. One day his brother Jerry and Jerry's wife, Carol, visited him at Cornell. As they took a walk together through a park in Ithaca, Dan mentioned various people on campus for whom he felt affection. "I've been saying good-bye," he told his brother and sister-in-law. He paused for moment and then explained in a subdued voice, "My friends want me to resist going to jail. They think I should hide for a while and see what happens." He did not elaborate, but Jerry understood the implication: his brother was thinking about going underground.[4]

In the spring of 1970, the surviving Catonsville demonstrators gathered at Viva House, the Catholic Worker residence in Baltimore, and discussed what they might do if their legal appeals fizzled and the federal government attempted to send them to prison. The activists realized that they were at an important crossroads: they could submit to the federal government, or they could continue to witness for peace outside prison. "There was a sense that we were facing both a great opportunity and a great danger," Dan Berrigan explained. "On the one hand, it was a strict canon of nonviolence that one took the consequences of illegal activity and paid up. On the other, there was the war." It concerned him that the Catonsville protest had failed to even momentarily slow down the progress of the war in Vietnam. "We had to admit it," he later wrote. "Our action at Catonsville, and all the draft board actions since then, had failed even to mitigate the war."[5]

During the discussion at Viva House, several of the activists struggled with the notion that they should acquiesce to the authority of the government that was responsible for the ongoing holocaust in Southeast Asia. If the war—an immoral and unconstitutional endeavor—continued to rage, perhaps they should continue to resist by refusing to report for their prison terms. Dan Berrigan later said that they were confronted with "a harsh dilemma, an utterly new field of moral decision." His brother Phil later described the choice they faced: "Should we surrender to a government that was committing genocide in Vietnam, or go underground and continue our resistance to the war?"[6]

For Phil, the correct choice was clear. "How could we allow ourselves to be shackled and led off to prison, when we had broken neither international law nor God's law?" he wrote. "Our actions were just; the law was unjust." He felt that the traditional approach to civil disobedience—"you have to take the consequences of your actions" and accept whatever punishment the state chose to dispense—was both superficial and, in this instance, far too limited. It was time to reject, "totally and unequivocally, the 'justice system,'" Berrigan concluded. By refusing to surrender to federal authorities, the Catonsville demonstrators would show that "we did not respect, and we could not obey, laws that condoned and courts that supported genocide."[7]

Dan Berrigan later described his own choice to go underground as having been fairly easy. Had he been faced with it earlier, he might have approached things differently. "If the decision had been made immediately after Catonsville, I would have surrendered too," he later explained. Submitting to the state's authority—and thereby conforming to the norms of civil disobedience—"would have been important to me then." Furthermore, he would have been drawn to the possibility of developing a ministry among draft resisters in prison. But now, almost a full two years after the raid on Local Board 33 in Catonsville, the circumstances had changed. The war had worsened, as had the poverty that plagued America's inner cities. To call attention to those ongoing problems, he had no choice but to engage in another form of resistance.[8]

Not all of the surviving Catonsville demonstrators reached their decision so easily. The meeting at Viva House went on for several hours. As they tried to determine a course of action, the activists talked, prayed, and reflected. It was clear from the beginning that "we would come to different decisions: some would choose to go to jail, some would not," Dan Berrigan recalled. The prospect of going underground and being cut off—from vocations, from friends, from families—simply was too daunting for some; others feared that they would expose fellow activists to prosecution for conspiracy by asking them for their support while underground.[9]

One thing was apparent: it wouldn't be a collective decision. "Catonsville was our thing as a group," John Hogan later said, "and it ended there." Hogan decided not to become a fugitive because he felt that he had fully expressed his opposition to imperialism and injustice by taking part in the Catonsville protest and then defending that action in court. "I didn't have any other statements to make," he later said. He really just wanted to get on with his life.[10]

In the end, the Berrigans, Mary Moylan, and George Mische chose to go underground. Mische—who would be traveling with his wife and children—had no illusions about his ability to evade the FBI for an extended period of time. "We knew we were going to get caught," he later said. "We weren't leaving the country. It was just a symbolic thing. We were going to keep things going as long as we [could]."[11]

Hogan, Tom Lewis (who had recently married a woman he had met in the peace movement), and Tom and Marjorie Melville would report for their prison sentences. The Melvilles would be given an extra week of freedom by the federal government so that they could complete some graduate coursework at American University. Tom Melville, a former priest, later said that he simply hoped to "go to jail and get it over with. I had been celibate long enough."[12]

A few days before the appointed date for surrender—April 9, 1970—Phil Berrigan gave an apparently valedictory interview with Weldon Wallace, the religion editor of the *Baltimore Sun*. If Wallace had expected to find Berrigan repentant about his scrapes with the law, he came away from the exchange disappointed. He wrote that the priest had "no regrets about taking part in the destruction of draft records in 1967 and 1968." Indeed, Berrigan said that he and his fellow activists would act in much the same way if they had the chance to protest again. "I don't know that we would do it today as we did it then," Berrigan said, "but we would certainly be involved in some form of protest."[13]

David Eberhardt (who had been sentenced for his role in the Baltimore Four protest at the Custom House), Hogan, Lewis, Mische, Moylan, and the Berrigans were supposed to surrender themselves to federal marshals in Baltimore at 8:30 A.M. on April 9. When that deadline arrived, only Hogan and

Lewis—along with a group of about two dozen supporters—presented themselves. Before entering the federal marshal's office and formally surrendering, Lewis kissed his new wife and spoke briefly about his love for painting. (He said he hoped he could continue to paint in prison.) For his part, Hogan flashed a peace sign before heading inside.[14]

When asked by reporters about the five activists who had failed to report, both Lewis and Hogan professed ignorance. They said they had no idea where their fellow protesters were.[15]

Eberhardt and Phil Berrigan soon made their intentions clear. In a statement released to the press, the two men announced, "We will . . . not surrender to the officers of this government. Rejecting this custody, we will seek the custody of peace people and resist one last time before jail." Instead of submitting to the federal government, they would endeavor to speak to "honest, serious people of their common state of oppression and their common fight for survival." They would, in short, continue to battle injustice as fugitives.[16]

This public statement was followed by a radio broadcast that aired on WBAI in New York. Interviewing each other from an undisclosed location, Berrigan and Eberhardt spoke of their reasons for going underground and explained how and when they might surrender to federal authorities. Berrigan insisted that it "ought to be done on our terms, not theirs."[17]

Such pronouncements failed to impress United States Attorney Stephen Sachs, whose office had successfully prosecuted both the Baltimore Four and the Catonsville Nine. "They are defendants who didn't come in," he said of the activists who had failed to report, "and we are going to arrest them." To that end, he asked that federal judges Roszel Thomsen and Edward Northrop, who had presided over the two Baltimore-area draft file destruction cases, issue warrants for the arrest of Eberhardt and the four Catonsville fugitives. Early in the afternoon of April 9, Thomsen and Northrop issued the warrants and handed them over to the federal marshal in Baltimore. The documents authorized the marshal and his staff, as well as other federal agencies (such as the FBI), to begin hunting for the fugitives. Thus began a search that would last for nine years.[18]

Even before the warrants were issued, the FBI began its efforts to apprehend the fugitives. Early on April 9, Claude DeLoach, J. Edgar Hoover's top aide, received a memorandum reporting that while Lewis and Hogan had surrendered as planned, "the others have indicated to the news media that they do not have any intention of surrendering to the court." Bureau agents in Baltimore guessed that the fugitives would "probably attempt to dramatize their arrest through the use of the various news media and might even possibly seek sanctuary." According to the memorandum, "just as soon as the bench warrants are issued, efforts will be made to locate and arrest these individuals but in doing so [FBI agents] will take every precaution to avoid a confrontation with followers of this group." This last note of caution was sounded throughout the hunt for the fugitives: they were to be captured, and quickly, but without coercion that might embarrass the bureau.[19]

A national manhunt began immediately. Hoover closely monitored the case and urged subordinates throughout the country to pay particular attention to pursuing leads that might bring it to a close. He was blunt in pressuring the special agents in charge (SACs) of the bureau offices in Baltimore and Albany, New York, to focus on the case. "You should afford this case close and continuous investigative attention," he wrote. The FBI director kept the SACs on a short leash, ordering them to submit to him a weekly update of their progress on the chase.[20]

As the search for the fugitives intensified, Hoover ordered his subordinates to go beyond cultivating their usual array of sources of information. "In view of the clerical status of the Berrigans," he noted at one point in the investigation, the Baltimore office "should consider contacting the Chancery Office for the Archdiocese of Baltimore to determine if they would cooperate in locating the subjects." One informant told the bureau that seeking such help probably would be futile: according to the Baltimore SAC, the source "advised that no priest would probably furnish information concerning the Berrigans in view of their clerical relationship and the fact that the Berrigans might seek confession, thereby establishing a privileged relationship."[21]

Religious buildings were kept under surveillance as well. In Baltimore, the FBI monitored the Josephite Fathers' residence on Calvert Street (where Phil Berrigan had lived) and St. Ignatius Church (the site of so many events during the week of the Catonsville Nine trial). Starting on April 9, "at least twice daily, spot checks and fisurs [physical surveillance] have been maintained at these locations with negative results," one FBI memo noted. The agency also conducted spot checks at the Cathedral of Mary Our Queen on Charles Street.[22]

During the first days of the manhunt, there was some concern that it soon might have to be expanded to include Tom and Marjorie Melville. The couple had been given permission to turn themselves in after they had completed the spring semester at American University. However, when Eberhardt and their fellow Catonsville defendants went underground, Sachs began to worry that they would bolt as well. According to FBI documents, he asked the bureau to keep tabs on the couple. The Baltimore SAC reported to Hoover that Sachs "has requested that spot surveillance be conducted on [the Melvilles] in view of the possibility they may disappear underground with the five other fugitives of this case at or about the time they are supposed to report to the US marshal's office in Baltimore." The FBI obliged, monitoring the Melvilles until their surrender later in April.[23]

The Melvilles' accomplices had been underground for only a few hours when people began to speculate about their plans. The most common guess: the fugitives would arrange to turn themselves in after they were able to pull off a final public act of resistance. "Although inquiries to various peace groups in Baltimore failed to disclose the whereabouts of the five," reporter Theodore Hendricks wrote in the *Sun*, "there was some speculation that they may plan a final demonstration, perhaps in a church, before being taken into custody." But days passed without any such protest taking place.[24]

As it became clear that the five draft board demonstrators were serious about remaining underground for an extended period, their fellow peace and social justice activists began to assess their decision. Michael Ferber, one of the Boston Five, was among those who disapproved. Ferber believed that Dan Berrigan in particular had made a mistake because he could have been far more valuable to the antiwar movement by operating inside the prison system. He also felt that the Jesuit might be grandstanding. "Dan is fostering a dangerous Che-type image that's falsely found—that he can survive in the underground," Ferber said, referring to the revolutionary icon Che Guevara. "People are bound to think he and the rest of the Catonsville escapees have gone nuts. If you haven't figured prison in your life, you shouldn't be in the movement."[25]

Jerry Elmer, who had been inspired by the Nine and took part in draft board demonstrations during the Vietnam era, disapproved as well. The Catonsville Nine always had "described their action as fitting squarely within the mainstream history of civil disobedience in the United States," he later wrote. Accepting the legal consequences of one's protest was a central element of that tradition. But some of the Nine, by becoming fugitives, now seemed to be repudiating that heritage. "By going underground instead of surrendering," Elmer concluded, "they undermined their own earlier arguments in favor of what they had done."[26]

Dan Berrigan had kept his colleagues at Cornell in the dark about his plans to become a fugitive. Without explaining where he was going, he had simply vanished from campus after walking into Anabel Taylor Hall and leaving his office keys on a secretary's desk.[27]

Berrigan began writing almost as soon as he went underground; he was jotting down notes just hours after he was supposed to surrender. The priest wrote that he had been unable to turn to either his own family or his religious order for shelter, his "family being powerless in this instance to help, the Jesuits unwilling." Instead, he found refuge in a rural area somewhere on the East Coast.[28]

In his first hours on the lam, Berrigan's thoughts turned to Dietrich Bonhoeffer, whose resistance to the tyranny of the Nazis had impressed all of the Catonsville Nine. "Bonhoeffer burned, sifted, removed," Berrigan wrote. "The task of a good man in a bad time was to despise, to put to naught, the tactics of evil power. He stepped time and again over the red herrings in his path, holding his nose against their stench." Berrigan prayed that he could muster as much courage over the coming days and weeks.[29]

On his second day underground, Dan Berrigan penned an open letter to his fellow Jesuits. In it, he explained why he and his brother had chosen "to resist the automatic claim on our persons announced by the U.S. Department of Justice." His rationale was straightforward: "We believe that such a claim is manifestly unjust, compounded by hypocrisy and repression of human and civil rights. Therefore only one action is open to us: to declare ourselves fugitives from injustice."[30]

The Jesuits' response was surprisingly warm: a "Jesuit Committee of Conscience" came into being. One member of the order's hierarchy—using the theme "Our Brother Is in Need"—led efforts to support Berrigan and raise money for his legal defense. "Where complete rejection had been feared," Berrigan's friend Jim Forest later wrote, "the final consequence was the first sign of official Jesuit support since Dan's first entry into the peace movement."[31]

At least initially, Berrigan believed that his time underground would be relatively brief—perhaps a period of a few weeks. Before making the decision not to report for his prison sentence, Berrigan had spoken with some antiwar friends who were organizing "America Is Hard to Find," a weekend protest celebration that was scheduled to held be at Cornell on April 17–19. "At this point," he later said, "I didn't think I'd be out beyond the Cornell thing." He thought that, having made his point by evading federal authorities for about 10 days, he might turn himself in at the festival itself, or immediately after.[32]

But Berrigan's thinking changed. During his first few days underground, he spoke with many supportive friends in the resistance community, antiwar activists who encouraged him to remain a fugitive for as long as possible. He also read his friend Howard Zinn's book *Disobedience and Democracy*. "For the crisis of our time," Zinn argued, "the slow workings of American reform, the limitations on protest and disobedience and innovation . . . are simply not adequate." Zinn further insisted that "the demands of our time will not be met by [a] narrow approach to civil disobedience."[33] Such passages appealed to Berrigan, who had been struggling with the notion of breaking with the standard practices of civil disobedience. With his resolve stiffened by reading Zinn and talking with fellow resisters, he began thinking about staying underground beyond the Cornell event in mid-April.[34]

Zinn's influence on Berrigan's evolving approach to civil disobedience was clear when the priest was interviewed by Philip Nobile for a lengthy article in the *New York Times Magazine*. He told Nobile that it was pointless to feel bound by the constraints imposed by a rigid understanding of the law. "There is very little you can do now within the law," he said. Berrigan claimed that the times called for "new actions outside the law which will create larger and larger communities dedicated to large nonviolent resistance. We simply must offer alternatives to the slavery and killing done in our name." This would involve moving beyond traditional conceptions of civil disobedience. "Before Catonsville, it was important to consider breaking human law for the sake of peace and decency," he told Nobile. "Now we are saying it is important deliberately to reject punishment for this lawbreaking."[35]

With numerous FBI agents looking on, Berrigan helped to kick off "America Is Hard to Find" by appearing at a "Freedom Seder" held on the first night of the raucous weekend festival at Cornell. As the priest—clad in a motorcycle helmet and sweater—made his way to the stage at the university's gymnasium, a great cheer rose from the crowd. Before long, most of the ten thousand people in attendance were on their feet, some even weeping and hugging one another in their excitement. A few young activists, eager to show their appreciation to the fugitive, clambered onto the stage to shake Berrigan's hand. "Bless you, bless you, Father Dan," one said as he greeted the fugitive. The effusive welcome had the FBI agents in the crowd rolling their eyes. "Bureau agents at the scene reported that many in the audience were overcome," the Albany SAC reported to Hoover. "Men and women were in tears, and some appeared to be on the verge of hysteria." The SAC had his suspicions about what might have contributed to this outpouring of emotion: "It was obvious," he told the FBI director, "that a large number present were intoxicated either from alcohol or drugs."[36]

Berrigan was his usual provocative self. He exhorted the crowd to follow his lead in resisting the war. "It is no more logical that a war resister obey a government order to surrender to American justice than that an American youth appear for induction into the military," Berrigan said. "I hope that I can, by example, encourage people to do what we did—to break the law in a way that is politically significant."[37]

Berrigan addressed his ongoing status as a fugitive. "If you think I should," he said from the stage, "I will surrender." The crowd's response was emphatic: cries of "Never! Never!" filled the gymnasium.[38]

From the stage, Berrigan could tell that he was being watched by a flock of agents dispatched by the FBI. "Presumably disguised," he recalled, "they were dressed incongruously in hippie garb, radio antennae sprouting about their heads like the feelers of insects." Berrigan considered surrendering himself to the laughably conspicuous agents after speaking and thus ending his stint underground.[39]

But "then came a strange turnaround of events," as Berrigan put it. After his speech concluded, musicians and performers from the Bread and Puppet Theater took the stage. Members of the troupe were slated to reenact (in mime) Jesus and his disciples at the Last Supper. After receiving some hurried instructions from supporters who wanted him to remain underground, Berrigan donned a comically oversized disciple costume (topped off by an enormous papier-mâché head). He then exited the stage, made his way out of the gym, and stumbled into a supporter's waiting panel truck. Before the FBI could determine what had happened, the vehicle sped away into the night. Berrigan spent the night in an empty cabin located about half an hour outside Ithaca; supporters then ferried him to a farmhouse.[40]

Although he had been considering the possibility for some time, Berrigan later described his choice that evening to remain a fugitive as "a spot decision," and he reflected on it frequently over the next few months. "I had ample time . . . to consider that night, that choice, its rightness or folly," he later wrote. "It came to me that something extremely simple was implied. I was trying, in a bad time rapidly worsening, to walk a consistent path." In his mind, consistency demanded that he continue to engage in resistance.[41]

Berrigan publicly explained himself in a statement that was read on the last day of "America Is Hard to Find." "Was it better to remain in Barton Hall, awaiting the moment when the hunters equipped with open season licenses, could take aim and bring me down?" he asked. "I chose once again to disappear, to guard my honorable status as a fugitive from justice."[42]

Hoover's frustrations over the manhunt—which was fast becoming a public relations debacle for the FBI—skyrocketed after Berrigan escaped at Cornell. It incensed him that "these subjects appear to be making a determined effort to avoid surrender and prevent arrest." He was livid that bureau agents apparently had botched a golden opportunity to take Berrigan into custody. "His arrest has not been effected to date, and his whereabouts [are] presently unknown," he complained to the Albany SAC after Berrigan made his escape. "It is expected that your plan as previously indicated by you be implemented with dispatch and that an all out effort be made to arrest [him] as soon as possible." But even as Hoover urged his subalterns to apprehend Berrigan immediately, he cautioned them to avoid engaging in heavy-handed tactics that might tarnish the bureau's reputation. "You must make certain that any arrest plan is well prepared and that the arrest can be carried out by your complete domination of the situation and without causing a direct confrontation with any group or groups sympathetic with [him]," he wrote. "It is incumbent upon your office to take an aggressive approach in this matter."[43]

While Dan Berrigan was eluding the FBI in Ithaca, his brother and Eberhardt were in New Jersey. Sister Liz McAlister offered to hide them in a summer home owned by her religious order. They stayed at the beachfront home for about two weeks before moving on—just a few steps ahead of the FBI, as it turned out. Soon after they had left, bureau agents, accompanied by police officers, broke into the retreat house. The rambling structure contained numerous bedrooms, and agents combed through them all. "No occupants were in the building during the search," according to the subsequent FBI report. "Evidence indicated that possibly subject Philip Berrigan and others may have recently been in building due to fresh garbage noted in a trash can located outside home."[44]

Although they had managed to narrowly escape the FBI in New Jersey, Phil Berrigan and Eberhardt's time as fugitives was drawing to a close. They were invited to an antiwar rally on April 21, 1970, at St. Gregory's, a church located on West 90th Street in Manhattan, and it seemed like an appropriate moment to end their sojourn underground. "One more rousing speech," Phil Berrigan recalled of their plans, "and we would submit to arrest." As it happened, Father

Harry Browne of St. Gregory's once had been a classmate of FBI agent Thomas Walsh, and the two old school chums apparently reached an understanding: the two fugitives would be allowed to address the rally, and then they would peacefully submit to arrest.[45]

But both sides developed second thoughts about this plan. Inspired by Dan Berrigan's escape a few days earlier in Ithaca, Phil Berrigan and Eberhardt decided that they would make a similar exit at the St. Gregory's event. At the rally's conclusion, two stand-ins would surrender themselves to the FBI while Berrigan and Eberhardt made their way out of the church, through a maze of nearby alleys, and into a getaway car. Helping to formulate these plans was a member of the Young Lords, a militant Puerto Rican nationalist group. While the two fugitives made their escape, members of the group were to create a diversion by starting a street fight near the church.[46]

The FBI, having been publicly embarrassed by Dan Berrigan's escape from Ithaca, was leaving nothing to chance. Even though agents had learned from Father Browne that Eberhardt and Phil Berrigan "wanted to be arrested in a public manner without any violence," as one bureau report later put it, they moved to take the two fugitives into custody prior to the evening rally. Several hours before that event was to begin, agents began scouring church property and nearby buildings for the two fugitives. (Phil Berrigan later claimed that one hundred agents had been deployed on the block surrounding the church.) At one point, FBI representatives inquired at the nearby headquarters of the Religious of the Sacred Heart of Mary. Said one, "This is the first time in twenty years with the bureau that I've ever had to search a convent."[47]

The search proved brief. At about 4:30 P.M., seven FBI agents approached a suite of rooms located on the third floor of the church's rectory. "After demanding in a loud voice that the door be opened to the FBI, and receiving no reply, the door was forced open and the agents rushed into the living room where two men were sitting upright at either end of a couch pretending to be asleep," according to an FBI report. Suspicious agents fanned out into the suite. Several entered a bedroom and found Father Browne "lying on top of the covers, fully dressed, also feigning sleep." Like all of the men in the suite, he told agents that he did not know where the fugitives were. "There is no else here besides those two," he said, motioning to the men on the couch. "You are welcome to look around."[48]

The agents took Browne up on his offer, opening cupboards and closets throughout the suite. "Father Dan, Father Phil—are you in there?" they asked, hopeful that they might snare both fugitive Berrigans. Agents opened one closet in Browne's room and discovered a locked inner closet. When Browne said he did not have a key for it, "the door was forcibly opened and the fugitives were found in the dark narrow confines of this inner closet," according to an FBI report on the search. "They were arrested without further incident."[49]

"It became terribly apparent that [the FBI] had no intention of allowing us at the rally in exchange for our surrender," Phil Berrigan complained. "And Browne had no place to put us but a closet. It was like trying to run in oversize pants with no belt." Hiding in the closet made him feel hunted, and as he crouched there with Eberhardt he "learned some sympathy for animals in traps as the dogs approach." When the agents moved to put the men in hand-cuffs, Berrigan objected, indicating that he posed no physical threat. They would have none of it. "Listen, big boy," one agent told him as the handcuffs were clamped over his wrists, "you're in our power now."[50]

The agents still hoped to find Dan Berrigan, whom they suspected was hiding elsewhere in the rectory. They remained throughout the day and into the evening, mingling with the crowd outside the church and observing the rally. Howard Zinn, who spoke that night, noted that "there seemed to be swarms of agents—trench coats, fedoras, the famous bureau wardrobe—circulating through the audience and around the platform." But Dan Berrigan never showed; he was in New Jersey.[51]

Eberhardt and Phil Berrigan were hustled to an FBI office on 69th Street in Manhattan and booked. As their initial reticence waned, agents chatted with the two men. "Their triumph complete," Phil Berrigan later wrote, "the agents were perfectly anxious to discuss themselves, politics, and the rising cost of sending their kids to Catholic schools." Inevitably, the talk turned to politics; the men discussed the nuclear arms race, the war in Vietnam, and the work of domestic activist groups of all ideological stripes. "We're out to defuse both sides, far right and far left," one agent said of the FBI's mission. "And we'll do it."[52]

After their capture and booking, Eberhardt and Phil Berrigan were brought before a federal district court judge. He turned them over to a U.S. marshal, who was responsible for transporting them to the federal penitentiary at Lewisburg. (This happened on May 1.) Eberhardt expressed his defiance as the former fugitives were escorted out of the hearing room, barking, "All power to the movement and to the brothers and sisters who will take our place!" At a rally held later by supporters, his wife read a statement express-ing Eberhardt's hopes for the peace movement. Berrigan's statement explained that his time on the lam had given him a unique opportunity to maintain his "balance under an entirely new set of stresses, joys, disappointments."[53]

The arrests rattled Dan Berrigan. "We were all distressed by Phil's sudden arrest," he wrote to his mother. Dan knew as well as anyone how much Phil loathed prison, and he was saddened to know that his brother would have to return to the pervasive tedium and oppression of Lewisburg. Dan was further unsettled by the realization that he too would have been captured if he had gone to St. Gregory's with Eberhardt and his brother. But he tried to spin things positively for his mother. "The main thing is that he went in good spirits and for a good cause," he wrote. "So there is no reason to be dismayed."[54]

For George Mische, simply being underground wasn't enough. "I want to be able to make a real dent in their ability to wage war and in their ability to repress the movement," he said while he was a fugitive. "I want tangible things in the underground that make our whole situation livable." He hoped that his ongoing witness would encourage other activists to mount antiwar actions that would be more impactful. "'Stand-by' actions now should be with great damage to property to insure a risk situation. This avoids nit-picking and engages in confrontation. For instance, you burn down the Bank of America and stand around and claim the action!" With the war worsening by the day, one thing was clear to him: "The day of symbolism is over."[55]

Midway through May 1970, Mische was staying in Chicago with a sympathetic former Jesuit. After leaving the priesthood, the friend had gotten married and had children, and Mische served as a kind of uncle to them. To Mische's horror, the children were present when FBI agents discovered him and came bursting into the apartment. The agents' guns were drawn, and Mische feared that the children present would find themselves in harm's way. As they converged on the fugitive, they demanded to know where Dan Berrigan was; they assumed that he and Mische were on the run together. But Mische remained mum about Berrigan and all of his activities as a fugitive. As the *Baltimore Sun* reported, "Mische refused to make any statement about how he had been living since he failed to report to the federal marshal in Baltimore to start his sentence."[56]

"We're Looking for Berrigan"

Howard Zinn spoke at St. Gregory's in New York City on the night that David Eberhardt and Phil Berrigan were arrested. Later that evening, he learned (through the byzantine channels that kept the Jesuit's whereabouts from being widely known) that "Dan Berrigan was hiding out in a house in New Jersey but that it was not safe," he later wrote. Zinn and a companion were given the address and told to move the priest elsewhere.[1]

The following morning, the two men rented a car in Manhattan and drove over to New Jersey. There they found a justifiably nervous Berrigan. According to Zinn, "He said getting out of there was urgent—across the street was the home of an FBI agent." The men decided that Berrigan should come to Boston, although he would not travel or stay with Zinn, who probably was under FBI surveillance. Together they put together a list of people in the Boston area who might be willing to step into the breach and harbor the fugitive. Zinn did not know what to expect when he approached these prospects, and their responses happily surprised him. "We knew that anyone who helped a fugitive was in danger of prison," he later wrote. "But none of those we asked to take Dan in—a young editor, an artist and her family, the family of two college professors—refused."[2]

Berrigan came to Boston and then shuttled between homes in the area. Zinn and a half-dozen other supporters formed an ad hoc support committee and managed, as best they could, his comings and goings. Berrigan's Boston advocates tried to control his movements in a manner that would not leave him exposed to unnecessary risk, but the priest sometimes bristled at their directives. Berrigan, Zinn later noted, "often refused to follow our 'orders.'"[3]

In Boston, Berrigan spent much of his time reading and writing—not only poems but also innumerable letters and public statements designed to articulate his reasons for continuing to defy the government's authority. But he also wanted to engage in everyday activities, such as seeing films in theaters and taking walks along the Charles River. Zinn and his colleagues, bowing to Berrigan's wanderlust, decided that they would disguise him for such jaunts around town. A wig was found, and Berrigan dutifully put it on—much to the merriment of his supporters. The priest looked so absurd that he spent an evening entertaining them by striking a variety of ridiculous poses.[4]

Berrigan (sans the preposterous disguise) managed to see several movies during his time underground. Perhaps not surprisingly, he enjoyed *Catch-22*, the black comedy that satirized the apparent madness of war. The fugitive also took in *Patton*, which presented a far different perspective on World War II. To Berrigan's friends, this seemed like a puzzling choice—he was, after all, one of the most famous pacifists in the country—but the priest explained that he saw the film because he wanted to better understand the perspective of Richard Nixon, who was said to have watched the picture repeatedly after its release in the spring of 1970.[5]

Attending to routine problems was a challenge for Berrigan during his time underground. At one point during his stay in Boston, the priest needed to have a tooth repaired. Zinn arranged an appointment with his own dentist: he explained that a friend who was visiting from out of town, "Mr. McCarthy," needed to be seen immediately. When Zinn and Berrigan arrived at the appointed time, they seated themselves in the waiting room and glanced down at some magazines that had been left out on a table. Opened before them was a recent *Time* magazine article on the priest, complete with a photograph bearing the caption "Fugitive Father Daniel Berrigan." Their hearts raced, but the dentist was unaware that "Mr. McCarthy" was wanted by the FBI.[6]

On several occasions that spring, Zinn found himself standing in for Berrigan at antiwar events in the Boston area. Early in May, more than 35,000 people crammed into Harvard's football stadium for a rally supporting a national student strike against the federal government's policies at home and abroad. A wide array of radical speakers addressed the throng: Black Panthers, representatives of the Socialist Workers Party, a high school student active in antiwar activities, and labor union representatives. When it was his turn at the rostrum, Zinn read a statement from Berrigan that called on fellow "bums, freaks, students and countrymen" to help make the strike a rousing success.[7]

As he taught political theory at Boston University (BU)that spring, Zinn's thoughts often turned to his fugitive friend. Zinn had his students read Plato's *Crito*, which examines why Socrates chose not to escape from prison and thereby evade punishment (in his case, death) at the hands of the state. Such were the obligations, according to Socrates, of an individual who had fully committed himself to civil disobedience. In his book *Disobedience and Democracy*, Zinn took issue with this stance, arguing that "there was no such obligation—that to evade prison was to continue civil disobedience, to continue the protest," as he later put it. To put his arguments in a contemporary context, Zinn mentioned Berrigan's ongoing resistance to the coercive power of the federal government. But Zinn never mentioned that the priest was in the Boston area—or that he was helping him evade the FBI.[8]

Zinn was not the only member of the BU community to be touched by Berrigan's decision to go underground. James Carroll—who had closely followed the trial of the Catonsville Nine in the fall of 1968—had been assigned to the university as a Catholic chaplain after his ordination in 1969. "Daniel Berrigan became my authority," he later wrote. "In relation to him I'd found a voice, and I used it against the war as forthrightly as I could, while he was underground and then when he was in prison."[9]

Inspired by Berrigan, Carroll spoke out against the war and participated in myriad antiwar demonstrations at BU. He also had the chance to serve as a surrogate for Berrigan during the Jesuit's time as a fugitive and prisoner. The Boston priest once received a call from a producer at the *Dick Cavett Show*, one of the leading variety television programs of its era. Cavett wanted to interview Berrigan, but his whereabouts were unknown. So the producer wondered if another antiwar priest—Carroll—would stand in for him on the show.[10]

Carroll was torn. He wondered if he was being brought onto the show because of the dramatic divisions within his own family. Here was a radical Catholic priest apparently modeling himself on Dan Berrigan—and his father had worked for decades for the FBI, the federal agency hunting the fugitive Jesuit. "They want me because of Dad," he thought, "the sensation it will cause." Despite the risk, he resolved to go ahead with the appearance; it seemed important that he use the opportunity to speak out against the war.[11]

The evening proved to be a donnybrook. Cavett was too ill to host the program, so one of the scheduled guests, the actor Jack Klugman, stepped in to replace him. Carroll was crestfallen. Waiting offstage, he became so unnerved that he spilled coffee all over the crotch of his pants when he heard himself announced as a guest.[12]

Carroll joined an unlikely group of guests onstage: the singer John Sebastian, the comedian Henny Youngman (whose signature line was, "Take my wife, please?"), and the actress Elizabeth Ashley. Klugman, noticing that Carroll was wearing a turtleneck (as Dan Berrigan himself surely would have), asked, "Where's your dog collar?" When the priest muttered that he didn't understand the question, Klugman said to him, "Your dog collar, Father. You know, woof-woof." The mockery did not faze Carroll; he stood his ground and launched into an extended expression of admiration for Dan Berrigan. His prolonged antiwar monologue stunned everyone. (Youngman was left speechless for one of the few times in his life.[13])

Berrigan did not leave everything up to proxies like James Carroll. He repeatedly issued public statements and granted interviews to journalists. At one point, he sat down for a long interview with reporter Bryce Nelson of the *Los Angeles Times*. Describing the genesis of his encounter with Berrigan, Nelson wrote that his initial contact was a nun who called herself "Sister Claudia"; she then handed him off to a priest named Charlie, who brought him to meet

Berrigan somewhere in an urban neighborhood. The elaborate security measures that marked Nelson's approach to Berrigan were not in place during the interview itself: as was his custom, the priest made no effort to disguise himself, wearing his signature black turtleneck and beret.[14]

In his talk with Nelson, Berrigan explained that he had experienced a transformation over the previous few years, thanks to his experiences in Hanoi and Catonsville and his time underground. "These last years have created something like an underground fire in me," he said. "I've had to deal with a great deal of anger, and the problem of how to make anger useful and not just burn up in it. I live with personal outrage about those I love." He would not douse those fires by capitulating to the federal government. "No, oh no," he said of the possibility of surrendering. "That's never been seriously considered." Still, he knew that he could not remain a fugitive forever; sooner or later, the FBI would catch up with him. "At some point, I'm going to be picked up. But that's something they're going to have to do. They're going to have to get to me. My friends and I are going to make that as embarrassing and unlikely as we can."[15]

In its search for the fugitive priest, the FBI cast a wide net. The search took agents to the Evanston, Illinois, home of actor and filmmaker Dick Cusack. Because Cusack had been Phil Berrigan's roommate at Holy Cross and remained close to the priest's family throughout his life, agents thought he might have some clue as to Dan's whereabouts. After they questioned Cusack and his wife, Nancy, she had to explain to their daughter Ann why the FBI had visited.

"These men are looking for Father Dan," she said.

"Why?" Ann asked.

"They think Father Dan has done something wrong."

"That can't be," Ann announced. "Father Dan wouldn't do anything wrong."[16]

The FBI believed that one of its best hopes for snaring Berrigan would come if he tried to make contact with his family. And he had ample reason to reach out to them: late in May 1970, his aging mother fell and hurt her hip. The injury required surgery, and the FBI closely monitored her hospitalization in the hope that it might draw the fugitive priest out from hiding.

The FBI's surveillance tactics were far from subtle. Agents approached Harold Weichart, the physician who was treating Frida Berrigan at St. Joseph's Hospital in Syracuse, and asked for his cooperation in apprehending her son. "The FBI wants me to watch for Dan coming here to see Frida," he informed the family, "and let them know." Weichart, an old family friend, wanted no part in the scheme, but other hospital staff proved far less protective of the Berrigans. Jerry Berrigan, Dan and Phil's brother, later wrote that nurses seemed bent on torturing Frida because of her son's purported lack of patriotism, at one point even refusing to help the frail woman leave her bed to go to the bathroom. "Oh Jerry, take me out of this hospital," she pleaded. "They don't want me here." All the while, agents lurked outside her room and inquired about her condition, apparently hoping that Dan would appear if things turned dire.[17]

The FBI maintained its surveillance at the hospital for several weeks, shadowing the family as it waited for Frida to recover. "For a month feds with crockery faces paced the corridors, strode the waiting rooms, peered in doors and up streets," according to Jerry Berrigan. "Collusion with nuns, nurses, administrators. Law 'n' order types, God and flag, heads all together: catch Father Dan and damn those other Berrigans, disloyal, godless people." But the agency's quarry knew better than to walk into such an obvious trap. As Jerry put it, "Dan stayed away. Blessedly."[18]

From underground, Berrigan wrote to his family and tried to explain why he found himself unable to reach his mother's bedside. "One can so long to be there and of course I do, and wish Phil also were at hand," he explained. "But then there are the times—deadly as they are—and our job—which we have not so much taken on ourselves as been summoned for. And I try to measure the pain of separation from you all, against the suffering of so many who are not only helpless and unable to cope, but (which I take to be most crushing to the spirit) have had no choice in their own fate, from birth to death." At least for the time being, he had grasped "the opportunity to choose something richer and wider than just one life. I take that as a great grace." The fugitive took comfort in the fact that the public remained interested in his ongoing witness against the war. "So beyond doubt does the FBI," he added.[19]

The family also communicated with Berrigan by telephone throughout his time underground. The weekly calls were relatively brief and short on details regarding his precise whereabouts, as everyone assumed that the FBI had tapped the family's phone. Nonetheless, the fleeting telephone conversations comforted the family. Jerry later said that "thanks to AT&T we had a lifeline, Dan and ourselves. Week by week we said to each other, 'We're still in the real world, we're making it!'"[20]

It was a world closely monitored by the FBI, which was under mounting pressure to apprehend Berrigan. A neighbor once approached Jerry's wife, Carol, with some concerns she had about the appearance of a strange man on their street.

"Did you see that man watching your house?" the neighbor asked. "Do you think he could be a pervert, after our kids?"

Carol could only make light of the situation. "Pervert? No! Feds," she informed the neighbor. "Our kids are being watched by the government, for free, as if they were kids of the Kennedys or Nixons. Isn't that wonderful?"[21]

The FBI also engaged in more heavy-handed efforts to find Berrigan through his family in the Syracuse area. One afternoon, two agents appeared at Jerry's front door. The men were so clean-cut that he initially thought they might be Mormon missionaries. When they stated their business—they were representing J. Edgar Hoover, not church elders—Berrigan shook his head and closed the door; he had no interest in speaking with men representing an agency that was hunting his brother and harassing his family. As the door closed, he could hear the agents rattling off the severe penalties he might face if he was found guilty of harboring or abetting a fugitive.[22]

The family soldiered on despite such threats. To stave off paranoia, they adopted a simple philosophy: "Ignore what you don't know; enjoy what you do!" as Jerry later described it. It was a process of self-discovery made easier by Dan's ongoing witness and its roots in the foundational teachings of Christianity. "We saw that he embodied joy because he was free. We learned that for one thing Dan saw the Sermon on the Mount not as a discussion club outline but as a guide for action."[23]

Berrigan's family members were not alone in facing scrutiny from the federal government during his time underground. Late in May 1970, NBC News interviewed the fugitive in a Connecticut hotel room. After portions of the interview aired, the FBI and the Justice Department asked to view unused segments of the interview and to question members of the crew that had filmed Berrigan. An agency spokesman said that the FBI was "seeing if anyone is willing to talk to us." The network, sensitive to the First Amendment implications of such an investigation, balked at the request. NBC's vice president for news announced that the network had told the government that "we did not think that [its request] was very sensible."[24]

The FBI's investigation was so far-ranging that it even reached a wedding in Baltimore. Unconcerned about disrupting the festivities, the agents left no stone unturned in their search for Berrigan at the church. "Someone even told me they looked for Dan under the pews," the bride later said.[25]

Berrigan was nowhere near the wedding, but he eventually learned how the FBI had disrupted it. He was told that a balloon had popped at one point during the agents' search for him. This innocuous accident had startled the agents; thinking it might be gunfire, they had drawn their weapons. Berrigan struggled to fathom why the agents would feel the need to arm themselves as they searched for an avowed disciple of nonviolence. "I don't believe I have ever held a gun," he said while underground. "I wouldn't know what to do with a gun if I had one."[26]

As the FBI pursued unproductive leads, Berrigan hopscotched among families who supported his ongoing witness. *Newsweek* estimated that "in all, some 300 persons, mostly urban families in the East and Midwest, provided [him] shelter" during his time underground. Traveling lightly, he brought along only the barest essentials: a Bible, a toothbrush, and a chaotic stack of poetry and prose manuscripts.[27]

The families harboring Berrigan learned that his status as a fugitive made some everyday tasks, such as making telephone calls, extraordinarily complicated. To avoid FBI wiretaps, only public telephones were used. One individual who sheltered the priest recalled that ferrying him to use a pay phone outside a large department store was a journey fraught with peril. "Outside, where other people moved with impunity, every stop at a traffic light was a menace to us," Berrigan's driver later said. "When I stepped with Dan into the street I felt directly the guilt and terror and madness of America waging war. Fugitives see clearly." In time, they found a row of telephone booths; they circled it once, just to make sure that they weren't being observed, before Berrigan exited the car and made his way to one of the phones. A police car cruised by, but the officers inside paid no attention to the prominent fugitive who sat just a few feet away.[28]

Berrigan returned to the car after a few moments. His smile seemed to indicate that the call had gone well and boosted his spirits. "No answer," he said, without a hint of melancholy. "There was no one there." The priest said he hoped to make the connection the next time he was able to make a call. But his companion realized that, because of his precarious existence underground, "we could have no idea when next time would be."[29]

Berrigan often felt painfully isolated. He later wrote that he sometimes seemed "like a ghostly ancestor in someone's attic, or pacing outdoors in a secluded yard." The families harboring him did their best to minimize his feelings of seclusion. A friend remembered taking him to the beach one day. The parents involved in this excursion worried over the possible risks involved, but not the fugitive Jesuit. When the group arrived at the beach, the children who had come along immediately began to frolic. Before the adults had time to register their objections, they looked over and saw that "Dan had already stripped down to a baggy borrowed bathing suit and chased after the kids, running into the cold water without breaking stride," one of them later said. "They played together in the surf, children and man, and we began to get some idea of what we were celebrating."[30]

Not all of Berrigan's underground interactions were so amicable. He once attended a meeting with some antiwar movement leaders, two Black Panthers, a few clergymen, and a former FBI agent. The Panthers took him to task—somewhat unfairly—for his alleged lack of concern for blacks and for his commitment to nonviolence, which seemed naïve to them. "You reacted toward Vietnam, but what about blacks?" he was asked. "If a white radical doesn't identify his action with the people at the bottom, then he's just shucking and jiving. You can't deal with violence and viciousness and fascism with morality. Then you only have six million people in gas chambers." Berrigan prided himself on his concern for racial justice, and he was taken aback by the accusations. "I'm working against a white war and war machine, and I don't know how the black community relates to that," he said. "But the minute we start saying that we're only being men when we're shooting, I begin to turn off."[31]

Early in August 1970, Berrigan surfaced long enough to make a dramatic public appearance in Philadelphia at the First United Methodist Church of Germantown. "I believe we are in such times as make it increasingly impossible for Christians to obey the law of the land and to remain true to Christ,"

Berrigan told the startled churchgoers, who had had been given no warning that he would appear. "And this is the simple word that I bring to you as a brother in Christ. I bring it with the full consciousness that in so doing I increase my own jeopardy. But I bring it, as I stated before, from my brother in prison, from all my brothers in prison, from all of those who suffer because children and the innocent die." Berrigan left the church abruptly after making his remarks, exiting through a side door and clambering into a waiting car, which quickly drove him away.[32]

Berrigan's puckish elusiveness made the FBI the object of no small amount of ridicule. In his widely syndicated column, conservative pundit William F. Buckley complained that the bureau agents were bumbling around while Berrigan was "thumbing his nose at American jurisprudence. . . . If you needed an extra speaker at your peace rally, an extra interviewee on your talk show, or an extra drummer at your rock festival, you could find Father Berrigan without any trouble; but for some reason, the FBI could not find him at all." Federal prosecutor Barney Skolnik summed up the prevailing view of the manhunt when he told *Newsweek*, "The FBI really had egg on its face on this one."[33]

Berrigan reveled in embarrassing the FBI. In interviews, he merrily noted the federal government's ineptitude in tracking him down, and he referenced it in letters home as well. He wrote in one buoyant letter, "I take perverse joy in knowing that I am on many charts and lists, and am causing a bit of sleepless attention to the law enforcers, and deflecting a bit of the military $$$ to my own person and whereabouts. Ha!"[34]

With public criticism mounting, the FBI redoubled its efforts to catch Berrigan, and agents finally closed in on their target. The end of his prolonged run as a fugitive came on Block Island, off the Rhode Island coast, early in August 1970. Berrigan went there to spend time with his friends William Stringfellow and Anthony Towne. They welcomed the priest warmly but also offered a trenchant critique of his role in the antiwar movement. Towne bluntly told him that "the movement badly needed depersonalization," he later wrote. "From the time of the Catonsville action the movement had depended too much upon the personalities of the Berrigans, and during the fugitive era it depended almost entirely on the personality of Daniel Berrigan." What would happen when, inevitably, the FBI captured him? The movement would be decapitated, Towne thought.[35]

On August 11, Towne saw something strange on their property: a man in an orange slicker. The man appeared to be a birdwatcher—he had field glasses— but something about the circumstances made him and Stringfellow suspicious. A northeaster appeared to be blowing in, and no one in his right mind would have been bird-watching in those blustery conditions.

After alerting Berrigan, Stringfellow ventured outside and approached the orange-clad figure. Soon, two cars appeared and sped past him toward the house.

"What are you doing here?" he demanded.

"Bird-watching," the man sheepishly replied.

"In a gale?"

The man then reached into his jacket and produced his FBI credentials. "We're looking for Berrigan," he told Stringfellow.

The two men then walked back to the house. Stringfellow realized that Berrigan's run was over, but he wanted to make sure that the federal agents were playing by the rules.

"You have any kind of warrant?"

"I don't," an agent told him. "We have a fugitive warrant, but I don't have a copy."

A fleet of cars pulled up to the house. About a dozen FBI agents—some in disguise—poured out and surrounded the residence.

Berrigan, who had watched from a window as the drama unfolded outside, made no effort to flee.

"I suppose you're wondering who I am," he said as he left the house. "I am Daniel Berrigan."

The agents frisked Berrigan, handcuffed him, and then pushed him into one of their cars. Despite the circumstances, the priest maintained his equanimity and graciousness. Before the car pulled away, he raised his shackled wrists and said, "God bless." As Berrigan was being led to the Coast Guard vessel that would take him back to the mainland, one of the FBI agents informed the priest that he had been schooled by the Jesuits. Savoring Berrigan's capture, he told the priest, "I said to myself when we took you, 'AMDG!'" (This was a reference to the Jesuit motto, ad majorem Dei gloriam—"for the greater glory of God."[36])

Such needling failed to dampen Berrigan's spirits. Pictures taken of the Jesuit being escorted by federal agents in Providence showed him grinning and raising his hands to offer the peace sign.[37]

Berrigan's supporters responded to his capture in a variety of ways. The Weather Underground praised him for having "refused the corruption of your generation." Some lashed out at the government for having pursued the priest so doggedly. "Father Daniel Berrigan has been taken away to prison for setting fire to draft board records and declaring 'Thou Shalt Not Kill,'" Howard Zinn, Noam Chomsky, and Robert S. Cohen declared in a joint statement. "He was captured by a government which, in violation of that Commandment, the Constitution, and international law, is carrying on a large-scale slaughter in Southeast Asia." Others took more direct action: in Manhattan, a group of seven pacifists protested Berrigan's capture by dumping fourteen gallons of animal blood on the steps of the federal courthouse in Foley Square.[38]

Not long after the FBI took Berrigan into custody, leaflets appeared on the streets of New York: "DAN BERRIGAN IS FREE," they read. "Would that more of us were as free of prison as is he."[39]

"The Impact of Such a Thing Would Be Phenomenal"

Prison was not an entirely new experience for Marjorie Melville. Like all of the Nine, she briefly had been incarcerated in the Baltimore County Jail after the Catonsville protest. But that fleeting taste of confinement had not fully prepared her for her second period behind bars, which began in April 1970 after she and her husband surrendered themselves to federal authorities in Baltimore. "This was a much harder experience," she later said, "in that I knew that this was the beginning of a long stretch." It would last until January 1971.[1]

Her second round of incarceration began with a two-week confinement in Baltimore's dank city jail, where she was held until her transfer to the federal women's prison camp in Alderson, West Virginia. The reality of her situation as a prisoner hit Melville at mealtimes in the jail. Either coffee or Kool-Aid were served to inmates in small metal dishes through the bars of their cells. The receptacles reminded her of the bowls that people used to feed their dogs. Their drinks were unpalatable, the food "absolutely horrible," she later said.[2]

When she arrived at Alderson, prison officials fingerprinted Melville, took her mug shot, and strip-searched her. She also was deloused—a necessary precaution, she understood, but humiliating all the same. Guards then shunted her off to a small, almost barren room. Clad in only a nightgown, she remained confined there for the better part of two days; no one ever explained why. So began a process of depersonalization that lasted for the duration of her prison term. "It makes you feel your powerlessness: like when you witness an accident and there's absolutely nothing you can do about it," she explained. "It's geared to de-humanize you and make you feel evil and guilty."[3]

Melville fought off the depersonalization—it included being identified by the Federal Bureau of Prisons as inmate 18096-170—with the help of some kindred spirits. Alderson also held two other women who had engaged in notable acts of political resistance: a woman who had raided a Chicago-area draft board and Lolita Lebrón, who had participated in a spectacular attack on Congress by

Puerto Rican nationalists in 1954. Melville did not feel that these political resisters were well understood by most of their fellow prisoners. "We have much
more reason to be in jail than most of the poor and the blacks," she explained.
"I chose deliberately to fight the society. But they're in because the society has
put them there."[4]

Melville felt that, because of the nature of their crimes, the political prisoners had some advantages over the general prison population. "The attitude about being there makes a big difference," she remarked. "Someone
there on narc[otics] charges is made to feel horribly guilty. But if you're there
because you chose to resist the system, they have a harder time making you
feel like nothing."[5]

Although some of them struggled to fathom her crime, Melville developed
close ties to many of the Spanish-speaking women in the prison. A few were
South Americans who had been caught in airports attempting to smuggle
narcotics. At Alderson, they forged lasting bonds as they knit or crocheted
together in the afternoons and evenings. These were intense, revealing sessions in which the women opened up and shared their experiences and beliefs.
Melville treasured how deeply the women came to know one another. "You
begin to penetrate each other's lives very intensely, much more than we do
normally—maybe husbands and wives do, but even some of them don't talk as
much as we do under those circumstances," she observed. "Every single day
for those long hours." This was possible only because the women learned to be
unguarded around one another. "It takes a long time to be able to have enough
confidence in someone so you can really talk about what you really feel. From
your own self you hide feelings many times, and there you could really talk."[6]

Melville joked with attorney Harold Buchman that Alderson was a country
club and assured him that prison authorities generally treated her well. She
found the toughest challenge in being separated from her husband. "What I've
missed so very much," she told Buchman in a letter, "is being away from Tom."
Their separation proved especially painful when she received word that her
father had passed away. She knew that her husband would have provided comfort and helped her through the grieving process.[7]

The separation also vexed Tom Melville (inmate 36761-133). After the couple
turned themselves in, he briefly lost track of his wife. "I have received no news
of Marjorie since we entered the marshal's office. Is she still in Baltimore City
Jail, or has she gone to Alderson?" he worriedly wrote to Buchman from the
federal prison at Lewisburg. "I am just a bit concerned about her—I know she
would have written to me by now if she could. These first days are the most
important and I need reassurance that she is adjusting adequately." He felt an
enormous sense of relief when he finally received a letter from her. He told
Buchman, "I've heard from Marjorie. She is fine, thank God."[8]

Aside from the anguish he felt over being separated from his wife, spending
a year and a half in federal prison did not prove to be especially difficult for

Melville. "Life could be worse here," he wrote. "They could have kept us in Baltimore City Jail." Having endured several years in a Catholic seminary as he trained for the priesthood, he was well prepared for the rigid order and monotony of prison life. Unbending schedules, bland food, limited personal autonomy—he already had lived through it all. For many years afterward, he would joke that his preparation for the priesthood had been the perfect training for spending a long period behind bars.[9]

For the most part, Melville steered clear of disciplinary troubles in prison. In time, he was rewarded with a job on the prison farm at Allenwood. Melville's seemingly mundane task—he ground corn for cattle feed—made him popular among his fellow prisoners. Many confined men taught themselves to be distillers, and they coveted Melville's corn because it could be transformed into home brew—"hooch," everyone called it. Before long, inmates were asking Melville to steal corn for them. He was confronted with an ethical quandary: he didn't want to disappoint his fellow prisoners, but he also didn't want to get caught stealing and have time added to his sentence. He resolved the dilemma by telling the men that although he wouldn't pilfer the corn himself, he would leave a particular silo unlocked when he left his post. If they wanted the corn, they could swipe it themselves, and he could deny knowing anything about it.[10]

This arrangement worked nicely until prison authorities busted an African American inmate for possessing hooch. Word spread that Melville had betrayed the man. Melville had established a friendship with a black inmate from Baltimore, and the man confronted him with the accusation and warned that Melville might be harmed if the claim proved to be true. Melville looked the inmate in the eye and assured him that he hadn't been the snitch. His word was enough; there were no reprisals against Melville for the incident.[11]

For a time, Melville drove a tractor at the prison farm. "It is a pleasant job," he wrote, "out in the fresh air and sunshine all day, admiring the rolling landscape that composes this area." He enjoyed the work until he developed a case of hemorrhoids. Melville had battled the ailment several times during his years in Guatemala, and he had no desire to repeat the excruciating experience. He reluctantly found other tasks. Given the condition of his posterior, "it's best to stay off the tractors," he joked.[12]

With the help of Brady Tyson at American University, Melville continued with his graduate studies from behind bars. Improvising a long-distance curriculum, Tyson dispatched parcels of books to Allenwood, and Melville pored over them whenever he could. The volumes had to pass muster with a guard who was responsible for keeping materials with potentially provocative ideological or political content out of the inmates' hands. Melville received so many hefty scholarly books from Tyson that the guard soon wearied of the task of closely inspecting them. Before long, he would merely glance at the books and mutter to Melville in perfunctory way, "Just tell me it's not against the U.S. government."[13]

While Tom was still behind bars, he and Marjorie managed to publish an account of their tumultuous time together in Guatemala and their participation in the Catonsville demonstration. The Melvilles promoted their book *Whose Heaven, Whose Earth?* by writing a joint opinion piece on the Catholic war resistance movement for the *New York Times*. In it, they asserted that such opposition to the war was making a real difference. "The purpose of Catonsville and the many draft board actions that followed was essentially didactic," they wrote. "We intended to demonstrate our belief that true loyalty to America as well as to Christ lies in active resistance to war and Nixon's propagation of it, as well as to other expressions of American hate, destruction and inhumanity. We know this message is getting across."[14]

When she was released from prison, Marjorie publicized the book by appearing on television and radio talk shows. The book's message—that the people of Guatemala were being denied fundamental human rights—sometimes got lost in these appearances; the questions often turned to her decision to marry or to her views on the Catonsville protest. She grew tired of repeatedly fielding the same inquiries, and she missed the companionship of her husband. Marjorie also found herself feeling out of place in the United States. "I think I'd prefer to have been released from jail in Mexico. I feel more at home there," she said. "Here I feel inferior. I don't know how to get along." This was apparent to a writer with whom she shared a lunch: as they left the restaurant, Melville got caught in a revolving door that spun too quickly.[15]

John Hogan, the Melvilles' fellow ex-Maryknoller in Guatemala, did his best not to make waves at Lewisburg and Allenwood. Getting to the federal prison facility proved to be a memorably sobering experience for him. Hogan and Tom Lewis were shackled for the trip north from Baltimore: handcuffed at the wrists, chained at the feet. When they stopped for a bathroom break, the federal marshals escorting them had to unlock everything—a long and tedious process that underscored for Hogan the boundaries of his new life as a prisoner. "This is crazy," he thought as he was slowly unshackled in the men's room. "This is nuts."[16]

When they arrived at Lewisburg, Lewis and Hogan showered and then received towels to dry off—a luxury that had not been afforded to them earlier in their journey, when they had bathed in Baltimore's fetid city jail. "The federal government," Hogan cracked, pretending to be impressed, "can afford towels."[17]

Hogan spent two weeks at Lewisburg before joining Tom Melville and Lewis at the adjoining Allenwood farm. Several of his fellow inmates were Italian Americans with ties to organized crime. Although Hogan never had been formally ordained as such, these Catholics dubbed him "priest" and peppered him with questions about religious doctrine and practice. He tackled such tasks as outlining for them the differences between the ascension of Jesus into heaven and the Assumption of Mary.[18]

There were quite a few small-time hoods at Allenwood—"mini-Mafias," Hogan called them. They seemed curious about what the Catonsville Nine had done to land themselves in prison, but his conversations with them seemed to lack any real depth. "They couldn't figure out what we were all about," he later said.[19]

Not all war resisters at Allenwood got along so well with the general prison population. About half a dozen Jehovah's Witnesses had been relegated there for violating draft laws, and they never quite fit in. Their faith, unlike Hogan's Catholicism, appeared strange and vaguely threatening. "I was always a little nervous for them," he later said. "They seemed very vulnerable being in jail."[20]

Like Melville, Hogan had some memorable alcohol-related experiences in prison. One night, some men received several cases of liquor that had been dropped over the fence by friends on the outside. (Security at Allenwood was notoriously lax.) Hogan was reading when the ensuing celebration began, but a fellow inmate soon asked him to join in and offered a large cup brimming with Scotch.

"I can't drink all of this," Hogan said.

"You ain't going nowhere," the inmate replied, grinning. "Take your time and enjoy it."

The party was interrupted for the nightly count of inmates. One man had gotten so loudly drunk that he threatened to expose the whole party to the guards, but one of Hogan's less pacifistic fellow prisoners fashioned a quick solution: he silenced the drunk with a roundhouse blow to the jaw. Prison officials eventually learned about the party. A search of the dorm the following day failed to produce any evidence, though, because the inmates had meticulously disposed of all the liquor bottles.[21]

Such experiences helped the inmates forge a cohesive and supportive community behind bars. Hogan found it congenial, for the most part. "I'm doing fine here, and have met some pretty great people," he wrote to attorney Harold Buchman. "I figured that would happen—but never thought there would be so many." Using the idiom of his generation, he told the lawyer that he had found "some great friends to groove with" at Lewisburg and Allenwood.[22]

Hogan, like Tom Melville, believed that his religious training had prepared him for life in prison, and he had few serious difficulties in adjusting to life behind bars. He found time to read and reflect on the events of the previous few years. "Funny thing, Harold—this whole thing has been blessed," he wrote to Buchman. "The act—the trial—and jail have carried a tremendous joy. No—don't mistake that word. There's no enjoying jail, but there sure is a strange good feeling that is wrapped up in it all."[23]

He told Buchman in another letter, "A world of light has appeared starting with Catonsville. Words are taking flesh and life is rich."[24]

Ambivalent about the terms he had handed down in the Catonsville case, Judge Roszel Thomsen urged all of the surviving defendants to write him letters explaining why their sentences should be reduced. Hogan suspected that the judge wanted him to apologize for his actions, but he told Buchman that doing so would be "totally impossible." He wrote a straightforward letter instead, telling Thomsen, "At present I can only say that I am living out that which I professed at Catonsville and the trial. I believe that the act, the trial, and now prison form for me a communion with people that stands for life. I neither regret nor deny that which I have done."[25]

Something in the letter must have resonated with Thomsen, because the judge cut Hogan's sentence from two years down to one. With time off for good behavior, he wound up serving only slightly more than nine months. (Melville also benefited from Thomsen's largesse: he served only about a year and a half.)

His wife, Joan, whom he met after being released, later said that she didn't think Hogan had been traumatized by his relatively brief time in prison. "He didn't think it was a bad experience," she said. "He got close to some of the people there. He enjoyed listening to their stories."[26]

Allenwood reminded Tom Lewis of his time in the Army—but only to a point. "The Penitentiary, the Army—one might say that I am the guest of the United States government," he wrote. "All expenses paid, free travel, clothes, food, lodging—it sounds like a Utopian travel poster. Almost. In the first case, honorably discharged after eight years service; in the second case, six years' prison sentence for protesting a genocidal war."[27]

Lewis shared a small, spartan room with four other men. There was little room for furniture in the cramped space: the men could wedge only a rickety card table in between their bunk beds. Decorations were few. "No posters, pictures or graffiti are allowed on the concrete block walls," he observed, "only a penitentiary-approved calendar." Nothing covered the concrete floor, and it turned into a freezing slab during the winter months.[28]

His days began at 6:30 A.M. Lewis usually awoke to sounds of the prison farm coming to life. Men murmured greetings to one another and shuffled into the communal bathroom. The relative cleanliness of this space came as a pleasant surprise to him. The latrines in the Army had smelled like "an Ohio backhouse [or privy] in mid-July," he quipped, but the inmates at Allenwood flushed frequently to minimize the stench.[29]

After breakfast, Lewis would clamber aboard a truck for the trip over to his job at the prison farm's piggery. The men who worked there tried to make the best of their miserable lot in life. In 1968, the Yippies famously had elected a pig—it bore the faux-Olympian name "Pigasus"—as president as part of their raucous protest at the Democratic convention in Chicago. Borrowing a page from this radical playbook, Lewis and his comrades in the piggery jokingly chose to nominate their own candidate, named "Runti." "A few campaign posters were tacked on the shoat lot, or pen, that Runti was in, and he was given a few pieces of candy by one of the crew that week," Lewis wrote.[30]

The men working in the piggery had some of the most undesirable jobs at Allenwood. They had to feed and clean up after the pigs before slaughtering (and later butchering) them. Donning black rubber aprons, they carried out this macabre task twice a week. "The pig is hoisted upon a chain by one foot, a knife is thrust into his throat, blood shoots out over the hand holding the knife," Lewis wrote. "When pigs are small, they bark like small dogs; when they are killed, they scream like people. It takes the pig anywhere from 15 to 30 seconds to die, screaming and jerking the whole time."[31]

Even in this gory environment, Lewis's mind turned to art. He was struck by how much the scene in the piggery reminded him of an image rendered by Rembrandt of a side of beef. The sounds of the abattoir also resonated: the pigs' screams made Lewis think of the people of Vietnam. "Always my thoughts go to the war in Vietnam and how the screaming of the people must sound during a bombing or napalm attack," he observed. "The sounds of the planes, the B-52's, must be deafening. One screaming pig sounds loud; 100 screaming people must be unbearable."[32]

In the morning, Lewis usually prayed in front of a favorite tree on the prison grounds before heading off to toil in the piggery. After work, he had ample free time to focus on his art—or even to just sit in the sun and think. Allenwood wasn't exactly idyllic, but for Lewis "it was actually a sane place to be in the late '60s and early '70s," when the outside world was so tumultuous. "Prison can be a sane place to be when times are insane."[33]

Lewis's stand against the war earned him the respect of his fellow inmates. There was a sense that they shared a common enemy: the state. "We are all in the same bag, so to say," he wrote. "The oppressing big brother is the government; it's government which keeps us behind the walls, and attempts to get our mind 'right' for when we leave." Lewis believed that the state utterly debilitated inmates and left them unprepared to resume normal, productive lives outside the prison walls. He viewed it as a kind of castration.[34]

It was Lewis's personal life, though, that proved to be the most emasculating. In the summer of 1968, he met a young woman who had joined the activist community supporting the Catonsville Nine. They married before he was sent to prison in the spring of 1970, but their union unraveled during his time at Allenwood. Through her involvement in the burgeoning women's rights movement, Lewis's wife had come to realize that she was a lesbian. She shared this revelation while visiting Lewis at the prison, and it devastated him. He thought about trying to exert some control over her—to command her to remain committed to their heterosexual union. But he realized that it would be pointless to issue such a mandate.[35]

As his marriage crumbled, Lewis ultimately surrendered his presumed authority as a male—something he thought more men should do in a variety of societal contexts. "I chose to give the power up," he later said. "And what I learned from that was . . . that men in this culture have to start by giving up power, and I mean power at all levels, and replace it with multiplicity—replace it, of course, with love."[36]

In prison, Lewis also learned how to accept suffering. "I don't want to say I invited the suffering," he later said. "I would say I accepted the suffering." He resolved to make the best of his oppressive circumstances by "growing as a Christian, as a Catholic. Reading the Bible. And being in support of other prisoners—draft resisters as well as other[s]."[37]

George Mische's stay at Allenwood and Lewisburg proved to be far more contentious than Lewis's. The most serious of his troubles began midway through the summer of 1971, when he was caught filching hard-boiled eggs from the mess hall at Allenwood. Although prisoners often took eggs that were about to be discarded, they were considered contraband, and Mische received a sixty-day suspended sentence in segregation as a penalty. Not long afterward, he was involved in a confrontation with a correctional officer. Their dispute arose when the guard inspected Mische's locker when the prisoner wasn't present. Mische asserted that, because of his political beliefs and interest in prison reform, the guard had conspired with a notorious prison informer to frame him for once again possessing contraband. The guard responded to this accusation by writing a misconduct report that cited Mische for insolence. The citation meant that Mische would be transferred over to Lewisburg to serve his stint in segregation for the earlier egg-stealing charge.[38]

But the first attempt to transfer him failed. Mische had emerged as a vocal advocate for prisoners' rights—he had even arranged for a congressman to visit the prison facility and hear prisoners' complaints of mistreatment—and there was a sense among his fellow inmates that his punishment was "a threat by the administration [of the prison] against anyone who said they would pursue decisions to higher authorities," as he put it. To show their support, a group of prisoners linked arms and blocked the truck that was transporting Mische over to Lewisburg. "The prisoners seemed bent on confrontation," a federal district court judge later wrote of the incident. "The situation became ugly. In my view, the prisoners were on the very edge of mutiny." Prison authorities defused the situation by keeping Mische at Allenwood—but only temporarily. The following day, a large contingent of armed guards moved him to Lewisburg, and no prisoners interfered.[39]

Mische's fellow inmates paid dearly for standing up for him. The men who had blocked the truck faced misconduct charges before the adjustment committee at Lewisburg. The penalties meted out were severe: one man was placed in segregation for two months, which resulted in his tentative release date being pushed back for close to a year; others were transferred to other prisons in the federal system. The sanctions set off another round of protests—both within the prison complex and beyond its gates. Inmates staged a brief work stoppage, and a group of roughly seventy-five protested outside the prison grounds. When the protesters tried to enter the facility, guards repulsed them with smoke bombs. There also were reports that guards beat a few of the demonstrators.[40]

Several of the men who were sanctioned, including Mische, subsequently filed a lawsuit against the Federal Bureau of Prisons. In it, they claimed that their right to due process of law had been violated during the disciplinary hearings at Lewisburg. The case did not get far; both a federal district court and the U.S. Court of Appeals for the Third Circuit ruled against them. The district court judge was especially hostile to the claims raised by Mische and his fellow prisoners, noting that they brought their action "without clean hands. A prison mutiny is a vicious thing."[41]

When he arrived at Lewisburg with his Baltimore Four partner David Eberhardt, Phil Berrigan assumed that, as a nonviolent offender, he would be dispatched to the prison camp at nearby Allenwood. His previous term there, in 1968, had been tolerable; he fondly recalled its "space, boredom, and cow manure." But Berrigan encountered troubles from the outset of his second stint at Lewisburg. The warden equivocated over whether he would be allowed to return to Allenwood, which was generally understood to be a less onerous place to serve time.

"You did abscond, you know," the warden told him, referring to his time underground. "How do we know you won't run again?"

"Absconding is the FBI's business; my conduct here is yours," Berrigan said. "And you have had no evidence, before or now, that I can't be trusted."

"Yeah? Well, we think that your conduct outside and here are linked. We wanna see, anyway."

Phil Berrigan wondered if the warden's decision was related to the fact that his brother remained a fugitive.

"Your decision or Washington's?"

"It's all one family," the warden responded. "I'll admit we'd like to see you all together again. You just wait a while, and we'll see how it works."[42]

From Berrigan's perspective, it worked poorly. Before his brother was apprehended, he felt that he was repeatedly punished for petty or simply trumped-up charges because federal authorities hoped to gain leverage on Dan. He engaged in a widely publicized hunger strike (in which he was joined by Eberhardt) and wrote letters of protest to numerous members of Congress, among them Senator Charles Goodell of New York. To Goodell, Berrigan recited a litany of complaints: "My mail has been tampered with constantly, stool pigeons encouraged to inform on me, guards instructed to report my every move, legitimate visits denied me, guards searching me, my quarters, the sacristy where I vest for Mass. In addition, I have been denied minimum security (one of the farm camps) usually accorded to political prisoners." There was an obvious explanation for the harassment. "The real reason is this—my brother, Father Daniel Berrigan, is still a fugitive, and everybody thinks that I can help apprehend him," the priest wrote.[43]

Writing to Goodell, Berrigan also bemoaned the length of his sentence—six years in prison "for burning paper rather than children." He angrily noted that an American soldier recently had been sentenced to only six months in prison for having murdered several Vietnamese civilians.[44]

Goodell knew of the Nine and respected what they had done. "I recognized their burning of draft records as an important symbolic act," he said. "Such acts are necessary when you reach a point of such great frustration that you don't think you can communicate any other way."[45] And so Berrigan's letter caught the senator's attention. He responded by telling the jailed priest that "your actions have shown a profound understanding of the paradoxes and contradictions of our country's position, both moral and political." He promised to contact Norman Carlson, the director of the Federal Bureau of Prisons, and urge him to place Berrigan, Eberhardt, and Mische in minimum security facilities, where they clearly belonged. Goodell also said he would ask Carlson to ensure that the prisoners' personal liberties were safeguarded.[46]

In his reply to Goodell, Carlson maintained that all of Berrigan's claims had been thoroughly investigated. The results of this inquiry showed, he said, that Berrigan's punishments had resulted from clear infractions of prison rules. Furthermore, the priest had not been harassed.[47]

Believing that they had proved their point, Berrigan and Eberhardt broke their fast. They were removed from isolation and rejoined the general prison population at Lewisburg shortly thereafter. "Our friends greet us joyously," Berrigan exulted, "and strangers stop us to inquire about our health." He took a clear lesson away from their protest: "The experience confirms me in nonviolent tactics even more profoundly."[48]

Phil Berrigan felt a combination of relief, shock, and disappointment when he learned that his brother had been captured on Block Island. Dan Berrigan had been on the run for almost four months, and his brother knew that he must have endured no small amount of anguish as he tried to elude the FBI and witness for peace. His capture, though saddening, had at least one salutary result: the brothers would be together once more. (They eventually were dispatched together to the federal penitentiary at Danbury, Connecticut, and served the bulk of their remaining sentences there.)

Early on, Phil Berrigan floundered in prison. In one letter to some members of his family, he apologized for "the periodic somberness from this quarter. I haven't quite pinned down its source—mostly the blob character of the institution, and the severe human damage that walks about, and the fact—at least, this is the present appraisal—that nothing moves, it just destructs."[49]

Seeing his brother confined in prison so saddened Dan Berrigan that he came to regret—at least momentarily—how the Catonsville witness had played out. He reflected that, if he had to do it all over again, "I would have fought not to have [Phil] go with us to Catonsville; he having done enough when he shook us alive." He likewise "would have tried to persuade him to turn himself in on the appointed date, not to go underground." His brother simply had paid too high a price.[50]

The brothers' time together in prison was not without friction. "I confess to harboring hobgoblins in my mind concerning Dan," Phil Berrigan wrote late in 1970. He zealously guarded his independence, and he felt that it was being compromised by his brother's presence. Matters came to a head when he accused Dan of egotism and "center-staging." Phil admitted that the two men "had it out, very painfully and sorrowfully"; Dan said that their relationship went through a "painful and fruitful revaluation." Things finally were smoothed over when the brothers realized that their differences were relatively petty.[51]

All of the prisoners at Lewisburg and Allenwood were aware of the presence there of Jimmy Hoffa, the Teamsters leader who had been convicted of jury tampering, attempted bribery, and fraud. Although Hoffa and his lieutenants exerted enormous influence among the prison population, the congenitally suspicious labor kingpin generally distanced himself from inmates who weren't part of his inner circle. But the Berrigans, Hogan, Mische, and Melville were different—they were fellow Catholics, and Hoffa seemed to think that they all were political prisoners. That they had vastly different perspectives on the war—Hoffa was a hawk—didn't seem to matter.[52]

If Hoffa had a criticism, it was tactical: he couldn't understand why the activists had waited around to be arrested after their raid in Catonsville. He felt that they should have wiped out the draft board and then made their escape. As Hogan summed up his approach, "If you're going to deal with the situation, deal with it. Never mind the symbolism."[53]

Hoffa took a particular interest in the welfare of Phil Berrigan. Not long after the Baltimore priest arrived at Lewisburg, Hoffa arranged a meeting in which he offered his assistance. "I tried to help," Hoffa explained to an interviewer, outlining for Berrigan "how to live in prison [and] who he should or should not talk to or be with—and last but not least, how to get along in prison." Berrigan recalled Hoffa saying that he "understood a lot of the crap from the prison authorities under which I would be operating, and that he had resources at his command to help me with this kind of pressure." Hoffa told him that if he encountered any trouble with prison officials or his fellow inmates, Hoffa's network would straighten it out. Berrigan, not unwise to the realities of prison life, took him up on the offer more than once. Throughout his time at Lewisburg, "the feedback to Hoffa was rather constant," he observed.[54]

Even with Hoffa's protection, Berrigan could not escape discord at Lewisburg. The worst of his woes arose from his failure to match Hoffa's circumspection in dealing with a fellow inmate named Boyd Douglas. Douglas approached most of the Baltimore-area draft protesters and told them that he enjoyed a range of special privileges at the prison; he even was allowed to leave the grounds to take classes at nearby Bucknell University. Douglas said he would be happy to share his good fortune by smuggling out letters for the men—communications that could be written more freely because they would not be reviewed by prison censors.

Most of the men smelled a setup. The FBI was smarting over Dan Berrigan's escapades as a fugitive, and it seemed well within the realm of possibility that the bureau might be seeking revenge by using Douglas to entrap the activists in some kind of illicit scheme for which they could be further punished. Both Melville and Mische flatly told Douglas that they wanted to have nothing to do with him. Melville later said he realized that "if they were letting [Douglas] go out with mail, then there's something wrong."[55]

Hoffa—something of an expert on such matters—kept his distance as well. He went to Berrigan and cautioned him about Douglas. "Here's a rat!" the union leader announced.[56]

But Phil Berrigan took the bait. Despite his friends' warnings, he began using Douglas to communicate with friends and confederates outside the prison walls. Berrigan went so far as to call him "the best thing hereabouts since polio vaccine." It was a colossal error in judgment.[57]

Before his capture, some of these messages concerned the underground maneuverings of Dan Berrigan. Using Douglas as a conduit, the brothers shared news and encouraged one another. At one point, the fugitive reported that he was "heartened to see what we hoped for at C[atons]ville is occurring and is mainly in younger hands, smart tough youngsters who are not afraid to try new things in the same spirit." Phil also used Douglas to communicate with like-minded activists such as Sister Liz McAlister. The letters between the two were often intimate; it was clear that they were developing a furtive bond. They also discussed Dan's whereabouts, explicitly considering if and how William Stringfellow might help the fugitive, with McAlister at one point even saying that "he's now or soon will be mixed up with" Dan.[58]

Other letters carried by Douglas revealed that Phil was brainstorming with fellow antiwar activists about staging a dramatic action that would demonstrate the continuing vitality of the antiwar movement. One idea floated by a collaborator named Eqbal Ahmad involved making a citizen's arrest of a prominent public official who was facilitating the war. At one point, Phil proposed that they "kidnap—in our terminology make a citizen's arrest of—someone like Henry Kissinger," Nixon's secretary of state. Before releasing him, Phil thought they could "hold him for about a week" and conduct a kind of trial in which Kissinger would be held accountable for the ongoing genocide in Vietnam. There also was talk in the letter of engaging in sabotage activities in steam tunnels in the nation's capital. "The impact of such a thing," the priest wrote, "would be phenomenal."[59]

The plot to kidnap Kissinger was too far-fetched to ever get off the drawing board, but the implications of the stillborn plan were disastrous. More a con artist than a committed activist, Douglas surreptitiously copied many of the documents he passed between Phil Berrigan and his supporters outside Lewis-burg, and he eventually turned them over to the FBI. It was through Douglas's cooperation—for which he was paid $200—that the federal government was able to arrest Dan Berrigan on Block Island and put an end to his time as a fugitive. Moreover, the letters outlining the plot to perform a citizen's arrest on Kissinger provided the basis for spectacular accusations leveled by J. Edgar Hoover. Appearing before a Senate subcommittee in November 1970, Hoover argued that the FBI needed millions of dollars in additional funding to fight the likes of the Berrigans, who were, in his words, ringleaders of "an anarchist group" that was "concocting a scheme to kidnap a highly placed government official" and sabotage various public works in Washington, D.C.[60]

Hoover offered the subcommittee no evidence to back up his claim (it would have consisted of nothing more than the letters that Douglas had copied), but it was a bombshell nonetheless; the charges appeared on the front page of the *New York Times* the following day. Early in 1971 the federal government obtained formal indictments charging seven people—including Phil Berrigan, McAlister, and Ahmad—with criminal conspiracy. (Although Hoover smeared him in his Senate testimony, Dan Berrigan never was indicted.)

The defendants and their champions mocked the charges as a transparent effort by Hoover to scare the Senate into giving the FBI more money. The news media was scarcely more kind: one newspaper called the indictment "one of the flimsiest on record." Respected columnist Tom Wicker warned that the charges might prove to be "another shocking example of the kind of official hysteria that so often damages individuals and clouds the public climate."[61]

Wicker's fears were borne out during the trial of the Harrisburg Seven (who took their name from the Pennsylvania city where the legal proceedings took place). The trial was an unmitigated disaster for the federal government. The prosecution's star witness, Douglas, was exposed as a greedy informer and a "pathological liar," as one of the defense attorneys put it. Such was the weakness of the government's case that the defense rested without putting on any evidence. The jury hung on the conspiracy charges, and the judge was forced to declare a mistrial. Berrigan and McAlister were found guilty of smuggling letters into and out of the prison, but an appellate court later threw out their convictions.[62]

Although the government was routed in the Harrisburg case, it also had damaging implications for the antiwar community that had coalesced around the Berrigans. The letters at the center of the case embarrassed Phil Berrigan in a variety of ways. Many people were dismayed that the defendants' far-fetched schemes had included unmistakably violent actions. Moreover, Berrigan and McAlister had not been completely transparent with their fellow activists about the deepening of their personal attachment. Berrigan—whose dis-missiveness of romantic entanglements was legendary—was viewed by some as a hypocrite for having carried on and concealed the relationship (which would culminate in the couple's marriage in 1973). Long-standing concerns about patriarchy within the Catholic left also bubbled over.[63]

"The ultra-resistance disintegrated at trial's end," according to Murray Polner and Jim O'Grady, who penned a masterful dual biography of the Berrigans, "exhausted and disillusioned by the ordeal." An era of antiwar activism—one that had begun in 1967 with the Baltimore Four's raid of the Custom House—effectively was over.[64]

Tom Lewis was released from federal prison on September 10, 1971. At first, he drifted back to Baltimore, where he found work teaching at an experimental high school and serving as an artistic consultant with a local theater. He then moved to Massachusetts—Cambridge first and then Worcester.

Lewis was mainly interested in resuming his career as an artist and teacher, but the FBI still kept tabs on him. In 1973 his FBI file contained a notation that he remained "potentially dangerous because of his background . . . or activity in groups involved in activities inimical to U.S." Agents wondered if he might be engaged in "revolutionary activity" in Cambridge, so they anonymously phoned Lewis's residence and workplace. The search turned up nothing. The investigation "failed to indicate in any way that the subject [Lewis] is involved in any radical type activity."[65]

Dan Berrigan was paroled from Danbury a few months after Lewis gained his release. The Jesuit's health had spiraled downward throughout 1971: he nearly had died after experiencing an allergic reaction to a Novocain shot during a dental procedure, and he had developed a laundry list of other ailments, including a painful kidney problem. The federal parole board decided to set him free in February 1972, after he had served eighteen months for his role in the Catonsville protest. Federal prosecutors Barney Skolnik and Stephen Sachs both wrote letters endorsing the move, with Sachs saying he was satisfied with Berrigan's "present attitude toward the law."[66]

A crowd of about two hundred people braved a snow squall to greet Dan Berrigan when he emerged from Danbury. He shouted, "Terrific, free!" upon leaving the prison grounds. Although his prison term nearly had killed him, Berrigan told reporters that he hadn't exactly done hard time. "It's a popsicle prison," he said of Danbury, "not like Attica."[67]

The federal government had given Berrigan its standard parting gift: $50 in cash. At the Mass he celebrated shortly after his release, he gave the modest bankroll to Dorothy Day, who had come to show her solidarity. She demanded that the money be cleansed with a sprinkle of holy water. "Now we can use this," she happily announced after the Jesuit performed the ritual.[68]

It took longer for Phil Berrigan to gain his release. Partly this was a result of his obstreperousness, but it also reflected the fact that he was serving concurrent sentences: six years for the Baltimore Four protest and three and a half years for the Catonsville Nine demonstration. (Without parole or time off for good behavior, his sentences for these crimes would have required him to remain behind bars until late in 1975.) His initial bid for parole was denied in July 1971. However, late in 1972, the eight-member United States Parole Commission announced that Berrigan would be set free on December 20.[69]

A crowd of several hundred supporters gathered outside Danbury to greet Phil Berrigan when he was released. The thirty-eight months he had spent behind bars had not cooled his passion: he told reporters that "men jailed for waging peace" were "homefront P.O.W.'s." Reflecting later on his prison experience, he drew further connections between injustices at home and oppression abroad: "At home, jails are looking glasses, images of our willingness to punish one another. But abroad, Indochina is the mirror of our violence and frenzy. Gazing at its misery is like sharing Dante's vision of hell and seeing ourselves there."[70]

The day after his release, Phil joined his brother Dan in New York City to celebrate a small Mass with Day and members of her Catholic Worker family. In her diary, Day noted Phil's robust health—he looked "wonderfully strong"—and the warmth of the occasion. "Everyone so happy," she wrote.[71]

"Being 'Underground' Is Strange"

Although she relished the opportunity to share her sentiments about peace and social justice with the wider world, Mary Moylan didn't enjoy sitting through the trial of the Catonsville Nine. "The courtroom mostly reeked of dry-as-dust justice," she wrote to a friend afterward, "as tho[ugh] blasted and mutilated bodies of the Vietnamese were baby dolls or puppets."[1]

She took solace in the fact that her witness in Catonsville—along with the earlier protest at the Custom House and the raid later conducted by the Milwaukee Fourteen—had shown that a variety of respectable people had committed themselves to reforming American society. Some conservatives scoffed that all antiwar protesters were sociopaths, but that argument fell apart when one considered the nurses, priests, and artists who were involved. These were serious folks and "great standing members of society," Moylan said.[2]

After the Nine were convicted in federal court and then sentenced to prison terms, Moylan remained devoted to peace and social justice causes. In the spring of 1969, she gave a talk on "Violence and the Pursuit of Justice" to a discussion group for employees at the U.S. Department of Health, Education, and Welfare in Washington, D.C. With two FBI special agents looking on and frantically scribbling down notes, Moylan touched on a wide variety of subjects. "She attacked the court system for not looking into the reasons behind the actions of the Catonsville Nine," according to the agents' report. "She also voiced concern over the use of napalm in Central and South America and indicated that this use was merely a further American attempt by the Central Intelligence Agency (CIA) to keep pro-American governments in power in those countries and thus help to maintain subhuman living conditions for the poor in that area of the world."[3]

Long committed to providing health care to the poor, Moylan lent her talents to the founding of the People's Community Health Center in Baltimore. The effort to establish the clinic brought together a number of activist groups, among them the Black Panthers, the Coalition of Women's Liberation, and the Baltimore Defense Committee.[4] One of Moylan's partners in this endeavor, Jim Keck, later said that Moylan worked tirelessly to help establish the clinic, which was designed to serve those on the lowest rungs of the city's socioeconomic ladder. "She was not just concerned with protest," said Keck. "She had a real strong desire to build a better society. I think Mary had the attitude that if you believed a certain thing, you had a responsibility to make it happen."[5]

As the Nine awaited the outcome of their legal appeal in 1969, Moylan also engaged in radical protest activities. Few of these were directed by Catholic groups or individuals. Moylan continued to drift away from the church, and she lost interest in partnering with fellow Catholics to protest the war or social injustice. "I became more involved with the [antiwar] movement," she later explained, "rather than Catholic groups." It was a measure of Moylan's increasing radicalization that she journeyed to Chicago in October 1969 to participate in the "Days of Rage." Designed to "bring the war home," this series of demonstrations and protests was organized by the Weatherman faction of Students for a Democratic Society (SDS).[6]

Although Moylan did not agree with everything the Weathermen were doing, she saw value in their provocative efforts in Chicago. "The Weatherpeople came to Chicago, and they said they were going to bring the war home," she explained. "Maybe you don't think that's a good idea, but it's the first time I've ever known SDS to do what it said it was going to do. And I'm not sure that's a bad idea." The Weathermen were not pacifists. As Moylan noted, in Chicago they smashed car and apartment windows and ran amok in the Loop. Although she was worried by some of the "insane fits" they experienced, such tactics didn't bother her. "I don't have any problem with that. . . . That's all right."[7]

To protect herself from the city's notoriously brutal police force, Moylan wore a helmet as she marched through the streets. What she described as "regulation dress" for the week also included shabby clothes. "I dressed," she joked, "as though I had no more than two cents to my name." She stayed with members of the anti-imperialist Revolutionary Youth Movement II (RYM II), a Maoist-oriented faction of SDS. RYM II believed that the white working class, in coalition with African Americans and students, could form the vanguard of revolutionary change. Significantly for Moylan, RYM II also foregrounded women's liberation and adamantly opposed patriarchy.[8]

Moylan became disenchanted with RYM II because of its passive reaction to the arrest of four Weathermen (two of whom she knew from Baltimore). It infuriated her that the RYM II contingent did little in response to the jailings. Factionalism within the protest movement apparently trumped genuine solidarity. "What the RYM people said to me, which freaked me out, was that the Weatherpeople were not 'ours' to begin with, so they could be picked up [by the police]," Moylan recalled. "The proper response, they said, was to get the badge number of the arresting officer and find out what the charge was."

Moylan wanted no part of such temerity: she informed members of RYM II that she "couldn't see any political reason to hit the streets with people who were going to let their own people be picked off."[9]

As she became increasingly radicalized, Moylan's most intense commitment was to the burgeoning women's movement. In a way that would far exceed her commitment to the antiwar cause, Moylan threw herself into the effort to ensure full social equality for women. Such was her dedication that Phil Berrigan—who probably never was described as being in the vanguard of the women's rights movement—later acknowledged that Moylan was an "ardent feminist."[10]

The attitudes and behaviors of men like Berrigan stoked Moylan's interest in promoting women's rights. "In my relations with men," she wrote in 1970, "I was becoming more and more aware of the fact that they were chauvinists—I guess that's the nicest thing I can say about them. It struck me that there were all of these men running around trying to build a human society who couldn't relate to a woman as a human being." And it wasn't just members of the establishment who treated women inequitably. She concluded that the members of SDS, one of the most vaunted radical groups of the 1960s, "were incapable of building a human society, in large part because they're incapable of dealing with women's liberation."[11]

As she immersed herself in the women's movement, Moylan admitted that her "gut reaction" was that she could "relate . . . only to sisters" as she moved forward with her activism. She was so disenchanted with the prospect of continuing to work with men that she expressed some ambivalence about her role in the Catonsville draft board raid. "I have to laugh when I think about the Catonsville action," she wrote in 1970. "I don't regret it at all. I'm very happy I did it, but it was totally insane." Her reservations centered less on what was done in Catonsville and more on with whom she had done it. "If I ever decided to go through [with] Catonsville again, I would never act with men: it would be a women's action for me or I wouldn't act."[12]

It was typical of Moylan, though, that she still maintained warm relationships with many men, including some of her compatriots in the Catonsville raid. After the Court of Appeals for the Fourth Circuit denied their legal appeal in October 1969, George Mische organized a kind of valedictory outing for the surviving members of the Nine. (Brother David Darst recently had died.) They gathered at a park in Maryland to picnic, swim, and reminisce. After they exited the park, the group decided to stop at a roadhouse to drink and dance. On the dance floor, Mische and his wife and Tom and Marjorie Melville enjoyed themselves, but Hogan hung back. Moylan noticed and approached him.

"I don't dance," Hogan shyly told her.

"Yes you do," she said with a smile, taking his hand and leading him out onto the dance floor.

That moment in the roadhouse long remained one of Hogan's fondest memories of Moylan. It seemed to symbolize her perfectly.[13]

By early 1970, it was obvious that the surviving members of the Catonsville Nine would not be meeting for many more picnics. As the date of their surrender approached, they gathered to discuss whether they would submit to imprisonment. Up until that point, Moylan had not really intended to become a fugitive for an extended period. She had considered engaging in nothing more than a brief act of defiance. "I hadn't intended at all to show up [to report for prison], but then neither had I intended to—so to speak—go underground," she later wrote. "To cooperate with such authority is to find yourself in a kind of weird position to begin with, and I had just planned to take a walk and smell the flowers and then they could come and pick me up when they so desired."[14]

But everything changed for Moylan when she learned that the Berrigan brothers and George Mische planned to go underground. She reconsidered her plans and "decided that because women's liberation is one of the most important issues being raised, I felt I had to do the same thing." As she later told journalist J. Anthony Lukas, "When I found out that . . . the men were going to become fugitives, I felt I had to try, too, if only to show a woman could do it." And not only would she become a fugitive; she would turn only to women to help her. "I wanted to rely exclusively on my sisters in the women's movement. I spoke with some of them and they said they'd help."[15]

Rosemary Ruether, who was acquainted with Moylan in this period, sensed that her decision to go underground was meant to signal a rebuke to the men who had participated in the Catonsville raid and their admirers. Ruether believed that Moylan had found that "her membership in the Catonsville Nine became increasingly enraging. She saw rampant clericalism and patriarchialism in the way the Berrigan brothers were in the center of attention. She was angered by the lack of equal regard for others, especially women like herself, who had taken the same risks but who remained in the shadows. She blamed not only the media but also the two priest-heroes"—the Berrigans. Going underground—and refusing the help of men while she was at it—thus proved an important point for Moylan. "She wanted to show [the Berrigans] that they were not the only ones who could take this further step of protest," according to Ruether. "She, too, could refuse to accept the unjust decree of the government and resist imprisonment."[16]

Moylan was explicit in stating that she meant to strike a blow for women. "It is not to escape or to revive the 'Catonsville 9' that I am not showing up [for prison]," she declared. "No, rather the opposite." Moylan insisted that she refused to turn herself in primarily because she wanted to show solidarity with women like Ericka Huggins (a Black Panther then on trial in New Haven, Connecticut) and Weathermen Kathy Boudin and Cathy Wilkerson (who were being sought by the FBI for their roles in an explosion at a Greenwich Village townhouse).[17]

Moylan's first weeks as a fugitive were unsettling. It was a confusing period in which she battled to make meaning of her resistance. "Being 'underground' is strange," she wrote shortly after she went on the lam. Because she was so isolated, simply getting through the day could be a challenge. "I live in an apartment with one bedroom, a kitchen, living room and hall," she related. "I spend my days reading, drinking, smoking and sleeping." Cut off from friends and family members—most of whom were being monitored by the FBI—she struggled with "being of out touch with many people, being inactive."[18]

As she wrestled with such issues, Moylan wondered how long she would be able to remain a fugitive. "It was really depressing," she wrote of her first few days underground. "I felt I was endangering sisters I really loved, afraid at any moment that the blankety-blank Feds would come knocking through the door." She weighed a variety of options, including just giving up. "I thought about going to some town and becoming the town librarian or a waitress, just going completely straight and waiting until the whole thing blew over. I even considered turning myself in, just going up to some F.B.I. man and saying, 'Here I am, sweetie.'"[19]

Moylan made her way to Canada and remained in hiding there for a few months. She "headed north and stayed with sisters in the woods, . . . vegetarians interested in survival techniques," as she described it. This was "rough living, to say the least." Plagued by feelings of isolation and worried about her friends (particularly the imprisoned ones), she reconsidered her approach to surviving the travails of being underground. She came to the conclusion that she could not "live any other way than as a participant in a revolution." Her fantasy of living as a librarian in a small town was quickly forgotten. For her there would be "no false ID and straight life in an unknown city." Moylan returned to the United States and resolved to reconnect with her "sisters" and the powerful movement they were creating.[20]

She would not let the possibility of capture control her life. Moylan explained to a journalist about her time in Canada: "I stayed up there for two months and pondered the whole situation. I asked myself, 'If you really believe in a human revolution, how do you remain [in] hiding from the Feds? Finally I decided that of course I'd have to take sensible precautions but I just couldn't spend all my time worrying about who was coming through the door."[21]

She came back to the United States in the summer of 1970 feeling much more at ease about her life as a fugitive and her ability to contribute to the women's movement. "I've kept on the move a lot but at a pretty easy pace," she explained after returning. "I travel pretty much by myself, but know at least one sister in each city I go to, and if I can't stay with her she arranges for me to stay with some other sister. The people I stay with usually provide me with good food and a little money and they look out for me. They are pretty careful about whom they invite when I'm with them."[22]

Moylan often reflected on the common motivations of the women who harbored her. "I think they share the usual things—opposition to the war, exploitation of the blacks and the poor, an outrage at the spoiling of our society—but mainly [the assistance has] been from sisters who have recognized that we have to first win our freedom as women." When she described women who aided her, Moylan talked of "straight ones and hip ones. Nuns and atheists. But sisters." In her first six months as a fugitive, Moylan moved to a new location every few days. She estimated that more than one hundred different women gave her shelter over that time.[23]

She settled into some routines: "I get up, have breakfast, read books, drink Scotch, turn on occasionally with pot or hash, see people, eat dinner, go to sleep." Keeping such habits allowed her to keep moving forward. "A human being can adapt to anything," Moylan explained, "and I've adapted myself to this."[24]

There were some tense moments. At one point relatively early in her time as a fugitive, a man paid a visit to the couple with whom Moylan was staying. "I think we know each other," he said upon meeting her. "Where are you from?"

Worried that she had been recognized, Moylan immediately blurted out that she hailed from Ames, Iowa—this despite the fact that she couldn't even find Iowa on a map. The ruse failed to deter the visitor; he was sure that he had run into Moylan previously.

"Have you ever been to Baltimore?" he asked.

Moylan admitted that she had passed through the city, and, luckily, that explanation seemed to satisfy him. She doubted that her interlocutor would have turned her in to the FBI if he had determined her identity, but the encounter nonetheless left her shaken.[25]

Moylan did not let her fear of being tracked down by the FBI completely circumscribe her life. She wrote several articles for publication and sat down for interviews with reporters Bernard Gavzer of the Associated Press and J. Anthony Lukas of the *New York Times*. Moylan agreed to the latter interview on the condition that a female reporter, Judy Klemesrud, ask the bulk of the questions. Their interview took place on the terrace of the Central Park Zoo cafeteria in Manhattan. In her discussion with Lukas and Klemesrud, Moylan seemed pleased to have eluded capture without the help of her more famous—and male—accomplices in the Catonsville Nine (all of whom had been captured by that point).

"The FBI really thought I was with Dan, because when they caught Phil and George they asked them whether I'd been with them or with Dan," she said. "I resented this automatic assumption that it was impossible for me to do it without a man. But now I think I've showed them."[26]

Lukas noted that Moylan had altered her most distinguishing physical feature: she had dyed her red hair, muting it into a dull black. She told him that this nod to discretion hadn't bothered her the most. "There is only one thing about myself that I'd rather change right now. I don't like wearing a skirt and blouse. I'd much rather be in dungarees," she explained. "And when I'm on the street, I always wear a bra. I'd rather not, but if you don't, it draws attention to you and I don't want to do that."[27]

It surprised Lukas that Moylan wasn't doing more to disguise herself, but she contended that elaborate precautions probably were unnecessary. "I don't worry about getting recognized on the street," she said. "I don't imagine the great majority of people have even heard of Mary Moylan, and I don't think there are too many photographs of me floating around." Nonetheless, Moylan knew that she couldn't evade the FBI forever. "Time is certainly on their side," she said. "Eventually they may catch up with me."[28]

Moylan insisted that the prospect of being captured and then imprisoned did not faze her. "I have no problem," she wrote in 1970, "with my own jail sentence. . . . The idea of jail doesn't bother me that much." If the FBI ever caught up with her, she would be dispatched to the Women's Federal Reformatory in Alderson, West Virginia, where Majorie Melville was incarcerated. The hardship of being in the reformatory would be mitigated somewhat by the presence of Melville and "a whole bunch of [other] sisters down there in that jail—sister criminals as a matter of fact." If nothing else, she no longer would be so isolated.[29]

But she mocked the high-minded notion of becoming a prisoner of conscience because of her radical beliefs. "I very definitely see myself as a criminal. I don't even know what the hell 'prisoner of conscience' means," she mused. "I think if we're serious about changing the society that's how we have to see ourselves. That 'prisoner of conscience'—if there is any such thing as conscience and if anybody has it—I guess all of us are prisoners of it, but it doesn't do anything politically to me at all. We're all out on bail, and let's all stay out."[30]

Moylan admitted that she had changed her stance on the usefulness and meaning of going to jail. "At the time of Catonsville, going to jail made sense to me, partially because of the black scene—so many blacks forever filling the jails and the whites being 'very concerned,'" she wrote. "Jail was not part of the scene for those whites." But by the time she had gone underground, Moylan's attitudes about the utility of jailing had changed. She came to see it as being almost self-indulgent. "I don't think it's a valid tactic anymore, because of the change in the country itself," she wrote in 1970. "I don't want to see people marching off to jail with smiles on their faces. I just don't want them going. The Seventies are going to be very difficult, and I don't want to waste the sisters and brothers we have by marching them off to jail and having mystical experiences or whatever they are going to have."[31]

During her time underground, Moylan also clarified her relationship—or lack thereof—with Catholicism and the pacifism espoused by such prominent peace and social justice activists as Dan Berrigan. Becoming increasingly radical, she cringed at accounts of the Catonsville Nine that inaccurately described her ideological leanings. Moylan wrote:

> The establishment press constantly described us, after Catonsville, as "Catholic pacifists," and that's when I stopped believing the establishment press. I'm much too Irish to be a pacifist, and my relationship with the Roman Catholic Church has been off and on, to say the least, for quite a while. Realizing that that was where I came from, the "Catholic" title bothered me less than the "pacifist" title. But it's even more difficult now because I have no relationship with the Catholic Church, nor do I want any. Everybody in the group, except George and me [as well as Tom Lewis], was either a priest or a brother or a sister or an ex-one-or-the-other. So everyone assumed when they met me that I was an ex-nun. I've had a lot of problems in my life, but that wasn't one of them.[32]

Moylan also seemed uneasy with how conventional the Catonsville protest now seemed. After the upheavals that had wracked American society over the previous few years, seizing and burning draft records seemed almost quaint. "The Catonsville 9 have always been in most people's minds the good guys; we've been socially acceptable," Moylan wrote while underground. "Most people wouldn't be too upset to have us to their house. . . . But if we think the establishment is illegal, then what are we doing making ourselves so legitimate and acceptable? It seems to me that we're playing the establishment game."[33]

While she moved away from her church and conventional forms of protest, Moylan felt the pull of the Weather Underground Organization (WUO), the loose-knit successor to the Weatherman faction of SDS. Fervently committed to revolutionary political change in the United States, members of the WUO mounted a series of covert and violent attacks on what they vilified as symbols or institutions of injustice. After declaring war on the American government in 1970, they engineered the prison break of LSD champion Timothy Leary and detonated bombs at both the headquarters of the New York City police and the Pentagon.[34]

In the periodic dispatches she penned during her time as a fugitive, Moylan frequently referenced the WUO and its members. She mentioned them favorably and reported that they were essential to her survival underground. "I have been living and working with Weatherpeople," she wrote in 1973, "for the most part with sisters."[35]

The FBI took Moylan's association with the WUO seriously. Throughout the early and mid-1970s, the bureau included her among the "Weathfugs" (for "Weatherman fugitives") it was monitoring. A typical memorandum from 1975 noted that "Moylan is apparently in Weather Underground at this time. . . . Furthermore, it is very possible she is in the company of Weathfugs, especially women." A year later, another memo noted that she was "traveling with and assisted by the Weatherman organization."[36]

For the FBI, Moylan's association with the WUO made her potentially dangerous. "In view of the fact MOYLAN is a member of the Weatherman," a 1975 memo reported, "it is believed she has a willingness and capability in engaging in acts which would result in interference with or a threat to the survival and effective operation of national, state and local governments. . . ." Another FBI report from this same period concluded that "inasmuch as MARY ASSUMPTA MOYLAN is reportedly in the company of WEATHFUG subjects and has embraced their ideology, she should be considered as armed and dangerous."[37]

As her association with the WUO deepened, Moylan grappled with her commitment to nonviolence. "One thing I'm still chewing on: . . . gun or no," Moylan wrote. If life was sacred, that principle had to apply to "the lives of the sisters and brothers" who were being gunned down by the police in the streets of America's cities. Like many in her generation of activists, Moylan reluctantly concluded that resorting to violence in self-defense was a morally permissible last resort for individuals who were facing annihilation themselves. And if the circumstances required it, she would be willing to resort to violence herself. "I will pick up the gun to fight alongside my sisters and brothers. I . . . can't say I'm happy about it but then no more can I stand my sisters and brothers being killed."[38]

While underground, Moylan was linked with at least one act of what WUO leaders called "symbolic violence." Living in Boston in the early 1970s, Moylan fell in with a small group of radical women called "the Proud Eagle tribe." This group—billed as the "women's brigade" of the WUO—attracted the likes of Kathy Boudin (who, along with Wilkerson, had survived the Greenwich Village explosion in 1970). The Proud Eagle tribe took responsibility for two bombings in the Boston area: the October 1970 bombing of Harvard's Center for International Affairs; and the October 1971 attack on the office of William Bundy, the former adviser to presidents Kennedy and Johnson and "one of the architects of the air war in Viet Nam," according to the group.[39]

The Boston-area bombers did not target people, and no one was physically harmed in the explosions they set off. The attack on Bundy's office occurred at 1 A.M.—after the women had called police and warned them to clear the building of all maintenance staff. ("Get the janitor out of there," they had warned.[40])

Moylan's main interest was in fostering relationships with her "sisters" and thereby advancing the women's rights movement. Not all of these interactions went smoothly. After she founded a small all-women's collective in Boston, Moylan had some awkward encounters with Janet Alpert, a radical activist who spent more than four years as a fugitive. In 1981—after she turned herself in and, in the eyes of many, betrayed her erstwhile colleagues in the underground—Alpert published an oddly mean-spirited account of these meetings, mocking Moylan's "homely, vegetarian-style community" and derisively noting her "plain Irish looks."[41]

Alpert might have been paying Moylan back for criticizing her widely circulated manifesto, "Mother Right: A New Feminist Theory." Moylan had responded to Alpert with a respectful but trenchant critique in which she boldly declared, "At this point in herstory I define myself as a radical feminist, which means to me fighting for reassertion of the feminine principle. I am committed to woman's revolution and to building women's culture." She framed her analysis of "Mother Right" by detailing her own experiences and ideological development. Moylan acknowledged that in the late 1960s, the sexist behavior of some radical men sometimes had turned her into "a screaming banshee. The sheer insensitivity and arrogant sexism of movement men almost drove me up a wall." Over time, however, she recognized the drawbacks of defining her commitment to other women in terms of her antipathy toward men. "I realize now that my fury at some men drained a lot of energy and ruled my life," Moylan wrote. "Gradually I learned to temper my anger and use it, instead of it using me. Slowly I understood that if the only reason I turned to sisters was out of anger at men, I was doing my sisters a disservice, because even if every man became nonsexist overnight, my commitment to women would remain."[42]

Moylan had much more congenial —if fleeting—relations with members of the activist community in Baltimore. Because of the possibility of FBI surveillance, her forays into the city were infrequent, but she did manage to pass dispatches back and forth. "People come up at demonstrations and say that they have a message," Liz McAlister said in 1978. "The messages aren't enough to give a real sense of her life. We receive a message and send greetings back. We don't probe."[43]

Moylan also met periodically with the likes of Grenville Whitman and Brendan Walsh and Willa Bickham of Viva House. When Moylan visited Whitman, he saw that his friend had been forced to disguise herself. "Her beautiful red hair was black; it was terrible," he later said. It was clear to him that the pressure of avoiding capture had begun weighing on Moylan. "She hated it," he recalled. "She wasn't her old self. She was fearful, anxious, and unhappy."[44]

Walsh and Bickham knew that the FBI was watching Viva House, and they never arranged to meet Moylan there. (She refused to go there anyway because she thought she might be putting the couple's child in jeopardy.) Instead, they rendezvoused in the Fells Point section of Baltimore or the city's Carroll Park. They also spent some time together at Rehoboth Beach in Delaware. "She just longed to be with old friends and have crabs and beer together," Bickham later said.[45]

Moylan missed more than mere food and drink. When her mother died in the early 1970s, she didn't return to Baltimore for the funeral because she knew the FBI would be watching. Agents were in fact on hand, and their obvious presence infuriated the Moylan family; it felt that the federal government had gone too far in its surveillance. They subsequently refused to cooperate with the FBI. When agents approached the family for a sample of Moylan's hand-writing, they were greeted with glowers and slammed doors. (The agency wound up unearthing a copy of Moylan's 1956 application to the Maryland state nursing board.) According to Moylan's FBI file, after the funeral incident agents in Baltimore "received no cooperation from the remaining members of her family."[46]

As it attempted to track down fugitives like Mary Moylan, the FBI had its hands full. J. Anthony Lukas reported in the *New York Times* in 1970 that the bureau had a whopping 75,000 fugitives of various kinds listed in its central database. Of these, more than forty were political fugitives, and the most prominent of this lot sometimes comprised half of the FBI's Most Wanted list. Chasing the likes of Eldridge Cleaver and Bernardine Dohrn vexed the bureau. In his account of the FBI's efforts to track down political fugitives, journalist Bernard Gavzer concluded that "the whereabouts of most of them are unknown."[47]

For all of Moylan's associations with the WUO, the FBI did not view appre-hending her as a matter of great urgency. One agent who worked on her case, Lane Bonner, later said that "Mary was not a top priority as we had other more important work to do." (In Maryland, this often meant grappling with the ram-pant political corruption that plagued the state.) And when its attention turned to political radicals, the FBI was "more interested in more violence-prone anti-war activists," Bonner recalled. He never thought she had a serious link—either ideologically or practically—to the WUO. "I have no reason to believe that Mary Moylan had any connection whatsoever to the very violence-prone Weather Underground," Bonner stated. "I believe that she very sincerely believed in what she was doing—opposing the war in Vietnam and the draft—[although she was] misguided."[48]

Still, the FBI monitored Moylan's whereabouts. On the anniversary of her mother's death, agents staked out the gravesite in the hope that the fugitive would appear. They also conducted surveillance on the homes of Moylan's sib-lings in Baltimore. And when Moylan's brother moved from Maryland to Maine, agents in Baltimore passed on leads to their colleagues in New Eng-land. Agents were so eager to ferret out information that they even interviewed a nun at St. Ursula School in Baltimore who had ties to the family.[49]

This work yielded little. When Bonner was working on Moylan's case, he never developed a single concrete lead on her whereabouts. As the years passed and it became clear that she was not seriously engaged in violent activities, the FBI's tracking of Moylan produced only tidbits of information. In 1974, for instance, it received word that she recently had been in Santa Fe, New Mexico, but the trail apparently went cold very quickly.[50]

And while the FBI's attention waned, so too did the interest of many of Moylan's erstwhile friends and allies. It wasn't a matter of people formally dissociating themselves from her; they merely moved on with their lives and lost touch with her. "Time went on and she slipped out of the mind of even many of those, like ourselves, who had been friends," Ruether later wrote. "From time to time, I would think of her, wonder where she was, what she was doing, how she was surviving."[51]

The truth was, Moylan was barely keeping her head above water. In the end, the pressure of being underground left her both physically and emotionally exhausted. In 1979, after nearly a decade as a fugitive, she contacted Bickham at Viva House in Baltimore and discussed how she might finally surrender to the federal government. They met with attorney Harold Buchman, who had so doggedly defended the Catonsville Nine. Moylan explained to him that she wanted to "surrender quietly, without any excitement," as he put it. He arranged for Moylan to give herself up at the federal courthouse in Baltimore on June 20, 1979.[52]

In a public statement, Moylan thanked her supporters and insisted that she had not grown weary of trying to dodge the FBI. "I did not turn myself in because I was tired of running," she wrote from Baltimore's city jail. "It was a political decision. A decision to be more deeply engaged in today's struggles, especially women's struggles and third world struggles." She hoped to draw attention to the plight of three other women who were still engaging in battles against oppression. Assata Shakur, Lolita Lebrón, and Yvonne Wanrow all were imprisoned, as Moylan knew she soon would be. "I turn myself in fully expecting to do time," she wrote, "and while it ain't my cup of tea, neither is it a big thing."[53]

Moylan still owed the government two years for her role in the Catonsville protest, but her defenders called for her to receive a pardon. "If President Carter can release Patty Hearst, . . . if he can honor human rights figures," Phil Berrigan said, "he can release Mary Moylan." Jimmy Carter rebuffed these entreaties, and Moylan was dispatched to the Alderson women's reformatory in West Virginia.[54]

While in prison, Moylan kept her distance from many of her old acquaintances. Isolated for so many years because of her status as a fugitive, she seemed unwilling—or unable, emotionally—to reconnect with many people she had known. "We tried to contact her several times in the Alderson women's prison where she was incarcerated," Ruether recalled. "But friends told us that she was embittered, that she did not want to hear from former friends."[55]

The Trial of the Catonsville Nine

The witness of the Catonsville Nine has been evoked in a diverse array of cultural forms that have kept the memory of their protest alive for the last forty years. These have ranged from the popular—the Nine were referenced in questions in the original version of the board game *Trivial Pursuit*—to the highbrow. An aspiring activist in Colum McCann's novel *Let the Great World Spin* hopes to march and display a banner for the Catonsville Nine, while a bomber pilot in Don DeLillo's *Underworld* lumps the activists together with the Vietcong. (For him, they are more or less the same thing—the enemy.) And the poet Adrienne Rich, a Baltimore native, grapples with the relationship between language and oppression in "The Burning of Paper Instead of Children."[1]

Detective fiction author Laura Lippman—who attended high school near Catonsville in Columbia, Maryland—also has referenced the Nine in her work, albeit in a slightly more lighthearted vein than Rich. Lippman's novel *No Good Deeds* features a running joke involving the Catonsville Nine and the Baltimore Four. Detective Tess Monaghan initially misunderstands her boyfriend when he says that he admires both groups of activists; for her, the "Baltimore Four" were the quartet of Baltimore Orioles pitchers who each won twenty games in 1971. When he explains who they are and what they did, the hardboiled Monaghan can only mutter in dismay, "You and the do-gooder crowd."[2]

Singer-songwriter Dar Williams paid tribute to the Catonsville Nine in her 2004 song "I Had No Right." Written from the point of view of Dan Berrigan, it explains the variety of paths taken by the activists on their way to Catonsville and then describes their destruction of draft files with a homemade batch of napalm. All the while, the activists attempt to figure out how to be both loyal Americans and good Christians—no small feat during the Vietnam era.[3]

Williams was only a toddler when the Catonsville Nine struck in 1968, but as she learned more about the 1960s she came to appreciate the stand they had taken for peace and social justice. "They went against the establishment in the name of religious belief," Williams said. "It was all too rare in this country to do that. That's why I wanted to write a song about them." She was particularly impressed by Dan Berrigan's choice to go to Catonsville: "His was a spiritually pure decision," she explained.[4]

But the most important and enduring cultural depiction of the Catonsville Nine essentially was rendered by the activists themselves. Midway through 1969, Dan Berrigan contacted all of his accomplices with the news that he had been negotiating with Boston's Beacon Press to publish "an edited version of the Catonsville Nine Court Record." Berrigan realized that the real message of their witness would be lost if he attempted to publish the massive trial transcript in its entirety. (The document produced by the court reporter was about one thousand pages long.) "Some compression and changes in the text will . . . be necessary," he explained. "I will do all I can to be faithful to the spirit which brought us together at Catonsville and in the Baltimore court."[5]

From the outset, it was clear to Jeremy Cott, Berrigan's editor at Beacon, that he wanted to complete the project as quickly as possible. When the two men discussed when in 1969 Berrigan could deliver the manuscript, the priest told him, "I can have it for you in late August."

"Fine," Cott said, "but late September is all right, too."

"No, late August. I might be in jail by September," Berrigan said.

"Well, then your manuscript is something of a risk, isn't it?"

"Yes, but then so is the entire peace movement."[6]

Not everyone fully approved of the project. George Mische was hesitant about the book because he feared it might mythologize the Nine as martyrs for peace. But he apparently did not register strong objections with Berrigan, who had pledged not to move forward without at least the implicit consent of all the Nine.[7]

The project kept Berrigan occupied throughout the summer of 1969. He hoped that the finished product would help young people who were struggling with their consciences in a time of moral chaos. But boiling down the enormous and unwieldy trial transcript into a coherent narrative proved to be a "nightmarish experience," he later told a friend. Berrigan admitted after shipping off the manuscript to his publisher, "I feel as though I have shaken a monkey or an angel from my back."[8]

With a few minor exceptions, Berrigan's abridgement remained true to the trial transcript. And his Herculean efforts paid handsome dividends. The slender book appeared in 1970 and drew favorable reviews from the likes of John Leonard, who wrote in the *New York Times* that it read like "letters from a world of moral desperation."[9]

Before the book was published, a copy of the galleys of *The Trial of the Catonsville Nine* wound up in the hands of director Gordon Davidson, who was quickly earning a formidable reputation for directing plays addressing significant contemporary social and political issues. Davidson hadn't closely followed the Catonsville case, but he was moved by Berrigan's text, which he devoured during a long airplane flight. He found himself in tears by the time his plane touched down. "As soon as the plane landed, before I got my luggage, I called Flora Roberts, the agent, and said, 'I don't know what this is, Flora, but I have to find a way to do it,'" Davidson later said. "She was very excited, and that started the whole journey."[10]

Essentially using Berrigan's text as a theatrical script, Davidson decided to stage *The Trial of the Catonsville Nine* as part of the "New Theater for Now" series at the Mark Taper Forum in Los Angeles. By the time it opened in the spring of 1970, the play was overshadowed by the still-unfolding saga of the activists it depicted. The playwright had gone underground, and the FBI monitored the nascent production in California in hopes of determining his whereabouts. "My phone was tapped," Davidson complained. "There was a nondescript repair truck curiously parked in front of my house for the entire duration of the rehearsal and the run of the play. It disappeared once the play closed." Many of the actors—including one who previously had been involved in radical political causes—were harassed by the FBI as well.[11]

The show went on, and Berrigan managed to stay connected to it, albeit at a distance. Davidson passed word to the fugitive that it was customary for a playwright to be present for a rehearsal. He wondered if Berrigan might want to bring this off via a taped communiqué. The priest obliged, sending the actors a long message in which he apologized for being confined by "this absurd underground existence." He told them, "We all share a certain hope that the Catonsville play might speak to people, might bring them to a more accurate, realistic, and painful sense of things. At the same time we wish to release a capacity of hope and joy. This was the spirit in which we carried off our Catonsville caper and faced its consequences—consequences which indeed have enlarged since then." Davidson later said that playing the message for the actors was a singularly moving experience. Berrigan also taped a message that was broadcast when the play opened in Los Angeles. "I hope it will become clear that at Catonsville we tried to deal with our fears," he said. "For weeks and months we allowed our fears to loom up before us with all their sinister claim on our souls. We faced them down, finally, and purged ourselves in the fire of a parking lot of a remote Maryland town." The sound of the fugitive's voice in the Los Angeles theater electrified the audience—and set off a stir among the phalanx of FBI agents in the crowd. An amused Davidson observed that the agents in attendance "leapt forward because they couldn't take the chance that [Berrigan] wasn't there speaking his line from the rafters like the Phantom of the Opera."[12]

Davidson was ecstatic over the results. Writing to Berrigan (who by then had been captured by the FBI), he exulted that "the staging of 'Catonsville' was perhaps the single most important thing we have ever done. It deeply affected the cast (as you predicted), the staff, and indeed the audience. There were some who didn't like it, but those who did were deeply moved and challenged. It wouldn't surprise me if for some it changed their lives."[13]

But even Davidson realized that this first production of *The Trial of the Catonsville Nine* was imperfect. One theater critic asserted that it "seemed provocative as a tract but static as a theater piece"; another said that it was a "sermon rather than a play, eloquent but long-winded." Davidson saw the validity of such critiques and resolved to reorganize the material. He brought in Saul Levitt (whose writing credits included *The Andersonville Trial*) to give the play more dramatic structure. The two men worked for long hours in Levitt's studio in New York's Greenwich Village, sitting on the floor and rearranging pieces of the script until it flowed more naturally.[14]

The reworked play's run in New York in 1971 prompted the playwright to reflect from his prison cell in Danbury. A melancholy Berrigan noted that the imprisoned brothers' initial reaction to the play's opening "is one of profound grief, on many grounds. We mourn for the war; that useless, grotesque, debilitating, downhill rampage; in spite of everything, the war goes on." Their witness in Catonsville, though powerful enough to merit treatment on stage, seemed not to have accomplished very much. "We mourn that our lives have made so little difference in the brute scales of power." Still, Berrigan remarked that "a serious effort to dramatize the Catonsville event must be accounted an important moment for all of us." For the imprisoned members of the Nine, the play stood as a "reminder that our action is not lost."[15]

Locked up in federal prison, the Berrigan brothers couldn't attend the play themselves. Dan figured that the next best thing would be for him to arrange for three prison employees to receive free tickets. But the men got cold feet at the prospect of picking up the tickets—which were under the name "Berrigan"—at the theater's box office. "Too much FBI surveillance," one sheepishly told Dan.[16]

The legendary producer Leland Hayward produced the play when it opened in New York early in 1971. Hayward's involvement in the play did not sit well with his wife, Pamela. Like many Catholics, she was bothered by the playwright's participation in the Catonsville raid and his subsequent decision to go underground. "She felt it was unethical," Brooke Hayward, her stepdaughter, later wrote. But Leland Hayward loved the material and went ahead with the play anyway. "Very gutsy man," he said of Dan Berrigan. "A lot braver than I could ever be. Besides, I don't think he's guilty." Hayward was hospitalized and missed the play's opening—a first in his long and storied career. (He would die a few months later.) But such was his devotion to *The Trial of the Catonsville Nine* that he kept track of the play's reviews from his hospital bed. When Brooke called him the morning after the play had opened, he exulted, "What about those notices! Great, huh?"[17]

And, indeed, the revamped play earned rave reviews. Perhaps the most ecstatic of these was penned by the critic John Simon. Simon hailed Davidson's production and lavished extraordinary praise on the Catonsville Nine themselves, saying that they were "as close to saints as anyone I have read about in the hagiographies. . . . I would like simply to canonize them." On the strength of such glowing reviews, the play became one of the hits of New York's theater season. It ran for 130 performances at the sanctuary of the Good Shepherd Faith Church, located near Lincoln Center, and then moved over to Broadway for 29 additional shows. The play earned three Obie Awards (including one for distinguished production), and Davidson garnered a Tony Award nomination for best director.[18]

Controversy dogged the play when it returned to Los Angeles later in 1971. The county board of supervisors fielded dozens of complaints from a group known as the Citizens Legal Defense Alliance that taxpayer dollars should not support such a radical, subversive, and biased play. (The Mark Taper Forum received some indirect support from the county.) Seconding those claims, a local lawmaker slammed the play as a "very slanted political documentary." Davidson adamantly defended the play itself and the theater's right to stage it. "Father Berrigan isn't asking you or me to burn draft cards," he insisted. "He's just saying that he made the decision to take a course of civil disobedience that others have taken during the history of this country." Ironically, the contretemps helped to draw larger crowds to the play: in the middle of the controversy, it set the Taper's single-day record for advance ticket sales.[19]

Over the last four decades, *The Trial of the Catonsville Nine* has been performed all over the world. In 1983 and 1984, it was staged in dozens of West German cities and "was adopted as the official voice of the resistance against nuclear missiles," according to Dan Berrigan, whose brother was in the audience when it premiered in Berlin. (Incredibly, it was the first time Phil Berrigan ever had seen the play in which he was portrayed. His frequent imprisonments had made it impossible for him to attend any earlier productions in the United States.) *The Trial of the Catonsville Nine* appealed to other Europeans as well. After the defeat of Greece's military junta in 1976, the play was staged in Athens by a group of actors who previously had been forced underground because of their political beliefs.[20]

The play has had a powerful impact on many who have seen it. Bruce Goldfarb sat in the audience when it was staged in Buffalo, New York, in the early 1970s. The teenager was floored. "I was intrigued by these people—particularly the brothers, the poet and the priest—who risked excommunication and imprisonment to make a statement and challenge the state," he later explained. "Then 14 or so years old, it was [my] first time being exposed to big thoughts like social justice, moral imperatives, civil disobedience. A light switch flipped on."[21]

According to Robin Andersen, director of Fordham University's Peace and Justice Studies Program, *The Trial of the Catonsville Nine* has become "part of a culture of resistance and wisdom" that has helped to sustain several generations of peace and social justice activists. Its ongoing resonance was demonstrated after the United States invaded Iraq in 2003. When the Lutheran School of Theology in Chicago mounted a production of the play that year, one of the organizers explained that it "is a stirring call to Christians to act on their beliefs and is particularly meaningful in the current climate of war, hate, and fear."[22]

The Trial of the Catonsville Nine was still relevant in the first decade of the twenty-first century, when the Actor's Gang—a Los Angeles theater ensemble led by actor Tim Robbins—staged star-studded readings from it as well as full productions. (One reading featured the likes of actors Sandra Oh, Martin Sheen, and Neil Patrick Harris.) "We were so moved by it, and the audience was so moved by it," Robbins said of the play, "we just understood how resonant it was for today and how the questions it was asking were so pertinent, so relevant to the questions we should be asking today."[23]

The Trial of the Catonsville Nine has been performed in the Baltimore area on numerous occasions. When the play first came to CENTERSTAGE the city's major theater, in the early 1970s, Mary Murphy refused to attend. The clerk who had so tenaciously resisted the Nine inside Local Board 33 worried that by buying a ticket she might provide financial support to Dan Berrigan and his allies. "I didn't feel like I wanted to contribute a cent to that cause," she later said. (Money apparently wasn't the only obstacle: she also refused complimentary tickets.) Murphy did agree to meet with an actor who was portraying her, and they spent a pleasant afternoon talking at the draft office in Catonsville (which by that time had moved down Frederick Road). Phyllis Morsberger, Murphy's draft board coworker, also spoke with an actor who was depicting her, but she also refused to attend performances of the play. "I lived it," she said. "I really don't have to see it."[24]

When the play came to Boston, Guy Darst had lunch with the actor who was portraying his brother. As they shared the meal, Darst was dismayed to learn that the actor seemed to be most worried about his billing in the production. "His ego stretched," Darst joked, "from Cambridge to the Canadian border." He seemed nothing like the humble and open-hearted man he was depicting on stage.[25]

During the play's run at the Mark Taper Forum in Los Angeles, a number of Hollywood heavyweights attended performances, including Gregory Peck, the venerated actor who was then beginning to make a name for himself as a director. "It was stimulating and emotionally engaging," Peck said of the play. "I found that my wife and I discussed it on and off for several days. We found it quite moving that a group of people would put their freedom on the line, would perform a symbolic act which involved breaking the law, knowing they'd be arrested." He immediately thought of the Boston Tea Party, another act of sabotage that had immediate and far-reaching political consequences. Peck concluded that the Nine, like their revolutionary forebears, were patriots.[26]

Peck, a Roman Catholic, was intrigued by what the Catonsville protest revealed about the changes that had been transforming his church. To him, the looting of Local Board 33 seemed emblematic of the reform spirit that had taken hold among Catholics, particular the young, in the wake of Vatican II. He found himself "increasingly stimulated by the ideas of the Catholic left" and the "new attitude" exhibited by younger Catholics toward social justice issues. For Peck, Berrigan's play showed how these impulses could transform America's social and political landscape.[27]

A five-time Academy Award nominee—he won the Best Actor award in 1962 for his iconic portrayal of Atticus Finch in *To Kill a Mockingbird*—Peck was a formidable figure in Hollywood. His liberal sympathies were no secret, but he felt that he had perhaps not done enough to express his opposition to the war in Vietnam. Turning Berrigan's play into a film could be his way of contributing to the antiwar cause. He thought it might "shake up a lot of people."[28]

Peck obtained the screen rights for *The Trial of the Catonsville Nine* and then set out to find backing from a studio. He met with executives from several, but none expressed much interest. Enthralled by the project, Peck decided to put together his own consortium of investors to fund the production of the film. The actor put up a large chunk of the $250,000 needed to get the movie off the ground; other backers included Roger Stevens of the Kennedy Center and film producer Ray Stark. None of them had any illusions about the film grossing millions of dollars. For practically everyone involved, it was to be a labor of love.[29]

The actors all worked for the minimum salaries mandated by the Screen Actors Guild. Gordon Davidson, making his film directorial debut, and cinematographer Haskell Wexler contributed their services without any salaries at all; they would be compensated by receiving a small percentage of the film's profits (if there were any). Wexler had to be argued into accepting even this slender prospect of pay.[30]

A number of prominent actors approached Peck about landing roles in *The Trial of the Catonsville Nine*, but he felt that using stars would draw attention from the script and thereby soften the play's moral and political message. (This stance applied even to himself: Peck flirted with, but ultimately scrapped, the idea of casting himself as Phil Berrigan.) The most familiar face in the cast probably belonged to William Schallert, who reprised his Obie Award–winning stage role as Judge Roszel Thomsen. Peter Strauss (who played Tom Lewis) later would become a bona fide Hollywood star, but at the time he was fresh out of Northwestern University and had only a handful of screen credits to his name.

They rehearsed for a week and then shot the entire film in eight days. Davidson stuck close to the script he and Saul Leavitt had crafted out of Dan Berrigan's original text. There were a couple of improvised scenes, including one showing the defendants talking during a recess at the trial. (This was shot in the studio's lunchroom while the actors were enjoying an actual meal.) Peck later said that the improvised scenes were included to show "the natural exuberance in the personalities of these people. We tried to . . . not get too solemn and dour."[31]

Having mounted the first theatrical production of Berrigan's play, Davidson already was familiar with the story of the Catonsville Nine. But directing the film touched him nonetheless, in part because of the uniquely cooperative and selfless spirit that pervaded the set. "Doing the film," he told Jerry and Carol Berrigan, "has been an extraordinary experience."[32]

Distributing the film proved troublesome. The major Hollywood studios weren't interested. Peck met with Robert Evans and Frank Yablans, of Paramount Studios, and screened it for them. Evans was ecstatic—"Everyone must see this picture," he said—but Yablans immediately dampened his enthusiasm by saying, "Not with my *Godfather* money." (Paramount recently had scored a major critical and commercial success with the first installment of the Mafia epic.) Peck finally struck a deal with a small chain of theaters, but the film languished. "Very few people saw it, but it was widely talked about in the press," he remarked. "All things considered, it may have shortened the war by about fifteen minutes."[33]

The film's release coincided with the end of Dan Berrigan's prison term. The *Trial of the Catonsville Nine* was screened at the Cannes Film Festival in the spring of 1972, and the French Association of Film Critics invited Berrigan there to screen it. Peck held his breath. Either underground or in jail for the previous two years, Berrigan never had seen a production of the play based on his Catonsville book—and now he would be viewing the film version. "It would have been profoundly embarrassing if he hadn't liked it," Peck later said. "That was our opening night, our toughest audience." When Berrigan expressed his approval, Peck breathed a sigh of relief.[34]

Other early reactions were similarly positive. Peck screened the film privately for the esteemed French actor Simone Signoret and the director Costa-Gavras, who recently had won plaudits for his political thriller *Z*. Signoret was so touched that she embraced Peck and exclaimed, "You're some kind of a cowboy, you are!" Costa-Gavras pumped Peck's hand and told him, "It's an act of courage, an act of courage!" Peck's European admirers were impressed that, in the United States, he had the artistic freedom to make such an overtly anti-war film. For them, the film "was a sign of our strength," Peck recalled.[35]

American movie critics responded to *The Trial of the Catonsville Nine* with somewhat less fervor. In the *New York Times*, Vincent Canby savaged the film from top to bottom. He mocked the script, saying that Berrigan's rendering of the trial testimony read "like rather bad collegiate poetry"; the acting he found "dreadfully sonorous" and "uniformly dreadful." Such was his distaste for Peck's film that he named it to his "ten worst" list for 1972. Canby's pillorying of *The Trial of the Catonsville Nine* occasioned a bitter exchange between him and Peck on the pages of the *Times*: Peck called the critic hopeless, but Canby stuck to his guns, insisting that it was "an awful film which does immense injustice to the defendants and to the event."[36]

The reservations of the film's most prominent critic were primarily political rather than artistic. The antiwar message of *The Trial of Catonsville Nine* helped to land Peck a spot on President Richard Nixon's enemies list.[37]

Jane Fonda believed that the story of Tom and Marjorie Melville merited a separate treatment on film. Late in 1971, the *New York Times* reported that Fonda and her sometime paramour, Donald Sutherland, "who have been known to participate in activities of a political nature, will soon participate in a movie about a pair of political activists"—the Melvilles. The proposed film was to be an adaptation of their account of their years in Guatemala, *Whose Heaven, Whose Earth?* Walter Bernstein was slated to write the screenplay, and Hannah Weinstein and Norman Eisner signed on to produce it. The headline of the *Times* story described how the film would be cast: "Sister Jane, Father Donald."[38]

As the project took shape, the Melvilles met with the principals at Weinstein's apartment on New York's Upper East Side. With Fonda and Sutherland sitting at their feet, the couple recounted their experiences among the peasants and revolutionaries in Guatemala in the 1960s. It was a heady experience for Tom and Marjorie. Here were two Hollywood stars hanging on their every word and preparing to bring their story to the big screen. Then, too, there was the money—$5,000 for the rights to their book.

But when their initial euphoria wore off, the Melvilles began to have second thoughts about the film. As they talked about the project with their friends, they began to worry that Hollywood would romanticize and perhaps distort the story of their years in Guatemala. They would have little input on how that story was told; the issues they cared passionately about—peace, social justice, equality—were likely to be obscured, if not simply ignored. Furthermore, they might become celebrities after the film was released—a prospect that they did not welcome. Swayed by these misgivings, they decided to pull out of the project.

Their decision occasioned a comical exchange with Fonda, who hoped to draw them back into the fold. The actress called them at their cramped apartment in Washington, D.C., but, apparently fearing that the phone might be tapped, she refused to use her full name.

"This is Jane," she said.

Not recognizing the voice, Tom Melville was puzzled. "Jane who?" he asked.

"You know, you met me in New York."

Once she had established her identity, Fonda arranged to meet the Melvilles to talk about the movie project. Her concern with secrecy extended only so far: on the appointed day, Fonda appeared in their hardscrabble Washington neighborhood in a chauffeured limousine. ("So much for keeping secrets," Tom Melville thought.) Fearing that their apartment might be bugged, she insisted on holding the discussion in the Melvilles' battered Ford sedan. As they drove around town, Fonda tried to assuage the couple's fears, promising that they would have input on the shape of the film. But the Melvilles stood firm, and the film project never got off the ground.[39]

"The Most Dangerous Time of My Life"

George Mische's turbulent experiences at Allenwood and Lewisburg, along with his earlier work with juvenile delinquents, shaped the career path he charted after his release from federal prison. After serving more than two years behind bars for his role in the Catonsville protest, he devoted his considerable energies to improving the lives of men who had run afoul of the criminal justice system.

In 1972 Mische investigated conditions at several federal penitentiaries and then made public some startling findings. His most sensational revelations concerned the federal penitentiary at Terre Haute, Indiana, where prisoners had lodged numerous complaints about brutality, corruption, and administrative unfairness. After visiting the prison, Mische confirmed that the charges were valid and then proclaimed that the facility was a powder keg. "Unless somebody steps in and does something, there may be another Attica there," he said. "That is a real hellhole." His ominous comments helped to precipitate a work stoppage at the prison; at its peak, according to one report, the protest involved almost 90 percent of the inmates at Terre Haute. But embarrassed administrators resisted Mische's call for reform, and conditions there remained wretched.[1]

When public exposure of prison abuses seemed to have little impact, Mische tried a different approach to correctional reform. He founded the National Coordinating Committee for Justice Under Law, a nonprofit organization devoted to providing vocational training and employment to men who had been convicted of nonviolent crimes. The group hoped to convince judges in several cities to assign nonviolent offenders to the program as an alternative to prison. No one could doubt that Mische and his staff were committed to the ethos of the project: they paid themselves the same wages earned by the men who were enrolled in the program.[2]

The National Coordinating Committee for Justice Under Law never quite gained a firm footing, and it ran out of money after a few years. Mische eventually returned to his hometown, St. Cloud, Minnesota, where he ran a tavern and worked as a labor organizer. Convinced that "the key right now is local government, grassroots," he ran for city council in 1976. Not surprisingly, he mounted a brash, antiestablishment campaign. "Who does this city belong to—the working people or the big corporations and a few rich cats?" he asked. The race was a bitter one—one sitting member of the council sniffed that Mische was unfit for public office and charged that his campaign brought politics in St. Cloud to a new low—but he scored a narrow upset victory.[3]

This proved to be the apogee of his political career in the city. Mische ran a failed campaign for mayor in 1980 and ultimately left the city council in the early 1980s. He eventually moved away from St. Cloud and settled down in Columbia Heights, just outside of St. Paul.[4]

As Mische moved on with his life after Catonsville, he heard many of his erstwhile comrades lionize Dan and Phil Berrigan. The brothers became objects of veneration among many aging radicals, symbols of a noble religious resistance to state tyranny. David Eberhardt, for instance, valorized Phil Berrigan, sometimes comparing his Baltimore Four compatriot to Old Testament prophets like Amos or Hosea or to John Brown, the great abolitionist. Although he always valued their undeniably significant contributions to antiwar and social justice causes, Mische was never quite as effusive in his praise for the Berrigans, and he did not maintain an especially close relationship with them as the years passed. He preferred to chart his own iconoclastic course.[5]

Baltimore activist Bill O'Connor—the peace and social justice stalwart who played a crucial behind-the-scenes role in both the Baltimore Four and Catonsville Nine protests—also pulled away from the charismatic brothers. Frustrated that Phil Berrigan had become intolerant and self-righteous, he decided to distance himself in the early 1970s.[6]

Although he respected Berrigan's accomplishments, O'Connor recoiled at his tendency to bring into his orbit of influence weak or naïve people. Berrigan recruited such pliable individuals, O'Connor believed, because they were easy to sway through "the moral pressure [and] the psychological manipulation" that he so often used to control people. O'Connor, who thought that he was made of sterner stuff, stubbornly resisted "the manipulations, the guilt trips, the moralizing" that Berrigan used "to trap people to make 'em feel inferior and yet bring 'em into the actions." O'Connor concluded that Berrigan was, in his words, simply "using people."[7]

If such fissures ever troubled Phil Berrigan, he never publicly acknowledged it. Supremely confident in the righteousness of his cause, he thundered against war and militarism for the rest of his life. His partner in this endeavor was Liz McAlister: he left the priesthood and married her in 1973. "We see our marriage as a radical assertion of our faith," they announced. "With God's grace and the help of our friends, we hope to continue to live the Gospels—in poverty, in community, and in nonviolent resistance, convinced of the contribution of religious resistance to humankind." They founded Jonah House, a faith-based, nonviolent resistance community in Baltimore. The group occupied a row house in West Baltimore for twenty-three years and then moved in the mid-1990s to St. Peter's Cemetery in the city.[8]

With Jonah House as his base, Berrigan devoted himself to battling the proliferation of nuclear weapons—what he considered to be the greatest single threat to peace that man had ever known. For him they were "the scourge of the earth; to mine for them, manufacture them, deploy them, use them, is a curse against God, the human family, and the earth itself."[9]

Operating under the banner of the Plowshares movement, Berrigan participated in numerous antinuclear protests in the 1970s and 1980s, among them a demonstration at a General Electric facility in King of Prussia, Pennsylvania, that evoked memories of the Baltimore Four and Catonsville Nine protests. The eight demonstrators poured several pints of their own blood on the nose cones of missiles and beat the weapons with hammers. In December 1999, Berrigan and others battered warplanes in an antiwar protest at a National Guard base in Maryland.[10]

His involvement in such acts of civil disobedience meant that Berrigan spent roughly a third of his final thirty years in prison. It amazed his children that he never seemed burdened by the weight of being behind bars. "Even in prison, even in those awful spaces, he was free," his daughters marveled. "In prison, as in the outside world, his work and life were to resist violence and oppression, to understand and try to live by God's word, to build community and help people learn to love one another."[11]

At the King of Prussia demonstration and many others, Phil Berrigan was joined by his brother Dan. The indefatigable Jesuit never seemed to slow down. He published poetry and prose, protested imperialism and social injustice, and tended to victims of AIDS at a New York City hospice. Over time, the priest became a kind of living saint for many liberal Catholics. The New York Times lauded him as "the granddaddy of the Catholic protest movement," and a celebratory book honored him as nothing less than an apostle of peace. But Berrigan was not one to rest on his laurels. He said in 2001 that he would stop agitating the day after he was embalmed.[12]

Dan Berrigan settled permanently in New York City in the mid-1970s and focused much of his activism there. In 2003, he was arrested protesting outside a military recruiting station in Times Square. Berrigan's bête noire in Manhattan apparently was the Intrepid Sea, Air and Space Museum—"a public disgrace," he called it. He was arrested in several protests there, including one staged just weeks before his eighty-ninth birthday in 2010.[13]

With war and injustice still so widespread, Berrigan felt that there remained a desperate need for such witnessing. "This is really the most dangerous time of my life," he said in 2004. "I have never seen this degree of irresponsibility, naked power, high-level duplicity, or the will to just own the world. I've never seen such blindness, and I'm scared, but it keeps me moving." The war in Iraq emerged as a particular source of concern for him, as it seemed to indicate that the nation had failed to glean much from the painful lessons of the war in Vietnam. "Well it's so insane that it defies description," he said. "It seems we've learned absolutely nothing from Vietnam except how to kill better."[14]

As he neared the end of his remarkable life, Dan Berrigan reflected on his regrets. Among the few was a nagging sense that he might have acted earlier and more urgently against the war in Vietnam. "I could have done sooner the things I did, like Catonsville," he acknowledged.[15]

Like the Berrigans, Tom Lewis also returned to jail periodically because of his ongoing commitment to antiwar and social justice causes. He eventually settled in Worcester, Massachusetts, where his career as an artist and teacher flourished. The flexibility afforded by this vocation allowed him to risk imprisonment for participating in a variety of protests. Even as he became a veteran of the criminal justice system, Lewis still felt some butterflies when he entered a courtroom. "Trials are always new and different," he admitted in the 1980s. "And the fear never wears off."[16]

Lewis was not content to keep fighting the same old battles; he kept his witnessing current. In 2005, for instance, he was arrested outside the Embassy of Sudan in Washington, D.C., for protesting the ongoing genocide in Darfur. Lewis also demonstrated against torture and called for the closure of the American detention camp in Guantanamo Bay, Cuba. When he wasn't out protesting, Lewis welcomed the poor into his home in Worcester and helped to feed the hungry at the nearby Mustard Seed soup kitchen.

There were times when Lewis's peace and social justice activities threatened to interfere with his professional life. He taught for many years at the Worcester Art Museum, and his periodic arrests sometimes meant that a substitute teacher had to be found on short notice. Usually, though, Lewis planned ahead. "He was so respectful always," said a museum staffer. "He would come into my office and say, 'I'm doing this and I don't expect to get arrested but if I do I've made arrangements and I'll have someone to cover the class and it probably wouldn't be longer than three weeks.'"[17]

John Hogan took a more subdued approach to addressing social justice issues. After being released from prison for his role in the Catonsville protest, he showed little enthusiasm for engaging in overtly political activities. "Not all life is political," he told a *Baltimore Sun* reporter in 1978. Hogan settled into a tranquil life in New Haven, Connecticut, in which he quietly served others. Putting his carpentry skills to good use, he worked for many years inspecting and repairing dilapidated public housing units in the city. (He did it all with gusto—except for painting. That was the one task Hogan didn't tackle with enthusiasm.) His labors benefited the poorest and most disadvantaged residents of New Haven—families receiving public assistance, the elderly, single mothers. He also volunteered with Interfaith Volunteer Caregivers.[18]

"I think that was an extension of what he did earlier," his wife said, "but in an everyday way." His work was meaningful, even if it wasn't done on a grand political scale. When she thought of her husband spending time with elderly public housing tenants or offering them rides around New Haven, she was reminded of an adage from Mother Theresa: "Don't look for big things; just do small things with great love."[19]

Hogan never lost interest in Central America. Later in life, he traveled to Nicaragua as a volunteer in the New Haven/Leon Sister Cities Project. It was like old times for him: he used his carpentry expertise to help facilitate a municipal construction project. And, like all of the Catonsville Nine, he continued to care deeply about issues of racial equality. Hogan once was called for jury duty in New Haven. During voir dire, he was asked if there was a reason he couldn't serve on the jury. Indeed there was: the defendant was African American, and Hogan believed that the man couldn't be tried by his peers because there were no blacks in the jury pool.[20]

Hogan's erstwhile colleagues in the Maryknoll order, Tom and Marjorie Melville, remained devoted to understanding the vast political and socioeconomic problems afflicting Central and South America. After Tom's release from prison, they traveled to Chile to research their joint doctoral dissertation, which focused on the social organization of the Mapuche Indians under the government of Salvador Allende. (They were saddened but hardly surprised when Allende was overthrown—with covert American backing—by strongman Augusto Pinochet.) As a professor at the University of Houston and then the University of California at Berkeley, Marjorie—who went by "Margarita" later in her life—focused her scholarship on Chicanas and the millions of refugees who were fleeing turmoil in Central America. Her book *Twice a Minority* was widely cited by other scholars. By the time she retired from Berkeley in the mid-1990s, she had risen to the post of associate dean of the university's graduate division.[21]

Tom Melville stayed focused on the region as well. He spent over a decade writing a biography of Father Ron Hennessey, a Maryknoll priest who battled Guatemala's repressive, American-backed oligarchy for many years. He promoted the book by delivering talks at colleges, churches, and bookstores across the country—often with his Catonsville Nine collaborator George Mische in tow.[22]

The two men spoke mainly about global issues of imperialism and militarism, but sometimes their thoughts turned to their witness in Catonsville. At a stop in Baltimore in 2007, Melville noted that he and Mische were not always remembered for what they had done at Local Board 33. "A lot of people we've spoken to," he said, "never have heard of the Catonsville Nine."

Melville shared his sentiments in a private conversation that same year with Hogan.

"John, how does it feel to be an asterisk in history now?" Melville asked him.

"What do you mean?" Hogan responded.

"People are forgetting about us, John," Melville told him. "They are forgetting about Catonsville. Some day when the whole story of the 1960s is written, there just will be a little asterisk for the Catonsville Nine."[23]

To help prevent the Catonsville Nine from being relegated to a historical footnote, in 1993 Melville attended a twenty-fifth anniversary celebration of the draft board protest. Six of the demonstrators—Melville, the Berrigans, Hogan, Lewis, and Mische—turned up for the gathering, which drew a crowd of about 250 people at Goucher College in Baltimore. The passing of time had not cooled the fires of their activism. "It is a lifetime responsibility and job to build a moral and just society for our children," Mische explained. "I believed it at Catonsville, and I believe it now." Phil Berrigan insisted that there remained an urgent need for protests like the ones he had engaged in a quarter century earlier. His brother agreed. "Things are worse than ever," Dan Berrigan said.[24]

The organizers of the reunion apparently were unable to persuade the increasingly reclusive Mary Moylan to attend. When she was released from prison, she tried to piece back together a life that had been put on hold for a full decade. Willa Bickham worked as a nurse in Baltimore, and she helped Moylan return to her former profession. Moylan's nursing license had lapsed, and she figured that, as an ex-con, she would need a sheaf of letters of support to regain it from the state nursing board. Bickham helped her obtain the documentation, but it proved unnecessary; Moylan merely had to pay the standard $5 fee. She subsequently worked at the People's Free Medical Clinic, which she had helped found in the late 1960s, and several hospitals in the Baltimore area. She eventually moved to coastal New Jersey and from there reconnected with the women's rights movement in New York City.[25]

Unable to readjust after her time as a fugitive and inmate, Moylan foundered after she left prison. She became isolated and attempted to soothe her turmoil with alcohol—with predictably grievous results. Dan Berrigan believed that being a fugitive for so long simply had left her broken. "I think she slowly went underground spiritually in a way that was very tragic," he said. "She was underground too long. By the time she turned herself in, the die was cast." And Moylan's struggles were physical as well as psychological. She had to contend with a variety of ailments, the most serious being a progressive eye disease that gradually robbed her of her sight. She found it increasingly difficult to recognize faces or read.[26]

Moylan found periodic work as a nurse but essentially withdrew from the world. "She was so successful in her Orphic descent underground that she lost contact with old comrades and her friends and her family," a *Baltimore Sun* reporter wrote. "Some of the people who loved her most never saw her again.

Lots of people knew a little bit about her, not many everything. She became a cherished, shadowy memory."[27]

When she died in Asbury Park, New Jersey, in 1995, Moylan was "poor, alone, forgotten," according to Rosemary Ruether, who had known her in Washington in the 1960s. There were small memorial services for her in New York and Baltimore, but her death attracted relatively little public notice. Marking her passing in a bittersweet remembrance in the *National Catholic Reporter*, Ruether felt that her old friend—"shattered and ground under by the trample of events"—should be counted as a kind of a casualty of war. "You, indeed, laid your life on the line for justice and were broken by it," she wrote of Moylan. "Perhaps we need an alternative Vietnam memorial bearing the names of all those whose lives were destroyed in protesting the war."[28]

Phil Berrigan's death garnered exponentially more attention than Mary Moylan's. A few days after he succumbed to kidney and liver cancer in 2002, a crowd of several hundred packed into a Baltimore church for his funeral Mass. The services were a celebration of Berrigan's unswerving commitment to peace. In his eulogy, Brendan Walsh recounted how, on the morning of the Catonsville raid, Berrigan had grabbed the car keys from him and insisted on driving over to the Knights of Columbus hall. "Talk about intensity," Walsh recalled. "I thought about Jesus overturning the tables of the temple." The encomiums for Berrigan came from both prominent activists and everyday people who had been touched by his activism. Howard Zinn argued, "Countless people all over the nation, and in other parts of the world, will remember Phil Berrigan as one of the heroes of our time." James Carroll dismissed the idea that Berrigan was a fringe figure whose time had passed, arguing that, "even in death, [he] has extraordinary relevance for . . . today's most urgent questions."[29]

Indeed, Phil Berrigan's passing and the onset of the American military invasion of Iraq just a year later seemed to rekindle public interest in the Catonsville Nine. Their witness for peace repeatedly was referenced as an example of how people should follow their consciences and battle injustices around the world. As the invasion loomed, Carroll noted Berrigan's prescience, terming the impending campaign "an exact instance of what Berrigan predicted—America going to war not because it needs to, but because it can."[30]

As the legacy of the Catonsville Nine has been reconfigured over the past four decades, the protesters have pondered the significance of their witness. Tom Melville has steadfastly refused to overstate its meaning or its impact on his life. "We were nobodies before and we're nobodies now," he said in 1993. "It was something I had to do. That's it." Looking back on the protest, he regretted that the demonstrators' concerns about Guatemala had been obscured: "What we had to say was largely lost."[31]

In a 1999 interview, both Tom and Marjorie Melville seemed wary of exaggerating the importance of what they had done at Local Board 33. She offered that she didn't think it was all that extraordinary, while he bluntly stated, "I don't see it as having any kind of historical significance at all." Both believed that their ongoing work on behalf of the people of Latin America had been of more lasting importance than their witness at Catonsville.[32]

Dan Berrigan and Hogan, however, viewed things differently. Both men believed that the Catonsville Nine had in fact made a significant difference in the world. "It didn't stop the war," Hogan said on the twenty-fifth anniversary of the raid in 1993, "but it contributed to [halting] it." Berrigan posited that the Nine were "an ingredient in the antiwar pot. All of us made it politically impossible to continue the war." He believed that the Catonsville protesters and their collaborators in the antiwar movement, in addition to expediting the war's end, had contributed to the demise of two presidents—Lyndon Johnson and his successor, Richard Nixon.[33]

Although the Catonsville Nine might have contributed to bringing the war to an end, they clearly failed in achieving their short-term goal: they didn't cripple the military draft. The Selective Service System did lose much of its effectiveness in the early 1970s, but, ironically, it was hamstrung by the kinds of conventional methods that the Nine had abandoned. According to one exhaustive study, the antiwar movement's "draft resistance goal was accomplished, but by members of the legal profession working within, not outside, the 'system.' . . . These lawyers, prosecutors, and judges did not draw public attention to the war in the manner of the draft-card burners and the Berrigans, but they did achieve the 'immense and provocative' results that activists found beyond their reach." It was this succession of legal attacks—and not the kind of extralegal activism practiced by the Nine—that eventually left the draft law in tatters.[34]

The Catonsville Nine might have impacted the Catholic Church more than they influenced government policy. As Father Mark Massa, dean of the School of Theology and Ministry at Boston College, has written in his incisive study of modern Catholicism, the raid on Local Board 33 "pluralized how, and in what ways, one could be a good Catholic. The events at Catonsville, undertaken by 'good Catholics'—among them priests and missionaries whom rank-and-file Catholics had always been taught to revere—opened the possibility of a new American Catholic identity because it witnessed to a different history of Catholic Christianity, one that evoked the 'dangerous memory' of Jesus." The provocative actions of the Nine showed that it was acceptable for Catholics to confront their government—even if it meant going to jail—when they believed it to be an agent of injustice. They thus helped to "crack the traditional conservatism of the Catholic community," as Howard Zinn put it.[35]

This influence manifested itself in a variety of ways. Young Catholics— particularly draft-age men—seem to have been impacted by the likes of the Catonsville Nine. According to the National Catholic Conference, only 0.5 percent of the young men applying for conscientious objector status in 1966 were Catholic. By 1969 that percentage had risen twentyfold, to 10 percent. Many of these draft resisters drew inspiration from the Catonsville Nine.[36]

Martin Sheen was an unknown young actor when he read a newspaper account of a reporter questioning Dan Berrigan before he was sent to prison for his part in the Maryland draft board raid. The reporter noted that it was perhaps easier for priests like Berrigan to engage in acts of civil disobedience because they wouldn't have to abandon any children if they went to prison. The skeptical newsman asked what would happen to his children if he went to prison for protesting injustice. Berrigan's answer was sui generis: "What's going to happen to them if you don't?"[37]

Berrigan's comment hit Sheen, a Catholic, "like a thunderbolt," as he described it. It "forced me to reevaluate everything about myself and the world in which I lived. Eventually it forced me to look at social justice in an entirely different light, and that light illuminated every political and social stand I would take for the rest of my life." And take them him he did: Sheen engaged in numerous acts of civil disobedience on behalf of peace, environmental, and social justice causes. Along the way, he was arrested more than sixty times.[38]

It wasn't just rank-and-file Catholics who were challenged by the Catonsville Nine to confront issues of peace and social justice. Bishops Thomas Gumbleton (Detroit) and Bernard Flanagan (Worcester) both said in the early 1970s that demonstrations like the Catonsville witness forced them to reflect on the morality of war and the Church's role in promoting peace. "I think people who are ready to put their whole lives on the line forced me to do some thinking," Gumbleton said. Pushed by the Nine and their partners in the Catholic peace movement, the American bishops issued a statement titled "The Challenge of Peace," which touted the potential of pacifism and nonviolence as essential methods of peacemaking.[39]

For Catholics like Father John Dear, the Jesuit peace and social justice activist, the witness of the Catonsville Nine continued to have meaning in the twenty-first century. On the fortieth anniversary of the protest, Dear wrote that "the Catonsville action pushed the U.S. Catholic church a large step forward. The action showed that we were not medieval, but involved, active, revolutionary. More, that the church was willing to take up where the Acts of the Apostles left off. We too could carry on the peacemaking life of the nonviolent Jesus." He argued that everyone should "be inspired by these heroic church folk to stand up and likewise be counted."[40]

The Catonsville Nine's reach extended well beyond the institutions and individuals in the Catholic Church. Their witness inspired several generations of peace and social justice activists to boldly and meaningfully confront injustice. Not long before his death in 2010, Howard Zinn praised the Nine for having fully devoted themselves to promoting peaceful resistance to evil. At about the same time, activist Shane Claiborne—a New Monasticism movement pioneer who was young enough to be Zinn's grandson—wrote of the Nine's actions, "It is acts of courage like this that the prophets were known for. And jailed for. They are an invitation to interrupt injustice with grace. They are an invitation to live with prophetic imagination."[41]

Joan Cavanagh was fourteen years old and living in the Baltimore area when the Catonsville Nine struck Local Board 33. She was amazed by the specter of Catholic clergy and laymen being involved in such a radical protest. "But more importantly, it was the symbol that was used—napalm," she later said. "[It] remains the most stirring image of my childhood, my young adulthood— it changed my life." Stirred by the witness of the Nine, she resolved to protest militarism and injustice herself. By 1973, she would be chaining herself to the White House fence as part of an antiwar demonstration—the first of many protest-related arrests she endured over the next four decades.[42]

The Catonsville Nine also invigorated Mitch Snyder. Imprisoned for auto theft in 1970, Snyder met Dan and Phil Berrigan during their term in Danbury Federal Penitentiary. Snyder was intrigued by the draft board protest and sought out Phil Berrigan, telling him, "I have a feeling that you know something that would be helpful to me." Snyder gravitated toward the brothers after joining their book group at the prison, and his outlook on issues of peace and social justice was transformed. From the Berrigans he gained clarity and direction. Snyder was radicalized—he participated in a month-long hunger strike to protest the initial denial of the Berrigans' parole—and drawn into an iteration of Catholicism grounded in the idea that "the Bible is in fact the blueprint for living—it's not symbolic," as he put it. After his release, Snyder became active in the Community for Creative Nonviolence and emerged as a leading advocate for the homeless. (In a neat bit of symmetry, Martin Sheen portrayed Snyder in the television movie that was made about his life.[43])

The lasting impact of the Catonsville Nine—both collectively and as individuals—was apparent even as their ranks thinned. When Lewis died in April 2008, the priest who celebrated his funeral Mass remarked that his antidraft protest decades earlier still ranked as the most powerfully symbolic Christian witness of the cleric's lifetime. His passing was mourned in both Worcester and Baltimore. "Tom was a saint, plain and simple," said Scott Schaeffer-Duffy, a longtime friend. "He's finally able to practice his art with all the masters in a place where there is no violence, war or injustice."[44]

Shortly after Lewis's death, his mother, brother, and sister represented the family at ceremonies in Baltimore marking the fortieth anniversary of the Catonsville demonstration. Hogan was the only surviving member of the Nine in attendance. Describing how he had gotten to the point of protesting the war, he said, "You think of the Vietnam War and you see at that time the pictures coming out of the place and you heard the reports, and the amount of men being killed, and the people over there being killed. It was just an enormous thing. How can you not react to it?"[45]

A few months later, Hogan was dead; a massive stroke took his life. At his tear-filled memorial service, Joan Cavanagh called him "an incredible inspiration." His voice freighted with sadness, Mische, Hogan's collaborator in Catonsville, offered, "John was the best."[46]

It wasn't only eulogies that kept memories of the Catonsville Nine from fading. In December 2010, federal authorities in Maryland charged a twenty-one-year-old man named Antonio Martinez with attempted murder of federal employees and attempted use of a weapon of mass destruction. Martinez—a recent convert to Islam who went by the name Muhammad Hussain—allegedly wanted to blow up Catonsville's Armed Forces Recruiting Center as an act of jihad, or holy war.[47]

Catonsville's military recruitment facility long since had moved out of the Knights of Columbus hall on Frederick Road. It was now located several miles away, on a busy highway crammed with commercial buildings. And Martinez allegedly was the antithesis of a nonviolent activist. (He reportedly told an undercover federal agent, "There will be no peace for the oppressors. . . . You will feel our bullets.") Nonetheless, his alleged plot stirred up memories of how, four decades earlier, Catonsville's military recruitment machinery had been targeted in a spectacular antiwar protest.[48]

Most news stories about the planned attack noted the obvious—if inexact—parallels between Martinez's scheme and the witness of the Catonsville Nine. What these accounts glossed over, however, were the deeper and more profound connections that linked the two events.

The Catonsville Nine decried imperialism because, in their worldview, it fueled the oppression of the world's underclass. They cautioned that unrest would continue to boil over—from Vietnam to Central Africa to Guatemala to urban America—if the core tenets of Christianity and representative democracy were not applied globally to alleviate the suffering of the poor and disenfranchised. In essence, they forewarned us about Martinez—a marginalized American Latino who was outraged by the oppression of his Muslim coreligionists in Chechnya, Pakistan, Iraq, and Afghanistan, among other places. The despair and alienation that have driven so many young men like him to lash out against the United States over the last two decades might seem unfathomable, but they resulted in part from a collective failure to heed the message that the Catonsville Nine delivered so poignantly on that May afternoon in 1968.

NOTES

Preface

1. The poem can be found in Daniel Berrigan, *Jubilee!*, New York: Hudson River Press, 1991.

Introduction

1. John P. Bauernschub, *The Knights of Columbus: Fifty Years of Columbianism in Maryland*, Rockville, MD: Wildside Press, 2008, 215–217; Marsha Wight Wise, *Images of America: Catonsville*, Charleston, SC: Arcadia Publishing, 2005, 126.

2. My reference to "kids" here is autobiographical. I walked atop the wall many times as a child.

3. Bauernschub, *Knights of Columbus*, 215–217.

4. Mark S. Massa, *The American Catholic Revolution: How the Sixties Changed the Church Forever*, New York: Oxford University Press, 2010, xiii, 1, 6.

5. Sheen writes movingly about Daniel and Philip Berrigan in Marlo Thomas, *The Right Words at the Right Time*, New York: Atria Books, 2002, 310–311.

6. I. F. Stone, "They Pleaded Guilty of Burning Paper Instead of Children," in Neil Middleton, ed., *The Best of I. F. Stone's Weekly*, New York: Penguin Books, 1973, 222–224; Harvey Cox, "Tongues of Flame: The Trial of the Catonsville Nine," in Stephen Halpert and Tom Murray, eds., *Witness of the Berrigans*, New York: Doubleday, 1972, 19–23. For a mystery novel with a Catonsville Nine reference, see Laura Lippman, *No Good Deeds*, New York: William Morrow, 2006, 10. A children's book referencing the Nine is Dorothy Lilja Harrison, *Peace, Be Still*, Seattle: CreateSpace, 2010.

7. K. T. Weidmann, "Gutiérrez, Gustavo," in Christian D. Von Dehsen, ed., *Philosophers and Religious Leaders* (*Lives and Legacies: An Encyclopedia of People Who Changed the World* series), Phoenix, AZ: Oryx Press, 1999, 79.

Chapter 1

1. *Baltimore Sun*, April 6, 2008; Donald Lewis to author, July 9, 2009 (in possession of author); "Reminiscences of Tom Lewis: Oral History," Oral History Research Office, Columbia University Libraries, CU, 1986 (hereafter Lewis oral history, CU), 2.

2. Lewis oral history, CU, 2; Tom Lewis, "Questions for Trial Testimony" [ca. September 1968], BC-CU.

3. Lewis oral history, CU, 33–34; "Thomas Pahl Lewis: Security Matter, Miscellaneous," July 15, 1968, TL-FBI.

4. Lewis oral history, CU, 34.

5. Ibid., 33.

6. "Thomas Pahl Lewis," TL-FBI; *BS*, November 18 and December 6, 1957.

7. Scott Schaeffer-Duffy, "Tom Lewis: An Artist/Activist," http://www.jonahhouse.org/LewisObit.htm (accessed January 12, 2010).

8. Lewis oral history, CU, 9; "Thomas Pahl Lewis," TL-FBI.

9. Schaeffer-Duffy, "Tom Lewis."

10. Lewis oral history, CU, 7–8.

11. *BS*, December 27, 1965; Lewis oral history, CU, 2–3.

12. Lewis oral history, CU, 2–3.

13. *Telegram and Gazette* (Worcester, MA), March 25, 1990; Lewis oral history, CU, 9; Lewis, "Questions for Trial Testimony," BC-CU.

14. Marianne Hinckle, "Lives of the Baltimore Saints," *Ramparts*, September 28, 1968, 11–16; *BS*, December 27, 1965, and January 25, 1967; *Worcester Telegram and Gazette*, March 25, 1990; Tom Lewis interview, *IOAF*, November 13, 1999.

15. *BS*, December 27, 1965, and January 25, 1967.

16. Barbara Mills, *"Got My Mind Set on Freedom": Maryland's Story of Black and White Activism, 1663–2000*, Westminster, MD: Heritage Books, 2002, 159.

17. Mills, *"Got My Mind Set on Freedom,"* 169–177; Mills, *And Justice for All: The Double Life of Fred Weisgal, Attorney and Musician*, Baltimore, MD: American Literary Press, 2000, 244–254.

18. Schaeffer-Duffy, "Tom Lewis."

19. Philip Berrigan, *Prison Journals of a Priest Revolutionary*, New York: Holt, Rinehart and Winston, 1970, 166.

20. Schaeffer-Duffy, "Tom Lewis"; Tom Lewis, "The Artist as Resister and Creator of Hope," talk delivered at New York Catholic Worker Friday Night Meeting, November 7, 1986, DD-CWC.

21. CTT, 564–601; Daniel Berrigan, *The Trial of the Catonsville Nine*, Boston: Beacon Press, 1970, 39; Mills, *"Got My Mind Set on Freedom,"* 161–163. Berrigan's account presents a generally reliable transcript of the Catonsville trial. However, the exigencies of rendering roughly 1,000 pages of trial testimony into a slender book forced him into editing and rearranging the sequence of some of the testimony. When possible, I have cross-checked it against multiple other sources, including the actual trial transcript (CTT), newspaper accounts, and *DD*.

22. Mills, *And Justice for All*, 292–293, 307; *Baltimore Afro-American*, April 23, 1966.

23. *Baltimore Afro-American*, May 24, 1966.

24. Ibid.

25. Lewis oral history, CU, 16–17, 42; Lewis, "Questions for trial testimony," BC-CU.

26. *TOTCN*, 40–41; Lewis oral history, CU, 21–22; CTT, 573; Lewis, "Questions for trial testimony," BC-CU.

27. *NYT*, October 5, 1965.

28. *NCR*, November 20, 1968, 4–5.

29. Lewis oral history, CU, 21, 41.

30. Ibid.

31. *BS*, January 25, 1967.

32. Schaeffer-Duffy, "Tom Lewis."

33. Lewis interview, *IOAF*; *PJ*, 165.

34. Schaeffer-Duffy, "Tom Lewis."

35. Lewis oral history, CU, 20.

Chapter 2

1. *FTLW*, 1–11.
2. Philip Berrigan, "Biographical Material" [ca. 1968], BC-CU.
3. *FTLW*, 1–11.
4. Ibid.
5. Ibid., 13–25.
6. "Report of IC [redacted]," November 9, 1967, PB-FBI; *FTLW*, 13–25.
7. "Philip Francis Berrigan, Security Matter—Miscellaneous," May 21, 1968, PB-FBI.
8. *FTLW*, 13–25; P. Berrigan, "Biographical Material," BC-CU.
9. *FTLW*, 27–45: P. Berrigan, "Biographical Material," BC-CU.
10. P. Berrigan, "Biographical Material," BC-CU.
11. *FTLW*, 47–77.
12. Ibid., 53–58.
13. Philip Berrigan, *No More Strangers*, New York: Macmillan, 1965, 115.
14. John W. O'Malley, *What Happened at Vatican II*, Cambridge, MA: Harvard University Press, 2008, 36–37.
15. Garry Wills, *Bare Ruined Choirs: Doubt, Prophecy, and Radical Religion*, Garden City, NY: Doubleday, 1972, 126; Warren Hinckle, "Left Wing Catholics," *Ramparts*, November 1967, 14–26.
16. *FTLW*, 152.
17. P. Berrigan, *No More Strangers*, 159–181.
18. *FTLW*, 35–36; William Appleman Williams, *The Tragedy of American Diplomacy*, 2d ed., New York: W. W. Norton, 1988.
19. *FTLW*, 58–64.
20. P. Berrigan, "Biographical Material," BC-CU.
21. *FTLW*, 80–84.
22. Ibid., 83; *PJ*, 21; Philip Berrigan to George O'Dea, October 31, 1965, and May 9, 1967, BMC.
23. *BS*, February 12, 1967; Author interview with George Giese, September 24, 2010 (in possession of author).
24. Dorothy Day recounts her remarkable career in *The Long Loneliness: The Autobiography of Dorothy Day*, which has appeared in numerous editions since its original publication in 1952. Another valuable resource for anyone interested in her life and work is: Day, *The Duty of Delight: The Diaries of Dorothy Day*, Milwaukee, WI: Marquette University Press, 2008.
25. Lewis oral history, CU, 23; Lewis, "Artist as Resister," DD-CW.
26. Lewis, "Questions for Trial Testimony," BC-CU.
27. Report of SA [redacted], October 30, 1967, PB-FBI; Charles Meconis, *With Clumsy Grace: The American Catholic Left, 1961–1975*, New York: Seabury Press, 1979, 18.
28. Meconis, *Clumsy Grace*, 18.
29. Ibid.
30. *DD*, 112.
31. *NYT*, December 31, 1966; Murray Polner and Jim O'Grady, *Disarmed and Dangerous: The Radical Lives and Times of Daniel and Philip Berrigan*, New York: Basic Books, 1997, 146.
32. Philip Berrigan to Dean Rusk, January 11, 1967, BC-CU.
33. Interfaith Peace Mission to Walt Rostow, April 22, 1967, BC-CU.

34. Ibid.

35. P. Berrigan, "Biographical Material," BC-CU; Polner and O'Grady, *Disarmed and Dangerous*, 146–148.

36. *FTLW*, 86; Polner and O'Grady, *Disarmed and Dangerous*, 146–148.

37. *FTLW*, 94; *PJ*, 19–20; *TOTCN*, 22–23.

38. *PJ*, 168.

39. Tom Cornell, "Catholic Worker Pacifism: An Eyewitness to History," http://www.catholicworker.com/peacetc.htm (accessed January 12, 2010).

40. *NYT*, March 18 and November 3, 7, 10, and 11, 1965.

41. Polner and O'Grady, *Disarmed and Dangerous*, 122–125.

42. Lewis oral history, CU, 47–48, 54–55.

43. Meconis, *Clumsy Grace*, 19–20; Lewis oral history, CU, 24.

44. Meconis, *Clumsy Grace*, 19–20.

45. Rosalie Riegle Troester, ed., *Voices From the Catholic Worker*, Philadelphia: Temple University Press, 1993, 42–43.

46. Little has been written about the Bondhus affair. I've drawn details from the contemporaneous newspaper articles posted on "The Fight Against Selective Service," http://www.selective-service.org/barry-bondhus-case.htm (accessed January 12, 2010).

47. *FTLW*, 87–88.

48. Meconis, *Clumsy Grace*, 19–20.

49. Troester, *Voices From the Catholic Worker*, 43.

50. Philip Berrigan to Daniel Berrigan [ca. October 1968], BC-CU.

51. Lewis oral history, CU, 50.

Chapter 3

1. *TOTCN*, 45–46; Troester, *Voices From the Catholic Worker*, 46.

2. Troester, *Voices From the Catholic Worker*, 42–43.

3. Philip Berrigan to Daniel Berrigan [ca. September or October 1967], BC-CU.

4. Interview with William J. O'Connor, November 14, 1975, H. Furlong Baldwin Library, Maryland Historical Society, Baltimore, MD (hereafter O'Connor oral history, MDHS), 1–25. (I am indebted to Joe Tropea for finding this document and sharing it with me.) The building often is referred to as the "Customs" House, but it is properly known as the "Custom" House.

5. O'Connor oral history, MDHS, 1–25.

6. Philip Berrigan to Daniel Berrigan [ca. September 1967], BC-CU.

7. O'Connor oral history, MDHS, 1–25; *FTLW*, 88; Polner and O'Grady, *Disarmed and Dangerous*, 171–173.

8. O'Connor oral history, MDHS, 1–25; *PJ*, 14–19.

9. Troester, *Voices From the Catholic Worker*, 43; Lewis oral history, CU, 50.

10. O'Connor oral history, MDHS, 1–25; *PJ*, 17.

11. O'Connor oral history, MDHS, 1–25.

12. Report of SA [name redacted], October 30, 1967, PB-FBI.

13. Ibid.

14. Ibid.

15. Philip Berrigan, *A Punishment for Peace*, New York: Macmillan, 1969, 147; Report of SA [name redacted], October 30, 1967, PB-FBI.

16. P. Berrigan, *Punishment for Peace*, 148.

17. Report of SA [name redacted], October 30, 1967, PB-FBI.

18. The entire statement is contained in Report of SA [name redacted], October 30, 1967, PB-FBI.

19. Ibid.

20. Ibid.

21. Ibid.

22. P. Berrigan, *Punishment for Peace*, 149.

23. Report of SA [name redacted], October 30, 1967, PB-FBI.

24. J. Edgar Hoover, "Memorandum for Mr. Tolson," October 27, 1967, PB-FBI.

25. "Report of the FBI Laboratory," October 30, 1967, PB-FBI.

26. Tom Lewis, "Some Reflections of a Catholic War-Protester While in Jail With Fr. Philip Berrigan," October 28, 1967, BC-CU.

27. P. Berrigan, *Punishment for Peace*, 150.

28. *FTLW*, 90.

29. *NYT*, October 28, 1967; *Washington Post*, October 28, 1967. The *Chicago Tribune* also covered the story, and it too highlighted Berrigan's prominent role, noting that the protest had been spearheaded by a "controversial Roman Catholic priest" (*Chicago Tribune*, October 28, 1967).

30. *NYT*, October 28, 1967.

31. Philip Berrigan to George O'Dea, October 28, 1967, BC-CU.

32. *NCR*, November 8, 1967.

33. Norman Mailer, *The Armies of the Night: History as a Novel, the Novel as History*, New York: Signet, 1968; Daniel Berrigan, *To Dwell in Peace: An Autobiography*, San Francisco: Harper & Row, 1987, 206–209; Daniel Berrigan to James Douglas, November 8, 1967, BC-CU.

34. *TDIP*, 206–210.

35. Ibid., 208–210.

36. *PJ*, xiv.

37. *NCR*, November 1, 1967.

38. Meconis, *Clumsy Grace*, 21–22.

39. Ibid.

40. Hinckle, "Lives of the Baltimore Saints," 11–16.

41. Report of SA [name redacted], October 30, 1967.

42. *NCR*, November 8, 1967.

43. Lewis oral history, CU, 28–29.

44. P. Berrigan, *Punishment for Peace*, 151–155.

45. Ibid., 152.

46. Ibid., 151–155.

Chapter 4

1. Interfaith Peace Mission to "Dear Friends," January 13, 1968, PB-FBI.

2. J. H. Gale to Claude DeLoach, February 14, 1968, PB-FBI; *BS*, November 1, 1967.

3. *BS*, April 1, 1968.

4. *BS*, December 2, 1967.

5. Philip Berrigan to Jim [Forest], December 2, 1967, BC-CU.

6. Jim Forest, "Phil Berrigan: Disturber of Sleep," in William Casey and Philip Nobile, eds., *The Berrigans*, New York: Avon Books, 1971, 166–179.

7. Mills, *And Justice for All*, 3, 496.

8. Ibid., 338.

9. Ibid., 338–339.

10. *BS*, December 23, 1967.

11. John Deedy, "News and Views," *Commonweal*, January 12, 1968, 426.

12. *FTLW*, 91.

13. CTT, 336–343.

14. *NCR*, April 10, 1968; *FTLW*, 91.

15. *PJ*, xvi.

16. *BS*, April 3, 1968; "Baltimore" to Director, FBI, April 3, 1968, PB-FBI.

17. *NCR*, April 17, 1968; *BS*, April 5 and 6, 1968.

18. *BS*, April 17, 1968.

19. My understanding of the Nazi war crimes trials has been informed by Joseph Persico's fine book *Nuremberg: Infamy on Trial*, New York: Penguin Books, 1995.

20. *NCR*, March 27, 1968.

21. *NCR*, April 17, 1968.

22. *United States v. O'Brien*, 391 U.S. 367 (1968).

23. CTT, 336–343.

24. *NCR*, April 17, 1968.

25. Ibid.

26. CTT, 336–343.

27. Ibid.

28. I derived this cursory account of the riots from the excellent website created by the University of Baltimore for its recent conference on the subject, "Baltimore '68: Riots and Rebirth." A wealth of material can be accessed at http://archives.ubalt.edu/bsr/index.html.

29. Giese interview.

30. CTT, 336–343.

31. Attending the trial must have been a formative experience for the child: he later became an attorney.

32. *BS*, April 16, 1968.

33. *BS*, April 17, 1968.

34. Ibid.

35. Mills, *And Justice for All*, 343.

36. Ibid.

37. *PJ*, xvii.

38. George Mische interview, *HAS*, November 13, 2007.

Chapter 5

1. Philip Berrigan to Daniel Berrigan [ca. April 30, 1968], BC-CU.

2. O'Connor oral history, MDHS, 1–25.

3. Lewis oral history, CU, 56.

4. *PJ*, 25.

5. Philip Berrigan to Karl Meyer, February 15, 1968, BC-CU.

6. G. Mische interview, *HAS*; "George Mische on U.S. Foreign Policy," Speech delivered at St. John's Methodist Church, Baltimore, MD, November 11, 2007, http://video.google.com/videoplay?docid=6386769262558826320# (accessed May 27, 2011).

7. CTT, 483–484.

8. Ibid., 484.

9. Ibid., 482–490.

10. *NCR*, May 29, 1968; Richard Curtis, *The Berrigan Brothers: The Story of Daniel and Philip Berrigan*, New York: Hawthorn Books, 1974, 83; *DD*, 126.

11. CTT, 489.

12. *TOTCN*, 69; John F. Kennedy, "Address at a White House Reception for Members of Congress and for the Diplomatic Corps of the Latin American Republics," March 13, 1961, in John T. Woolley and Gerhard Peters, *The American Presidency Project*, http://www.presidency.ucsb.edu/ws/?pid=8531 (accessed July 24, 2010).

13. CTT, 491.

14. "Discussion of Catonsville Action by Rev. Paul Mayer, Mary Moylan, and George Mische," Milwaukee, Wisconsin [ca. July 1968], audio recording, Michael Dennis Cullen Papers, Department of Special Collections and University Archives, Marquette University, Milwaukee, WI (hereafter Cullen Papers).

15. *TOTCN*, 70; *DD*, 191–192.

16. CTT, 496–498.

17. *DD*, 192–193.

18. SAC, Minneapolis, to Director, FBI, July 8, 1968, JMD-FBI.

19. *DD*, 190–191.

20. SAC, Minneapolis, to Director, FBI, July 8, 1968, JMD-FBI.

21. *TOTCN*, 72–74.

22. G. Mische interview, *HAS*.

23. Rosemary Bannan, Interview with George Mische, October 8, 1968, BC-CU. Although it is not clearly marked as such, this appears to be one of the many interviews that Bannan conducted with the Nine for her book (with John Bannan) *Law, Morality and Vietnam: The Peace Militants and the Courts*, Bloomington: Indiana University Press, 1974.

24. CTT, 508; G. Mische interview, *HAS*.

25. William O'Connor interview, *IOAF*, February 1, 1999; Thomas Melville and Marjorie Melville interview, *IOAF*, July 17, 1999.

26. "The Washington Newsletter," July 1968, BC-CU.

27. Thomas Melville and Marjorie Melville, *Whose Heaven, Whose Earth?*, New York: Alfred A. Knopf, 1971, 7.

28. *WHWE?*, 11–12.

29. Thomas Melville, "Thomas R. Melville" [ca. 1968], BC-CU. This is one of the many autobiographical statements that the lawyers defending the Catonsville Nine asked them to prepare as they readied for their trial and subsequent sentencing.

30. *WHWE?*, 15.

31. Richard Ostling, "Those Beleaguered Maryknollers," *Time*, July 6, 1981, 36.

32. *TOTCN*, 51.

33. *NYT*, June 16, 1968.

34. T. Melville, "Thomas R. Melville," BC-CU; Hinckle, "Lives of the Baltimore Saints," 11–16.

35. *WHWE?*, 22–24.

36. Ibid., 30–31.

37. Ibid., 70–83.

38. *TOTCN*, 52.

39. *WHWE?*, 128–129.

40. Ibid., 153.

41. Ibid., 39.

42. *WHWE?*, 62–63.

43. T. Melville, "Thomas R. Melville," BC-CU; *WHWE?*, 62–63.

44. *WHWE?*, 62.

45. Rosemary Bannan, Interview with Thomas and Marjorie Melville, May 26, 1969, BC-CU, 1–28.

46. *WHWE?*, 100–102.

47. Ibid., 155–171.

48. Ibid., 215–216; Bannan, Interview with Thomas and Marjorie Melville, 1–28, BC-CU.

49. *WHWE?*, 227–228.

50. Denis Carroll, *What Is Liberation Theology?* Dublin: Mercier Press, 1987, 7–30.

51. Gustavo Gutiérrez, *Gustavo Gutiérrez: Essential Writings*, Maryknoll, NY: Orbis Books, 1996, 28–30.

52. *WHWE?*, 263–264. I use the terms *peasant* and *peasantry* occasionally to reflect the language used by the Melvilles at the time.

53. Hinckle, "Lives of the Baltimore Saints," 11–16.

54. *WHWE?*, 266–267; Bannan, Interview with Thomas and Marjorie Melville, 1–28, BC-CU.

55. *WHWE?*, 268.

56. CTT, 606–608.

57. Ibid.

58. "Eulogies Honoring John Hogan," October 2008 (private video recording in possession of author).

59. CTT, 609; John Hogan, Oral History Interview with Joan Cavanagh, Greater New Haven Labor History Association, March 10, 2005 (hereafter Hogan oral history). I am grateful to Cavanagh and Joan Hogan for their help in accessing this invaluable resource.

60. T. Melville, "Thomas R. Melville," BC-CU.

61. CTT, 611–612.

62. T. Melville, "Thomas R. Melville," BC-CU; CTT, 611–612.

63. CTT, 607–613; Hogan oral history.

64. Hogan oral history; Robert McAfee Brown, Abraham J. Heschel, and Michael Novak, *Vietnam: Crisis of Conscience*, New York: Association Press, 1967.

65. Hogan oral history.

66. *WHWE?*, 268.

67. Ibid., 269–270.

68. *NYT*, January 19, 21, and 22, 1968.

69. Hogan oral history.

70. Report of John Mulvaney, "Registration Act—Guatemala," April 17, 1968, JMD-FBI. This report quotes the February 28, 1968, issue of *Siempre*.

71. *NCR*, January 31, 1968.

72. *Los Angeles Times*, April 5, 1968.

73. Ibid., February 11, 1968.

74. Hogan oral history; SAC, New York, to SAC, Baltimore, May 22, 1968, JMD-FBI.

Chapter 6

1. *NYT*, May 4, 1968, 10.
2. *WHWE?*, 290–291.
3. Melville and Melville interview, *IOAF*.
4. Hogan oral history.
5. Ibid.
6. Ibid.; John Hogan interview, *IOAF* [ca. 1999].
7. Hogan oral history; Hogan interview, *IOAF*.
8. Hogan oral history; Hogan interview, *IOAF*.
9. Melville and Melville interview, *IOAF*.
10. Mary Moylan, "Being Underground," *Peace News*, July 3, 1970, 2. I also have relied on slightly different versions of Moylan's account that have been reprinted in Rosalyn Baxandall and Linda Gordon, eds., *Dear Sisters: Dispatches From the Women's Liberation Movement*, New York: Basic Books, 2001, 42–43; and (with the title "Underground Woman") in Mitchell Goodman, ed., *The Movement Toward a New America: The Beginnings of a Long Revolution*, Philadelphia: Pilgrim Press, 1970, 61–63.
11. *BS*, November 25, 1961. Joseph Moylan sometimes has been referred to as a "reporter for the *Baltimore Sun*," but that description seems to conflate two separate jobs. He did work for the paper, but as a secretary, before he began working as a court stenographer.
12. *BS*, July 14, 1995.
13. *BS*, September 26, 1962.
14. Ibid.
15. Ibid.
16. Piero Gleijeses, "'Flee! The White Giants Are Coming!': The United States, the Mercenaries, and the Congo, 1964–65," *Diplomatic History* (Spring 1994): 207–237.
17. Ibid.
18. Moylan, "Being Underground," 2. Moylan wrote that the American planes were "piloted by Cubans," but this might have been a misapprehension on her part. Cubans proxies were fighting in the Congo—it was said that Che Guevara was among them—but they were fighting for the rebels.
19. Moylan, "Being Underground," 2; Moylan, "Underground Woman," 61–63. These two essays are similar but not identical; they appear to have been edited differently. I've chosen to rely on both.
20. CTT, 545–548; Moylan, "Being Underground," 2.
21. *NCR*, November 10, 1995, 14.
22. Helene Mische interview, *HAS* [ca. 2007].
23. H. Mische interview, *HAS*; Moylan, "Underground Woman," 61–63; Moylan, "Being Underground," 2.
24. H. Mische interview, *HAS*; Moylan, "Underground Woman," 61–63; Moylan, "Being Underground," 2.
25. H. Mische interview, *HAS*; Grenville Whitman interview, *HAS*, August 5, 2009.
26. H. Mische interview, *HAS*; *BS*, July 14, 1995.
27. Ibid.
28. *TOTCN*, 64.
29. Moylan, "Underground Woman," 61–63; Moylan, "Being Underground," 2; *TOTCN*, 64; CTT, 541–563.

30. CTT, 554–555.

31. "Discussion of Catonsville Action," Cullen Papers.

32. CTT, 554–555.

33. "Discussion of Catonsville Action," Cullen Papers.

34. Rosemary Bannan, Interview with Mary Moylan [ca. 1969], BC-CU, 1–23.

35. CTT, 556–557; *TOTCN*, 65–66.

36. Bannan interview with George Mische, BC-CU.

37. Hogan oral history; Hogan interview, *IOAF*.

38. Ibid.

39. Theodore Draper, *Abuse of Power*, New York: Viking Press, 1967.

40. Hogan oral history; Hogan interview, *IOAF*.

41. Ibid.; Rosalie Troester, Interview of Tom Lewis, June 10, 1988, DD-CWC. An edited version of this interview appears in Troester, *Voices From the Catholic Worker*, and I have cited that separately where appropriate.

42. Brother David Darst, "Some Thoughts on Burning Draft Files," *WIN*, July 1968, 4–5.

43. *WHWE?*, 295.

44. G. Mische interview, *HAS*.

45. O'Connor oral history, MDHS; Joe Tropea, "Hit and Stay: The Catonsville Nine and Baltimore Four Actions Revisited," *Baltimore City Paper*, May 14, 2008, available at http://www.citypaper.com/news/story.asp?id=15722 (accessed August 4, 2010).

46. *WHWE?*, 295.

47. Hogan oral history; Hogan interview, *IOAF*.

48. *WHWE?*, 295–296.

49. Ibid., 294–296; Hogan oral history.

50. Richard McSorley, *My Path to Peace and Justice: An Autobiography*, Marion, SD: Fortkamp/Rose Hill Books, 1997, 118–120.

51. *WHWE?*, 296.

52. Ibid., 296–297.

53. Ibid.

54. Melville and Melville interview, *IOAF*.

55. Ibid.

56. *WHWE?*, 297–298.

57. Ibid., 298–299.

58. Ibid., 298–299.

59. CTT, 635.

60. *WHWE?*, 299.

61. H. Mische interview, *HAS*.

62. Lewis oral history, CU, 57.

Chapter 7

1. *TDIP*, 33, 53; Daniel Berrigan, "Pretrial Statement" [ca. 1968], 1–16, BC-CU.

2. *TDIP*, 78–86; Polner and O'Grady, *Disarmed and Dangerous*, 63–66.

3. *TDIP*, 84–86; Polner and O'Grady, *Disarmed and Dangerous*, 63–66.

4. *TDIP*, 98–99; P. Berrigan, "Pretrial Statement," 1–16.

5. *TDIP*, 104–105.

6. Ronald Knox, *God and the Atom*, London: Sheed & Ward, 1945.

7. *TDIP*, 106–108; Daniel Berrigan, "Peace Preacher," in Jeff Kisseloff, ed., *Generation on Fire: Voices of Protest From the 1960s, An Oral History*, Lexington: University Press of Kentucky, 2007, 106.

8. *TOTCN*, 34; *DD*, 67; Polner and O'Grady, *Disarmed and Dangerous*, 88–92.

9. *DD*, 67–69; D. Berrigan, "Peace Preacher," 108; Daniel Berrigan and Robert Coles, *The Geography of Faith: Conversations Between Daniel Berrigan, When Underground, and Robert Coles*, Boston: Beacon Press, 1971, 120–121.

10. *DD*, 67–69; Polner and O'Grady, *Disarmed and Dangerous*, 90–91.

11. *DD*, 69–70.

12. *DD*, 71; D. Berrigan, "Pretrial Statement," 1–16.

13. *DD*, 72.

14. *TDIP*, 161.

15. Polner and O'Grady, *Disarmed and Dangerous*, 107–108.

16. *TDIP*, 170; D. Berrigan, "Pretrial Statement," 1–16.

17. Mitchell K. Hall, *Because of Their Faith: CALCAV and Religious Opposition to the Vietnam War*, New York: Columbia University Press, 1990, 15.

18. *NYT*, December 5 and 12, 1965; *DD*, 102; *TDIP*, 180–182; D. Berrigan, "Pretrial Statement," 1–16.

19. D. Berrigan, "Peace Preacher," 108–109; George Anderson, "Dan Berrigan's Latin American Exile," *America: The National Catholic Weekly*, November 5, 2010, http://www.americamagazine.org/blog/entry.cfm?blog_id=2&entry_id=3502. This episode also has been described as having happened in Lima, Peru.

20. *TDIP*, 183–185.

21. *NYT*, March 11, 1966.

22. Hall, *Because of Their Faith*, 24–25; *NYT*, May 16, 1966.

23. *NYT*, February 1, 1967.

24. Polner and O'Grady, *Disarmed and Dangerous*, 156–157.

25. *TDIP*, 206–214.

26. *NCR*, December 20, 1967.

27. Howard Zinn, *You Can't Be Neutral on a Moving Train: A Personal History of Our Times*, Boston: Beacon Press, 1994, 126–128.

28. Zinn, *You Can't Be Neutral*, 126–128.

29. D. Berrigan, "Peace Preacher," 108.

30. Daniel Berrigan, *Night Flight to Hanoi: War Diary With 11 Poems*, New York, Harper & Row, 1968, 40; Berrigan, "Peace Preacher," 111.

31. Polner and O'Grady, *Disarmed and Dangerous*, 183.

32. *TDIP*, 216–217; *DD*, 131.

33. *FTLW*, 91.

34. *TDIP*, 218.

35. D. Berrigan, "Peace Preacher," 111–112; Polner and O'Grady, *Disarmed and Dangerous*, 196.

36. Daniel Berrigan, "Open Sesame: My Life and Good Times," *Katallagete* (Winter 1968–1969): 19–25; *BS*, May 18, 1998.

37. Troester, Interview of Tom Lewis, DD-CWC.

38. Ibid.

39. D. Berrigan, "Pretrial Statement," 13, BC-CU.

40. Author interview with Tom Melville, June 28, 2010 (in possession of author); Charles Meconis, Interview with George Mische, November 1975, Murray Polner Collection, DePaul University Special Collections and Archives, Chicago, IL, 1–4.

41. *PJ*, 15.

42. Troester, *Voices From the Catholic Worker*, 45; *TOTCN*, 44.

43. David Maraniss, *They Marched Into Sunlight: War and Peace Vietnam and America October 1967*, New York: Simon & Schuster, 2003, 72–73.

44. *WHWE?*, 300; *TOTCN*, 33–34.

45. Troester, *Voices From the Catholic Worker*, 45.

46. Melville and Melville interview, *IOAF*; O'Connor interview, *IOAF*.

47. *TOTCN*, 33–34; Polner and O'Grady, *Disarmed and Dangerous*, 196.

48. Tropea, "Hit and Stay," *City Paper*.

49. *DD*, 130.

50. *NYT*, November 14 and December 1, 1967, and January 3, 1968; SAC, Baltimore, to Director, FBI, June 13, 1968, JMD-FBI.

51. G. Mische interview, *HAS*; Troester, *Voices From the Catholic Worker*, 45; Lewis oral history, CU, 58.

52. D. Berrigan, "Peace Preacher," 112.

53. *WHWE?*, 299.

54. *TOTCN*, 93–94.

55. *DD*, 132.

56. *NCR*, November 12, 1969.

57. Lewis oral history, CU, 59–60; Daniel Berrigan, *Lights On in the House of the Dead*, New York: Doubleday, 1974, 213.

58. Lewis oral history, CU, 59–60.

59. Tropea, "Hit and Stay," *City Paper*.

60. Melville and Melville interview, *IOAF*; O'Connor interview, *IOAF*.

Chapter 8

1. Mary Murphy interview, *IOAF* [ca. 1999]; Interview with Mary Murphy, Friends of the Catonsville Library Oral History Program, November 2, 1972, Friends of the Catonsville Library Collection, Baltimore County Public Library, Catonsville Branch (hereafter Murphy oral history, FCLC). I am grateful to the Catonsville Library for granting permission to use this interview and myriad other materials relating to the Catonsville Nine.

2. Murphy interview, *IOAF*; Murphy oral history, FCLC.

3. Ibid.

4. Ibid.

5. Ibid.

6. CTT, 309; *Catonsville Times* [n.d. clipping ca. March 1972], FCLC.

7. Murphy interview, *IOAF*; Murphy oral history, FCLC; *Catonsville Times* [n.d. ca. March 1972].

8. CTT, 318; Katherine Kindervatter, "Procedures to Follow If a Local Board Picketed or Sit-Down Strike Occurs on Local Board Premises," July 28, 1967, FCLC.

9. Katherine Kindervatter, "Safeguarding Cover Sheets, Registration Certificates and Local Board Stamps," March 6, 1968, FCLC.

10. O'Connor interview, *IOAF*; Tropea, "Hit and Stay," *City Paper*; Polner and O'Grady, *Disarmed and Dangerous*, 197–198; Memorandum, "FBI New York," June 10, 1968, JMD-FBI.

11. *WHWE?*, 300.

12. Moylan, "Being Underground," 2.

13. Ibid.

14. Murphy interview, *IOAF*; Murphy oral history, FCLC.

15. *DD*, 45–46.

16. G. Mische interview, *HAS*.

17. Murphy interview, *IOAF*; Murphy oral history, FCLC.

18. Hogan oral history; Hogan interview, *IOAF*.

19. Ibid.

20. Murphy interview, *IOAF*; Murphy oral history, FCLC.

21. Report of SA John Hanson, May 23, 1968, JMD-FBI; Hogan oral history; Hogan interview, *IOAF*.

22. Murphy interview, *IOAF*; Murphy oral history, FCLC.

23. Interview with Phyllis Morsberger, Friends of the Catonsville Library Oral History Program, October 25, 1976, FCLC (hereafter Morsberger oral history, FCLC).

24. Report of SA John Hanson, JMD-FBI; Morsberger oral history, FCLC; Moylan, "Underground Woman," 61–63.

25. *BS*, May 25, 2008; Murphy oral history, FCLC; Morsberger oral history, FCLC.

26. Murphy interview, *IOAF*; Murphy oral history, FCLC.

27. Morsberger oral history, FCLC.

28. Patrick McGrath, "Napalm in Baltimore," *Ave Maria*, June 8, 1968, 16–17, 21.

29. Ibid.

30. Ibid.

31. Author interview with Grenville Whitman, July 14, 2009 (in possession of author); Grenville Whitman interview, *HAS*, August 5, 2009.

32. *TDIP*, 220–221.

33. *NCR*, May 29, 1968.

34. Ibid.

35. Ibid.

36. Ibid.

37. Ibid.

38. McGrath, "Napalm in Baltimore," 16–17, 21.

39. Ibid.

40. Hogan oral history; Hogan interview, *IOAF*.

41. G. Mische interview, *HAS*.

42. Ibid.

43. Murphy interview, *IOAF*; Murphy oral history, FCLC.

Chapter 9

1. McGrath, "Napalm in Baltimore," 16–17, 21.

2. Sachs, *IOAF*. The DVD version of Sachs's film includes a separate segment featuring the unedited footage shot by WBAL-TV, titled "News Footage: Patrick McGrath."

3. "News Footage: Patrick McGrath."

4. *Baltimore Peace and Freedom News*, May 23, 1968, 12.

5. Brendan Walsh interview, *HAS*, September 1, 2008.

6. Murphy interview, *IOAF*; Murphy oral history, FCLC.

7. Interview with Jean Walsh, Friends of the Catonsville Library Oral History Program, March 30, 1973, FCLC (hereafter Walsh oral history, FCLC).

8. Walsh oral history, FCLC.

9. Ibid.

10. Ibid.

11. "News Footage: Patrick McGrath."

12. Moylan, "Being Underground," 2.

13. John Hogan interview, *HAS*, May 17, 2008; Hogan oral history; Hogan interview, *IOAF*.

14. "Report of Fire," Baltimore County Fire Department, May 17, 1968, JMD-FBI.

15. Melville and Melville interview, *IOAF*.

16. Report of the FBI Laboratory, May 28, 1968, PB-FBI.

17. Ibid.

18. *DD*, 47.

19. *BS*, May 18, 1968.

20. Walsh oral history, FCLC.

21. Ibid.

22. Ibid.

23. *WHWE?*, 5.

24. Ibid.

25. Walsh oral history, FCLC.

26. *FTLW*, 96; G. Mische interview, *HAS*.

27. "Daniel Berrigan on the Catonsville Nine," Extended interview to accompany *William Kunstler: Disturbing the Universe*, http://www.pbs.org/pov/disturbingtheuniverse/interview_berrigan.php (accessed January 31, 2011).

28. Morsberger oral history, FCLC.

29. Hogan interview, *IOAF*.

30. Bannan, Interview with Thomas and Marjorie Melville, 1–28, BC-CU.

31. Report of SA [redacted], May 20, 1968, JMD-FBI.

32. G. Mische interview, *HAS*.

33. *BS*, May 19, 1968.

34. *FTLW*, 97.

35. Ibid.

36. Moylan, "Being Underground," 2.

37. Ibid.

38. *Washington Post*, May 30, 1971.

39. Rosemary Bannan, Interview with Mary Moylan [ca. 1968], BC-CU, 1–23.

40. *DD*, 49; *PJ*, 22.

41. *BS*, May 19, 1968.

42. Daniel Berrigan, *America Is Hard to Find*, New York: Doubleday, 1972, 180; Daniel Berrigan interview, *IOAF* [ca. 1999].

43. D. Berrigan, "Pretrial Statement," 13.

44. *DD*, 49; Brother David Darst to Joann Malone, May 21, 1968, in Charles Darst, ed., *All in the Passing of Now: The Collected Writings of James McGinnis Darst*, [unpublished ms., ca. 1975], 36. Chuck Darst has my thanks for generously sharing this incredible source.

45. Brother David Darst, "Some Thoughts on Drastic and Public Civil Disobedience From the Baltimore County Jail," *Ave Maria*, July 20, 1968, 8–10.

46. Philip Berrigan, "Letter from a Baltimore Jail," *Christianity and Crisis*, July 22, 1968, 168–170.

47. *BS*, May 20, 1968.

48. *BS*, May 23 and 25, 1968.

49. Ibid.; Philip Berrigan to Daniel Berrigan, May 28, 1968, BC-CU.

50. *Baltimore Peace and Freedom News*, June 6, 1968, 1–2.

51. Lewis oral history, CU, 61–62.

52. *BS*, May 25, 1968.

53. Newspapers are quoted in John Deedy, "News and Views," *Commonweal*, June 21, 1968, 394.

54. Dorothy Day to Daniel Berrigan, May 31, 1968, BC-CU.

55. *BS*, May 30, 1968.

56. Tom Lewis, "A Free Ride to Lewisburg Prison Compliments of the U.S. Government" [ca. 1968], BC-CU.

Chapter 10

1. Dan Finnerty, "Catonsville 9 vs. Boston 5: A Question of Tactics," *Philadelphia Resistance Review*, October 1968, 1–3.

2. *Evening Sun* (Baltimore), May 21, 1968.

3. McGrath, "Napalm in Baltimore," 21.

4. Cheryl Dunigan, "Expressions of Faith," *Catonsville Patch*, December 10, 2010, available at http://catonsville.patch.com/articles/expressions-of-faith (accessed February 3, 2011).

5. *Catonsville Times*, October 10 and 24, 1968.

6. *BS*, May 20, 1968.

7. [Redacted] to J. Edgar Hoover, May 21, 1968, PB-FBI; J. Edgar Hoover to [redacted], May 28, 1968, PB-FBI.

8. Mills, *And Justice for All*, 344.

9. *BS*, May 5, 1998.

10. J. Justin Gustainis, "Crime as Rhetoric: The Trial of the Catonsville Nine," in Robert Hariman, ed., *Popular Trials: Rhetoric, Mass Media, and the Law*, Tuscaloosa: University of Alabama Press, 1990, 164–178; "Has the Church Lost Its Soul? *Newsweek*, October 4, 1971, 188–189.

11. Giese interview.

12. John F. Hanson, Memorandum, June 27, 1968, JMD-FBI; *Evening Sun* (Baltimore), May 21, 1968.

13. *NCR*, June 5, 1968; Philip Berrigan to Daniel Berrigan, June 10, 1968, BC-CU.

14. *Catholic Review*, quoted in "Paper Assails Draft Protest," May 27, 1968, PB-FBI.

15. Walker Percy, "Walker Percy," *Commonweal*, September 4, 1971, 431.

16. Penelope Adams Moon, "Loyal Sons and Daughters of God? American Catholics Debate Catholic Anti-War Protest," *Peace & Change* 33 (2008): 1–30.

17. Moon, "Loyal Sons and Daughters," 12.

18. Berrigan and Coles, *Geography of Faith*, 12.

19. Ibid., 13.

20. Ibid., 12; Coles, "Thinking About Those Priests," in Casey and Nobile, *Berrigans*, 214–219.

21. "Civil Disobedience at Catonsville," *America*, October 26, 1968, 372–373.

22. "The Spoken Word, the Printed Word . . . and Napalm?" *Ave Maria*, June 8, 1968, 4.

23. *NCR*, June 5, 1968.

24. Ibid.

25. Michael Novak, "'Blue-Bleak Embers . . . Fall,'" in John C. Raines, ed., *Conspiracy: The Implications of the Harrisburg Trial for the Democratic Tradition*, New York: Harper & Row, 1974, 37–71.

26. Michael Novak, "Talkin' 'Bout My Generation," *First Things*, April 2009, 39–42.

27. *NCR*, July 10, 1968.

28. Robert Drinan, *Vietnam and Armageddon: Peace, War and the Christian Conscience*, New York: Sheen and Howard, 1970, 142.

29. *DD*, 50.

30. "Jesuits Voice Support for Fathers Berrigan and Companions," May 22, 1968, JMD-FBI.

31. Tom Cornell, "Nonviolent Napalm in Catonsville," *Catholic Worker*, June 1968, 1–2, 8.

32. Dorothy Day to Daniel Berrigan, May 31, 1968, BC-CU.

33. *DD*, 162–163.

34. Paul Elie, *The Life You Save May Be Your Own: An American Pilgrimage*, New York: Farrar, Straus and Giroux, 2004, 408–409; Nancy Roberts, *Dorothy Day and the Catholic Worker*, Albany: State University of New York Press, 1985, 160.

35. Roberts, *Dorothy Day and the Catholic Worker*, 160.

36. Thomas Merton, "Blessed Are the Meek: The Roots of Christian Nonviolence," *Fellowship*, May 1967, 18–22.

37. Thomas Merton to Daniel Berrigan, October 10, 1967, in *The Hidden Ground of Love: The Letters of Thomas Merton on Religious Experience and Social Concerns*, New York: Farrar, Straus and Giroux, 1985, 96–98.

38. Elie, *The Life You Save*, 408–409.

39. Merton's piece for *Ave Maria* is republished as part of "The Burning of Papers, the Human Conscience, and the Peace Movement," *Fellowship*, March 1969, 5–9, 30.

40. Daniel Berrigan, *Portraits of Those I Love*, New York: Crossroad, 1982, 13; *FTLW*, 98.

41. Lewis interview, *IOAF*.

42. SAC, Baltimore, "Investigation at Scene," May 20–24, 1968, PB-FBI.

43. Ibid.

44. Report of SA John F. Hanson, May 23, 1968, JMD-FBI.

45. Murphy interview, *IOAF*; Murphy oral history, FCLC.

46. CTT, 292–332.

47. "Baltimore Nine" to Local Board 33 Clerks [ca. May 1968], FCLC.

48. *PJ*, 116–118.

49. P. Berrigan, "Napalming Draft Files," 20–21.

50. Mary Murphy, Statement, November 27, 1968, BC-CU; Mary Murphy to Nathan Walkomir, October 28, 1968, FCLC.

51. Tom Lewis to Mary Murphy, November 2, 1968, FCLC.

52. Philip Berrigan to "Miss Murphy," November 1, 1968, FCLC.

53. Murphy interview, *IOAF*; Murphy oral history, FCLC.

54. Ibid.

55. Murphy Statement, BC-CU.

56. Murphy interview, *IOAF*; Murphy oral history, FCLC.

57. Ibid.

58. *BS*, May 27, 1968; Walsh oral history, FCLC.

59. Walsh oral history, FCLC.

60. Morsberger oral history, FCLC.

Chapter 11

1. William Kunstler, *My Life as a Radical Lawyer*, Secaucus, NJ: Carol, 1994, 57.

2. Ibid.

3. Ibid., xiii; William Kunstler, *Politics on Trial: Five Famous Trials of the 20th Century*, New York: Ocean Press, 2003, ix.

4. Kunstler, *My Life*, xiv–xvi; David J. Langum, *William M. Kunstler: The Most Hated Lawyer in America*, New York: New York University Press, 1999.

5. Kunstler, *My Life*, 166.

6. Kunstler, "Some Thoughts About the Berrigans et al.," in Halpert and Murray, eds., *Witness of the Berrigans*, 166.

7. Ibid., 167.

8. Ibid.

9. Ibid.

10. Father Robert Drinan often was referenced as another member of the defense team, but there is little evidence to suggest that he actively participated in the case.

11. *NYT*, December 23, 1955; Newsletter, Syracuse Peace Council, November 23, 1962, BC-CU.

12. Harrop A. Freeman, "The Constitutionality of Peacetime Conscription," *Virginia Law Review* 40 (1944–1945): 40–82.

13. *Los Angeles Times*, April 24, 1966.

14. *Florence* (Alabama) *Times and Tri-Cities Daily*, February 14, 1980.

15. Ibid. Buchman's radical activities are discussed capably in Vernon L. Pedersen's *The Communist Party in Maryland, 1919–57*, Urbana: University of Illinois Press, 2001.

16. *Chicago Sun-Times*, August 11, 1989; *Chicago Tribune*, February 25, 1970.

17. Harrop Freeman to Harold Buchman, September 14, 1968, BC-CU.

18. Mills, *And Justice for All*, 346–347.

19. Philip Berrigan to Harold Buchman [ca. August, 1968], BC-CU.

20. Daniel Berrigan, "Some Pertinent Facts: Catonsville Nine Action" [ca. 1968], BC-CU.

21. D. Berrigan, "Some Pertinent Facts," BC-CU.

22. Ibid.

23. Kunstler, "Some Thoughts About the Berrigans," 170.

24. Kunstler, *My Life*, 188–189.

25. Ibid., 189.

26. Kunstler, "Some Thoughts," 168–170.

27. Kunstler, *My Life*, 188–189; Kunstler, "Some Thoughts," 168–170.
28. *PJ*, 66–67; Philip Berrigan interview, *IOAF* [ca. 1999].
29. O'Connor oral history, MDHS, 1–25; O'Connor interview, *IOAF*.
30. Philip Berrigan to Daniel Berrigan [ca. September 1967], BC-CU.
31. *PJ*, 100–106.
32. Ibid.
33. Ibid., 103–105.
34. Philip Berrigan to Daniel Berrigan [ca. August 1968], BC-CU.
35. Mills, *And Justice for All*, 344–351.
36. Ibid.
37. *Washington Post*, March 18, 1986; *BS*, November 19, 1969.
38. *BS*, November 19, 1969.
39. Stephen Sachs interview, *HAS*, August 29, 2009.
40. *BS*, May 17, 1993.
41. Rosemary Bannan, Interview with Stephen Sachs, May 13, 1969, BC-CU.
42. *Baltimore Afro-American*, January 16, 1960 and June 17, 1978.
43. *PJ*, 114; G. Mische interview, *HAS*.
44. Author interview with Barnet Skolnik, June 21, 2010 (in possession of author).
45. Ibid.
46. Ibid.
47. Ibid.
48. Spiro Agnew, *Go Quietly . . . or Else*, New York: Morrow, 1980, 50.

Chapter 12

1. Author interview with Chuck Darst, January 15, 2010 (in possession of author); author interview with Guy Darst, January 8, 2010 (in possession of author); Brother David Darst Center, "Background on Brother David Darst," 2007, available at http://www.brdavid-darstcenter.org/david_darst.html (accessed January 7, 2010).
2. C. Darst interview; G. Darst interview; Darst Center, "Background."
3. Ibid.
4. Ibid.
5. Ibid.
6. Ibid.; Brother David Darst, "The Love Letter of 1967," in *AITPN*, 1–5.
7. John Koller to Brother David Darst Center [n.d.] (in possession of author).
8. John Ortbal, "The Catholic Radical Left of the Sixties: A Failed Revolution but a Moral Victory?" unpublished paper, University of Chicago Divinity School, March 13, 1996, 7, 9; Author interview with Joseph Forgue, June 3, 2010 (in possession of author).
9. Brother David Darst, "The Brother," *Commonweal*, June 4, 1965, 366–367.
10. *NCR*, November 12, 1969. Shortly after Darst's death in 1969, *NCR* published an extensive interview that Darst had completed with Harry Cargas of St. Louis University. It ran under the title "The Legacy of Brother David Darst."
11. "David Darst" [interview transcript ca. 1968–69], BC-CU.
12. Michael Novak, "Draft Board Theology," *Commonweal*, July 28, 1967, 467–468; *NCR*, November 12, 1969; David Darst, "Letter to a Young Bozo on Life as a Journey Into Mystery," in *AITPN*, 7–9. The "bozo" to whom the letter is affectionately addressed apparently is his brother, Chuck.

13. CTT, 391; Darst, "Letter to a Young Bozo," 7–9.

14. SAC, St. Louis, to SAC, Baltimore, May 21, 1968, JMD-FBI.

15. *NCR*, November 12, 1969; "David Darst," BC-CU.

16. C. Darst interview; *NCR*, November 12, 1969.

17. *NCR*, November 12, 1969.

18. Ibid.

19. Ibid.

20. Darst, "Some Thoughts," 4–5.

21. *NCR*, June 12, 1968; "David Darst," BC-CU.

22. Report of SA [redacted], June 10, 1968, JMD-FBI; *NCR*, November 12, 1969.

23. David Darst, "Notes From the St. Louis City Jail," June 19, 1968, in *AITPN*, 38–43.

24. Ibid.

25. Ibid.

26. Ibid.

27. Ibid.

28. Ibid.

29. Ibid.

30. Ibid.

31. *NCR*, August 7, 1968.

32. Ibid.

33. Ibid.

34. *NCR*, August 21, 1968.

35. Ibid.

36. *NCR*, September 4, 1968.

37. G. Darst interview.

38. Brother David Darst, "Non-Marital Sexual Expressions as Play and Humor in a Serious Society: Some Reflections on Contexts and Sexual Morality," *Pastoral Psychology*, March 1969, 52–55.

39. I have referenced a reprint of the article in Brother David Darst and Joseph Forgue, *Sexuality on the Island Earth*, New York: Paulist Press, 1970, 24–25.

40. James Forest, "Daniel Berrigan: The Poet and Prophet as Priest," in Halpert and Murray, *Witness of the Berrigans*, 84–110.

41. Meconis, *Clumsy Grace*, 25.

42. Ibid., 26.

43. Ibid., 26–27.

44. "An Interview with Robert Cunnane," in Halpert and Murray, *Witness of the Berrigans*, 45–46.

45. Meconis, *Clumsy Grace*, 27.

46. Francine du Plessix Gray, "The Ultra-Resistance," in Noam Chomsky, ed., *Trials of the Resistance*, New York: New York Review Books, 1970, 125–161.

47. Meconis, *Clumsy Grace*, 31.

Chapter 13

1. Meconis, *Clumsy Grace*, 24–26; "Discussion of Catonsville Action," Cullen Papers.

2. James Forest interview, *HAS*, October 11, 2009; Meconis, *Clumsy Grace*, 24–26; "Discussion of Catonsville Action," Cullen Papers.

3. Forest interview, *HAS*; Meconis, *Clumsy Grace*, 24–26; "Discussion of Catonsville Action," Cullen Papers.

4. *NCR*, September 18, 1968.

5. Randolph Lewis, *Emile de Antonio: Radical Filmmaker in Cold War America*, Madison: University of Wisconsin Press, 2000, 77.

6. SAC, Baltimore, to Director, FBI, October 1, 1968, BDC-FBI.

7. Albany to SAC, Baltimore, and Director, FBI, October 5, 1968, BDC-FBI.

8. Los Angeles to SAC, Baltimore, and Director, FBI, October 3, 1968, BDC-FBI.

9. Whitman interview.

10. Baltimore Defense Committee, "A National Call" [ca. 1968], BDC-FBI.

11. Baltimore Defense Committee, "Manifesto" [ca. 1968], BDC-FBI.

12. Baltimore Defense Committee, "Catonsville Nine Trial Set; Aggressive Confrontation Expected" [ca. 1968], BDC-FBI.

13. For this thumbnail sketch of Agnew's political career, I have relied primarily on Jules Witcover, *White Knight: The Rise of Spiro Agnew*, New York: Random House, 1972, and Richard Cohen and Witcover, *A Heartbeat Away: The Investigation and Resignation of Vice President Spiro T. Agnew*, New York: Viking Press, 1974.

14. Witcover, *White Knight*, 24.

15. Rick Perlstein, *Nixonland: The Rise of a President and the Fracturing of America*, New York: Simon & Schuster, 2008, 258.

16. Baltimore Defense Committee, "Catonsville Nine Trial Actions Set," September 25, 1968, BDC-FBI.

17. *NCR*, September 25, 1968.

18. Daniel Berrigan to Jim [Forest], September 10, 1968, BC-CU. Copies of this letter were sent to, among others, Howard Zinn, William Sloane Coffin, Gordon Zahn, Sister Corita, Dorothy Day, Robert Lowell, Rabbi Abraham Joshua Heschel, and Bishop James Pike.

19. Thomas Merton to Daniel Berrigan, September 10, 1968, in Merton, *Hidden Ground of Love*, 101.

20. *DD*, 155.

21. Laurie Dougherty, "Alpha & Omega: The Trial of the Catonsville Nine," *WIN*, November 1, 1968, 9–10.

22. *BS*, October 5, 1968.

23. *BS*, October 7, 1968.

24. O'Connor interview, *IOAF*; O'Connor oral history, MDHS, 1–25.

25. Garry Wills, *Nixon Agonistes: The Crisis of the Self-Made Man*, New York: Mariner Books, 2002, 44; Harold Buchman to Samuel Green, October 4, 1968, BC-CU.

26. Wills, *Nixon Agonistes*, 42–44.

27. Ibid.

28. *BS*, October 5, 1968.

29. Ibid.

30. *BS*, October 5 and 6, 1968.

31. *BS*, October 7, 1968.

32. Kenneth Durr, *Behind the Backlash: White Working-Class Politics in Baltimore, 1940–1980*, Chapel Hill: University of North Carolina Press, 2003, 131–132.

33. *BS*, May 9, 1995.

34. Whitman interview.

35. *Catholic Review* (Baltimore), October 11, 1968.

36. Wills, *Nixon Agonistes*, 42–46.

37. Anthony Towne, "Reflections on Two Trials," *Christian Century*, December 4, 1968, 1535–1539.

38. Wills, *Nixon Agonistes*, 42–46.

39. Michael Ketchum, "Baltimore," *Catholic Worker*, October, 1968, 1, 2.

40. Wills, *Nixon Agonistes*, 42–46; *BS*, October 7, 1968.

41. Ibid.

42. *Catholic Review* (Baltimore), October 11, 1968; *BS*, October 7, 1968.

43. Wills, *Nixon Agonistes*, 42–46.

44. Ibid.

45. William Stringfellow and Anthony Towne, *The Death and Life of Bishop Pike*, Garden City, NY: Doubleday, 1976, 39–41. I have drawn my entire anecdote about Pike's trip to Baltimore from this entertaining source.

Chapter 14

1. *BS*, March 12 and 13, 1992.

2. Ibid.

3. Roszel C. Thomsen, "The Integration of Baltimore's Polytechnic Institute: A Reminiscence," *Maryland Historical Magazine*, Fall 1984, 235–238.

4. *The Capital* (Annapolis, MD), June 23 and July 28, 1954; *BS*, March 12 and 13, 1992.

5. John Lewin, *The Baltimore Briefs*, Bloomington, IN: Trafford, 2009, 32–33; *BS*, July 3, 1994.

6. Lewin, *Baltimore Briefs*, 32–33.

7. James F. Schneider, "A Guide to the Clarence M. Mitchell, Jr., Courthouse, Baltimore, Maryland," Baltimore Courthouse and Law Museum Foundation, Inc., 2009, available at http://www.baltocts.sailorsite.net/about/courthouseguide.pdf (accessed August 23, 2010).

8. *NCR*, October 16, 1968.

9. Stringfellow and Towne, *Death and Life of Bishop Pike*, 39–41.

10. *DD*, 166.

11. Thelma Nason, "The Trial of the Catonsville Nine," *Johns Hopkins Magazine*, Fall 1968, 27–32.

12. *DD*, 166.

13. CTT, 93–107.

14. *Washington Post*, October 8, 1968; *DD*, 172.

15. *NYT*, October 8, 1968.

16. TOTCN, 3–4.

17. TOTCN, 4–9.

18. TOTCN, 4–9; *NYT*, October 11, 1968.

19. Day, *Duty of Delight*, 429–430.

20. CTT, 202–209.

21. *Washington Post*, October 8, 1968; *BS*, October 8, 1968.

22. Baltimore Defense Committee, "Pine Trees, Rattlesnakes and Revolution: A Word About Our Flags" [ca. 1968], BDC-FBI.

23. *Washington Post*, October 8, 1968; *BS*, October 8, 1968.

24. Barbara Deming, "Trial by Autopsy," *Liberation*, December 1968, 6–11.

25. Elizabeth Fee, Linda Shopes, and Linda Zeidman, eds., *The Baltimore Book: New Views of Local History*, Philadelphia: Temple University Press, 1991, 197–199.

26. *Baltimore City Paper*, May 21, 2008.

27. *Washington Post*, October 8, 1968; *BS*, October 8, 1968.

28. Nason, "Trial of the Catonsville Nine," 27–32.

29. *Baltimore City Paper*, May 21, 2008.

30. Report of SA [redacted] on Baltimore Defense Committee, January 31, 1969, BDC-FBI.

31. *BS*, October 8, 1968; *NCR*, October 16, 1968.

32. Dougherty, "Alpha & Omega," 9–10.

33. Wills, *Nixon Agonistes*, 45–46.

34. Nason, "Trial of the Catonsville Nine," 27.

35. Meconis, *Clumsy Grace*, 33–34.

36. Ibid., 34; *NYT*, February 21, 1971.

37. James Carroll, *House of War: The Pentagon and the Disastrous Rise of American Power*, Boston: Houghton Mifflin, 2006, 320.

38. Nason, "Trial of the Catonsville Nine," 27–32.

39. Ibid.

40. Philip Berrigan, "Statement—Phil Berrigan SSJ—Catonsville Nine Rally," October 7, 1968, BC-CU.

41. Federal Bureau of Investigation, "Baltimore Defense Committee," October 9, 1968, BDC-FBI.

42. *Washington Post*, October 8, 1968; *BS*, October 8, 1968.

43. Ibid.

44. *BS*, October 8, 1968; Dougherty, "Alpha & Omega," 9–10.

45. Dougherty, "Alpha & Omega," 9–10.

46. Wills, *Nixon Agonistes*, 47–48.

47. Deming, "Trial by Autopsy," 6.

48. *Catholic Review* (Baltimore), October 11, 1968.

49. Report of SA [redacted] on Baltimore Defense Committee, January 31, 1969, BDC-FBI; Stringfellow and Towne, *Death and Life of Bishop Pike*, 42–44.

50. *NCR*, October 16, 1968; *DD*, 162–163.

51. *DD*, 162–163.

52. *DD*, 163–164.

53. *DD*, 163–165.

54. Ibid.

55. Wills, *Nixon Agonistes*, 49–50; *Baltimore Afro-American*, October 8, 1968.

56. *Baltimore Afro-American*, October 8, 1968; Wills, *Nixon Agonistes*, 49–50.

57. Wills, *Nixon Agonistes*, 58.

58. Ibid.; *DD*, 164–165.

Chapter 15

1. Dan Finlay, "Notes on the Catonsville Trial" [ca. 1968], BC-CU.

2. *NYT*, October 16, 1968.

3. Ibid.

4. CTT, 214–224.

5. *PJ*, 115.

6. CTT, 252–292.

7. Ibid.; *DD*, 173.

8. CTT, 236–252; *PJ*, 116–117.

9. CTT, 269–270.

10. Dougherty, "Alpha & Omega," 9–10.

11. *DD*, 173.

12. CTT, 292–332; *TOTCN*, 13–15; Murphy oral history, FCLC.

13. CTT, 292–332; *TOTCN*, 13–15.

14. Ibid.

15. CTT, 292–332; *TOTCN*, 13–15; Murphy oral history, FCLC.

16. *PJ*, 117–118.

17. Ibid.

18. Daniel Berrigan and Tom Lewis, *Trial Poems*, Boston: Beacon Press, 1970, n.p.

19. Murphy oral history, FCLC.

20. CTT, 332–355.

21. Ibid.; Morsberger oral history, FCLC; *DD*, 173–174.

22. *DD*, 174.

23. CTT, 229–230.

24. *NYT*, October 9, 1968.

25. *DD*, 169; *Washington Post*, October 9, 1968.

26. *BS*, October 9, 1969.

27. CTT, 224–235.

28. Ibid.

29. *DD*, 177.

30. CTT, 386–421; *TOTCN*, 33–34; *BS*, October 9, 1969.

31. CTT, 386–421.

32. CTT, 386–421; *TOTCN*, 33–34; *BS*, October 9, 1969.

33. CTT, 386–421; *DD*, 177–179; *TOTCN*, 33–34.

34. CTT, 386–421; *DD*, 177–179; *TOTCN*, 34–37.

35. Ibid.

36. Ibid.

37. CTT, 395–399.

38. CTT, 386–421; *TOTCN*, 34–37.

39. Koller to Darst Center; *DD*, 177–179.

40. Ibid.

41. *BS*, October 9, 1968.

42. Ibid.; Baltimore Peace Action Center, "You Don't Have to Go!" [ca. 1968], BDC-FBI.

43. *PJ*, 118–119.

44. Towne, "Reflections on Two Trials," 1535–1539.

45. FBI, "Baltimore Defense Committee," October 9, 1968, BDC-FBI.

46. Baltimore Defense Committee, "Schedule of Activities During Catonsville 9 Trial Week" [ca. 1968], BDC-FBI.

47. Dougherty, "Alpha & Omega," 9–10; *BS*, October 9, 1968.

48. Ketchum, "Baltimore," 1–2; *BS*, October 9, 1968.

49. Dougherty, "Alpha & Omega," 9–10; Towne, "Reflections on Two Trials," 1535–1539.

50. Troester, *Voices From the Catholic Worker*, 46; Meconis, *Clumsy Grace*, 34.

51. Deming, "Trial by Autopsy," 11.

52. *DD*, 174–175.

53. *DD*, 175.

54. Deming, "Trial by Autopsy," 6.

55. *BS*, October 9, 1968.

Chapter 16

1. Nason, "Trial of the Catonsville Nine," 29; *DD*, 197.

2. Troester interview with Tom Lewis, DD-CWC.

3. CTT, 424–481; *DD*, 203.

4. CTT, 424–481; *DD*, 204.

5. CTT, 424–481; *DD*, 203–207; *TOTCN*, 21–31; *BS*, October 10, 1968; *NYT*, October 10, 1968.

6. *DD*, 203–207; *TOTCN*, 21–31; *BS*, October 10, 1968; *NYT*, October 10, 1968.

7. *PJ*, 119–120.

8. Richard Shaull, "Resistance and the Third World," in Catonsville Nine–Milwaukee Fourteen Defense Committee, *Delivered in Resistance*, New Haven, CT: Advocate Press, 1969, 60–64.

9. CTT, 481–512; *DD*, 190–194; *TOTCN*, 69–75; *BS*, October 10, 1968; *NYT*, October 10, 1968.

10. Ibid.

11. Ibid.

12. Ibid.

13. CTT, 498–499.

14. *DD*, 190–194; *TOTCN*, 69–75; *BS*, October 10, 1968; *NYT*, October 10, 1968.

15. CTT, 509; *DD*, 190–194; *TOTCN*, 69–75; *BS*, October 10, 1968; *NYT*, October 10, 1968

16. CTT, 509.

17. *DD*, 195.

18. *PJ*, 120; CTT 512–540; *DD*, 181.

19. CTT 512–540; *TOTCN*, 56–57.

20. CTT 512–540; *TOTCN*, 56–57; *DD*, 182.

21. CTT 512–540; *DD*, 182–184.

22. CTT, 538–539.

23. Ibid.

24. D. Berrigan interview, *IOAF*.

25. Here I have relied on Lynne Sachs, *Mary Moylan: Nine Years Underground*, multimedia biography, 2001. Sachs's website reproduces several of the postcards sent by Moylan, including one she dispatched to her friend Ann Perkins, which I have quoted here. The image is accessible at http://www.lynnesachs.com/wp-content/uploads/2009/08/mary-moyland-post2forweb.jpg.

26. CTT, 541–563; *DD*, 187–190; *TOTCN*, 63–66; *BS*, October 10, 1968; *NYT*, October 10, 1968.

27. Ibid.

28. Ibid.

29. Ibid.

30. CTT, 564–601; *DD*, 196–198; *TOTCN*, 41–43.

31. CTT, 564–601; *TOTCN*, 43–44.

32. CTT, 564–601; *TOTCN*, 45–46.

33. CTT, 564–601; *TOTCN*, 46.

34. CTT, 564–601; *TOTCN*, 48.

35. Ibid.

36. CTT, 564–601; *TOTCN*, 48–49.

37. Ibid.

38. CTT, 564–601; *TOTCN*, 49.

39. Hogan interview, *IOAF*.

40. Ibid.; Hogan oral history.

41. CTT, 602–621; Hogan interview, *IOAF*; Hogan oral history.

42. CTT, 618–619.

43. CTT, 602–621; *TOTCN*, 78.

44. Hogan interview, *IOAF*; Hogan oral history.

45. Stanley Spector, "A Meditation on Catonsville," *Bulletin of Concerned Asian Scholars* (October 1968): 4.

46. *DD*, 184.

47. Nason, "Trial of the Catonsville Nine," 28.

48. Melville and Melville interview, *IOAF*.

49. Ibid.

50. CTT, 621–637.

51. Ibid.; *DD*, 184–187; *TOTCN*, 51–60; *BS*, October 10, 1968; *NYT*, October 10, 1968.

52. Ibid.

53. CTT, 637–719; *PJ*, 119–120.

54. CTT, 637–719; *TOTCN*, 81–95; *DD*, 198–203; *BS*, October 10, 1968; *NYT*, October 10, 1968.

55. Ibid.

56. Ibid.

57. Ibid.

58. Ibid.

59. *BS*, October 10, 1968.

60. Whitman interview; *BS*, October 10, 1968.

61. *BS*, October 10, 1968.

62. *Baltimore City Paper*, May 21, 2008.

63. *BS*, October 10, 1968.

64. William Stringfellow, *A Keeper of the Word: Selected Writings of William Stringfellow*, Grand Rapids, MI: William B. Eerdmans, 1996, 68–70.

65. Stringfellow, *Keeper of the Word*, 68–70.

66. *BS*, October 10, 1968.

Chapter 17

1. *PJ*, 121–122.

2. Ibid.

3. *DD*, 209.

4. Ibid.

5. CTT, 749–763; *PJ*, 121–122; *DD*, 209–210; *TOTCN*, 99–101; *Washington Post*, October 11, 1968; *BS*, October 11, 1968.

6. CTT, 749–763; *DD*, 209–210; *TOTCN*, 99–101; *Washington Post*, October 11, 1968; *BS*, October 11, 1968.

7. Ibid.

8. CTT, 760–761.

9. CTT, 762–763.

10. Charles McCarry, "A Few Soft Words for the Rabble-Rousers," *Esquire*, July 1969, 106–108, 132–135.

11. CTT, 763–794; *DD*, 209–210; *TOTCN*, 99–101; *Washington Post*, October 11, 1968; *BS*, October 11, 1968.

12. Ibid.

13. Ibid.

14. CTT, 780–781; *DD*, 209–210; *TOTCN*, 99–101; *Washington Post*, October 11, 1968; *BS*, October 11, 1968.

15. Ibid.

16. CTT, 780–781; *NYT*, October 11, 1968; *DD*, 209–210; *TOTCN*, 99–101; *Washington Post*, October 11, 1968; *BS*, October 11, 1968.

17. CTT, 782–784; *NYT*, October 11, 1968; *DD*, 209–210; *TOTCN*, 99–101; *Washington Post*, October 11, 1968; *BS*, October 11, 1968.

18. *NYT*, October 11, 1968; *DD*, 209–210; *TOTCN*, 99–101; *Washington Post*, October 11, 1968; *BS*, October 11, 1968.

19. Ibid.

20. CTT, 763–794; *TOTCN*, 105.

21. CTT, 763–794; *TOTCN*, 105–106.

22. Brother David Darst, "Flying Back From Baltimore, Lines to William Kunstler" [ca. October, 1968], in *AITPN*, 80; Kunstler, "Catonsville—Twenty-Five Years Later, 1968–1993," in *Hints and Allegations: The World in Poetry and Prose According to William M. Kunstler*, New York: Seven Stories Press, 2003, 37.

23. *DD*, 212–213.

24. CTT, 794–809; *DD*, 212–213.

25. Ibid.

26. Ibid.

27. *DD*, 213.

28. *PJ*, 122–123.

29. Ibid.

30. CTT, 810–812.

31. CTT, 814–817.

32. Ibid.

33. *PJ*, 122–123; *DD*, 213.

34. *DD*, 215.

35. CTT, 818–820; *NCR*, October 16, 1968; *Washington Post*, October 11, 1968; *DD*, 215.

36. CTT, 818–820; *DD*, 214–215; *BS*, October 11, 1968.

37. CTT, 818–820; *DD*, 214–215.

38. *PJ*, 123.

39. *TOTCN*, 111.

40. Ibid.

41. *TOTCN*, 111–112.

42. *TOTCN*, 113.

43. *TOTCN*, 114; *DD*, 216–219.

44. *TOTCN*, 114; *DD*, 216–219; *BS*, October 11, 1968; *NCR*, October 16, 1968.

45. Ibid.

46. *TOTCN*, 114; *DD*, 216–219; *BS*, October 11, 1968; *NCR*, October 16, 1968.

47. *TOTCN*, 115; *DD*, 216–219; *BS*, October 11, 1968; *NCR*, October 16, 1968.

48. *TOTCN*, 117.

49. *DD*, 220.

50. *TOTCN*, 117.

51. *TOTCN*, 118; *DD*, 220.

52. Ibid.

53. *PJ*, 123–124.

54. *DD*, 221–222.

55. Kunstler, *My Life*, 190; Sachs interview, *HAS*.

56. *DD*, 221–222.

57. Ibid.

58. Hogan interview, *IOAF*.

59. Kunstler, *My Life*, 190.

60. Sachs interview, *HAS*.

61. CTT, 862.

62. CTT, 863–873; *DD*, 223–224.

63. CTT, 873; *PJ*, 124.

64. CTT, 873; *BS*, October 11, 1968.

65. *NYT*, October 11, 1968; *DD*, 224–225.

66. CTT, 874–888.

67. *DD*, 225.

68. *NCR*, October 16, 1968.

Chapter 18

1. Mary Moylan to Friends, October 25, 1968, BC-CU.

2. Daniel Berrigan to Friends, [ca. October 1968], BC-CU.

3. Tom Lewis and Phil Berrigan to Daniel Berrigan, November 1968, BC-CU.

4. Tom Lewis, "Introduction," in Berrigan and Lewis, *Trial Poems*, n.p.

5. Lewis, "Artist as Resister," DD-CW; Lewis, "Introduction," n.p.

6. McCarry, "Few Soft Words," 106–108, 132–135; *BS*, November 7, 1968; *NCR*, November 13, 1968.

7. McCarry, "Few Soft Words," 106–108, 132–135.

8. *BS*, November 9, 1968; *San Mateo* (California) *Times*, November 9, 1968.

9. *NCR*, November 13, 1968.

10. McCarry, "Few Soft Words," 106–108, 132–135.

11. United States District Court for the District of Maryland, Transcript of Sentencing, *United States of America v. Daniel Berrigan, et al.*, Criminal No. 2811, November 8, 1968, BC-CU, 1–74; McCarry, "Few Soft Words," 106–108, 132–135; *BS*, November 9, 1968.

12. *United States v. Berrigan*, Transcript of Sentencing, 1–74; *NCR*, November 20, 1968.

13. Ibid.

14. Ibid. In *TOTCN*, it appears that some of Phil Berrigan's comments here at sentencing are grafted onto his earlier trial testimony.

15. *NCR*, November 13, 1968.

16. *BS*, November 9, 1968; *Newark* (Ohio) *Advocate*, November 11, 1968; *NCR*, November 13, 1968.

17. *United States v. Moylan et al.*, 417 F.2d 1002 (4th Cir. 1969); *BS*, November 9, 1968; *NCR*, November 13, 1968.

18. *Times* (London), November 9, 1969; *NYT*, March 6, 1969.

19. *Albuquerque Tribune*, October 15, 1968.

20. *NCR*, November 13, 1968.

21. *BS*, December 13, 1968; *Hagerstown* (Maryland) *Morning Herald*, December 13, 1968.

22. *BS*, December 14, 1968, and February 15, 1969.

23. D. Berrigan, "Some Pertinent Facts," BC-CU.

24. Ibid.

25. United States Court of Appeals for the Fourth Circuit, Brief for Appellants, *United States of America v. Philip Berrigan, et al.*, Filed April 1, 1969, PB-FBI, 53–55, 77.

26. Clarence M. Kelley to Director, U.S. Secret Service, December 18, 1973, TL-FBI.

27. Kelley to Director, U.S. Secret Service, December 18, 1973.

28. Daniel Berrigan to Stephen Sachs, March 26, 1969, BC-CU.

29. "Reverend Philip Francis Berrigan et al.," October 28, 1969, PB-FBI.

30. John Deedy, "News and Views: Berrigan, Darst, et al.," *Commonweal*, November 21, 1969, 236; Tom Cornell, "Milwaukee 12," *Catholic Worker*, June 1969, 1.

31. "Stipulation of Facts," November 27, 1968, BC-CU; *NYT*, June 5, 1969.

32. *BS*, June 5 and 6, 1969.

33. Circuit Court for Baltimore County, Transcript of Trial, *State of Maryland v. Thomas Robert Melville et al.*, June 4 and 6, 1969, BC-CU; *News American* (Baltimore), June 4, 1969.

34. *News American* (Baltimore), June 6, 1969; *Hagerstown* (Maryland) *Morning Herald*, June 7, 1969. The Maryland Special Court of Appeals later affirmed the robbery convictions and one count of assault and battery. However, the court vacated the convictions for the second count of assault and battery. See *Thomas Melville et al. v. Maryland*, 268 A.2d 497 (1970).

35. Lewis, "Introduction," n.p.

36. Ibid.

37. T. Melville interview; *Washington Post*, February 2, 2003.

38. O'Connor oral history, MDHS, 4–5, 15–18.

39. Ibid.

40. Phillip Berrigan to Daniel Berrigan, June 23, 1968, BC-CU.

41. O'Connor oral history, MDHS, 4–5, 15–18.

42. Ibid.

43. Ibid.

44. Philip Berrigan to Jim [Forest], May 21, 1969, BC-CU.

45. Joseph Tropea, "Hit and Stay: The Baltimore Four, the Catonsville Nine and How They Sustained the American Peace Movement," unpublished master's thesis, University of Maryland–Baltimore County, 2008.

46. Patricia McNeal, *Harder Than War: Catholic Peacemaking in Twentieth-Century America*, New Brunswick, NJ: Rutgers University Press, 1992, 196–199.

47. *Milwaukee Sentinel*, September 4, 1970; *NYT*, September 8, 1970.

48. D. Berrigan, "Peace Preacher," 111–112.

49. Daniel Berrigan to [the Catonsville Nine], May 22, 1969, BC-CU.

50. *Milwaukee Sentinel*, September 4, 1970; *NYT*, September 8, 1970.

51. Ibid.

Chapter 19

1. Brother David Darst, "Letter to an Unseen Friend" [ca. 1969], in *AITPN*, 85–87.

2. Brother David Darst to Debbe Orenstein, August 25, 1969 (in possession of author). I am grateful to Debbe Orenstein Fate for generously sharing with me dozens of pieces of correspondence from Darst.

3. Author interview with Debbe Orenstein Fate, June 7, 2010 (in possession of author).

4. Darst, "Letter to an Unseen Friend," 85–87.

5. Brother David Darst, "Dialogues with Debbe [Orenstein] and Stan [Brostowksi]," October 1969 (in possession of author). These "dialogues" were a series of letters written by Darst to his friends over the months leading up to his death.

6. Forgue interview; Brother David Darst to Debbe Orenstein, September 15, 1968 (in possession of author).

7. Brother David Darst to Daniel Berrigan, May 23, 1969.

8. Darst, "Dialogues."

9. Ibid.

10. Brother David Darst to Debbe Orenstein, July 4, 1969 (in possession of author); Darst, "Dialogues."

11. Brother David Darst to Debbe Orenstein, July 28, 1969 (in possession of author); Darst, "Dialogues."

12. Darst, "Dialogues."

13. Ibid.

14. Ibid.

15. Ibid.

16. Brother David Darst, "A Passing Thought," in *AITPN*, 120–121.

17. Kunstler to Harold Buchman, March 24, 1969, BC-CU.

18. *BS*, June 11, 1969.

19. Philip Berrigan to Dick and Nancy Cusack, February 7, 1970, BMC; Bannan, Sachs interview, BC-CU.

20. Lewin, *Baltimore Briefs*, 31; Michael Mayer, "Simon Sobeloff Biography," University of Maryland School of Law Thurgood Marshall Law Library, http://www.law.umaryland. edu/marshall/specialcollections/sobeloff/index.html (accessed September 20, 2010).

21. *United States v. Moylan*, 417 F.2d 1002 (4th Cir. 1970). On the same day, the Fourth Circuit handed down its opinion in *United States v. Eberhardt*, the appeal in the Baltimore Four cases. The convictions were affirmed, but the case was remanded for further consideration of the sentences (417 F.2d 1009 [4th Cir. 1969]). On June 11, 1970, the district judge held a hearing on the motion for reduction of sentences. James Mengel's sentence was suspended, and Tom Lewis's was reduced from six to three years. The judge refused to alter the sentences of Phil Berrigan and Dave Eberhardt (*United States v. Philip Berrigan et al.*, 437 F.2d 750 [4th Cir. 1971]).

22. *United States v. Moylan*, 417 F.2d 1002.

23. *Pittsburgh Press*, October 28, 1969.

24. Darst, "Dialogues."

25. Interview with C. Darst.

26. Darst, "Dialogues."

27. Ibid.

28. Ibid.

29. Ibid.

30. Brother David Darst, "Instant Replay," in *AITPN*, 136. For the background on Darst's hospital visit, I've also relied on his brother's marginal comments that accompany the poem.

31. *Lincoln* (Nebraska) *Star*, November 1, 1969; *NCR*, November 12, 1969.

32. State of Nebraska Department of Public Health, Certificate of Death, David Darst, November 3, 1969, BC-CU.

33. C. Darst interview.

34. Ortbal, "Catholic Radical Left," 3–4, 13.

35. Ibid.

36. Ibid.

37. Fate interview.

38. Ibid.

39. D. Berrigan, *Lights On*, 245.

40. D. Berrigan, *America Is Hard to Find*, 179–191.

41. "Report of SA [Redacted]," February 28, 1970, PB-FBI.

42. SA [redacted], "Thomas Pahl Lewis," TL-FBI, 1–7.

43. SAC, Honolulu, to Director, FBI, April 8, 1970, PB-FBI.

44. *Honolulu Star-Bulletin*, March 26, 1970.

45. Francine du Plessix Gray, "Phil Berrigan in Hawaii," in Casey and Nobile, *Berrigans*, 159–160.

46. Memorandum, SAC, Washington, to Director, FBI, February 20, 1970, PB-FBI.

47. Harold Buchman to Harrop Freeman, December 9, 1969, BC-CU.

48. *NYT*, January 16, 1970.

49. *Moylan v. United States*, 397 U.S. 910 (1970); *Berrigan v. United States*, 397 U.S. 909 (1970); J. H. Gale to Claude DeLoach, February 24, 1970, PB-FBI.

50. D. Berrigan, *America Is Hard to Find*, 31.

51. SAC, Baltimore, to Director, FBI, March 18, 1970, PB-FBI.

Chapter 20

1. William Stringfellow and Anthony Towne, *Suspect Tenderness: The Ethics of the Berrigan Witness*, New York: Holt, Rinehart and Winston, 1971, 21–23.

2. Stringfellow and Towne, *Suspect Tenderness*, 21–23.

3. Ibid.

4. Jerome Berrigan, "Introduction," in Berrigan, *America Is Hard to Find*, 7.

5. *TDIP*, 238–239.

6. *FTLW*, 117–118.

7. Ibid.

8. *NYT*, April 16, 1970.

9. *TDIP*, 238–239.

10. Hogan oral history; Hogan interview, *HAS*.

11. *St. Cloud* (Minnesota) *Times*, January 29, 2010.

12. Hogan interview, *HAS*; T. Melville interview, *HAS*.

13. *BS*, April 8, 1970.

14. *BS,* April 10, 1970.

15. Ibid.

16. Ibid.

17. "The Catonsville 9: Father Philip Berrigan and David Eberhardt," interview broadcast on WBAI, New York, NY, April 1970, Pacifica Radio Archives.

18. *BS*, April 10, 1970.

19. J. H. Gale to Claude DeLoach, April 9, 1970, PB-FBI.

20. J. Edgar Hoover to SACs, Baltimore and Albany, NY, April 14, 1970, PB-FBI.

21. SAC, Baltimore, to J. Edgar Hoover, April 17, 1970, PB-FBI.

22. Ibid.

23. SAC, Baltimore, to J. Edgar Hoover, April 13, 1970, PB-FBI.

24. *BS*, April 10 and 12, 1970.

25. *NYT*, June 28, 1970.

26. Jerry Elmer, *Felon for Peace: The Memoir of a Vietnam-Era Draft Resister*, Nashville, TN: Vanderbilt University Press, 2005, 126–127.

27. Daniel Aloi, "From Vietnam to Redbud Woods: Daniel Berrigan Launches Events Commemorating Five Decades of Activism at Cornell," *Cornell University Chronicle Online*, April 4, 2006, http://www.news.cornell.edu/stories/April06/berrigan.0406.html (accessed April 20, 2011).

28. D. Berrigan, *America Is Hard to Find*, 39–49.

29. Ibid.

30. Ibid., 35–38.

31. Forest, "Daniel Berrigan: Poet and Prophet as Priest," 109.

32. *NYT*, June 28, 1970.

33. Howard Zinn, *Disobedience and Democracy: Nine Fallacies of Law and Order*, Cambridge, MA: South End Press, 2001, 7.

34. *NYT*, June 28, 1970.

35. Ibid.

36. SAC, Albany, to J. Edgar Hoover, April 21, 1970, PB-FBI.

37. *NYT*, April 18, 1970.

38. *Cumberland* (Maryland) *Sunday Times*, April 19, 1970.

39. *TDIP*, 244.

40. Ibid.; Polner and O'Grady, *Disarmed and Dangerous*, 223–224.

41. *TDIP*, 244–5.

42. *Herald-Journal* (Syracuse, NY), April 20, 1970.

43. J. Edgar Hoover to SAC, Albany, April 20, 1970, PB-FBI; J. Edgar Hoover to SAC, Baltimore, April 20, 1970, PB-FBI.

44. SAC, Newark, to J. Edgar Hoover and SAC, Baltimore, April 21, 1970, PB-FBI.

45. *FTLW*, 119.

46. Ibid.

47. "Bulls and Berrigans," *Newsweek*, May 4, 1970, 106; Philip Berrigan, *Widen the Prison Gates: Writing From Jails, April 1970–December 1972*, New York: Touchstone Books, 1973, 15–16.

48. Report of [redacted], April 27, 1970, PB-FBI.

49. Ibid.

50. P. Berrigan, *Widen the Prison Gates*, 15–16.

51. *FTLW*, 119; "Bulls and Berrigans," 106; Zinn, *You Can't Be Neutral*, 135–138.

52. P. Berrigan, *Widen the Prison Gates*, 15–16.

53. *BS*, April 23, 1970.

54. D. Berrigan, *America Is Hard to Find*, 49.

55. Daniel Berrigan, George Mische, Dave Eberhardt, and Philip Berrigan, "Underground and Action," *WIN*, June 15, 1970, 17–18.

56. *BS*, May 19, 1970; G. Mische interview, *HAS*.

Chapter 21

1. Zinn, *You Can't Be Neutral*, 135–138.

2. Ibid.

3. Ibid.

4. Ibid.

5. "The Taking of Father Dan," *Newsweek*, August 24, 1970, 37.

6. Zinn, *You Can't Be Neutral*, 135–138.

7. *Harvard Crimson*, May 9, 1970.

8. Zinn, *You Can't Be Neutral*, 135–138.

9. James Carroll, *Constantine's Sword: The Church and the Jews*, New York: Houghton Mifflin, 2001, 48–49.

10. James Carroll, *An American Requiem: God, My Father, and the War That Came Between Us*, New York: Houghton Mifflin, 1996, 224–227.

11. Carroll, *American Requiem*, 224–227.

12. Ibid.

13. Ibid.

14. *Los Angeles Times*, July 12, 1970.

15. Ibid.

16. Garry Wills, *Outside Looking In: Adventures of an Observer*, New York: Viking, 2010, 60–61. Several of Cusack's children, including Ann, Joan, and John, have followed in his theatrical footsteps.

17. Jerome Berrigan, "Introduction," in Berrigan, *America Is Hard to Find*, 7–11.

18. Ibid.

19. Berrigan, *America Is Hard to Find*, 58–59.

20. J. Berrigan, "Introduction," 7–11.

21. Ibid.

22. Ibid.

23. Ibid.

24. *NYT*, June 6, 1970.

25. Paul Cowan, "Catholic Left Says the Heat's On," *Village Voice*, July 16, 1970, 19, 26.

26. Berrigan and Coles, *Geography of Faith*, 35.

27. "Taking of Father Dan," 37.

28. "Four Sketches by People Who Sheltered Him: Dan Berrigan With Families Underground," in Casey, *Berrigans*, 191–202.

29. "Four Sketches," 191–202.

30. *TDIP*, 245; "Four Sketches," 191–202.

31. *NYT*, June 28, 1970.

32. *NYT*, August 3, 1970; Daniel Berrigan, "Sermon from the Underground, August 2, 1970," in Halpert and Murray, *Witness of the Berrigans*, 140–141.

33. "Taking of Father Dan," 37; Buckley quoted in David L. Anderson, *The Human Tradition in America Since 1945*, Lanham, MD: SR Books, 2003, 89.

34. Daniel Berrigan to Jerry, Carol, and Frida Berrigan, May 1, 1970, BC-CU.

35. Stringfellow and Towne, *Suspect Tenderness*, 43.

36. Lee Lockwood, "How the 'Kidnap Conspiracy' Was Hatched," *LIFE*, May 21, 1971, 24–30.

37. Robert Wool, "The Harboring of Daniel Berrigan: An Exercise of Christian Charity," *Esquire*, November 1971, 156–161, 206. Here I have closely followed Wool's excellent account.

38. *NYT*, August 14 and 23, 1970; "Weatherman on Berrigan," *Village Voice*, January 21, 1971, 21.

39. Forest, "Daniel Berrigan," 109.

Chapter 22

1. *Washington Post*, May 30, 1971.

2. Ibid.

3. Mariett Wickes, "Tear Down the Walls!" *Off Our Backs*, April 15, 1971, 2; *Washington Post*, May 30, 1971.

4. Wickes, "Tear Down the Walls!," 2; *Washington Post*, May 30, 1971.

5. Ibid.

6. *Washington Post*, May 30, 1971.

7. Marjorie Melville to Harold Buchman, May 16 and 26, 1970, BC-CU; Dave and Jan Hartsough to "Dear Friends," June 19, 1970, BC-CU.

8. Thomas Melville to Harold Buchman, April 24 and May 11, 1970, BC-CU.

9. Thomas Melville to Harold Buchman, June 27, 1970, BC-CU; T. Melville interview, *HAS*.

10. T. Melville interview, *HAS*.

11. Ibid.

12. Dave Hartsough and Jan Hartsough to "Dear Friends," June 19, 1970, BC-CU.

13. Interview with T. Melville.

14. *NYT*, April 27, 1971.

15. Rachel Cowan, "Guatemala to Catonsville," *Village Voice*, May 20, 1971, 32, 52.

16. Hogan interview, *IOAF*.

17. Ibid.

18. Ibid.

19. Hogan oral history.

20. Hogan interview, *IOAF*.

21. Ibid.

22. John Hogan to Harold Buchman, June 30 and September 30, 1970, BC-CU.

23. Hogan to Buchman, September 30, 1970.

24. Hogan to Buchman, June 30, 1970.

25. John Hogan to Harold Buchman, May 23, 1970, BC-CU; John Hogan to Roszel Thomsen, May 25, 1970, BC-CU.

26. *New Haven Register*, October 17, 2008; Hogan interview, *HAS*.

27. Tom Lewis, "Reflections From the Pig Farm," *Commonweal*, September 24, 1971, 499–500.

28. Lewis, "Reflections," 499–500.

29. Ibid.

30. Ibid.

31. Ibid.

32. Ibid.

33. Troester, Interview with Tom Lewis, DD-CWC.

34. Lewis, "Reflections," 499–500.

35. Troester, *Voices From the Catholic Worker*, 309–310; Lewis oral history, CU, 64–65.

36. Lewis oral history, CU, 64–65.

37. Ibid.

38. Philip Withim, "Chronology and Background of the Events at Allenwood Prison Camp, July and August, 1971," BC-CU; *Washington Post*, August 9, 1971; *Braxton v. Carlson*, 340 F. Supp. 999 (Mid. District PA 1972), 999–1000; *Braxton v. Carlson*, 483 F. 2d 933 (3rd Cir. 1973), 934–942.

39. *Washington Post*, August 9, 1971; *Braxton v. Carlson*, 340 F. Supp. 999–1000; *Braxton v. Carlson*, 483 F. 2d 934–942.

40. *Simpson's Leader-Times* (Kittanning, PA), August 2, 1971; *Washington Post*, August 9, 1971; *Braxton v. Carlson*, 340 F. Supp. 999–1000; *Braxton v. Carlson*, 483 F. 2d 934–942.

41. *Braxton v. Carlson*, 340 F. Supp. 999–1000; *Braxton v. Carlson*, 483 F. 2d 934–942.

42. P. Berrigan, *Widen the Prison Gates*, 23–24.

43. Philip Nobile, "Phil Berrigan in Prison," in Casey and Nobile, *Berrigans*, 125–126.

44. Ibid.

45. Ibid.

46. *FTLW*, 122; Nobile, "Phil Berrigan," 129.

47. Nobile, "Phil Berrigan," 130–131.

48. P. Berrigan, *Widen the Prison Gates*, 46–47.

49. Philip Berrigan to Carol and Jerry Berrigan, October 11, 1970, BC-CU.

50. D. Berrigan, *Lights On*, 107–108.

51. P. Berrigan, *Widen the Prison Gates*, 89–89; D. Berrigan, *Lights On*, 102–103.

52. *PJ*, 45–46.

53. Hogan oral history.

54. *PJ*, 45–46; Polner and O'Grady, *Disarmed and Dangerous*, 267; Jack Nelson, Interview with James R. Hoffa, October 2, 1972, BC-CU.

55. T. Melville interview.

56. Nelson, Interview with Hoffa, BC-CU.

57. T. Melville interview; Polner and O'Grady, *Disarmed and Dangerous*, 266–267.

58. Jack Nelson and Ronald J. Ostrow, *The FBI and the Berrigans: The Making of a Conspiracy*, New York: Coward, McCann & Geoghegan, 1972, 71, 88.

59. Nelson and Ostrow, *FBI and the Berrigans*, 116.

60. Polner and O'Grady, *Disarmed and Dangerous*, 269, 295

61. *NYT*, January 14, 1971; Nelson and Ostrow, *FBI and the Berrigans*, 162.

62. Polner and O'Grady, *Disarmed and Dangerous*, 296–297.

63. McNeal, *Harder Than War*, 208.

64. *DAD*, 298–299.

65. SAC, Baltimore, to Director, FBI, April 23, 1971, TL-FBI; Clarence Kelly to Director, U.S. Secret Service, December 18, 1973, TL-FBI; SAC, Boston, to Acting Director, FBI, May 1, 1973, TL-FBI.

66. Stephen Sachs to George Reed, December 15, 1971, BC-CU; Polner and O'Grady, *Disarmed and Dangerous*, 260–261.

67. *NYT*, February 25, 1972.

68. Polner and O'Grady, *Disarmed and Dangerous*, 262.

69. *NYT*, July 29, 1971; *BS*, November 30, 1972.

70. *NYT*, November 30, 1972; Philip Berrigan, "Prisons and War," *Fellowship*, Winter 1973, 12.

71. Day, *Duty of Delight*, 518.

Chapter 23

1. Sachs, *Mary Moylan*. Sachs used video, audio, postcards, and artifacts for this piece, which premiered at the Maryland Film Festival in 2001. Additional information can be accessed at http://www.lynnesachs.com/medium/multimedia/mary-moylan-nine-years-underground-08082001/?fcat=4.

2. Rosemary Bannan, Interview with Mary Moylan [ca. 1969], BC-CU.

3. SAC, Washington, to Director, FBI, May 6, 1969, PB-FBI.

4. *BS*, July 14, 1995.

5. Ibid.

6. Moylan, "Underground Woman," 61–63; Moylan, "Being Underground," 2.

7. Ibid.

8. Rebecca Klatch, *A Generation Divided: The New Left, the New Right, and the 1960s*, Berkeley: University of California Press, 1999, 209; *Caller-Times* (Corpus Christi, Texas), October 25, 1970. The latter source is a lengthy and rich Associated Press story by reporter Bernard Gavzer titled "The New Fugitives in America."

9. Moylan, "Underground Woman," 61–63; Moylan, "Being Underground," 2.

10. Ibid.; Philip Berrigan interview, *IOAF* [ca. 1999].

11. Moylan, "Underground Woman," 61–63; Moylan, "Being Underground," 2.

12. Ibid.

13. Hogan interview, *IOAF*; *BS*, July 14, 1995.

14. Moylan, "Underground Woman," 61–63; Moylan, "Being Underground," 2.

15. Ibid.; *NYT*, December 13, 1970. Here I have relied on J. Anthony Lukas's excellent piece for the *New York Times Magazine*, "On the Lam in America."

16. *NCR*, November 10, 1995.

17. Mary Moylan, "Catonsville 9 Go Underground," *WIN*, Jun 1, 1970, 14–16.

18. Moylan, "Underground Woman," 61–63; Moylan, "Being Underground," 2; Moylan, "Catonsville 9 Go Underground," 14–16.

19. *NYT*, December 13, 1970.

20. Mary Moylan, "A Woman's Work Is Never Done," *Off Our Backs: A Women's News-journal*, September 30, 1970, 1.

21. Moylan, "A Woman's Work Is Never Done," 1; *New York Times*, December 13, 1970.

22. *NYT*, December 13, 1970.

23. *Caller-Times*, October 25, 1970; Moylan, "Underground Woman," 61–63; Moylan, "Being Underground," 2.

24. *NYT*, December 13, 1970.

25. Ibid.

26. Ibid.

27. Ibid.

28. Ibid.

29. Moylan, "Underground Woman," 61–63; Moylan, "Being Underground," 2.

30. Ibid.

31. Ibid.

32. Ibid.

33. Ibid.

34. *NYT*, December 5, 2008.

35. Moylan, "Mary Moylan's Letter to Jane Alpert," in Jonah Raskin, ed., *The Weather Eye: Communiques from the Weather Underground, May 1970–May 1974*, New York: Union Square Press, 1974, 80–83.

36. SAC, Baltimore, "Mary Assumpta Moylan," July 15, 1975, MM-FBI.

37. SAC, Baltimore, to Director, FBI, July 15, 1975, MM-FBI; SA [redacted], "Mary Assumpta Moylan," November 21, 1975, MM-FBI.

38. Moylan, "A Woman's Work Is Never Done," 1; Bannan, Interview with Mary Moylan, BC-CU.

39. Bernardine Dohrn, Bill Ayers, and Jeff Jones, eds., *Sing a Battle Song: The Revolutionary Poetry, Statements, and Communiques of the Weather Underground, 1970–1974*, New York: Seven Stories Press, 2006, 62–63; *Harvard Crimson*, October 15, 1970, and June 3, 1996.

40. Susan Braudy, *Family Circle: The Boudins and the Aristocracy of the Left*, New York: Alfred A. Knopf, 2003, 247.

41. Jane Alpert, *Growing Up Underground*, New York: William Morrow, 1981, 332–339.

42. Alice Echols, *Daring To Be Bad: Radical Feminism in America, 1967–1975*, Minneapolis: University of Minnesota Press, 1989, 249–253; Moylan, "Mary Moylan's Letter to Jane Alpert," 80–83.

43. *BS*, July 22, 1978.

44. Whitman interview, *HAS*; ibid.

45. *BS*, July 14, 1995; Willa Bickham interview, *HAS*, September 1, 2008.

46. SAC, Baltimore, to Director, FBI, June 3, 1971, MM-FBI.

47. *NYT*, December 13, 1970; *Caller-Times*, October 25, 1970.

48. Lane Bonner to author, July 10 and 12, 2009 (in possession of author).

49. SAC, Baltimore, to Director, FBI, August 18, 1976, MM-FBI.

50. Lane Bonner to author, July 10 and 12, 2009; SAC, Baltimore, to Director, FBI, May 19, 1975, MM-FBI.

51. *NCR*, November 10, 1995.

52. *Washington Post*, 21 June 1979; Willa Bickham interview, *HAS*; *BS*, July 14, 1995.

53. Mary Moylan, "Statement from Balto. City Jail" [ca. 1979], BC-CU.

54. *Washington Post*, June 21, 1979.

55. *NCR*, November 10, 1995.

Chapter 24

1. Colum McCann, *Let the Great World Spin*, New York: Random House, 2009, 89; Don DeLillo, *Underworld*, New York: Simon & Schuster, 1998, 612; Adrienne Rich, *The Will to Change: Poems, 1968–1970*, New York: W. W. Norton, 1971, 15–18.

2. Lippman, *No Good Deeds*, 10.

3. Dar Williams, *The Green World*, CD, Razor & Tie, 2000.

4. Alex Teitz, "Dar Williams," http://www.femmusic.com/darwilliamsint.htm (accessed January 20, 2011); *Seattle Post-Intelligencer*, October 6, 2000.

5. Daniel Berrigan to Catonsville Nine, May 7, 1969, BC-CU.

6. *NYT*, July 12, 1970.

7. G. Mische interview, *HAS*.

8. Daniel Berrigan to George Lawler, September 15, 1969, BC-CU.

9. *NYT*, April 1, 1970; G. Mische interview, *HAS*; Berrigan and Lewis, *Trial Poems*, n.p.

10. Arthur Bartow, *The Director's Voice: Twenty-One Interviews*, New York: Theatre Communications Group, 2002, 67–68, 74–77.

11. Ibid.

12. Ibid.; D. Berrigan, *America Is Hard to Find*, 87–91.

13. Gordon Davidson to Daniel Berrigan, September 4, 1970, BC-CU.

14. Bartow, *Director's Voice*, 67–68, 74–77; *Los Angeles Times*, August 10, 1970, and June 18, 1971.

15. D. Berrigan, *Lights On*, 109–110.

16. Ibid., 135–142.

17. Brooke Hayward, *Haywire*, New York: Vintage, 2011, 285–286.

18. John Simon, "Saints for Our Time," *New York*, February 22, 1971, 66; M. Paul Holsinger, "The Trial of the Catonsville Nine," in M. Paul Holsinger, ed., *War and American Popular Culture: A Historical Encyclopedia*, Santa Barbara, CA: Greenwood, 1999, 420.

19. *Los Angeles Times*, May 26 and July 8, 1971.

20. *TDIP*, 220.

21. Bruce Goldfarb, "Finding the Catonsville Nine," http://welcometobaltimorehon.com/finding-the-catonsville-nine?replytocom=7729 (accessed May 13, 2011).

22. Robin Andersen, "Preface to the Fordham University Press Edition," in Daniel Berrigan, *The Trial of the Catonsville Nine*, Fordham University Press Edition, New York: Fordham University Press, 2004, xi–xvi.

23. "Actor, Director Tim Robbins Takes Up Historic Vietnam War Protest in Production of 'The Trial of the Catonsville Nine,'" broadcast on "Democracy Now! The War and Peace Report," August 27, 2009, http://www.democracynow.org/2009/8/27/actor_director_tim_robbins_takes_up (accessed February 1, 2011).

24. Murphy oral history, FCLC; Morsberger oral history, FCLC.

25. G. Darst interview.

26. *NYT*, May 21, 1972; Gary Fishgall, *Gregory Peck: A Biography*, New York: Simon & Schuster, 2002, 278–279.

27. *NYT*, May 21, 1972.

28. *Los Angeles Times*, December 31, 1971.

29. *NYT*, May 21, 1972.

30. *Los Angeles Times*, December 31, 1971.

31. Ibid.

32. Gordon Davidson to Jerry and Carol Berrigan, November 11, 1971, BC-CU.

33. Lynn Haney, *Gregory Peck: A Charmed Life*, New York: Carroll & Graf, 2004, 355–356; Fishgall, *Gregory Peck*, 279–280.

34. *NYT*, May 21, 1972.

35. Ibid.

36. *NYT*, May 28 and June 11, 1972, and January 7, 1973.

37. Louis Liebovich, *Richard Nixon, Watergate, and the Press: A Historical Retrospective*, New York: Praeger, 2003, 10.

38. *NYT*, December 5, 1971.

39. T. Melville interview.

Chapter 25

1. National Coordinating Committee for Justice Under Law, *An Investigation and Analysis of Federal Prison Strikes*, Washington, DC: National Coordinating Committee for Justice Under Law, 1973, 34–42.

2. *Frederick* (Maryland) *News*, April 10 1975.

3. *BS*, July 22, 1978; *Washington Post*, May 14, 1978.

4. *St. Cloud* (Minnesota) *Times*, January 29, 2010; Tropea, "Hit and Stay," 67–68.

5. *BS*, May 17 and 24, 1993. Eberhardt describes his feelings about the Berrigans (and recounts his many discussions with Mische about them) in his work "m'vt and other memoirs," which is available at his website, http://davideberhardt.webs.com/.

6. O'Connor oral history, MDHS, 1–26; O'Connor interview, *IOAF*.

7. Ibid.; *BS*, February 16, 1977.

8. Berrigan, *Widen the Prison Gates*, 259–261.

9. Howard Zinn, "A Holy Outlaw," *Progressive*, February 2003, 14.

10. *NYT*, April 11, 1990; *BS*, December 10, 2002.

11. Kate and Frida Berrigan, "Kate and Frida's Eulogy," http://www.jonahhouse.org/eulogy.htm (accessed January 5, 2011).

12. *NYT*, May 13, 2001.

13. *New York Daily News*, November 3, 2008; John Dear, "On the Road to Peace: Daniel Berrigan at 89," *NCR*, May 4, 2010, http://ncronline.org/blogs/road-peace/daniel-berrigan-89 (accessed January 20, 2011).

14. Carl Kozlowski, "Q&A: Daniel Berrigan," *Progressive*, March 2004, 15; *New York Daily News*, November 3, 2008.

15. George M. Anderson, "Looking Back in Gratitude," *America*, July 6, 2009, 25–27.

16. Troester, Interview with Tom Lewis, DD-CWC.

17. *Telegram & Gazette* (Worcester, MA), July 17, 2008.

18. *BS*, July 22, 1978, and October 5, 2008; *New Haven Register*, October 17, 2008.

19. Rafael Alvarez, "John Hogan: A Carpenter for Peace," October 12, 2008, http://washingtonexaminer.com/local/john-hogan-carpenter-peace (accessed April 20, 2011); Brian Kolodiejchuk, ed., *Mother Teresa: Come Be My Light: The Private Writings of "The Saint of Calcutta,"* New York: Doubleday, 2007, 34.

20. *Record-Journal* (Meriden, CT), October 6, 2008; "Eulogies Honoring John Hogan."

21. Diane Telgen and Jim Kamp, eds., *Notable Hispanic American Women*, Book One, Detroit, MI: Gale Research, 1993, 270–271; Thomas Melville and Marjorie Melville, *Guatemala:*

Another Vietnam?, New York: Penguin, 1971; Tropea, "Hit and Stay," UMBC thesis, 67–68; *NYT*, June 23, 1991; Margarita Melville, *Twice a Minority: Mexican American Women*, St. Louis: Mosby, 1980, 1.

22. Thomas Melville, *Through a Glass Darkly: The U.S. Holocaust in Central America*, Bloomington, IN: Xlibris, 2005.

23. Thomas Melville, "Insurgency and Counterinsurgency," speech delivered at St. John's Methodist Church, Baltimore, MD, November 11, 2007, http://video.google.com/vide oplay?docid=-211874374465883204# (accessed April 7, 2011).

24. *BS*, May 17 and 24, 1993; *Washington Post*, May 27, 1993.

25. Bickham interview, *HAS*, September 1, 2008.

26. Bickham interview, *HAS*; D. Berrigan interview, *IOAF*.

27. *BS*, July 14, 1995.

28. *NCR*, November 10, 1995.

29. *BS*, December 7 and 10, 2002; *Boston Globe*, December 10, 2002; Zinn, "Holy Outlaw," 14.

30. *Boston Globe*, December 10, 2002; *BS*, May 16, 2008.

31. *NCR*, Mary 21, 1993.

32. Melville and Melville interview, *IOAF*; T. Melville interview, *HAS*; T. Melville interview.

33. *BS*, May 17 and 24, 1993; Berrigan, "Peace Preacher," 117.

34. Lawrence Baskir and William Strauss, *Chance and Circumstance: The Draft, the War, and the Vietnam Generation*, New York: Alfred A. Knopf, 1978, 67–68.

35. Massa, *American Catholic Revolution*, 124, 127–128; Howard Zinn, *A People's History of the United States, 1492–Present*, New York: HarperPerennial, 2005, 490.

36. *BS*, June 14, 1971.

37. "Martin Sheen," in Thomas, *Right Words at the Right Time*, 311–312.

38. "Martin Sheen," 311–312.

39. *NCR*, February 11, 1972.

40. *NCR*, May 20, 2008.

41. Shane Claiborne, "Holy Mischief: 40 Years after the Catonsville 9 and the 'Fracture of Good Order,'" http://blog.beliefnet.com/godspolitics/2008/05/40-years-after-the-catons-ville.html (accessed January 27, 2011).

42. "Eulogies Honoring John Hogan"; *Yale Daily News*, September 25, 2010.

43. Victoria Rader, *Signal Through the Flames: Mitch Snyder and America's Homeless*, Kansas City, MO: Sheed & Ward, 1986, 43–45; *FTLW*, 137.

44. *Telegram & Gazette* (Worcester, MA), April 6, 2008.

45. *NCR*, June 2, 2008.

46. "Eulogies Honoring John Hogan."

47. *NYT*, December 8, 2010; *BS*, December 8, 2010.

48. Ibid.

A NOTE ON SOURCES

In researching and writing this book, I have been helped immeasurably by the work of two talented documentary filmmakers. I can't thank them enough for their help.

I learned a great deal about the Catonsville Nine from watching Lynne Sachs's excellent *Investigation of a Flame* (2001). What's more, Sachs has made available, on VHS tapes, much of the raw interview footage that she shot for her film. I have relied on those tapes here and cited them accordingly (using the abbreviation *IOAF*). I am grateful for the access to these tapes, which was provided on several separate occasions by the Catonsville Branch of the Baltimore County Public Library and the Friends of the Catonsville Library.

I similarly benefited from the work and counsel of Joe Tropea, whose forthcoming film (on the Catonsville Nine protest and other antidraft demonstrations of the Vietnam era) bears the title *Hit and Stay*. Tropea made available to me transcripts of several interviews he conducted for the film, and they helped me immensely. (I have cited those transcripts by using the abbreviation *HAS*.) Joe also shared ideas and critiques that helped me to sharpen my focus.

Over a period of several years, I obtained thousands of pages of materials on the Catonsville Nine from the Federal Bureau of Investigation. Using the Freedom of Information Act, I filed separate requests for materials related to: the Baltimore Defense Committee; Philip Berrigan; James McGinnis Darst (Brother David Darst); John Hogan; Tom Lewis; and Mary Moylan. Each request yielded several hundred pages of documents. For the sake of economy, I have relied on the abbreviations listed in the Abbreviations section when referencing those individual files.

I have relied extensively on the actual court transcript of the trial of the Catonsville Nine (the edited version of which comprises Dan Berrigan's *The Trial of the Catonsville Nine*). To my knowledge, the only extant copy of this massive document (abbreviated in the notes as CTT) can be found in the Daniel and Philip Berrigan Collection at Cornell University.

A Note About Names

The names of two of the Catonsville Nine changed slightly over time. James McGinnis Darst was not known as "David" or "Brother David" until he joined the Christian Brothers religious order, and his family members still sometimes refer to him as "Jim" or "Jimmy." (To make matters even more confusing, one of those family members has the given name of "David.") For the sake of consistency, I have referred to the Catonsville Nine participant as "David" or "Brother David" in describing his life after he joined the Christian Brothers.

Fixing a single name on Marjorie Melville has proven to be similarly challenging. At various times, she has been called "Marjorie," "Margie," "Sister Marian Peter" (the name she took as a nun), and "Margarita" (the name she has gone by for the last several decades). To avoid confusion, I have stuck with "Marjorie" because that is the name most commonly associated with her around the time of the Catonsville demonstration.

Throughout the book, I have chosen to refer to the Berrigan brothers as "Dan" and "Phil." This seems consistent with how they referred to themselves during the events described here.

BIBLIOGRAPHY

Books

Agnew, Spiro. *Go Quietly . . . or Else.* New York: William Morrow, 1980.

Alpert, Jane. *Growing Up Underground.* New York: William Morrow, 1981.

Anderson, David. *The Human Tradition in America Since 1945.* Lanham, MD: SR Books, 2003.

Bannan, John F., and Rosemary S. Bannan. *Law, Morality and Vietnam: The Peace Militants and the Courts.* Bloomington: Indiana University Press, 1974.

Bartow, Arthur. *The Director's Voice: Twenty-One Interviews.* New York: Theatre Communications Group, 2002.

Baskir, Lawrence, and William Strauss. *Chance and Circumstance: The Draft, the War, and the Vietnam Generation.* New York: Alfred A. Knopf, 1978.

Bauernschub, John. *The Knights of Columbus: Fifty Years of Columbianism in Maryland.* Rockville, MD: Wildside Press, 2008.

Baxandall, Rosalyn, and Linda Gordon, eds. *Dear Sisters: Dispatches From the Women's Liberation Movement.* New York: Basic Books, 2001.

Berrigan, Daniel. *America Is Hard to Find.* New York: Doubleday, 1972.

———. *Jubilee!* New York: Hudson River Press, 1991.

———. *Lights On in the House of the Dead: A Prison Diary.* Garden City, NY: Doubleday, 1974.

———. *Night Flight to Hanoi: War Diary With 11 Poems.* New York: Harper & Row, 1968.

———. *Portraits of Those I Love.* New York: Crossroad, 1982.

———. *To Dwell in Peace: An Autobiography.* New York: Harper & Row, 1987.

———. *They Call Us Dead Men: Reflections From a Life of Conscience.* New York: Macmillan, 1968.

———. *The Trial of the Catonsville Nine.* Boston: Beacon Press, 1970.

———. *The Trial of the Catonsville Nine.* Fordham University Press Edition. New York: Fordham University Press, 2004.

Berrigan, Daniel, and Robert Coles. *The Geography of Faith: Conversations Between Daniel Berrigan, When Underground, and Robert Coles.* Boston: Beacon Press, 1971.

Berrigan, Daniel, and Tom Lewis. *Trial Poems.* Boston: Beacon Press, 1970.

Berrigan, Philip. *Fighting the Lamb's War: Skirmishes With the American Empire.* Monroe, ME: Common Courage Press, 1996.

———. *No More Strangers.* New York: Macmillan, 1965.

———. *Prison Journals of a Priest Revolutionary.* New York: Holt, Rinehart and Winston, 1970.

———. *A Punishment for Peace.* New York: Macmillan, 1969.

———. *Widen the Prison Gates: Writing From Jails, April 1970–December 1972.* New York: Touchstone Books, 1973.

Braudy, Susan. *Family Circle: The Boudins and the Aristocracy of the Left.* New York: Alfred A. Knopf, 2003.

Brown, Robert McAfee, Abraham J. Heschel, and Michael Novak. *Vietnam: Crisis of Conscience.* New York: Association Press, 1967.

Carroll, Denis. *What Is Liberation Theology?* Dublin: Mercier Press, 1987.

Carroll, James. *An American Requiem: God, My Father, and the War That Came Between Us.* New York: Houghton Mifflin, 1996.

———. *Constantine's Sword: The Church and the Jews.* New York: Houghton Mifflin, 2001.

———. *House of War: The Pentagon and the Disastrous Rise of American Power.* Boston: Houghton Mifflin, 2006

Casey, William, and Philip Nobile, eds. *The Berrigans.* New York: Avon Books, 1971.

Catonsville Nine–Milwaukee Fourteen Defense Committee. *Delivered in Resistance.* New Haven, CT: Advocate Press, 1969.

Chomsky, Noam, ed. *Trials of the Resistance.* New York: New York Review Books, 1970.

Cohen, Richard, and Jules Witcover. *A Heartbeat Away: The Investigation and Resignation of Vice President Spiro T. Agnew.* New York: Viking Press, 1974.

Curtis, Richard. *The Berrigan Brothers: The Story of Philip and Daniel Berrigan.* New York: Hawthorn Books, 1974.

Darst, Brother David, and Joseph Forgue. *Sexuality on the Island Earth.* New York: Paulist Press, 1970.

Day, Dorothy. *The Duty of Delight: The Diaries of Dorothy Day.* Milwaukee, WI: Marquette University Press, 2008.

DeLillo, Don. *Underworld.* New York: Simon & Schuster, 1998.

Deming, Barbara. *Revolution and Equilibrium.* New York: Grossman, 1971.

Dohrn, Bernardine, Bill Ayers, and Jeff Jones, eds. *Sing a Battle Song: The Revolutionary Poetry, Statements, and Communiques of the Weather Underground, 1970–1974.* New York: Seven Stories Press, 2006.

Draper, Theodore. *Abuse of Power.* New York: Viking Press, 1967.

Durr, Kenneth. *Behind the Backlash: White Working-Class Politics in Baltimore, 1940–1980.* Chapel Hill: University of North Carolina Press, 2003.

Echols, Alice. *Daring To Be Bad: Radical Feminism in America, 1967–1975.* Minneapolis: University of Minnesota Press, 1989.

Elie, Paul. *The Life You Save May Be Your Own: An American Pilgrimage.* New York: Farrar, Straus and Giroux, 2004.

Elmer, Jerry. *Felon for Peace: The Memoir of a Vietnam-Era Draft Resister.* Nashville, TN: Vanderbilt University Press, 2005.

Fee, Elizabeth, Linda Shopes, and Linda Zeidman, eds. *The Baltimore Book: New Views of Local History.* Philadelphia: Temple University Press, 1991.

Goodman, Mitchell, ed. *The Movement Toward a New America: The Beginnings of a Long Revolution.* Philadelphia: Pilgrim Press, 1970.

Gray, Francine du Plessix. *Divine Disobedience: Profiles in Catholic Radicalism.* New York: Alfred A. Knopf, 1970.

Gutiérrez, Gustavo. *Gustavo Gutiérrez: Essential Writings.* Maryknoll, NY: Orbis Books, 1996.

Hall, Mitchell K. *Because of Their Faith: CALCAV and Religious Opposition to the Vietnam War*. New York: Columbia University Press, 1990.

Halpert, Stephen, and Tom Murray, eds. *Witness of the Berrigans*. New York: Doubleday, 1972.

Haney, Lynn. *Gregory Peck: A Charmed Life*. New York: Carroll & Graf, 2004.

Hariman, Robert, ed. *Popular Trials: Rhetoric, Mass Media, and the Law*. Tuscaloosa: University of Alabama Press, 1990.

Harrison, Dorothy Lilja. *Peace, Be Still*. Seattle: CreateSpace, 2010.

Hayward, Brooke. *Haywire*. New York: Vintage, 2011.

Holsinger, M. Paul, ed. *War and American Popular Culture: A Historical Encyclopedia*. Santa Barbara, CA: Greenwood, 1999.

Kisseloff, Jeff, ed. *Generation on Fire: Voices of Protest From the 1960s: An Oral History*. Lexington: University Press of Kentucky, 2007.

Klatch, Rebecca. *A Generation Divided: The New Left, the New Right, and the 1960s*. Berkeley: University of California Press, 1999.

Knox, Ronald. *God and the Atom*. London: Sheed & Ward, 1945.

Kolodiejchuk, Brian, ed. *Mother Teresa: Come Be My Light: The Private Writings of "The Saint of Calcutta."* New York: Doubleday, 2007.

Kunstler, William. *Hints and Allegations: The World in Poetry and Prose According to William M. Kunstler*. New York: Seven Stories Press, 2003.

——. *My Life as a Radical Lawyer*. Secaucus, NJ: Carol, 1994.

——. *Politics on Trial: Five Famous Trials of the 20th Century*. New York: Ocean Press, 2003.

Langum, David. *William M. Kunstler: The Most Hated Lawyer in America*. New York: New York University Press, 1999.

Lewin, John. *The Baltimore Briefs*. Bloomington, IN: Trafford, 2009.

Lewis, Randolph. *Emile de Antonio: Radical Filmmaker in Cold War America*. Madison: University of Wisconsin Press, 2000.

Liebovich, Louis. *Richard Nixon, Watergate, and the Press: A Historical Retrospective*. New York: Praeger, 2003.

Lippman, Laura. *No Good Deeds*. New York: William Morrow, 2006.

Maraniss, David. *They Marched Into Sunlight: War and Peace, Vietnam and America, October 1967*. New York: Simon & Schuster, 2003.

Massa, Mark. *The American Catholic Revolution: How the Sixties Changed the Church Forever*. New York: Oxford University Press, 2010.

McCann, Colum. *Let the Great World Spin*. New York: Random House, 2009.

McNeal, Patricia. *Harder Than War: Catholic Peacemaking in Twentieth-Century America*. New Brunswick, NJ: Rutgers University Press, 1992.

McSorley, Richard. *My Path to Peace and Justice: An Autobiography*. Marion, SD: Fortkamp/Rose Hill Books, 1997.

Meconis, Charles. *With Clumsy Grace: The American Catholic Left, 1961–1975*. New York: Seabury Press, 1979.

Melville, Margarita. *Twice a Minority: Mexican American Women*. St. Louis: Mosby, 1980.

Melville, Thomas. *Through a Glass Darkly: The U.S. Holocaust in Central America*. Bloomington, IN: Xlibris, 2005.

Melville, Thomas, and Marjorie Melville. *Guatemala: Another Vietnam?* New York: Penguin, 1971.

————. *Whose Heaven, Whose Earth?* New York: Alfred A. Knopf, 1971.

Merton, Thomas. *The Hidden Ground of Love: The Letters of Thomas Merton on Religious Experience and Social Concerns.* New York: Farrar, Straus and Giroux, 1985.

Middleton, Neil, ed. *The Best of I. F. Stone's Weekly.* New York: Penguin Books, 1973.

Mills, Barbara. *"Got My Mind Set on Freedom": Maryland's Story of Black and White Activism, 1663–2000.* Westminster, MD: Heritage Books, 2002.

————. *And Justice for All: The Double Life of Fred Weisgal, Attorney and Musician.* Baltimore: American Literary Press, 2000.

National Coordinating Committee for Justice Under Law. *An Investigation and Analysis of Federal Prison Strikes.* Washington, DC: National Coordinating Committee for Justice Under Law, 1973.

Nelson, Jack, and Ronald J. Ostrow. *The FBI and the Berrigans: The Making of a Conspiracy.* New York: Coward, McCann & Geoghegan, 1972.

O'Malley, John W. *What Happened at Vatican II.* Cambridge, MA: Harvard University Press, 2008.

Pedersen, Vernon L. *The Communist Party in Maryland, 1919–57.* Urbana: University of Illinois Press, 2001.

Perlstein, Rick. *Nixonland: The Rise of a President and the Fracturing of America.* New York: Simon & Schuster, 2008.

Persico, Joseph. *Nuremberg: Infamy on Trial.* New York: Penguin, 1995.

Polner, Murray, and Jim O'Grady. *Disarmed and Dangerous: The Radical Lives and Times of Daniel and Philip Berrigan.* New York: Basic Books, 1997.

Rader, Victoria. *Signal Through the Flames: Mitch Snyder and America's Homeless.* Kansas City, MO: Sheed & Ward, 1986.

Raines, John C., ed. *Conspiracy: The Implications of the Harrisburg Trial for the Democratic Tradition.* New York: Harper & Row, 1974.

Raskin, Jonah, ed. *The Weather Eye: Communiques From the Weather Underground, May 1970–May 1974.* New York: Union Square Press, 1974.

Rich, Adrienne. *The Will to Change: Poems, 1968–1970.* New York: W. W. Norton, 1971.

Roberts, Nancy. *Dorothy Day and the Catholic Worker.* Albany: State University of New York Press, 1985.

Stringfellow, William, and Anthony Towne. *The Death and Life of Bishop Pike.* Garden City, NY: Doubleday, 1976.

————. *Suspect Tenderness: The Ethics of the Berrigan Witness.* New York: Holt, Rinehart and Winston, 1971.

Telgen, Diane, and Jim Kamp, eds. *Notable Hispanic American Women. Book One.* Detroit: Gale Research, 1993.

Thomas, Marlo. *The Right Words at the Right Time.* New York: Atria Books, 2002.

Troester, Rosalie Riegle, ed. *Voices From the Catholic Worker.* Philadelphia: Temple University Press, 1993.

Von Dehsen, Christian D., ed. *Philosophers and Religious Leaders.* Phoenix, AZ: Oryx Press, 1999.

Williams, William Appleman. *The Tragedy of American Diplomacy.* 2d ed. New York: W. W. Norton, 1988.

Wills, Garry. *Bare Ruined Choirs: Doubt, Prophecy, and Radical Religion.* Garden City, NY: Doubleday, 1972.

———. *Nixon Agonistes: The Crisis of the Self-Made Man.* New York: Mariner Books, 2002.

———. *Outside Looking In: Adventures of an Observer.* New York: Viking, 2010.

Wise, Marsha Wight. *Images of America: Catonsville.* Charleston, SC: Arcadia, 2005.

Witcover, Jules. *White Knight: The Rise of Spiro Agnew.* New York: Random House, 1972.

Zinn, Howard. *Disobedience and Democracy: Nine Fallacies of Law and Order.* Cambridge, MA: South End Press, 2001.

———. *A People's History of the United States, 1492–Present.* New York: HarperPerennial, 2005.

———. *You Can't Be Neutral on a Moving Train: A Personal History of Our Times.* Boston: Beacon Press, 1994.

Articles

"Actor, Director Tim Robbins Takes Up Historic Vietnam War Protest in Production of 'The Trial of the Catonsville Nine.'" *Democracy Now! The War and Peace Report,* August 27, 2009. http://www.democracynow.org/2009/8/27/actor_director_tim_robbins_takes_up (accessed February 1, 2011).

Aloi, Daniel. "From Vietnam to Redbud Woods: Daniel Berrigan Launches Events Commemorating Five Decades of Activism at Cornell." *Cornell University Chronicle Online,* April 4, 2006. http://www.news.cornell.edu/stories/April06/berrigan.0406.html (accessed April 20, 2011).

Anderson, George M. "Dan Berrigan's Latin American Exile." *America: The National Catholic Weekly,* November 5, 2010. http://www.americamagazine.org/blog/entry.cfm?blog_id=2&entry_id=3502 (accessed June 29, 2011).

———. "Looking Back in Gratitude." *America: The National Catholic Weekly,* July 6, 2009. http://www.americamagazine.org/content/article.cfm?article_id=11747 (accessed November 1, 2011).

"Background on Brother David Darst." Brother David Darst Center, 2007. http://www.brdaviddarstcenter.org/david_darst.html (accessed January 7, 2010).

Berrigan, Daniel. "Open Sesame: My Life and Good Times." *Katallagete* (Winter 1968–1969): 19–25.

Berrigan, Daniel, George Mische, Dave Eberhardt, and Philip Berrigan. "Underground and Action." *WIN,* June 15, 1970, 17–18.

Berrigan, Kate, and Frida Berrigan. "Kate and Frida's Eulogy." Jonah House, 2002. http://www.jonahhouse.org/eulogy.htm (accessed January 5, 2011).

Berrigan, Philip. "Letter From a Baltimore Jail." *Christianity and Crisis,* July 22, 1968, 168–170.

———. "Napalming Draft Files—A Letter From Jail." *Liberation,* July/August 1968, 20–21.

———. "Prisons and War." *Fellowship* (Winter 1973): 12.

"Bulls and Berrigans." *Newsweek,* May 4, 1970, 106.

"Civil Disobedience at Catonsville." *America,* October 26, 1968, 372–373.

Claiborne, Shane. "Holy Mischief: 40 Years After the Catonsville 9 and the 'Fracture of Good Order.'" *God's Politics,* May 19, 2008. http://blog.sojo.net/2008/05/19/holy-mischief-40-years-after-the-catonsville-9-and-the-fracture-of-good-order-by-shane-claiborne/ (accessed January 27, 2011).

Cornell, Tom. "Catholic Worker Pacifism: An Eyewitness to History." *Catholic Worker,* 2006. http://www.catholicworker.com/peacetc.htm (accessed January 12, 2010).

——. "Milwaukee 12." *Catholic Worker*, June 1969, 1.

——. "Nonviolent Napalm in Catonsville." *Catholic Worker*, June 1968, 1–2, 8.

Cowan, Paul. "Catholic Left Says the Heat's On." *Village Voice*, July 16, 1970, 19, 26.

Cowan, Rachel. "Guatemala to Catonsville." *Village Voice*, May 20, 1971, 32, 52.

"Daniel Berrigan on the Catonsville Nine." Extended interview to accompany *William Kunstler: Disturbing the Universe*. Public Broadcasting Service, POV: Documentaries With a Point of View, 2010. http://www.pbs.org/pov/disturbingtheuniverse/interview_berrigan.php (accessed January 31, 2011).

Darst, Brother David. "The Brother." *Commonweal*, June 4, 1965, 366–367.

——. "Non-Marital Sexual Expressions as Play and Humor in a Serious Society: Some Reflections on Contexts and Sexual Morality." *Pastoral Psychology*, March 1969, 52–55.

——. "Some Thoughts on Burning Draft Files." *WIN*, July 1968, 4–5.

——. "Some Thoughts on Drastic and Public Civil Disobedience From the Baltimore County Jail." *Ave Maria*, July 20, 1968, 8–10.

Deedy, John. "News and Views." *Commonweal*, January 12, 1968, 426.

——. "News and Views: Berrigan, Darst, et al." *Commonweal*, November 21, 1969, 236.

Deming, Barbara. "Trial by Autopsy." *Liberation*, December 1968, 6–11.

Dougherty, Laurie. "Alpha & Omega: The Trial of the Catonsville Nine." *WIN*, November 1, 1968, 9–10.

Dunigan, Cheryl. "Expressions of Faith." *Catonsville Patch*, December 10, 2010. http://catonsville.patch.com/articles/expressions-of-faith (accessed February 3, 2011).

Finnerty, Dan. "Catonsville 9 vs. Boston 5: A Question of Tactics." *Philadelphia Resistance Review*, October 1968, 1–3.

Freeman, Harrop. "The Constitutionality of Peacetime Conscription." *Virginia Law Review* 31 (1944–1945): 40–82.

Gleijeses, Piero. "'Flee! The White Giants Are Coming!': The United States, the Mercenaries, and the Congo, 1964–65." *Diplomatic History* (Spring 1994): 207–237.

Goldfarb, Bruce. "Finding the Catonsville Nine." Welcome to Baltimore, Hon!, April 5, 2010. http://welcometobaltimorehon.com/finding-the-catonsville-nine?replytocom=7729 (accessed May 13, 2011).

"Has the Church Lost Its Soul?" *Newsweek*, October 4, 1971, 188–189.

Hinckle, Marianne. "Lives of the Baltimore Saints." *Ramparts*, September 28, 1968, 11–16.

Hinckle, Warren. "Left Wing Catholics." *Ramparts*, November 1967, 14–26.

Ketchum, Michael. "Baltimore." *Catholic Worker*, October 1968, 1–2.

Kozlowski, Carl. "Q&A: Daniel Berrigan." *Progressive*, March 2004, 15.

Lewis, Tom. "Reflections From the Pig Farm." *Commonweal*, September 24, 1971, 499–500.

Mayer, Michael. *Simon Sobeloff Biography*. University of Maryland School of Law, Thurgood Marshall Law Library, 2006. http://www.law.umaryland.edu/marshall/specialcollections/sobeloff/index.html (accessed September 20, 2010).

McCarry, Charles. "A Few Soft Words for the Rabble-Rousers." *Esquire*, July 1969, 106–108, 132–135.

McGrath, Patrick. "Napalm in Baltimore." *Ave Maria*, June 8, 1968, 16–17, 21.

Merton, Thomas. "Blessed Are the Meek: The Roots of Christian Nonviolence." *Fellowship*, May 1967, 18–22.

——. "The Burning of Papers, the Human Conscience, and the Peace Movement." *Fellowship*, March 1969, 5–9, 30.

Moon, Penelope Adams. "Loyal Sons and Daughters of God? American Catholics Debate *Catholic* Anti-War Protest." *Peace & Change*, 2008, 1–30.

Moylan, Mary. "Being Underground." *Peace News*, July 3, 1970, 2.

———. "Catonsville 9 Go Underground." *WIN*, June 1, 1970, 14–16.

———. "A Woman's Work Is Never Done." *Off Our Backs: A Women's Newsjournal*, September 30, 1970, 1.

Nason, Thelma. "The Trial of the Catonsville Nine." *Johns Hopkins Magazine*, Fall 1968, 27–32.

Novak, Michael. "Draft Board Theology." *Commonweal*, July 28, 1967, 467–468.

———. "Talkin' 'Bout My Generation." *First Things*, April 2009, 39–42.

Ostling, Richard. "Those Beleaguered Maryknollers." *Time*, July 6, 1981, 36.

Percy, Walker. "Walker Percy." *Commonweal*, September 4, 1971, 431.

Schaeffer-Duffy, Scott. "Tom Lewis: An Artist/Activist." Jonah House, 2008. http://www.jonahhouse.org/LewisObit.htm (accessed January 12, 2010).

Schneider, James F. "A Guide to the Clarence M. Mitchell, Jr., Courthouse, Baltimore, Maryland." Baltimore Courthouse and Law Museum Foundation, Inc., 2009. http://www.baltocts.sailorsite.net/about/courthouseguide.pdf (accessed August 23, 2010).

Simon, John. "Saints for Our Time." *New York*, February 22, 1971, 66.

Spector, Stanley. "A Meditation on Catonsville." *Bulletin of Concerned Asian Scholars* (October 1968): 4.

"The Spoken Word, the Printed Word . . . and Napalm?" *Ave Maria*, June 8, 1968, 4.

"The Taking of Father Dan." *Newsweek*, August 24, 1970, 37.

Teitz, Alex. "Dar Williams." Femmusic.com: The Place for Emerging Women in Music. http://www.femmusic.com/darwilliamsint.htm (accessed January 20, 2011).

Thomsen, Roszel C. "The Integration of Baltimore's Polytechnic Institute: A Reminiscence." *Maryland Historical Magazine* 79 (Fall 1984): 235–238.

Towne, Anthony. "Reflections on Two Trials." *Christian Century*, December 4, 1968, 1535–1539.

Tropea, Joe. "Hit and Stay: The Catonsville Nine and Baltimore Four Actions Revisited." *Baltimore City Paper*, May 14, 2008. http://www.citypaper.com/news/story.asp?id=15722 (accessed August 4, 2010).

Wickes, Mariett. "Tear Down the Walls!" *Off Our Backs*, April 15, 1971, 2.

"Witness to Catonsville Nine Dies at 92." *Register (Selective Service System)*, January–February 2002, 3.

Wool, Robert. "The Harboring of Daniel Berrigan: An Exercise of Christian Charity." *Esquire*, November 1971, 156–161, 206.

Zinn, Howard. "A Holy Outlaw." *Progressive*, February 2003, 14.

Unpublished Papers and Manuscripts

Darst, Charles, ed. "All in the Passing of Now: The Collected Writings of James McGinnis Darst." Unpublished manuscript, ca. 1975.

Ortbal, John. "The Catholic Radical Left of the Sixties: A Failed Revolution but a Moral Victory?" Unpublished paper, University of Chicago Divinity School, March 13, 1996.

Tropea, Joseph. "Hit and Stay: The Baltimore Four, the Catonsville Nine and How They Sustained the American Peace Movement." Unpublished master's thesis, University of Maryland–Baltimore County, 2008.

Films, Videos, and Other Media

Davidson, Gordon. *The Trial of the Catonsville Nine*. RCA/Columbia Pictures Home Video, 1983.

"Eulogies Honoring John Hogan." October 2008. Private video recording in author's possession.

Melville, Thomas. "Insurgency and Counterinsurgency." Speech delivered at St. John's Methodist Church, Baltimore, MD, November 11, 2007. http://video.google.com/videoplay?docid=-211874374465883204# (accessed April 7, 2011).

Mische, George. "George Mische on U.S. Foreign Policy." Speech delivered at St. John's Methodist Church, Baltimore, MD, November 11, 2007. http://video.google.com/videoplay?docid=6386769262558826320# (accessed May 27, 2011).

Sachs, Lynne. *Investigation of a Flame: A Documentary Portrait of the Catonsville Nine*. First Run/Icarus Films, 2001.

———. *Mary Moylan: Nine Years Underground*. Multimedia biography, 2001.

Tropea, Joe. *Hit and Stay*. Forthcoming.

Williams, Dar. *The Green World*. CD, Razor & Tie, 2000.

INDEX

ML

6-12